The Origins of Deconstruction

The Origins of Deconstruction

Edited by

Martin McQuillan
Professor of Literary Theory and Cultural Analysis, Dean of Arts and Social Sciences, Kingston University, UK

Ika Willis
Lecturer in Reception, School of Humanities, University of Bristol, UK

First published 2010 by
PALGRAVE MACMILLAN

Palgrave Macmillan in the UK is an imprint of Macmillan Publishers Limited,
registered in England, company number 785998, of Houndmills, Basingstoke,
Hampshire RG21 6XS.

Palgrave Macmillan in the US is a division of St Martin's Press LLC,
175 Fifth Avenue, New York, NY 10010.

Palgrave Macmillan is the global academic imprint of the above companies
and has companies and representatives throughout the world.

Palgrave® and Macmillan® are registered trademarks in the United States,
the United Kingdom, Europe and other countries.

ISBN-13: 978–0–230–58190–6 hardback

This book is printed on paper suitable for recycling and made from fully
managed and sustained forest sources. Logging, pulping and manufacturing
processes are expected to conform to the environmental regulations of the
country of origin.

A catalogue record for this book is available from the British Library.

A catalog record for this book is available from the Library of Congress.

10   9   8   7   6   5   4   3   2   1
19   18   17   16   15   14   13   12   11   10

Printed and bound in Great Britain by
CPI Antony Rowe, Chippenham and Eastbourne

Contents

Foreword: 'Taught by Love'

Martin McQuillan

The story of Butades is well known, the Corinthian maid (sometimes called 'Dibutades', Butades being her father's name) who draws the outline of her lover's shadow on the wall so that she might remember him when he has gone. The story provides a mytho-poetic 'origin of painting', most heavily invested in by eighteenth- and nineteenth-century traditions of art history. For a philosophical, if no less allegorical, understanding of such shadow play one might look to Plato's treatment of the Cave in *The Republic*. The questions raised by both Plato and Butades are significant and many: the origin of representation as such, the origin of representation as a category, the originariness of representation, and the representation of origins. The story of Butades is perhaps most interesting in this last respect. As a myth of origins it carries a certain poetic charm – art after all is erotic in origin. However, the story also tells us that the very idea of the origin is caught up in the problem of representation, not just that the narrative of an origin must be somehow secondary but that the idea of an origin is itself a retrospective, if fundamental, constitution of the conditions of that which it originates. The iconographic tradition of Butades is not about capturing the likeness of the real but about the erotic attachment to something that in itself has no substance (shadow, memory, art, representation). The 'origin' is, however, neither the shadow nor the lover but the act of drawing, which as an incomplete process is the origin of something other than itself, namely the completed outline (art, painting). Drawing cannot present itself as an adequate origin of art because the idea of art (the completed outline as *aide mémoire*) must be presupposed in order to imagine the process of its completion (Butades' drawing). In other words, Butades must be making art even before she draws and so art pre-exists its own origin. This is consequently complicated by the many belated works of art which depict Butades making art as the origin of the art of making. While the idea of the origin, traditionally understood, requires a single source of unmediated primacy, the story of Butades, and her pictorial history, shows that the origin of representation as a representation of origins knows itself to rely upon a certain *trompe l'oeil* whereby that which has no presence and is only ever an event of difference (drawing or marking) takes on the identity of a pure mimesis. However, what is interesting about Butades as a drawn figure herself, is that each representation of her must make visible the diremption between lover and shadow and the further displacement of that relation into the hand which marks the drawing on the wall, taking its departure from a prior *différance*, which at once puts in play the differential system of marks and simultaneously recuperates the effects of that difference by retrospectively installing the historically secondary act of drawing as the constitutive origin of the art which seemingly legitimates the notion of drawing.

The origins of deconstruction are by definition overdetermined and, by analogy to Butades, similarly complex. There could be no single origin, not even the biography of the late Jacques Derrida, which could satisfactorily provide a point of fixity for deconstruction in this way. Like the process of drawing, deconstruction has no substance of its own. It is rather the process of what happens and any attempt to install retrospectively a starting point, to create an outside or beyond, and so a time before deconstruction, similarly runs the risk of presenting a secondary effect as the origin of its cause. Of course, this may well be the case as certain nostalgic if bad-tempered academics will remind us there *was* a time before deconstruction, even if deconstruction shows that this time was always already in deconstruction. Any attempt to sketch an origin for deconstruction (although one day an institutional history must be written) will leave the reader like a spectator to the Butades paintings, observing the belated mystification, or a mythologization as a demystification, of that which already presents itself as mystifying demystification in process. Rather than offer one origin of deconstruction this book provides fourteen, deconstructing the idea of the origin as much as demystifying the origins of deconstruction. For deconstruction does have origins (many in fact), some of which, like the art of Butades, have been 'taught by love'. That is, love as the betrayal of the lover in the least bad way. Butades loves her drawing, it is a narcissism par excellence. Like the story of Toth and the origins of writing in the *Phaedrus*, who betrays memory by the mnemonic device of writing, to speak of the origins of deconstruction is already to betray a certain idea of deconstruction and yet we must speak of such things ('in loving memory' as the phrase goes). Because the origins of deconstruction have no presence does not mean that they do not exist; deconstructing them is the task set by this book.

The editors would like to thank Daniel Ferrer for kind permission to reprint the two interview texts which make up the prologue section of this volume. I would also like to thank Hugh Silverman and the members of the Executive Committee of the International Association for Philosophy and Literature who first suggested that this book be written, for my part it is dedicated as a reminder of the friendships afforded by the IAPL.

Notes on Contributors

Claudia Baracchi is Associate Professor of Philosophy at the New School for Social Research, New York. Her publications include *Of Myth, Life, and War in Plato's Republic* (2002). Her most recent book is *Aristotle's Ethics as First Philosophy* (2008).

Gérard Bucher was Melodia E. Jones Professor of French at SUNY (Buffalo). He now researches in Paris at the Collège International de Philosophie. His principal publications are *La vision et l'Enigme* (1989), *Le Testament poétique* (1994) and *L'Imagination de l'Origine* (2000).

Claire Colebrook is the Edwin Earle Sparks Professor of English Literature at Penn State University. Her recent publications include *Irony in the Work of Philosophy* (2002) and *Milton, Evil and Literary History* (2008).

Hélène Cixous is Professor of Literature at the Université Paris VIII. One of today's most important writers and theorists, her recent publications in English include *Portrait of Jacques Derrida as a Young Jewish Saint* (2004) and *Hélène Cixous: The Writing Notebooks* (2004).

Jacques Derrida (1930–2004) was Director of Studies at the Ecole des Hautes Etudes en Sciences Sociales and Professor of the Humanities at the University of California, Irvine. His contribution to contemporary thinking is immeasurable.

Thomas Docherty is Professor of English and Comparative Literature at the University of Warwick. His principal publications include *Alterities: Criticism and Modernity* (1996), *After Theory* (1997) and *Aesthetic Democracy* (2005).

Robert Eaglestone is Professor of Contemporary Literature and Thought at Royal Holloway College, University of London. His publications include *Ethical Criticism: Reading after Levinas* (1997) and *The Holocaust and the Postmodern* (2004).

Daniel Ferrer is Director of Research at the Institut des Textes et Manuscrits Modèrnes at the Centre National de la Recherche Scientifique in Paris. His publications in English include *Virginia Woolf and the Madness of Language* (1990) and *Genetic Criticism: Texts and Avant-Texts* (2004).

Marc Froment-Meurice is Professor of French at Vanderbilt University, Nashville. His principal publications include *Solitudes, from Rimbaud to Heidegger* (1995), *That Is to Say: Heidegger's Poetics* (1998) and *Incitations* (2002).

Margret Grebowicz is Associate Professor of Philosophy at Goucher College, Baltimore. She is the editor of *Gender after Lyotard* and *SciFi in the Mind's Eye: Reading Science through Science Fiction* (both 2007).

John P. Leavey is Professor of English Literature at the University of Florida (Gainesville). His translations of Derrida include *Edmund Husserl's 'Origin of Geometry'* (1978), *The Archeology of the Frivolous* (1980) and *Glas* (1986).

Martin McQuillan is Professor of Literary Theory and Cultural Analysis, Dean of Arts and Social Sciences, Kingston University, UK.

Paul Patton is Professor of Philosophy at the University of New South Wales. His principal publications include *Deleuze and the Political* (2001), *Between Deleuze and Derrida* (2003) and *Deleuzian Concepts: Philosophy, Colonization, Politics* (2010).

Jean Michel Rabaté is Vartan Gregorian Professor in the Humanities at the University of Pennsylvania. His recent publications include *Joyce and the Politics of Egoism* (2001), *Jacques Lacan and Literature* (2001), *The Future of Theory* (2002) and *The Cradle of Modernism* (2007).

Lynn Turner is Lecturer in Visual Culture at Goldsmiths College, University of London. Her current book project is entitled *Machine-Events: Autobiographies of the Performative*.

Ika Willis is Lecturer in Reception at the University of Bristol. She is the author of numerous articles on deconstruction, queer theory, Latin poetry and fan fiction.

Julian Wolfreys is Professor of Modern Literature and Culture at the University of Loughborough. His work on deconstruction includes *Deconstruction: Derrida* (1998) and *Occasional Deconstructions* (2004).

Introduction: The Origins of Deconstruction – Derrida's Daughters

Ika Willis

> You claim that there is no given starting point, so you start in the most traditional way imaginable with the problem of beginning, and you proceed with a game that is puerile and predictable, reflexive, narcissistic, you attempt to enclose us from the start in writing and the text, a whole complacent baroque discourse based on well-known and quite banal paradoxes of self-reference.
>
> Jacques Derrida[1]

The origins of deconstruction

Why, then, start at the beginning? The choice of a starting place can never be justified ('at most one can give a strategic justification for the procedure'); but neither can we *not* choose, pretend to be starting 'just anywhere', for the 'just anywhere' already presupposes a map of the terrain into which we jab the blind pin: and the origin is that which will have instituted the map on which the origin is located *in the first place*. Which is to say that the origin comes both before and after the first place. The origin partakes of the circularity of the *logos* which deconstruction diagnoses as a time which is out of joint.

For deconstruction, the origin is 'the very order, reason and meaning of *logos*'[2]. Instituting an 'order of continuous derivation',[3] a linear temporal path along which a self-identical object is presumed to travel in a predetermined direction, the origin is the apparatus which unifies a thing's essence with its history: it is the 'before' and the 'from-since' which 'draw in time or space an order that does not belong to them',[4] the organization of time and space according to the order of the *logos*. From the very beginning, therefore, of course, we are always already involved in iteration, as well as in the structure of *différance* and of hauntology. The origin is the very order of logos; it is that supplement which comes from the outside to fill a plenitude's lack; it is *difference*...The problem of the origin, then, *is* the problem

1

of deconstruction: a formulation (x *is* deconstruction, deconstruction *is* x – justice, for example[5]) which will be familiar to anyone who has followed the changing names and quasi-transcendentals of deconstruction over the years since – to take a starting point at random – the 1976 publication of Gayatri Spivak's English translation of *Of Grammatology*.[6]

The writers in this volume suggest various ways of thinking the origin *in* deconstruction and various origins *for* deconstruction. Among the latter are Algeria; the Holocaust; Husserl's *Origin of Geometry*; Rousseau's 'Essay on the Origin of Language'; the fourth book of Vergil's *Aeneid*; and Plato. Many of these origins, therefore, are located outside the temporal field which would be plotted by an analysis seeking to map the continuous derivation of Jacques Derrida's work from its origin. Since deconstruction is *first and foremost* a reading, a response to a prior text, it always comes from outside itself and therefore has no origin proper to itself.

This volume as a whole seeks both to attend to and to resist, *through* that attention, the desire to 'ground' deconstruction through reuniting it with its origin in the biography and bibliography organized under the proper name *Jacques Derrida*.

It cannot be the case, of course, that the proper name Jacques Derrida marks the limits of the field of deconstruction, not least because deconstruction disorganizes inside/outside and persistently destabilizes what can be thought of as being proper to a text. The writers in this volume, then, take seriously our responsibility to betray Derrida by remaining faithful to a deconstruction which is not the straightforward ideology critique which frequently takes place under the same name as that mode of thinking from which we seek to differentiate it here: and in our desire (not) to bound the field of deconstruction by, to bind it *to*, the name Jacques Derrida, we are rigorously faithful to Derrida.

For property, boundaries, language, the name – all these inextricably interwoven terms – are gathered at and mark, according to Rousseau (according to Derrida), the fall into spacing. Spacing, in the 'Essay on the Origin of Language', as traced laboriously in *Of Grammatology*, is *both* an accident befalling speech from the outside *and* that monstrosity which haunts speech from within and which the *logos* can therefore neither contain nor break with. The fall into spacing is thus one of the origins of deconstruction – in both senses of that ambiguous genitive. It is at the beginning of deconstruction, in that it is a scene of origin where deconstruction is already at work; and it is one of deconstruction's origins, in that it conforms to the deconstructive thinking of the origin as that which 'comes from the outside as accident or catastrophe or is at work on the inside as monstrosity'.[7]

In other words, deconstruction might be said to begin at the origin of language – or at least at the 'Origin of Language'. Or, at least, one of the origins with which deconstruction is concerned is the origin of language, of spacing, and of the sign.

Derrida's daughters

In Derrida's work, a series of female or feminine bodies figure the origin of spacing and the work of memory as/in the absence of the thing remembered: Gradiva, for example, in *Archive Fever*, whose footstep is 'this irreplaceable place, the very ash, where the singular imprint, like a signature, barely distinguishes itself from the impression'; yet 'this uniqueness is not even a past present... would have been possible, one can dream of it after the fact, only insofar as its iterability... haunted it from the origin'.[8] Or Butades, through whose 'exemplary narrative' the origin of painting in the iconographic tradition substitutes memory for perception, the impression for the imprint:

> In this [iconographic] tradition, the origin of drawing and the origin of painting give rise to multiple representations that substitute memory for perception. Firstly, because they are *re*presentations, next, because they are drawn most often from an exemplary narrative (that of Butades, the young Corinthian lover who bears the name of her father, a potter from Sicyon), and finally, because the narrative relates the origin of graphic representation to the absence or invisibility of the model.[9]

Butades appears both in *Of Grammatology* and in *Memoirs of the Blind*: in both texts Derrida cites Rousseau's reference to the story of Butades in his appeal to 'Love' as the originator of drawing:

> Love, it is said, was the inventor of drawing... How many things the girl who took such pleasure in tracing her Lover's shadow was telling him! What sounds could she have used to convey this movement of the stick?[10]

The question 'Where does it come from?', with its echo of the primal scene, must already be caught up in a metaphorics of 'love' – that is, of reproductive heterosexuality in its relation to reproduction, kinship and filiation.

To trace Butades back to the first surviving attestation of her existence, in Pliny's *Natural History*, is to find not only that the original exemplary purpose served by her narrative is not the one to whose service she has been put in the iconographic tradition but also that Butades' origin – Butades *as* origin – is, appropriately enough, strikingly secondary, lacking, belated, rewritten, generationally confused. For the *Natural History* is a radically secondary text, deriving from multiple, discontinuous and effaced origins – on the most literal level, pointing to the textual sources for Pliny's claims, most of which have not survived. The *Natural History* is frequently read as nothing but the archive of other texts, a collection of traces from what would have been a non-erased origin.

Moreover, although in Rousseau's 'Essay on the Origin of Languages' as it comes down to us through Derrida, Butades is the origin of *painting* or *drawing*, she is originally (in the *Natural History*) no such thing: she is not an origin at all. The origin which this narrative exemplifies is that of sculptor, and the originator is Butades-the-father. Pliny introduces the anecdote with these words, making it clear that the anecdote is *not* about painting or drawing: 'Enough and more than enough has now been said about painting. It may be suitable to append to these remarks something about the plastic art'; sculpture is introduced, as in the anecdote itself, as a secondary effect of drawing/painting.

> It was through the service of that same earth that modelling portraits [*similitudines*] from clay was first invented by Butades, a potter of Sicyon, at Corinth. He did this owing to his daughter, who was in love with a young man; and she, when he was going abroad, drew in outline [*circumscripsit*] on the wall the shadow of his face thrown by a lamp. Her father pressed clay on this and made a relief, which he hardened by exposure to fire with the rest of his pottery.
>
> Pliny, *NH* 35.151

Remarkably, in the Butades story as it organizes an origin for the iconographic tradition, Butades' father (and the practice of sculpture) is effaced from the scene of drawing – and, perhaps, from the family scene as well, since his daughter (unnamed in Pliny) begins to bear his name without alteration. The iconographic tradition which places the daughter of Butades at the origin of drawing, naming *her* Butades and effacing her father and the place of sculpture in the scene, executes a point-by-point reversal of the original anecdote. The daughter, in the original scene only instrumental to her father's invention, becomes the origin herself – the secondary, derivative art of sculpture is excised from the scene of original drawing – and appropriates her father's name.

In *Derrida: The Movie* (Kirby Dick, Amy Ziering Kofman, 2002) Jacques Derrida is asked which philosopher could be his mother; he answers that only a philosopher to come, only his philosophical daughter or granddaughter, could be his mother. Is Derrida's – and therefore deconstruction's – origin, then, Derrida's daughter?

* * *

The first set of essays in this volume take up the question of the origins of deconstruction in these terms of gendered embodiment, reproduction and filiation. These follow a Prologue that opens with Daniel Ferrer's interview with Jacques Derrida, which addresses the technicity of the writing body and the material practices of reading and writing around deconstruction, which is followed by a conversation between Ferrer and Hélène Cixous about reading, writing, and the space of books in which Cixous locates herself. In the first essay of the 'Incubation' section Marc Froment-Meurice proceeds from the paradoxes generated by his titular pun on 'dating deconstruction' to articulate the implication of gender, heterosexuality and reproduction in the cyclical/linear temporality of dates. Lynn Turner's chapter, which grafts Derrida's critique of communication in 'Signature – Event – Context' onto Levi-Strauss's model of the 'communication of women', proposes a similiarly grafted new beginning in its complex pun *Les Jeune Nées*, a pluralizing return to Cixous' *'newly born woman'*; Ika Willis's essay, on the deployment of figures of the female body in the construction of originary autochthony and the thinking of sovereignty, rereads the undecidable hymen of 'The Double Session' in the terms of the undecidable marriage between Dido and Aeneas in Vergil's *Aeneid*. It is Thomas Docherty who poses the question of the origin of deconstruction in the form 'Where does deconstruction come from?'; he unfolds from this point a complicated discussion of *nostalgerie*, which thinks the determination of the present by the past through the interrelation of suicide, sovereignty and subjectivity. Finally, Jean-Michel Rabaté's essay, as if in response to Docherty's framing of the question, poses the origin of deconstruction as the marriage of Husserl and Joyce and rigorously plays out the consequences of this move.

This piece also serves as a transition to the second part of this volume, 'Inauguration', whose first two chapters explore the consequences of positing, as the origin of deconstruction, the 'first' book by the 'author' of deconstruction – Derrida's Introduction to Husserl's *Origin of Geometry*. Claire Colebrook gives a clear and rigorous account of the relationship of deconstruction to transcendental phenomenology, showing how Derrida's work is on both sides of the transcendental question and project at once; Margret Grebowitz gives a meticulous account of the way that scholarship on Derrida prefers *Speech and Phenomena* to the 'Introduction' to the *Origin of Geometry* as an origin to deconstruction, and traces what is at stake in this choice for the thinking of the origin and of deconstruction by taking seriously Derrida's claim that *Speech and Phenomena* is only a supplement to the 'Introduction'. Paul Patton's chapter, by contrast, relates Derrida's work on beginnings and differential repetition to that of his contemporary Gilles Deleuze, and shows, through a reading of J. M. Coetzee's novel *Disgrace*, how both Derrida and Deleuze use the notion of *becoming* to complicate linear time and political foundation.

The impossibility of linear temporality opens 'Installation', the third and final part of this volume, to a concern with time and space – before/after, inside/outside, and their organization and disorganization through the appeal to the origin. John P. Leavey's chapter sets up the terms of the debate by discussing the temporality of reading, which is marked by a radical *secondariness* with respect an originary illegibility, in terms of the work of Walter

Benjamin and the impossibility of beginning (in its complicity with ending) Italo Calvino's novel *If on a Winter's Night a Traveller*. Julian Wolfreys, arguing that there is no singular 'deconstruction' which is repeated in different temporal contexts, asks what its origin(s) could be, if it 'is' only where it 'takes place' – and where it takes place is *between*? In this case, the origin is already a *response* to an impossible injunction, and therefore always secondary, split and outside itself. This complexity of the inside/outside relation is taken up in Robert Eaglestone's chapter, which characterizes deconstruction as an *exorbitant* mode of thought and, in tracing its relationship to the ethical demands of the Holocaust, shows how deconstruction is structured by an attention to the inadequacy of a critique originating *either* from within *or* from outside the system which produces it. Claudia Barrachi similarly puts the inside and the outside of systems, and the linear consequentiality of historical time, into question, but now by returning to the concerns with which this book opened. Barrachi organizes her reading of the *Phaedrus* around the term *inspiration*: breathing – the passage of air into and out of the speaking/writing body – becomes a figure for the originary undecidability of the origin of speech. Finally, Gérard Bucher's essay, taking up Barrachi's concern with the *spirit*, finds the origin of art – and thus the beginning of differentiation between animal and human – between Heidegger and Bataille.

Notes

1. Geoffrey Bennington and Jacques Derrida, *Jacques Derrida*, trans. Geoffrey Bennington (Chicago and London: University of Chicago Press, 1993), 19–20.
2. Bennington and Derrida, *Jacques Derrida*, 18.
3. ibid., 19.
4. Jacques Derrida, *Memoirs of the Blind: The Self-Portrait and Other Ruins*, trans. Pascal-Anne Brault and Michael Naas (Chicago: University of Chicago Press, 1993), 55.
5. Jacques Derrida, 'Force of Law: The "Mystical Foundation of Authority"', in Drucilla Cornell, Michel Rosenfeld and David Gray Carlson (eds), *Deconstruction and the Possibility of Justice* (London and New York: Routledge, 1992), 3–67.
6. Jacques Derrida, *Of Grammatology*, trans. Gayatri Chakravorty Spivak (Baltimore: Johns Hopkins University Press, 1976).
7. Bennington and Derrida, *Jacques Derrida*, 16.
8. Jacques Derrida, *Archive Fever*, trans. Eric Prenowitz (Chicago: Johns Hopkins University Press, 1995), 92.
9. Derrida, *Memoirs of the Blind*, 49.
10. Jean-Jacques Rousseau, *Essay on the Origin of Languages*, cited in *Memoirs of the Blind*, 52, and *Of Grammatology*, 234.

Prologue

A. 'Between the writing body and writing…': Jacques Derrida

*An interview with Daniel Ferrer**

Jacques Derrida is arguably the philosopher who has shown the greatest interest in the form of writing. For the first time, he has agreed to describe in detail his own working practice and the concrete organization of the scene of writing (and reading) which has always preoccupied him.

Daniel Ferrer: *Two years ago, we opened the first session of this seminar series, 'Writers' Libraries' with a beautiful quotation from one of your texts on 'The Invention of the Other'.[1] We chose as our starting point the hypothesis that the writer's library, whether real or virtual, is the privileged space in which to observe how the writer 'receives the other within the economy of the same'. There would be many questions to ask about this topic but today you have agreed to speak to us, on a more personal note, about your own library and your own writing and reading practices.*

Jacques Derrida: The exercise I have been invited to perform is formidable. It is a call for a somewhat indecent gesture, a gesture that some might well interpret as narcissistic, exhibitionist, even nudist. What is at stake here is speaking of that which in each of our lives represents the most secret, the most intimate: what we do when we're alone, at home, a moment which is heavily invested with eroticism, maybe even auto-eroticism, when we prepare, with all sorts of writing instruments and materials, what is already an exhibition: our publications. These machines of pleasure or auto-erotic torture are what I have to exhibit, since I have to speak of my library, of my way of writing, taking notes, using my 'word-processing' instruments. I used the big words 'narcissism', 'voyeurism', 'exhibitionism'…The most appropriate word in this case, however, would probably be 'fetishism'. The objects and things of which I'll speak are for all of us objects of a heavy fetishistic cathexis. All these objects, from paper to computer, are objects that can be fetishized more easily than others. I have to speak of all of this: narcissism, exhibitionism, autoeroticism, fetishism…And all this is prepared within our private space with a view to publication. It is the fate of all of us, of everyone present

9

here. We are beings of publication who in secrecy, at night, sharpen all kinds of instruments of pleasure and torture.

There is another scruple which makes it difficult for me to speak here and that's the hesitation before the *typical*, before that which is common to us all because fundamentally we are part of the same social and professional group, but also of the same generation. Everything I'm going to say has been marked by a history which, for this whole generation, has been the scene of profound and radical transformations. I'll therefore waver between the description of typical traits and structures, certain generalities, and the description of more idiomatic things, more singular, more personal. I don't want to hide personal matters, because I imagine that you have invited me out of curiosity to see in what way I'm part of a typical, general movement, while at the same time also marking my distance. I'll thus try to steer clear of these two pitfalls, of the shabbily and generally typical, and the purely idiomatic, which is very difficult to grasp. I'll thus testify by speaking at the crossroads between singularities and common traits.

I have two letters by Daniel Ferrer in front of me. The first alludes to 'the way in which writing in progress articulates onto the already-written'. This is a rule I'll adhere to, that I've received, but in order to comply I'll rely on another already-written, a second letter by Daniel Ferrer, which I received only recently and in which he sends me a list of questions to which I feel I should reply. I'll try to reply to each question he asks me, with special reference to the already-written.

But before I come to these questions, and after some general remarks on the anxious and turbulent history of my reading and writing experience, on certain points of reference, certain general scansions, I would like to tell you, in all naïveté, what I remember of my past in terms of writing, reading, books, materials, etc.

Like all of us, I suppose, I observe myself when I work, whether I'm reading or writing. And this process of observing is an essential part of the experience. I observe my body – because it is of the body I'll have to speak – the position of the body. Ever since I've been interested in the question of writing, a question I have probably given more attention to than many, the question of the writing body has always worried, interested me. It has always been a place of experimentation and observation; and, for example, the question of how one should write, in what position one should write: lying down, sitting or standing. Thus, one of the texts that developed out of the work you did last year, and which Daniel Ferrer gave me to read, the text on Nietzsche's library, opens with a quotation from Nietzsche: 'One can only think and write while sitting down ...' And I remember that in my first publication, in 1962, I quoted this text and commented on it by saying that, and please allow me to quote so that I can then expand on what has been my own experience of the 'lying-sitting-standing' with regard to writing. With reference to Flaubert, quoted by Nietzsche, who says that: 'Flaubert is always despicable, the man is nothing, the work is all...', I then added:

> We would have to choose then, between writing and dance. Nietzsche recommends a dance of the pen in vain: '...dancing with the feet, with ideas, with words, and need I add that one must also be able to dance with the pen – that one must learn how to write?' Flaubert was aware, and he was right, that writing cannot be thoroughly Dionysiac. 'One can only think and write sitting down,' he said. Joyous anger of Nietzsche: 'Here I have got you nihilist! A sedentary life is the real sin against the Holy Spirit. Only those thoughts that come when you are walking have any value.' But Nietzsche was certain that the writer would never be standing; that writing is first and always something over which one bends. Better still when letters are no longer figures of fire in the heavens.[2]

These different movements are also the movements of my interminable hesitation between writing-lying, writing-sitting and writing-standing. It sometimes happens that I write lying down, taking notes when I wake up from a dream. But most of the time, like all of us, I write sitting down, but with the feeling that nothing very important happens when I write sitting down. When I write sitting down I merely administer my thoughts, ideas, thinking processes, which always come to me while I'm standing, or doing something else, like walking, driving or running. The most organizing things and ideas always used to come to me while I was running (I've stopped now). So I sometimes went running with a piece of paper in my pocket to take notes. Afterwards, when I sat down at my table in front of my computer I simply administered, exploited these furtive, cursory and sometimes dazzling things I always received on the run.

I quickly became conscious of the fact that it was while I was standing that these good things could happen to me. I thus put up a shelf in my first office (I have four or five offices) at chest height, slightly tilted, thinking that it would be better if I could manage to write standing up (I used to write with a pen then). I tried very hard but it didn't lead anywhere. This is just to illustrate that the position of the body is something I'm very mindful of. When I write sitting down I'm suffering all the time. But I understand very well Nietzsche's and also Flaubert's protest that a certain kind of work presupposes immobility, the being-seated.

After this detour, which should merely remind us that what we're speaking of is a certain desiring, writing, suffering body, I'll have to return to my early childhood, since the question was about writing. The first violence I felt with regard to this was *one* of the forms of violence I experienced in school (there were many): very early, in primary school, I was a very good pupil (this deteriorated somewhat later) except for writing and there were times, during the break, when the schoolmaster, knowing that I was best of the class, would say to me: 'Come back up and write this again. This is illegible. When you're in secondary school you'll get away with writing like that, but for the moment this is just not acceptable.' So very early I encountered the ordeal of the illegibility of my handwriting, something that, unfortunately, has not improved since. My writing has remained difficult to read to an extent that some of my friends have to have my letters deciphered by 'experts'. This has always worried me, and there are some handwriting instruments that preserve the normal form of my writing, illegible as it may be, and others which do not. For example, a pencil does not respect my writing and quills do not either. I've had very few pens in my life, and I can see that my writing has changed since when I was a young lecturer or student. It used to be much sharper then and disjointed, but equally illegible. You get the impression of an archive when you notice the transformation of your handwriting.

To come back to the question of the instrument and the writing materials, for a very long time I could only write with a nib pen, dipped into ink (not with a fountain pen). I brought my inkpot with me to the exams and the *concours*, with a specific quill. I did this for a very long time, even when I started publishing. I could only write the first version of a text on large paper and with a pen. When I was a child, a teenager, locking myself in my room (very early, writing for me became a kind of imprisonment, withdrawal, retreat), locked up in my room I wrote in my exercise books – I mean school notebooks which I used as diaries – or onto other kinds of material. I can still remember a table in El Biar, in Algeria, which served as my desk, in a small room; it was covered in pink paper, that looked like a tablecloth, and little thoughts I'd put on those papers. Afterwards I cut them out and I remember very well cutting with a pair of scissors all those things I'd written at this table out of the pink paper.

The same history of instruments and materials, I think, has been common to all intellectuals of my generation. It had to be a dip pen, not a fountain pen, a dip pen for the first version of texts, even when I started publishing. My first books were written with a pen. I only used a typewriter for the final version. I bought my first typewriter in the United States in 1956. I had to do the typing. That's when I learned typing. I type very fast, very badly, with many mistakes. I learned to type fast and badly at Cambridge and Harvard where I spent a year after I'd finished school. At the time, my wife – we didn't have much money – translated a Russian novel and I typed her translations. So I bought a small Olivetti 32 with an international keyboard because I couldn't find a French keyboard over there, which meant that for many years, from 1957 to the seventies, I had to take advantage of every visit to the United States to find another one of these international keyboards to which I had got used to. I'd never typed on a French keyboard till then. Every time, I replaced one small Olivetti by another small Olivetti.

To summarize in broad strokes, after the pen, I used the Olivetti, from my first publications beginning of 1960, until 1979. For almost 20 years. In 1979

I bought an electric typewriter and *The Post Card*[3] was written on an electric typewriter, at a different rhythm. I thus made my workshop electric in 1979, and since then, always resisting (I still resist modernization and technological progress), I started organizing my resistance towards the computer from 1984–85 onwards. In 1985, the difficult but decisive experience happened when Jean-François Lyotard, who was organizing his exhibition 'Les Immatériaux' at the Centre Pompidou, signed me on to a group of people who were supposed to correspond with each other by defining a certain number of words – he had made a list of them – communicating through linked-up computer terminals sponsored by Olivetti who, as a publicity stunt, had distributed twenty-six of these computers. Everyone was supposed to produce their own definitions and communicate them to the others. I installed this machine at home and when it entered the house I got the impression that I had let in a monster. And, of course, I was completely incapable of using it. I gave up and I told the organizers that I would use my electric typewriter instead and that they would have to transcribe the thing themselves. And this is what happened. 'I'll never collude with this thing,' I said to myself then.

Nevertheless, witnessing, especially abroad with my American friends, how this thing kept progressing, and realizing the assistance it provided to them, I asked to be initiated. I bought a computer. There were some disasters which should have been enough to make me relinquish definitively, but which, on the contrary encouraged me to take more precautions and, from this moment on, the whole thing became instead a question of managing the dependency of a drug-addict. I don't even understand anymore how I could have worked with an electric typewriter. I can go back to handwriting letters, because it's more economical. The drive towards the manuscript is very much alive in me, but I could never again use a typewriter, whether mechanical or electric. Every time I try I get the impression that it's like using a pneumatic drill. So now it is a hesitation between word-processors, as the curious expression goes, and handwriting.

I often get asked whether the use of the computer has changed the way I write. I don't really know what to answer. Yes and no. No, in so far as something continues to prompt me with words, the rhythm of a sentence, etc. Yes, undeniably, in so far as it has changed the economy of composition. I write all my seminars, everything I teach, on the computer, and I see that when I want to organize a session, which involves moving things around, moving something from the end to the beginning, that from that point of view I do things that I would never have been able to do before, that sometimes I would never even have thought of doing by hand or even with the typewriter. Undeniably, as far as composition, flexibility, speed of writing are concerned, things have profoundly changed. As far as sentence structure, movement or the relationship between body and writing are concerned, I'm not so sure.

Allow me to tell you a little story about this: one day, over dinner, a discussion starts between Jean Genet, Paule Thévenin and me, around this topic. Jean Genet, who'd never even touched a typewriter, says to me: 'But you can't possibly write on a typewriter. You must have noticed that it kills your sentences. It's an unacceptable violence, it's a question of the body, etc.' And a long discussion follows, a whole evening, during which I try to convince him that probably the interposition of the machine, whatever kind, does transform the writing body, the relationship between the body and the letter and the sentence, but it is a transformation that doesn't interrupt, doesn't cut the body off from the writing. And anyway, a certain interruption even exists if you use a pen or a pencil. In any case, there's an interruption and that's why ideas come to you not when you're writing but rather while you walk, run or drive. I drive a lot and it's often while I drive that I have the best ideas. There is thus an interruption when you write with a pen or a quill, there is an interruption when you write with a machine, but these are two different types of interruptions which nevertheless allow something of the body to pass into writing. It is another order of interruption. We had a discussion the whole evening about this. 'I'm saying that the machine doesn't preclude anything; you're saying it stops the poetry, it stops the literature, it stops the flow of the sentence...No, it's just another body.' He wasn't convinced. He left at about midnight, with Paule Thévenin, with whom I saw him quite often. When they got back to Paris, Paule told him: 'You know, I think Jacques is right.' But the next morning, very early, he rang me to tell me roughly this: 'In fact, I think you're wrong.' It's an interminable discussion about what happens between the writing body and the writing, depending on what happens to intervene between them and then, of course, what manages to intervene very often is also in fact someone who does the intervening. In this scene of writing, which has always interested me, there are of course figures, characters, forces, which are embodied, instrumentalized in all these instruments and that must be dealt with.

Now, to give you an impression of how big a neurotic I am with regard to the scene of writing, I'll tell you about how terrorized I've been of losing texts ever since I've had a computer, a kind of terror that stems from initial traumatic experiences (I've lost texts like everybody else), a terror I could have felt while writing on paper, too, because you can easily lose paper. Nevertheless this form of terror is about losing text as such. As a result I confess that I have at home three computers, two of which have a zip drive, a supplementary hard disk – the word 'supplement' is a magnificent way to express this – and when I'm writing a long text, which takes a long time before going into print, I never leave the house, because I was once burgled, my computers were stolen, and so I never leave the house without having made multiple copies of this text, one, two, three, four... at least ten copies, which I leave in different places because apart from burglary there is of course also the risk of fire, and so on. And I have here in my briefcase essentially what is in progress, not a copy of everything. Everything that is awaiting completion is in this briefcase.

This is the kind of neurosis that develops alongside technology. I didn't have this kind of worry when I was using handwriting. I don't even remember making photocopies of my first texts. I had one carbon copy, that was it. Today, despite all this, once I've finished a long text, an article or a book, after it's printed, I take it to the photocopier and run off a copy for myself.

Now, after these general points – because they really are general, even though some pathological traits are of course my own, but there are many aspects that you've probably recognized as being part of your own writer's universe – I will try to answer the more specific questions that Daniel Ferrer put to me.

'Do you read pen in hand?' – Yes, sometimes, but I don't take notes when I read, there is no notepaper placed next to the text. I use a pencil to ill-treat the book, to scribble, to underline, to draw arrows. I brought some samples of books thus tortured by me, when I was a student but also very recent ones. But in general I don't take any notes alongside, or what you'd call reading notes. I did do that when I was a young student. Sometimes I note down those things that I know I'll need, but not actually while I'm reading through a book. This actually provokes some irony and criticism in my family, because I have two sons who, quite unlike me, treat books with great respect, they are very bibliophile. I'm not, I don't have a religious respect for books or for the beauty of the book-object. My sons don't want to use my books, they prefer to buy their own copies because they see the traces of my violence, the pencil stabs, exclamation marks, arrows, underlinings.

'If so, what material do you write on? In the book itself, in a notebook, on cards?' – It varies. I read with a project in mind. I rarely read aimlessly, I'm almost always looking for something because I've got work in progress, a seminar, so that I'm reading actively, selectively, too selectively and not passively. Thus I'm looking for things and I sometimes note references, stick in Post-its, or write this or that word or idea in the back of a book, a page number. These are not indexes, but just reminders where to find things in the book, where I can find a specific idea again, a problem, a word. What I often write down when I'm not at my desk but behind the wheel, waiting at a set of traffic lights, what I note, what I find, is a word, an inductive or formalizing word, an economical word, nothing else.

As far as index cards are concerned, there is no regularity. I did use some cards a long time ago when I was working on *Of Grammatology*,[4] on writing as it happens. At that time, I accumulated Bristol Board cards that went into wooden boxfiles which I bought at Gibert, like people who write their thesis. I don't anymore. What sometimes happens now when I'm in the process of writing something, a project that takes some time, is that I travel with some notebooks. I love notebooks with thick paper, I just carry them around with me. For a very long time in my life when I was preparing a book that I never actually wrote, on circumcision, of which only the little text called *Circonfession*[5] remains; for years, I kept filling notebooks of a certain type, in a not exactly random way but quite far removed from the point of actual writing, potential notes, very virtual. I took notes of everything which one day might be related to circumcision. These could be reading notes or thoughts that just occurred to me. I have a great number of these notebooks. They were drawing sketch books, Canson sketch books, beautiful paper. They each started with a letter of the Hebrew alphabet. I can't write Hebrew but I learned the word for circumcision, which is *mila* and in these sketch books, drawing books, I wrote at great length in a handwriting that is no longer quite my own.

'When you take notes do you already know exactly what they are for?' – Yes, in principle. Except for the case I just mentioned, but even then I knew that the notes were either directly or indirectly related to circumcision, otherwise, yes. I take notes that follow on from the things that are in progress. Most of the time for my teaching, actually, because what occupies me most, the best part of the year, is the seminar that I'm teaching. At the moment, everything that concerns the pardon or the death penalty. I scribble something that is utterly illegible for anyone else. But it's a kind of reminder, an *aide mémoire*, so that I can go and find the passage in question.

'Do your notes leave traces that can be located in your drafts?' – I don't have drafts. In the beginning, the 'protohistory' I referred to, there were several stages of a text, and I used to rewrite things. I didn't make many corrections, I rewrote the entire text. I even rewrote an entire book by hand once. I remember that I recopied by hand my first book, the Introduction to Husserl's *The Origin of Geometry*,[6] which is about two hundred pages long, before typing it. This is over now. Since everything is on the computer there are no more drafts but only several formats of a text on a disk, which I don't usually keep. A couple of times I kept several stages, notably for *Circonfession*. But for most of the texts I don't keep anything, they are transformed without leaving any trace.

'Do you read different kinds of books differently?' – Of course. Having answered in the affirmative I don't really know how to pursue this question any further. It is a question of rhythm. To tell you the truth about the way I read, I must admit that I read very impatiently, very fast and that this selective impatience costs me dearly, notably in many injustices and neglects. But very often when I open a book, in the middle, this impatience leads me straight to what I'm looking for, or what I didn't even know I was looking for – while still finding it. Thus this very impatient, selective (much too selective) way of reading is a price I have to pay. What makes me suffer, however, is that even though this speed may sometimes serve me well for philosophical texts, it's completely unjustifiable in the case of novels or poetry, literary texts. In those cases I must say that to read, to read a literary text properly, means that I have to slow down, decrease my normal reading rhythm.

I often notice that it's while writing *about* a literary text that I begin to read and that my first reading consisting of intermittent flashes of understanding was very incomplete. In a word, my experience is basically that I can only be just and faithful in my readings, that I can only do justice to the text I read, when I am teaching and writing about it, and when I'm thus interested in a specific passage of a text. Rousseau's *Contrat social*, for example which I read and studied for my *agrégation* [professorial exams], suddenly appears afresh under my reading lamp when I prepare a reading of a passage for my students, and I have the impression that I'm reading it for the first time. And only then am I reading it at the rhythm it demands and I would never have been able to read it like that, from beginning to end, impossible. I sometimes start with a reading or writing hypothesis formulated without sufficient time and then reread exhaustively in order to verify that hypothesis. For example, I counted the 'yes' in *Ulysses* after I'd started writing a text on the 'yes' in *Ulysses*, but once I'd formulated my hypothesis, I had to reread everything. So I read the whole thing again in French and in English annotating every 'yes' in both versions. And their equivalents. On that occasion I read with great pain and patience, which is really not my normal rhythm of reading. That wasn't the way I'd first read *Ulysses*[7] but I had obviously missed a lot of things the first time.

Thus I only read when I work, even texts that seem to be extremely far removed from any idea of work, poetic texts, prayers, mystic texts; I only read them, receive them, when I'm working or teaching with them. In fact, it's the teaching that makes me read.

'Does the way you classify books in your library, whether it's premeditated or by chance, have an influence on your thinking?' – Yes, very much. It's like the body, the way in which books are positioned in the house, at home. This is something that has always exercised me a lot, and even though I've never lived in great luxury as far as space is concerned, I've always been very attentive to this. The topology of things is at once rational and empirical, it's stratified and retains marks of my life-story, and the places where I live. When I think back to my adolescence, I grew up in a family without many books, some, rather bad, novels, which I read of course, Paul Bourget . . . and that was all. I bought my first books in Algiers with the money my father gave me for the week. Hence, extreme fetishism: above my bed there were Baudelaire's *Les Fleurs du mal*, Gide, for whom I had a great passion. I had maybe ten, fifteen, twenty . . . books. I carried them around with me and I brought them here into this building [The Ecole Normale Supérieure, 45 rue d'ulm, Paris]. I had all my books in Paris, and when I went to the United States I left a case full of books (about a hundred or a hundred and fifty) in the attic and I never found them again when I came back. I'm still weeping at having lost these books, the stolen books of my youth.

Afterwards I started reconstituting a small library without stratification – empirical topology. In the beginning, in my home (as it first was a suburban house) my library consisted of shelves on bricks. These books that I took with me when I moved in 1968 were either works of philosophy or just my favourite books, literature, or books that I began to receive. Gradually the house started to be organized like this: in the attic, of which I took possession, because there was not enough space elsewhere, were all the philosophical books I needed for my work (I worked in what I called my *sublime*, an attic only accessible with a ladder). For ten years I worked in there, and it contained all the books for my work, the great philosophers: Plato, Kant, Marx, Husserl, Heidegger, etc. Downstairs were the books I started being sent, dedicated books. I don't throw any books away, and I'm being sent quite a few, more and more, in fact. So all the dedicated books stand together in alphabetical order. There are now many rooms full of dedicated books. When my two sons left the house I occupied their rooms. Now there are the attic and three rooms on the first floor filled with these books. Literature is on the ground floor. There are some shelves with foreign literature, literature written in English has a place of its own, art books and then my favourites, Mallarmé, Artaud, Ponge, Blanchot, Bataille, Kafka...

The latest piece of news is that since the house couldn't take any more books we added a room which extends the house into the garden and is going to be my studio apartment. There for the first time in my life I'll have enough room. It's a large room with a very high ceiling and a mezzanine floor, shelves and ladders that go right to the top and I'm in the process of completely changing the order of my library. In brief, the current plan is that the philosophical works will go down into this apartment where I'm working on one of my computers. I won't say anything of that which takes up most of the space apart from the books: cardboard boxes full of papers, manuscripts and correspondence. As it happens – another confession I'm making – since the last three or four years there has been a Franco-American project to accommodate my archive and a few years ago the University of [California at] Irvine, where I teach, proposed, and I finally accepted, to accommodate all the paper copies, a large amount of the notes (for my seminar which I've been teaching for thirty-five years), typewritten scripts, a lot of early handwritten material, the originals of which go there, while I only keep a copy. And there is also an agreement with the IMEC[8] and this American archive to arrange for everything to be duplicated, in order to share these things or at least the access to them, especially the correspondence. I now have somebody who comes to help me classify, order, make an inventory of everything and send it either to Paris or Irvine, this whole archive of manuscripts, proofs and notes.

Question from the floor: *You said that during the phase of conception, before the actual writing, you jot down a word: what do you mean by that?*

JD: This word is somewhat other than a word. It's a word that in the best of cases has the ability to formalize, or maybe is the future of a thought, a word which is a theoretical matrix or which allows me, through condensation, to say more, more quickly. I'm circling around a hypothesis, a logic, an explanation and suddenly a word seems right to me because of its economy to formalize, to capitalize. It's not a word but a concept. But it's not only a concept either; it's inseparable from the body of a word in French. What I'm feeling then is not that I've invented or that I've been the first active user of this thing, but rather that I've received it by chance. This word comes to me through the French language, like something that had been in reserve and which now suddenly formalizes and liberates at the same time a kind of theoretical potential. I'm not saying that this happens very often, but this is the way in which the best things happen in my work. In these moments I discover this word to which I never before seem to have paid any attention and then, all of a sudden, it arrives and is the response to my waiting.

Question from the floor: *Do you see any link between these words and your impatient reading?*

JD: The word-unit remains what guides me like a beacon in my impatient reading. There are more and more books which I don't have time to read. So I flick through them and while I do so, using this mixture of blindness and lucidity of which I spoke earlier; words, not long sentences, jump out at me. And I'm often surprised myself by a certain assurance – inseparable from chance, however – in this encounter with the word I was looking for. When I work I have a kind of programme that is running, a certain set of themes I'm interested in, an organizing principle and as a result, with anything I open, book or newspaper, this programmatic set of themes operates like the search function on my computer. So I know what I'm looking for, the computer starts working, I open a book and bang! At that very moment, whatever I happen to look at, I go straight to the thing that matters for me. And this process depends on words. It is words that come right towards me.

Question from the floor: *In this geography of books you described, this developing organization, is there any room for emotion? Is there any room for books which are not being used for your work? Which books do you have in your bedroom?*

JD: Everything is full of emotion, everything, even the philosophy books, the technical books. On my bedside table there are some books I browse in every night. I can't read for a long time. Every night I read a little before I fall asleep, and there are some books with which I fall asleep. These are never philosophy books, nor books I use for work, because they would put me in the kind of active state that would harm my sleep. There are books from which I expect affective gratification, pleasure even. They might be books written by people I know, or to whom I have a personal relationship, who are important to me. Often this is also the time when I flick through the newspapers. Generally, there is not just one but four or five books next to me, which I open one after the other, five minutes each. But I'm not a leisurely reader [*liseur*]. The books at my bedside are not leisurely reads.

Question from the floor: *Where does your reluctance to throw away books or paper come from?*

JD: I began by talking about fetishism and autoeroticism. It is obvious that those things we write on, these traces, are pieces of our own desiring body, eroticized. It's narcissism. Even if I keep books by other people, this is not without narcissism. It's always a little bit of self-preservation.

The big phantasy (let's call it a phantasy, for want of a better explanation) which is always actively, topically and thematically present to me, is that all these papers, books, texts or disks are already surviving me. They are already witnesses. I'm thinking of this all the time, that someone will come after my death and will look at this book for example, which I read in 1953, and will ask: 'Why did he tick this, or put an arrow there?' I'm obsessed with this surviving structure of any of these bits of paper, of these traces. It's the structure of the trace which is survival as such. And this house for me is already a place which I imagine people (and I'm mistaken of course and I know it), probably my family, will be interested in. I'm telling myself that they will come to archive, reclassify, inspect everything they didn't see while I was alive. I'm obsessed by this scene, of that which already dispenses with me, which already survives me. But I don't believe anything of this, of course.

Question from the floor: *You talked about the relation between the body and writing, is this not also a matter of age?*

JD: Of course! What I tried to describe in an extremely broad way earlier on is at once the historical and technical transformation of the thing, the development from pen to computer, and also the movement from one age to the next. And since I'm also obsessed with death and survival I observe myself growing old through my writing. I'm always looking out for signs of change in the way I read, in the way I write – not so much with regard to the way I write in terms of style or thinking, but technically, in relation to memory. I'm constantly watching the workings of memory and that which, in my case, has always taken the form of an extremely active form of forgetting. A moment ago I spoke of selecting and filtering. Selecting and filtering of course are not only what happens while I open a book in the present, it's also about what I retain from the past. I've obviously got an absolutely astounding ability for amnesia, which is also what allows me to move on, to continue. Amnesia with regard to what I've read but also to what I've written. And this is not just a question of age: I've always been operating on forgetting just as much as on remembering. Which means that very often I retake the same routes, and I keep finding the same things. It's a very strange scenario: I am in a specific film sequence and suddenly I realise that I revisit, in a different form, a very familiar text-scene which I'd totally forgotten. This can be the text of an author, but also a way of formulating a reading hypothesis. So I start the same thing all over again, the thing I had forgotten.

Notes

*This and the following interview with Hélène Cixous first appeared in *Genesis*, 17 (2001), 59–72.

1. Jacques Derrida, 'Psyche: Inventions of the Other', in Lindsay Walters and Wlad Godrich (eds), *Reading de Man Reading* (Minneapolis: University of Minnesota Press, 1989), 25–65.
2. Jacques Derrida, 'Force and Signification' in *Writing and Difference*, trans. Alan Bass (London: Routledge, 1990), 29.
3. Jacques Derrida, *The Post Card: From Socrates to Freud and Beyond*, trans. Alan Bass (Chicago and London: University of Chicago Press, 1987).
4. Jacques Derrida, *Of Grammatology*, trans. Gayatri Chakravorty Spivak (Baltimore: Johns Hopkins University Press, 1976).
5. In Jacques Derrida and Geoffrey Bennington, *Jacques Derrida*, trans. Geoffrey Bennington (Chicago: University of Chicago Press, 1993).
6. Jacques Derrida, *Edmund Husserl's The Origin of Geometry: An Introduction*, trans. J. P. Leavey (Lincoln: University of Nebraska Press, 1989).
7. Jacques Derrida, 'A Number of Yes', trans. Brian Holmes, *Qui Parle*, 2 (2), 1988, 120–33.
8. The *Institut mémoires de l'édition contemporaine*; see www.imec-archives.com

B. 'I am an archreader':[1]
Hélène Cixous

An interview with Daniel Ferrer

A writer of fiction, playwright, critic – and also a teacher, one who has taught several generations of postgraduates (including this interviewer) and those attending her seminars to read – Hélène Cixous has agreed to give a detailed description of her personal library and to reveal to what extent, and in what ways, reading leaves its mark on her own creative activity.

Daniel Ferrer: *When one undertakes a range of activities – those of critic and teacher, writer of theatre and fiction, does this imply several different modes of reading?*

Hélène Cixous: This morning, we thought about potential questions and, to be honest, I had not thought of that one, and yet it is absolutely pertinent, although I did think to myself that there are several, I nearly said readers in the masculine, no, women-men readers,[2] several people reading in me, that's certain. But ultimately I had never wondered, until now, about the plurality of those reading. Therefore, I am being cautious: there must be a small trace of sexual difference in the positioning of the reader: who is reading for whom? Who in me is reading what for whom else in me? For me there are two scenes of reading; one is my relationship to reading in general which I have already had occasion to discuss: the other is very ritualized because it is linked to the subject of my Saturday seminar, for which I read specifically, in a very ritualized manner, throughout the two preceding days, normally the Thursday and the Friday.

Thus I should distinguish between these two scenes which are radically different and talk to you about different kinds of reading. But perhaps I should start by stating that I am an archreader, everything began through reading. Legend has it in my family that, when I was very young and ill one day with a sore throat, that I learnt to read on my own in twenty-four hours and that I could read perfectly before I was four. This is

22

probably true because I have always been mad about books for a multitude of reasons that I have discussed in different texts. I immediately realized, before starting school, that the *other world*, what was for me anyway, the world of salvation, was the world of the book. I believe that the most urgent thing that structured me is this – the need for books born of a tragic view of the world, and I could speak at length about my need for books and the way in which this need has continued throughout my life. The need for books works (me) like a charm and keeps me well.

I am a reader before I write. Writing for me is born of reading. And I never write without reading. I am always accompanied by reading and furthermore I believe that when I write I am reading, I mean to say that everything that I write is but reading. This is clearly banal, but it seems to me that when I am writing, I am in the process of reading what has not yet been written, that what I am in the process of doing is transcribing. Thus I read the invisible book before me and am accompanied by visible and readable books which surround me. The act of writing is an act of reading, I leaf through some kind of cosmic book and I copy it down. I am really a copyist of the invisible book.

In order to be more specific, I noted down my everyday library, that which constitutes my room. I need the place in which I write to be empty, I need it to represent the blank page, I don't want to be surrounded by things to look at, instead it is completely covered by books. The *presence* of books around me, even if I don't read them, is essential to me, essential to my physical existence. I might say, switching between metaphors, that if I am a knight the shelves full of books are my armour or, if I am a bird, then they are my feathers. In any case it is part of the body, it is my other body, my double from which I am inseparable. I cannot imagine myself writing in a place that was not, as part of its very nature, full of books. I cannot write without being in a situation that is almost ritualized. I need all my books around me, I need a world to be created, I need the world of literature to be there. I have sometimes written in hotels, taken notes. But that is not writing, it is quick notation, the text would not get off the ground if there were not this invisible army of books around me, walking alongside me.

So my surroundings are simply part of my bodily furniture.[3] It is sacred, which means that there are no books around me that I don't like. That would not be possible. I will even tell you some secrets: I receive lots of books, some of them I like, many of them I don't like. They stay with me for a very brief period, because the space around my reading self is sacred. So if I don't like them, I immediately put them in another room, those books cannot have access to that which is so much a part of my body that I couldn't say that I make love to them: they are me, they make me up, they dream me.[4] And, as they are (so much to) me, they are always there.

I have noticed some quite strange things about this – these are such ancient habits that I had never analysed them. But in stepping back to observe I realised: that's it, there are certain books which are always in front of me. I have two writing desks – one in Paris and one in my house in the South West of France where I go to really write – and both of them, whilst being entirely different from each other, have the same structure. In both cases my desk is in front of the window, and so I direct myself towards a particular space, towards the distance, *towards the faraway* and, in front of the window, I have a row of books which I consider as *the closest*, the closest to me physically and spiritually, my secret books.

Through the book-window I approach the faraway, I fish for it with books. To my left I have other books, to my right I have others, and behind me there are some more. In the two places of writing I have more or less the same books. I cannot duplicate them all because that would be too many and some of them are rare, have become impossible to find, perhaps because I am lazy, I have no idea, but there are more or less the same books in the two places and I bring those with me which are not in the second place as I run a shuttle of books from one place to the other.

Those books in front of me have a sort of longevity. I no longer even know what is there. But I do know that when a book wins a place in front of me it is because it has touched me deeply. After that I can go without reading it for a long time. But it stays there. Higgledy-piggledy. I have no system. I have seen other peoples' libraries: how do you organize books? Very often it's done alphabetically – but how can you put books in alphabetical order? Which element is alphabetized – the author's name, the title? I carry the location of all my books within me through my memory: a sensual geobibliography.

In front of me is Dante, there is *Paradiso*. Two or three random volumes of Artaud as I have Artaud's complete works in the old Gallimard edition, but not all of Artaud is in front of me. Those in front of me are chance volumes. Then there is Dante's *Inferno*, Mandelstam's *The Egyptian Stamp* (actually there is a lot of Mandelstam), there is Thomas Bernhard, the interviews, *The Voice Imitator*, two or three volumes of Thomas Bernhard, this is also a synecdoche, as all of Thomas Bernhard is behind me. The fact that there is some Thomas Bernhard in front of me means that I must have a very intimate relationship with Thomas Bernhard. There is a book by a Czech poet, Vladimir Holan, a book entitled *Douleur* which I think is sublime. There are two slim volumes of Ingeborg Bachmann: *The Good God of Manhattan* and the other one I think is a volume of her lectures. This represents my relationship with Ingeborg Bachmann, the rest is elsewhere. There is a completely worn out volume of Théophile de Viau that I love and that has been with me for thirty or forty years. There is Mandelstam's *Tristia*; two anthologies of Chinese poetry; a recent volume from a Serbian writer, David Albahari, a very beautiful book entitled *Bait*, the Pléiade edition of Rimbaud, and Montaigne from whom I am never separated. There is Derrida's *The Gift of Death*; the *Oresteia* in various translations; a volume by the Swedish poet Edith Södergran, *The Land Which Doesn't Exist*; there is Nelly Sachs, *Enigmes en feu*, all of Shakespeare, four or five volumes of Levinas, the complete works of François

Villon and *The Song of Roland*. That's what is in front of me, they make up my 'Contemporary'. I note that there is a lot of poetry here. The books from which I am inseparable are often books of poetry, even though I don't write in this form, at least not explicitly.

On the left is the shelf I would label 'correct usage'. There is a Grevisse, *Latin Words, Greek Words*, a Benveniste, a Morier, the dictionary of poetics and rhetoric, several volumes of Bernhard which are there by accident, there is a German etymological dictionary, a series of tiny basic dictionaries of several languages, because the big ones are behind me, that's it.

Higher up on the left, there is my stock of theatre, but this is my emergency shelf, if I can put it like that, because the theatre is also elsewhere. Up there are those that I love, in one way or another: there is Chikamitsu in French, which is now a complete set, whereas for a long time it was almost unobtainable and for twenty years I dragged around an old, completely worn-out volume of the first translations. There is some Strindberg, not all – here also there is a reserve, there is some Zeami; there is a large volume of Noh which I love.

Behind me there is a wall covered in shelves, on them there are a huge number of books. But the ones which I find indispensable have to be there, even if I only use them sporadically. I cannot bear the idea of not being reassured by them. There is a *Bailly, Gaffiot, Harrap's, Oxford* and large dictionaries of Russian and Portuguese. There is a book that I have been searching for desperately, it is impossible to find so if you come across it buy it as a matter of urgency, it's the *Boissière, The Analogical Dictionary of the French Language*, which is an absolute wonder, unfortunately now impossible to find. I found it secondhand fifteen or twenty years ago and, since then, when anyone asks to borrow it, I refuse, I never lend my *Boissière*. Then there is a *Littré* and a *Larousse* of the nineteenth century.

Also near me, always behind me, in the place of the unconscious or of the future in progress, is the whole of Derrida's oeuvre, from the beginnings, and the beginnings are very ancient, from the first offprints to the most recent works. Then there is a row of books which are very important to me, as familiar as books from childhood. They are in fact the childhood of literature: a large number of epics, Homer, of course, in different translations, two volumes of the Talmud, the Bible, the Gospels, all of Saint Augustine, all of Saint Francis of Assisi, the *Egyptian Book of Death*, the *Tibetan Book of the Dead*, two or three versions of *Gilgamesh* (there are now very beautiful translations of all these books), the Vedas, Chrétien de Troyes.

This is my luggage, which can remain silent for a long time. But I cannot separate myself from it because, when I'm writing, I might need to go over there and consult them. I will tell you about them later. Of course there is all of Proust, all of Stendhal, only half of Rousseau's works, which have always fascinated me, but that's just how it is. I have a passion for Rousseau, but it must be a half-passion. All of Genet, all of Ingeborg Bachmann, in French and in German, all of Kafka, in French and in German, all of Bernhard, in French and in German, all of Clarice Lispector, in French, in Portuguese, in English. There are often English translations because, for the seminar, I sometimes work with comparative translations: I want to see how a text has been (c)harmed in this or that language. There is all of Tsvetaeva in French and in Russian, the same for Akhmatova. There is all of Celan, in French, in German and sometimes in other languages too. Then the German Romantics. And then my treasures, perhaps what is most secret to me, as these are the books that I adore but are not liked or even known by many, for example, the work of Selma Lagerlöf. I insist on her place here and this represents an exception to the general rule that governs my choice, most of the books which I have and love are adventurous, daring, deconstructing texts which play with meaning, but this is not at all the case with Selma Lagerlöf. We could talk about this.

There is *The Tale of Genji*, there is Isaac Babel, all of Pirandello, all of Rilke, Ibsen, Brecht, a quarter of Brecht but all of Ibsen. All of Dostoevsky, all of Pushkin, and all the other Russians that I try to collect whenever possible from Platonov to Pasternak.

There is yet another shelf, the lower one. There is a little Joyce. I admit to having relegated my enormous Joycean library to another room, but it is not far away. I rarely use it, but cannot be separated from it either. There are five or six shelves of history books or books on music which I need from time to time. I use history a lot, but in a particular way as it is linked to theatre. I have books either on the Middle Ages, or on very recent events. Always theatre. And if I now move to another room, which doesn't mean going very far away, as these are communicating rooms, at this particular moment I have almost all of classical psychoanalysis, and the same can be said for classical philosophy. There may be gaps of course, more Joyce, and then a series of Pleiade editions.

That is the very rough description of what surrounds me. Then there are thousands of books that make up what is left. For example, all my library of English and American literature (which I never open, but I haven't thrown them away) that dates from my Anglicist period and which slumbers under a thick layer of dust. A sort of hotchpotch which represents the sedimentation of my own academic history. I should say (and am gripped by remorse): that in a forgotten corner there are books by women. I am also ashamed to say that, at one point, I had opened my own 'women's' section, in this case also for academic purposes. But it is significant nevertheless. For example, I have not much in common with Nathalie Sarraute and Marguerite Duras, even though I have and love[5] their books. They are elsewhere alongside a wide range of others. There are a few volumes of Madame de Staël, a few volumes of George Sand, or even Karen Blixen, of whom I am immensely fond, but in this emergency situation, as the shelves are full, she has found herself a little further back.

So this is the very general map of the library that accompanies me. I have told you which are the closest to me. It is not perhaps what you might have imagined, but that's how it is.

DF *Is it fixed or does it evolve? Are there books which are suddenly promoted to the first row, or which disappear without a trace?*

HC Amongst those that I love, there are none that vanish completely. On the other hand there is a chronological order of arrival, as much on my bookshelves as in my texts. I did not get to grips with Stendhal until quite late. I couldn't put a date to it, but about fifteen years ago he became one of my favourites. Now I never go a year, and certainly not a summer (the time for writing), without conversing with Stendhal. There are events of reading whose origins I cannot trace. They happened so long ago. The books that are closest to me, which are amongst my oldest encounters, are the German Romantics, all the great epics, the Bible etc. These are my prehistory; books that I started to read as soon as I could get my hands on them, from a very long time ago. In the case of Derrida, this has been from the point he began to write as I have followed him since 1963 without ever 'missing' a single text. My relationship with Freud is a very particular story. I can see myself now, reading Freud for the first time at the age of eighteen with, unfortunately, the mistaken idea, the naivety, of thinking that he would tell me everything, I had an image of him as a prophet, I had always thought that he would know everything and the first question I asked him was: 'What is a woman?' It was disastrous as I had gone straight to the texts which dealt with female sexuality and I got a terrible shock: I had never dared think that Freud could be challenged, and so I concluded therefore that I must be a strange and abnormal being who did not correspond to this description of women. This was so painful that I closed Freud and put him aside completely. Later, I must have already been twenty-five, I returned to Freud. Then I had the good idea of reading *The Interpretation of Dreams* and I found myself at home. It's only in this second period of reading that I have made friends with Freud, with whom I always had the feeling of sharing family ties, fantastical ones of course, but explicable nonetheless as my own family shares his socio-historical and geographical origins. Every time I flicked through the family photograph album, I thought: 'Ah, that's him, right there!' He looked just like my great uncle. I felt as if I was being reunited with a member of my family and he is very present in my texts but in a way which is not always noticeable. I amuse myself by implicating him as a character in my texts, or even as the strange poet that I seek out in order to stage a literary discussion, an exchange.

My memory on these matters is very clear, I could almost date the point at which these companions entered my life. The only one who has a slightly singular fate is Joyce, but not to any great extent. I spent ten years of my life as close as possible to Joyce, ten years of intense study, in absolute proximity. Joyce is the only one whose manuscripts I have consulted. It is he who gave me the taste for manuscripts. When I began to work on Joyce there was nothing in France and I set off to do research. I thus travelled around the universe. Joyce's manuscripts were scattered, some in the British Museum, some in the library in Buffalo, and some in the library at Yale. I went on a pilgrimage to all these sanctuaries and this was very important for me. When I was near Joyce's manuscripts I enjoyed an intimate and loving relationship with him. I spent a long time with them as, at that time, there was no other way of doing things. You were not allowed to make photocopies, yet you held the manuscript in your hands, it's a very necessary experience for researchers and I believe that everything is transmitted from hand to hand or from body to body.

So this is someone with whom I have spent many years, but strangely, he has never been my heartfelt favourite. For me, there has always been something missing in Joyce's work. You cannot blame him for this absence. I could say that there is no Levinas in Joyce. I will be told: but yes, you only have to look... No, there is no Derrida there either. And in Joyce there is an element missing that is absolutely vital to me, that of tragedy, of human suffering. And so this is someone with whom I have not become allied. But on the other hand, I feel infinite friendship, loyalty and faithfulness towards his tremendous textual adventure and, obviously, I feel great admiration as this explorer has always enchanted and amused me. But I have never in my life written a book with Joyce. He is not there. From time to time I call him, I invite him to visit me with my researchers because he has this unique genius of signifying. I had great fun this year with extracts from *Finnegans Wake*. It must be said that wherever this kind of gigantic genius at forgery of the unconscious produces the effects of the unconscious – it remains unimaginable. He is unique in this way – and this interests me enormously and so, from time to time, I seek him out, I distribute a text, I share his hostilities with my students. He is the only one to have this very particular fate of becoming a distant relative. The others I mentioned just now are close to me in an entirely different way.

DF *Apart from this sense of physical presence, how, in concrete terms, does the exchange with books take place?*

HC There are different versions. For example, in my own texts, in certain books, books are present, other books. I have always practised intertextuality from my very earliest writings, because I always felt that literature was not the invention of one individual, but that it was this immense river swelled by tributaries and converging currents. Last week I was at Montaigne's tower near Bordeaux. I always had the feeling that when I wrote I was not alone, I knew that Montaigne was just over my shoulder and that Homer was to my right and so on. I never write without these 'present-s'. This presence, which for me is ever-presence, within the space and time of the work that I am writing, allows me to feel constantly part of an immense genealogical or creative network. Sometimes there are books within my books. For example, Freud is directly there in *Portrait du Soleil*. It's either the work that makes its way into my books or the author of the texts who appears. If we look for the work, for example, in the *The Third Body* I had amused myself by rewriting, by completely replaying several texts by Kleist. I turn my own text into a mixture by taking the text with which I am in correspondence and by editing it, transforming it, translating it into my own text. Sometimes authors become characters in my texts: Mandelstam or Akhmatova. For me, this is also a phenomenon of reading. For me there are immense works that are encapsulated in their author, for example, Stendhal. There are others in which the author doesn't exist for me: Racine for example. For me, Racine is this or that great play, but I never think of Racine. On the other hand there are works which I cannot disassociate from their origins and, when I read them, the author, for example Mandelstam or Thomas Bernhard, is right beside me, watching me read, I am in the middle of talking to him or her and I have the impression of accommodating them, of sheltering them, of giving them somewhere to stay. I become the dwelling place of people who are sometimes my contemporaries, this is what is so strange: I read their books, I hear their heart beating, their passions course through me, their illnesses affect me. I don't keep them separate and so when I write with them, I write with the text and with the author that I imagine. Thomas Bernhard might come in and say to me: 'But that's not it at all.' But well, in the end that is not important, he is not here to stop me playing with who he is. It must be noted that this fantastical presence is supported by the fact that these are people who left an awful lot of traces, of 'autobiographical' accounts, without of course suggesting that I am taken in by the myth of autobiographical truth. As soon as you write you are in *otherbiography*. But I am sensitive, probably because of a certain affinity, to all works where the author was, or is, caught up in the political and historical whirlwind of their epoch and their country, as in the (melo)dramatic crucible of the unconscious.

DF *In the light of this, in which category do we find Mr Shakespeare?*

HC I don't know Shakespeare. He is perhaps amongst the very first others. As I would do with others, Joyce enjoyed constructing his Shakespeare, inventing his Shakespeare, by biographing him, by biografting him, in *Ulysses*. I do nothing of the kind. For me, Shakespeare is rather like the Bible, he is one of the great cradles of all literature. It is his plays that are always with me. I do not know them all by heart, but I do know a great many almost by heart. I open the store cupboard, there are a certain number of works which I know intimately and which are indelibly present with me, so much so that when I am writing this or that kind of text, I realise 'So, I am on this philosophical track' (it is often the philosophical that directs me), I am in the process of writing from my own material and I hear Shakespeare say to me: 'Yes, but this is what I think.' Or perhaps I hear Montaigne say: 'Yes, but here's my view on that matter.' And I remember it clearly. And that which I do not remember perfectly, it could be just a turn of phrase, an amphibology, I will find it in an instant, straight away. I need to hear them and to rework such and such a theme, taking into account their thoughts on it. Amongst those whom I question most frequently is Montaigne. (I don't do anything without Montaigne, not even for my seminars.) I am constantly leafing through his work, because I know that everything is in Montaigne, just as everything is in Shakespeare. There is not a single human situation that has not been grasped and shown anew, illustrated, incarnated, by Montaigne and then by Shakespeare. That is absolutely certain. To these, I would add Kafka, to whom I feel an extremely profound attachment, but Kafka did not say everything: he did not have time. And then there are areas of thought, of experience that are not part of his universe. But he remains, nonetheless one of those with whom I converse most frequently.

There are other interlocutors who do not occupy the same role as absolute predecessors. For me they are the gods of writing, both because of their immensity, the extraordinary profundity of their human thought and because of their textual power. There is literally no-one more modern than Shakespeare or Montaigne. You cannot say that about every author. These are people who will surprise us at any moment by the inventiveness of a phrase, the general linguistic metabolism which is theirs alone. It is astounding. It nourishes me. At any moment I can pick up these texts, open them at any page, and *laugh*, because I want to laugh, I want to be exultant, to admire human genius. It is here that I find it. Then I am subject to other encounters, it is very mysterious, I call them the inflamers, that is to say when I read them, it is as if I were receiving a wink of complicity that tells me 'yes, writing exists', as if they were a demonstration, as if they were proof of the existence of writing. As soon as I read a newspaper, I begin to doubt the existence of God. So luckily there are books to reassure me. In this category, Stendhal shines out. When I despair, when I think: 'No, the world is finished', I only have to open Stendhal in order to be gripped by *elation*, to reassure myself that any situation, the most base (that is what is so wonderful about Stendhal) – the most sordid, the most stupid, the most banal, can be transcended through a genius of writing. 'There, it's alright, writing is magical, you can get on it anywhere, there's a lift, there's a ladder, there is no shortage of transport.' Because Stendhal remains nevertheless someone who, in his personal writings and in his correspondence, deals with our experience: taking the metro, encountering idiots, wishing that the tiresome intruder on the bus would disappear, finding that

Shakespeare tastes like spinach or, conversely, finding spinach sublime, everything is in his books. So you are confident, because he takes next to nothing and turns it into something absolutely magnificent.

There is an entirely different mode of reading, one which is more aligned with incantation, similar to prayer, and moreover corresponds to cheating, I have to confess, when I happen to read Chinese poetry or Noh. I say it's cheating because I have to read them in French. A falsification of which I am very aware, but something remains which comes from the Chinese or Japanese culture and way of thinking: a sort of extraordinary economy, of condensing, of restraint, of which there are other examples, not only in painting. The character, but not only the character, that which is allusive, that which is unfinished, that which is left in the air are absolutely indispensable and corrective traits of this writing. The brevity, the economy, the thrift, the slightness of the oeuvre in these cultures, which in no way signifies that it is spiritually lacking in soul, rather that these are the workings of the sublime. It is absolutely essential for us in our cultures of excess. We write expansively. Except for a particular poetry with a slender scan. The first book in this tradition which I have dragged around with me my whole life was this poor old volume of Théophile de Viau, which I must have bought at a second-hand bookstall on the banks of the Seine, in Paris, at the age of nineteen. There is a brevity in Théophile de Viau as there is in Villon, which I find brilliant and necessary. And one that we have a tendency to lose, to dilute.

I should also add that very often I leaf through Derrida, even though I know it by heart. I would say that if he were not so close, so immediately contemporary, he would have had for me, or will have in a few centuries' time, the status of Montaigne, in so much as his project also consists of dealing with all that is human. If I happen to 'open him', I know exactly where, in the precious treasure chest, to find this or that remark.

I have not talked about Dostoevsky, despite the fact that I adore him, that I read him a lot, but my worry, here also, is that I am not a Russianist and every time that I read him, I am tormented by the knowledge that I am reading the affects, the dramatic art, and his economy of thought which I think I have properly understood, an economy of diversibility, and he is the most diverse author that one could ever come across in the world . . . but I feel grief-stricken because throughout my whole life I have lived with Dostoevsky in French or in English, which is, it must be said, disfiguring, for me at least. Yet I need that which he shares with Stendhal, which is diversibility. Plus the dimension of tragedy that cannot be found in Stendhal.

What do I do when I start to write a book? It varies greatly. I think I am always accompanied when I write. But this is not something that I can plan, I start writing my text and, on the way, I hear the others. And I go to find them. This happens in a way that I can only describe with uncertainty: I have never filmed myself doing that. In general the work that seems to be the neighbour, friend, or enemy of the text that I am writing comes and takes its place in front of me. This does not mean that I am going to read it whilst I am writing. It's rather as if it comes through to me like a telephone call, as if I were telephoning someone else or as if he were telephoning me, then, at a certain moment, suddenly things come together. There are always coincidences that I seek out or go and consult. But there are also other ways of proceeding. Sometimes I find myself taking notes, extremely precise notes, having some kind of route mapped out, having reread this or that text. It could be Kafka, or Montaigne, or Shakespeare. I make notes in an academic manner, that is, with the exact reference, or I put 'see this chapter, at this point', and that doesn't mean that it will finish up in the book. That means that there is an encounter and that maybe, yes, maybe will stay there. Or then again sometimes I use quotations. It often happens that I lift a phrase and either I will rush it straight into my text, but without marking the quotation because I will replay it immediately, or I will transpose it, that is, I will take a phrase and make substitutions, I change the subject, I anacoluth, I asyndetonate. It's a process of transposition, of distortion, which is obviously conscious, willed, and which may go on to be replayed throughout the entire text. That happens quite frequently, but it is not a regular practice.

DF *You mentioned worn-out copies of texts. What do you put them through? Do you write things in them?*

HC That's a very interesting question: well, I don't! And I wonder: 'But, why not?' I sometimes tick books, and I tick with a pencil, which is ridiculous, because in this case I know why: I tell myself that I will rub it out. It's ridiculous because I don't rub anything out. I don't return to the book later and erase. Deep down I am afraid of marking the book. For me there is some kind of taboo around it. But let's move on to discuss the seminars, as I work very intensely on the texts in the seminars: I don't make any marks in my books. Each time I work on a text, I make, twenty, thirty or forty-page copies of texts for my own use and there, in contrast, it's a precise method, a technique, and I mark it in a thousand ways, and obviously it is aimed at the students. For example, I could take a period of Derrida's *Circonfessions*, and I work on it in minute detail, annotating, I always leave myself blank spaces around the text, here in the margins and everywhere. I very quickly note the general directions of the reading, be they philosophical or linguistic, and I cover the text with the traces of my reading using highlighter pens, that means, for example, working through, and marking in one colour, all the traces of a phonic signifier. An example would be the 'ri-re' in Derrida's work during 1991, this whole period is played out through 'le rire' (the laugh). It's anagrammaticized in every way possible, there are thirty or forty occurrences that are completely covered up by the ordinary textual process. But with my three, four, five different colours, I can render visible that which, when reading the text, is unheard (we should have eyes which are ears). I want to make heard in colour that which is otherwise inaudible but which remains all the same the message hidden in the text. I do this for the seminar, I don't do it for myself.

DF *But you don't hand this out, it's a score that you interpret, for the seminar audience?*

HC Yes, but on the other hand I render it in part of the seminar, by showing the trajectory, because if I gave it out already done, no one else would make the slightest effort at deciphering it. I wait for it to be deciphered. For myself, when I am all by myself and running through the seminar with myself, I don't do this, simply because I can hear it myself, but when I read for myself, I have two modes of reading: a rapid mode of reading, I cut across, I skim, but when I stop on a page, I undertake this read-analysis. I hear everything, I see everything, I see how it has been put together, and I also understand very well that this has not been consciously planned by the author, even if what was the work of the unconscious does sometimes return towards the conscious.

My mode of reading for myself is very different from my mode of reading for the seminars as deep down I have a fantasy for the seminar, a double impulse. One impulse is to make the message reappear or rise up, that's why I tire of Joyce, because it happens very, very quickly, you very quickly cover what he has to say, but I work on texts which have a high philosophical content, which I want to make heard, which I want to decipher. But my fantasy is that you must honour the author whilst revealing their craft. Through showing the smallest, the tiniest effect of the text, this is what makes up the genetics of the text. This is what a text is made for. Unfortunately we never read like that. It is as if I were studying a cathedral with a magnifying glass. You need long-distance vision but you also need the magnifying glass on the cathedral, always. It's my fantasy, I am not saying that I would preach it to everyone, but I do find it indispensable. I work on a text poetically. I work through a lengthy text as if each paragraph were a poem. But when I am reading just for myself, it's different. I must say that when I read, I read very, very quickly, I read a page at a glance, what matters to me is discursive position taken, the engagement, it's the question of life and death experienced by each author.

But what also interests me, is the absolute artistic singularity of each one. For example, the unbelievable cheek of Stendhal when he peppers his text with 'etc'. In one move he blows apart the 'well turned out' of his day, for no-one dares to write 'etc' in mid text like that, no, one takes the trouble to finish. What I like is the step of the non-finished. I adore them, those who do not finish, those who leave you high and dry, and who make it into an art, because it clearly is an art. What overwhelms me, is always the way in which the author gets out of the text: hey presto! It's finished. An author who manages this so admirably is Clarice Lispector. All of a sudden she returns and she leaves the text. Sometimes she goes away, sometimes she is in the text, sometimes she addresses the reader and then she says: 'Wait there, carry on, I'll be back', and the text goes off like that, on its own, and hey presto! she returns a few paragraphs further on.

What matters to me is the extreme freedom of texts and everything that is normally neglected, everything that is ambiguous, undecidable, everything that plays with genre/gender, that which for me is life itself.

The poetry that I love has this. Celan; he who in an absolutely inspired way, broke, cut the thread of German poetic discourse, which doesn't at all mean that he de-poeticised it, quite the contrary. He found another form of poetry. This is what I search for myself, for myself, between me and myself. I search for the split, for the rupture. Yet another way has been found of defaulting.

DF *In what way is the rupture of the Other useful to you?*

HC It's because I am aware of the opposite instinct in me, a kind of instinct to make connections between things, thus from time to time I become Proustian, everything follows on, there are infinite infibulations, invaginations…This is a tendency that I recognize. I could say, from an analytic point of view, that it's a binding drive, that it's simply what life is. I cannot let go of it. However, it is also that which kills things off. And to be able to begin again, that's the secret of the oeuvre, you have to cut, you have to stop and set off again. I know that that exists as part of me. It's a battle, a struggle between these two movements.

I am not a model reader. Because there are several texts that I can take pleasure in reading, but for me they are not extraordinary. This doesn't mean that it's not good, it means that it's not Rimbaud, it doesn't allow me to cross a mountain or a century. I am like this because I write, I was born a reader-writing.

When I write for the theatre, I have a different system of reference that I use to help me to find this rigour, what I call this cruelty that is needed for the stage. That is when Selma Lagerlöf comes in. I am telling you all my secrets. She doesn't write for the theatre, far from it, she is a great narrator. But she is someone who possesses a Shakespearean heart – by this I mean that everything she writes takes place in the depths of the heart. You remember Yeats' phrase: 'The foul rag-and-bone shop of the heart.' All is rags, everything that has been ripped, torn away, you can find it in her work, and I always read Selma Lagerlöf when I am writing a play. It's long, it's heavy, it's not elegant, but it is solely about the heart. Dostoevsky is also like that, but less than her.

DF *Let's imagine the researcher working on the manuscripts that you are in the process of giving to the Bibliothèque nationale. Will they find the tracks of your reading? Will they be able to say, without your assistance, that this comes from there ...?*

HC I think so, yes. They will see the tracks of the work that accompanies my writing or my preparatory work – except for those that I threw away, because there was a period in my life when I didn't think about such things, and so everything went in the wastepaper basket. And I regret this enormously because I myself would be interested in it. But I was in an unreflective period during which I felt that I was not writing. For a long time, I had the feeling that there was someone who was writing and I did not dare to say out loud that *it was not me*, but I was absolutely convinced of it. I was rather ashamed when people spoke to me as if I myself had written what had been written there: at first I was incapable of realizing, then I knew that it was not me but the other. For a long time I felt ill at ease, I felt like a fraud. At this time I threw things away, because I thought that everything that was a transitional step, that was misshapen ... was for the dustbin. I thought that even the final version could also be thrown away. Moreover, I have been known to throw away unpublished texts, it was all the same to me, I didn't think that it was me that wrote them and so I wasn't at all attached to them. My narcissism in relation to this was very slight – it has grown since then ...

But for the last twenty years, as far as the theatre is concerned, Ariane Mnouchkine has kept an eye on me: having discovered that I was throwing everything away she began to howl in outrage. This was not at all because she thought that things should be kept for the Bibliothèque nationale, but for her. These were versions that she thought she might eventually use. And so it was as if I had woken up with a start. I decided that I shouldn't throw things out, in this way, that I should keep them. Now I am fairly scrupulous about keeping things, even if in a disorderly fashion. I preserve my tracks. When there are references to texts, as it was the material to be worked on, I have noted the exact reference myself, there are tracks. It is not necessarily filed within the text, but I know that Marie-Odile Germain [the head librarian in control of the classification of the collection] will be able to find her way, with the reference she could find the right path straight away. Otherwise there are quotations which are in the notebooks. Therefore, the preparatory materials are accessible, readable, exactly as I was able to read Joyce's manuscripts. I read them because I had read the finished texts, but I could not read the finished texts, at least not in the way I wanted to read them, until I had had access to his manuscripts. It felt like a sudden illumination. It's something I firmly believe in ... I think that the published text is like a conjuring trick, the work in progress is missing. I have always needed the workshop, the work in progress. It is the same in the theatre. I have always had one regret. What is played out on stage is the final point of culmination, of development, of refinement, of a clean-up. I think that all the work that took place behind the scenes was so beautiful... I cannot do without the forge. And it makes me sad. The poor audience! What they see or read is the final photograph. That's my preference, but perhaps there are people who prefer the end product.

DF *It's not for us to contradict you on that point*[6] *... Do you therefore experience no regrets in parting with all your documents?*

HC I told Marie-Odile that I needed two things. Firstly a copy, because I realized at this point that I become used to *living with manuscripts*. It's like a familiar animal that I never look at, but it's as if I had a kind of divine cat always nearby and I didn't want to be separated from it. This may seem ridiculous, as I never look at them. It's as if it were the materialization of my memory, which is only a forgetting, but I cannot be apart from my memory, I want it to stay near me. At the moment, something horrible is happening, photocopies are being made, and in addition I know that photocopies have no future, as I have already seen over the past few years how photocopies deteriorate. But I am undertaking another horrible task which I suppose is part of an experience common to many, which is that I have to be selective because a great many of my manuscripts – varying from fifteen to sixty pages – are extremely private documents which I cannot give to the Bibliothèque nationale at this time. Some are pages from my personal notebooks, some very often are notes of dreams. In both cases they cannot be made available. So I am holding them back.

DF *Do you not, like some other writers, feel some reticence faced with the idea that Hélène Cixous' 'forge' of writing will become known?*

HC On one hand it gives me great pleasure! I mean, through an identification with others. In the case of the theatre, you do not see the work in progress which is the period of rehearsal and which is very long in our Théâtre du Soleil, and sends me to the ends of the earth a dozen times. These expeditions, it's *The Odyssey*, the Argonauts, it's devastating. For months everybody suffers, but this devastation is sublime. It produces so many acts, creative actions, which are failures – but failures are the portals of discovery, as Joyce would say. I find this the most moving part. It's the research that interests me the most. This is perhaps why I love *Remembrance of Things Past*, because it is the book that is the closest to the movement of writing, that is, to research.

And each time I am grief-stricken. I think if only the public could see these moments be they comic or tragic, they are always epic! But no, the public sees the published book. It's a strange phenomenon, this homogenization, which is that of the market of course. Everything will have the same look. It's a shame; *what's left over* is so extraordinary. Work in progress lacks order, supreme harmony, but I find that the period of disorder has something more to offer, I think that it's very important that we, as humans, are aware of this. It demolishes the image of the artist's mastery. This is not true. The artist is a bungler.

I had my own personal experience of manuscripts which was a very liberating and enriching moment for me. I always think this must be the same for those around me, academics and researchers. I have never been able to imagine that you could undertake a thesis without going to consult the manuscripts, if they exist. Only, they have to exist, to be accessible. This is not always the case.

DF *There are some authors who donate their manuscripts after having carefully refined them in order to give a certain image. Except for that which is private, the communication of which you are deferring, are you donating everything?*

HC Yes. I think that this is out of respect for the creative process, not simply of my own oeuvre. Kafka's work in progress, the unpublished, that's what would interest me most in the world. Marie-Odile showed me some manuscripts at the Bibliothèque nationale and some of them overwhelmed me. Let's take one example: Flaubert's famous phrase 'He travelled' ('*Il voyagea*'). It's a sentence with the power of Noh. This is absolute purity, the purity of the simplest sentence. Then you see how Flaubert put it together, how this sentence was manufactured. He writes on large pages: the choice of material, the format, is a choice of body, it's absolutely fascinating. And to see that it took ten, fifteen, thirty attempts and rejections, to realise either a very complicated sentence or, on the contrary, a very simple one... Both are needed: the path taken is as fascinating as the final achievement, I am someone who is very moved by this kind of work, work wracked by division, the work of dissatisfaction, of an infinite tearing apart...

Translated by Julia Dobson

Translator's notes

1. The term used in the title is '*lisante*', a neologism which foregrounds the grammatical feminine whilst avoiding the use of '*lectrice*' or '*liseuse*'. Its roots in the present participle of the verb '*lire*', to read, foreground the process and unending nature of reading.
2. The term '*lectrices-lecteurs*' insists upon a combination of genders and plurality.
3. The French insists upon a stronger link between '*décor*' (surroundings) and '*du corps*' (of the body).

4. The wordplay between 'are me' – '*me sont*' and 'dream me' – '*me sont je*' recurs throughout Cixous's writing.
5. The French '*j'ai / me*' insists upon the textual connection of having and loving.
6. This interview was conducted within the premises of the Institut des Textes et Manuscrits Modernes, a research institution devoted to the study of the writing process.

Part I
Incubation

1
Dating – Deconstruction

Marc Froment-Meurice

I Where are we now?

To begin with – where are we now? First things first: before even asking
for information or looking at the map, we need to know what our final
destination is. We need to start from this point on, but as we did not get
there (otherwise we would not be wondering where we are now wandering),
we will have to leave our position in an uncomfortable indetermination.
Perhaps there is, at least for us, no way to decide as to whether we should
follow or not this *pas à suivre*. Had I to translate the title – which I would
prefer not to – I would be torn between two opposite directions: either *pas
à suivre* means that what is following is the right way, which we should
therefore follow; or, on the contrary, that it is not to be continued, because
this way is a dead end (in German, *Holzweg*). We stand at this critical point,
hesitating between two contradictory steps: either we go forward or we go
backward, depending on the meaning of the word *'pas'*, 'step' or 'not'.[1]

'Do (not) follow me', this would be the word from the title (not) to be
followed. But then either we follow, and therefore we do not follow, the step
(not) to be followed; or we follow, and therefore we do not follow, the same
step: in both cases, we have to break the law that we are required to follow
(*or not*)...Perhaps the only way to get out of the quagmire would be to be
firmly determined to stay in this indetermination up to the end and even
beyond, if indeed the place where we stand, as if paralyzed, is the end of the
road. In order to begin, we need more than simply keeping an eye to this
end; we need to be *at* the end, be it only in a thinking way, but then what
possibility is left, if the road is always already ended before we even start to
move on? How to follow anything when the next step is the last one?

Future, *à venir*, is what is intolerable to the gods and, by extrapolation, to
the so-called masters of the world. What I find most appealing in *Being and
Time* is that Dasein is conceived primarily in terms of its future. Of course,
it is its death, which means that Dasein's future is the absolute impossibility
of any future for Dasein. Dasein not to be continued, Dasein interrupted,

41

finished, and this ending is not even a completion or an accomplishment. No, simply, Dasein, as 'is', is over. The only future that opens Dasein to its being is – no future. But precisely this 'no' [*ce pas*] is what Rimbaud, at the end of his 'Farewell' (*Adieu*) to Hell, calls 'the winning step', *le pas gagné*. A step that is won only inasmuch as it stops on the threshold of the promised land, and, instead of entering there, calls for thinking, if only about the next (last or not) step.

If we are to follow Heidegger's *Denkweg* [pathway], then we first have to stop – *halten* – and even turn backward, re-turn. In a lecture given on 30 October 1965, 'Das Ende des Denkens in der Gestalt der Philosophie',[2] Heidegger describes the next step, the step after the end of philosophical thinking, as *der Schritt zurück aus der Philosophie*. It is a step backwards, turning onto itself, to the point of stepping out of philosophy. It steps out of it precisely to step into that which philosophy comes to be: not its ground, but the bottomless place that the word *Lichtung* indicates and which is nothing but the place where we already dwell.

> That which becomes necessary is rather the step that returns from philosophy. It is the coming-back-into [*Einkehr*] the field that we are merely indicating with the word of *Lichtung*: there, where we, human beings, constantly already dwell.

Where we have to go [*là où il y a lieu d'aller*] is where we always have been. This place is not an unknown or foreign location but the proper place of our own being. However, this place or site (*Ort*) 'was in no way sufficiently far enough thought', namely, with the name of 'Dasein'. In the end, with 'Dasein', all has been said and done, and yet nothing at all has been said as long as we *stay* there. For Dasein is not (yet) there, but *has to be* 'the-there', as Heidegger says 'in a turn that is probably impossible in French': *le-là*, the *Lichtung*.[3] However, since Dasein's destination is also its ending, one could argue that once the Dasein gets there, there is no longer any Dasein ... The original trope is this turn of the screw, and the step backwards may resemble, in a schizoid way, the dialectical process in which the *telos* determines in advance the point of departure, except that in this case there is no real progression or mediation. If Dasein is *constantly and essentially* not yet there, it will *never* be there; in other words, it will be forever not yet there. 'Not yet' will never be present except at the 'instant of my death' which by the same stroke means the end of any possibility of still being there.

Clearing up all that has been said before, in order to repeat all that has been said: repetition that erases everything at the same time that it reinscribes the same as the utterly other, I say: (Heidegger states that) the step backwards, which starts from the end of philosophy, does not return to its starting point, since in fact the starting point was already missing the point: Plato already thrown into the oblivion of Being. Philosophy starts from the end, that is, from the illusion that not-yet will turn into *parousia*. On the one hand, Heidegger is right in putting an end to 'philosophy' (which he reads as the exhaustion of every possibility): make no mistake, we are going nowhere with something as worn out as 'philosophy', and we should experience as a dead end the *way* of thinking that until now has worked out 'so well' that no one has any longer to look for his or her way: it all comes down to the same automatic self-programmation. This is a massive *fact* and I wonder how we could not agree with what is seemingly the last word: today, the day we see, philosophy has not taken a single step since Heidegger. Not one step. *Pas un pas.* (What is loosely called 'deconstruction' is a different step, different in the sense that it is not *one* step, does not lead into a single direction or horizon, and does not even have the unity that the name 'deconstruction' seems to ensure.) On the other hand, there is no other place than this 'nowhere'. In other words, the step backwards does not open up any other dimension for a way of thinking that would not be still determined and contained in this end of philosophy. It is something that Heidegger recognizes in asserting the finitude of thought as such. Thinking takes place only in the experience of the irreducible finitude (of Dasein in 'man'), an experience of aporia that is 'much more difficult than the display of any Absolute'. But that also amounts to saying that there is no other place than this end, no other thinking than the one that experiences thinking as always already finite, indeed, that there is no other (possible) at all. Only the same is the element of thought: thinking and Being as this same, *tauton* according to Parmenides. Any thinking that claims to be 'of' (from or for) the Other is not thinking or if it is, is not *of* the Other.

If we are to find our way, we first have to recognize the point where we now stand: at the end, but this end is far from meaning 'impotence and decadence' as long as we can retrieve the original meaning of the *word* 'end', in German *Ende*: the place, *Ort*. As the translator says: 'At the origin *Ort* designates the cutting edge of a sharp object, and also the point that results from the sharpening – the point of a spear, for example. This signification shows an affinity with *Ecke* (corner, angle) in the primary meaning of what is sharpened, cutting, acute, pointed.' It is the ideal corner, so to speak, the wedge [*coin*] to be inserted and even hammered down to the bottom, right to the core of philosophy, in order to push its way of thinking to its last and extreme possibility, i.e., to the impossible. Yet, Heidegger continues, in the end philosophy is not 'abandoned or doomed to disappear from the memory of the thinking man'. But no more is philosophy 'sublated in the sense of a dialectical process of history such as Hegel thought of'. Neither a loss nor a redemption, but the need to confront with the *pointed (w)edge* of the end, as this point where philosophy is reduced to its ultimate possibility, but which *points* toward something utterly other in the very impossibility of finding it*self*. We still have to experience the impossible as that which is pointed by the exhaustion of every (other) possibility. Philosophy is still incomplete as long as it never reaches this point and above all never inhabits the place where it came to end up. Despite all the warnings given by thinkers such as Hegel, Nietzsche and Heidegger, we still believe in an infinite set of possibilities left for philosophy, be that of a bad infinity as with the transformation of absolute knowledge into a techno-scientific process driven by the globalization of 'cultural' resources and socio-economic means to secure the one-way mode of thinking. In this depressing marketing context, 'philosophy' is completely forgotten, or rather no longer needed, since it has accomplished its mission at every moment and in every circumstance, in our everyday 'life': the global one-way mode of thinking has installed everywhere its final shape and print as the dominant 'truth' that we encounter in every object or subject (no difference at this point), at every corner of the streets and at every moment of the day or night. Philosophy can close its doors since techno-beings are open 7/7, 24 hours a day.

Mais y a-t-il lieu de penser? 'But is thinking necessary?' Not only in a different mode from the one that is now prevailing in the total programming of whatever, but is thinking *überhaupt* necessary? Is it the right path to follow, if the goal is to arrive 'where we, human beings, always already dwell'? Is not thinking already a sign that we are lost, looking for our way while this search can do nothing but aggravate the loss?

Y a-t-il lieu de penser?, another untranslatable question, asks after a place, a possible site for what is called thinking. A radical question that, while remaining a question – that is, simultaneously insisting on and existing out of any given place – gives way to the answer, in a double step: beyond and not beyond, there and here, on the cutting edge where thinking places itself as the dis-placement that points toward its own place (out of place). The proper place or site of thinking cannot be found anywhere insofar as it takes place apart from any place (is this Khora?): not only without a place, but without the need [*le lieu*] for a place – or as Without as the only place left.

II What time is it?

'The Origins of Deconstruction': this how I entitled Chapter 6 of my French translation of Rodolphe Gasché's *The Tain of the Mirror*.[4] Originally, the title evoked a remarkable Trinity: '*Abbau, Destruktion*, Deconstruction.' Two German words, and then an English one, itself a transliteration of the French.

'Before engaging in a detailed analysis of Derrida's philosophy [...], let us first examine the conceptual filiation of this notion of deconstruction, which for many has come to designate the content and style of Derrida's thought'.[5] According to Gasché, 'deconstruction' is a philosophical concept that is originated in other concepts 'generated' in other 'philosophies'. 'Filiation', a word that I rendered through the Greek 'genealogy', comes directly from the Latin '*filius*', meaning 'son' ('*fils*' in French). How a 'concept' (or 'notion') could be a son, and why not a daughter? Even if 'deconstruction' could be taken as a concept as we could find in traditional philosophy, are concepts like human beings? Then, it should have a father *and* a mother. Yet in philosophy, for obvious reasons dating back to Plato and Parmenides' 'parricide', the sexual or generic difference had to be obliterated or neutralized. Logos is a male, a father, and thus we should assign two fathers to deconstruction – two German fathers (Husserl and Heidegger) but no mother. (Mother is 'indeconstructible' because she is not part of the philosophical 'conception'.)

The very notion of a 'conceptual filiation' seems even more problematic if we want to apply it to the 'case' of deconstruction, insofar as deconstruction starts with deconstructing the unity and the purity of *just any* philosophical concept – and since there is no other way of conceptualizing, such 'filiation' is doomed to become fiction, which would certainly not please the creator of deconstructive 'infrastructures'. Even if we could do *as if* such fiction were at least very close to the 'truth', we would still stumble over a major dilemma: which of the two fathers should be deemed the most legitimate? With which one should we start, Husserl or Heidegger? Gasché picks Husserl, in spite of the chronological order, since the 'concept' of *Abbau* appears only in 1938, more than ten years after the explicit task of 'Destruktion': 'Although Husserl's notion of *Abbau* appears for the first time in *Experience and Judgment* (1938), and thus later than Heidegger's notion of *Destruktion* in *Being and Time* (1927), it should be discussed first, for, in spite of some essential difference, it is in large part another name for phenomenological reduction.'[6] We could agree that in philosophy 'chronology' is merely empirical, and that on the 'transcendental' level (of pure Ideas) Husserl with 'his' phenomenological reduction precedes Heidegger and 'his' destruction (of the history (of ontology)) 'since Heidegger's method of destruction...must be viewed against the backdrop of the epochal process of discovery'.[7] Yet, if I may speak in all 'objectivity', phenomenology does not allow much room for historicity, at least in the Husserlian use that is dealing not with *Dasein* but with a transcendental ego. Not only is the Husserlian reduction thoroughly anhistoric, but by making it more 'original' than the ontological destruction, Gasché accomplishes a real tour de force or even a violent coup: he reverses the sense of precedence by 'lending' a possible 'borrowing' by Heidegger (supposedly the son) to Husserl-the-Father: 'Heidegger may have borrowed this concept from Husserl, who referred to the forms of reduction, bracketing, or epoche as "mental destructions".'[8] However, very soon after this hypothesis, 'borrowing' becomes 'anticipating' a concept that Husserl (the father or lender) 'was not to make his own until 1938'. In other words, the son borrowed from his father a 'concept' that the father had not yet made his own?

I think it is in our best interest to 'bracket' the Husserlian *filiation* since its legitimacy is far from being proven. Furthermore, Derrida 'himself' never mentioned Husserl when he had to justify his use of the word 'decon-struction', a French (Latin) word constructed from the Latin word for 'destruction', as is the 'concept' of structure. But since Derrida started his 'philosophy' by 'deconstructing' Husserl in *The Voice and the Phenomenon*, Gasché is convinced that it is primarily in Husserl that we can find the 'roots' for the 'method' of deconstruction. He fails to see how two close 'concepts' may radically differ according to their use and position with regard to all the other ones in a given 'context'. For example, 'phenomenology' finds itself displaced into a foreign body as soon as it is envisioned as a method in the service of *Destruktion* in order to 'retrieve' a genuine sense of Being, and certainly not to get a direct access to the 'world of life' that lies concealed 'under a coat of ideas'. Thus it is only after having presented the 'double task' of the research – namely, the analytics of *Dasein* and the Destruction of the history (of ontology) – that Heidegger addresses the demand for a method appropriate for this double task (Chapter 7, 'The Phenomenological Method of the Investigation', in which Heidegger develops a 'pre-concept' or 'proto-concept' of phenomenology, based on the reinterpretation of 'logos' as 'making manifest').

In his discussion of the previous chapter, Gasché insists on the 'positive' aspects in the 'concept' of *Destruktion*. Destruction should not be considered as a 'violent act'. However, Gasché reminds us that in 1929, when opposed to Cassirer, a dominant representative of philosophical tradition, 'Heidegger employed the much more forceful German word *Zerstörung*, as opposed to its Latinization in *Being and Time*, to designate the radical dismantling of the foundations of Occidental metaphysics'.[9]

Undoubtedly *Destruktion* is *not* a purely negative action, according to Hei-degger: 'To bury the past in nullity is not the purpose of this destruction; its aim is positive; its negative function remains unexpressed and indirect.' But if the 'intent' is a positive one, the *action* of 'destroying' cannot be lessened and alleviated without doing violence to its *historical* necessity. 'History' (of ontology) has to be destroyed because it is made out of destruction, through a process of self-destruction and self-deception. The necessary (though not intentional) violence of phenomenological destruction corresponds to the violence of metaphysical constructions which each time have buried the (temporal) meaning of Being under an unquestionable 'evidence'. Minimiz-ing the necessity of the *task* of destruction, Gasché did not pay enough attention to what is actually said in *Being and Time*:

> The tradition that hereby gains dominance makes what it 'transmits' so little accessible that initially and for the most part it covers it over instead. What has been handed down it hands over to obviousness; it bars access to those original 'wellsprings' out of which the traditional categories and concepts were in part genuinely drawn. The tradition even makes us

forget such a provenance altogether. Indeed, it makes us wholly incapable of even understanding that such a return is necessary.[10]

Not only tradition does not deliver what it is supposed to transmit, but it is tradition that must be 'delivered' and therefore entirely deconstructed insofar as it blocks access to these 'wellsprings'. Tradition is destructive in a so radical manner that it obstructs tradition 'itself'.

How to account for such destructive power embedded in tradition? Heidegger responds by referring to the existential structure of *Verfallen*: a structure of de/structuration that could be retraced to an 'original sin' or at least to a *défaut de naissance* (birth defect) intrinsic to philosophy. It is the tragic birth of philosophy (out of Socrates' death) that at the 'same' time opens up the space for a weird survival, between life and death or even neither living nor dead. On the one hand, philosophy is born from a loss: once upon a time there was, that is, there *is* no Being, no self-present, eternally co-substantial and simple origin. On the other hand, this 'not' (*pas*), as it shows the only left trace of Being, of its proper meaning that is presently gone, effaced or forgotten, gives the departure for the quest for the meaning and truth of Being. We must pass through the initial aporia, and cross this 'not' (crossable), by clearly marking the way of return as crossed out, forbidden, which in its turn will allow, through this interdiction (since only re-Turning opens the true way, the experience of self-return), to posit Being at the origin, as erasing any trace of *not*-being. 'Not' constitutes the founding step, responsible for the origin (to be), the erection of the onto-theological Tower through the turn or trope of the re-turn. Such turn is made possible by what the deconstructor of the Tower calls, among other words, 'iterability', a word in which we can barely read, half-effaced, the trace of the other (*alter*), covered by the '*iter*', the way, the method, the engaging process which is supposed to provide the first thesis on Being, Being as its own thesis, as 'absolute position' (Kant): a point of departure that should have effaced any 'other' precedence, that is, any otherness, by giving itself as without-origin inasmuch as origin of itself. The Origin will not have had any origin outside of its 'without'-origin. The quest for the forgotten 'meaning of Being' announces its own ruination, in that it is still a move, a tension *toward* ... a pre-tension claiming to the presence of sense as pre-sense, and thus an implicit recognition of its 'original' absence: from the outset there will have been a stable position only by way of a retroaction, an original feedback or after-the-fact, before even it started.

Dasein is 'thrown' into a preexisting 'sense' (understanding) that

> grows into a customary interpretation of itself and grows up in that interpretation. It understands itself in terms of this interpretation at first, and within a certain range, constantly. This understanding discloses the

possibilities of its being and regulates them. Its own past – and that always means that of its 'generation' – does not follow after *Dasein* but rather always already goes ahead of it.[11]

Not only is 'our' past not even passed, but it stands clearly in our way. The pre-formatted 'intelligence of being' stands close to a 'prejudice' (*préjugé*) that we have to get rid of, *prior to* any further 'investigation' into the (lost) meaning of Being. Such pre-sense precedes us insofar as it has grown into a stable ground, given as self-comprehensible, a so-called 'common sense' that is laid not only under our current judgments but ahead of each of us.

On the other hand, *Destruktion* does not either intend to restore an ideal and genuine purity. A restoration presupposes an original integrity that in fact is the product of a fantas-mythical reconstruction for the purpose of exorcism or of sacrificial cleansing. Yet in order to see how purity (full self-presence, pure-and-simple Being) is constituted from the impurity at the outset, we must have like Oedipus 'an eye too many', but it is no longer the same one. And perhaps it is not an eye, but rather an alien sense, the sense of *sans* (without). Such sense would be sensitive to that which the eye to excess (for ideality) implies, and this is why deconstruction is possible only *from within* the 'construction', because it retraces what has been effaced and given for obvious, natural, indisputable.

When does it 'appear', deconstruction? Even though it does never appear as such, the question seems difficult to avoid. Any question starting with 'when' is exposed to madness, in German, *Wahnsinn*. When Heidegger encounters the word '*Wahnsinnige*' in Trakl's poem, commonly understood as 'crazy, nonsensical, aberrant', he 'destructures' it in two parts: first, *wahn*, which, referred back to its etymon, is the same as *ohne* ('without') and, second, *sinnige*, which obviously refers to *Sinn*, 'sense'. Therefore, in all logic, the word should really mean 'without sense'. But no, that would be too simple, it would amount to the same common meaning of madness that Heidegger wants precisely to avoid. Poets such as Trakl or Hölderlin *cannot* be 'simply' insane, their poetic words must (should, ought to) make sense – otherwise all that Heidegger said about poetry and its 'mission' might appear to make as little sense as their poems make. Heidegger tries to show that in fact 'sense' is not sense, by explaining that *sinnige* does not refer to the noun *Sinn* but to the verb *sinnen*, meaning (like *besinnen*) 'to meditate', and then to the Indo-European root *set*, which means *Weg*, 'way'. Thus the *Wahnsinnige*, far from being insane, is the one who is searching for another sense (and above all, another sense of words and of sense). Like Derrida, I find rather extravagant such recourse to etymology in order to establish a different and more 'prior' sense of sense. But even if we could manage to extract another sense for the second part of the word, the first one would stay unaltered. What about the *Wahn* supposed to mean 'without'? And then, in a flash, I translated *Wahnsinn*, 'madness', by '*sans-sens*', not that it is *sans le sens*, without a sense, but because *sens*, 'sense' 'is' *sans*, 'without'.

What time is it?

'Time' – Heidegger puts quotation marks on almost every word in this sentence – 'is neither "inside" nor "outside", and it "is" "*prior*" to every subjectivity and objectivity, because it presents the condition of the very possibility of this "prior". Does it then have any "being" at all? And, if not, is it then a phantom or is it "more in being" than any possible being?'[12]

Notes

1. See Maurice Blanchot, *Le Pas au-delà*, trans. as *The Step (Not) Beyond*, trans. and with an introduction by Lycette Nelson (Albany: SUNY Press, 1992).
2. Published in 1984 with the title *Zur Frage nach der Bestimmung der Sache des Denkens*. See Martin Heidegger, *L'Affaire de la Pensée*, trans. A. Schild (Mauvezin: T.E.R., 1990), 27–8.
3. See the letter to Jean Beaufret in *Letter on Humanism*, in David Farrell Krell (ed.) *Basic Writings: Martin Heidegger* (London: Routledge, 1993), 213–66.
4. See Rodolphe Gasché, *Le Tain du miroir. Derrida et la philosophie de la déconstruction*, trans. Tilman Küchler and Marc Froment-Meurice (Paris: Galilée, 1995).
5. Rodolphe Gasché, *The Tain of the Mirror. Derrida and the Philosophy of reflection*, (Cambridge MA, London: Harvard University Press, 1986), 109.
6. ibid.
7. ibid.
8. ibid., 111–12.
9. ibid., 113.
10. Martin Heidegger, *Being and Time*, trans. Joan Stambaugh (Albany: SUNY Press, 1996), 19.
11. ibid., 17–18.
12. ibid., 384–5.

2
The Course of a General Displacement, or, the Course of the Choreographer

Lynn Turner

> In contrast to the spasmodic chronological progression of tragedy, the Trauerspiel takes place in a spatial continuum, which one might describe as choreographic. The organizer of its plot, the precursor of the choreographer, is the intriguer.
>
> *Walter Benjamin*[1]

In his seminal work on the structural analysis of kinship, Claude Lévi-Strauss once wrote, '[...] women themselves are treated as signs, which are misused when not put to the use reserved to signs, which is to be communicated'.[2] And Jacques Lacan reciprocated, agreeing that the 'communication' of women between set groups of men would 'guarantee that the voyage on which wives and goods are embarked will bring back to their point of departure in a never-failing cycle other women and other goods, all carrying an identical identity'.[3] This communicant, however, wishes not simply to herself communicate but to radically alter the structure of this kinship system.

While I continue to find the structural analysis of kinship compelling in the sense of a persuasive account of the organization of culture, it is also compelling in the sense of exerting coercion. Moreover, I also find it politically problematic in terms of the compulsory heterosexuality it would institute and theoretically untenable in terms of the certainty of communication anchoring the circuits it claims to describe. Step one of the course of this paper, the point of its new departure, is to interrupt the latter in order to open up some play in the former. Rather than keep to the constituent elements of structural and psychoanalytic analyses of kinship as many feminist critics have – particularly within the realm of film theory – I prefer to pursue the deconstructive critique of communication. Emphasizing communication as a trope of transportation and opening questions of destination, the reliability of the 'compass' and the coherence of the 'cargo',[4] I appropriate Jacques Derrida's suggestion that language is subject to an 'essential drifting' and consider what would happen if the 'cargo' should drift off course.[5]

The second step takes this transfigured communication into the land of translation, the Benjaminian land that refrains from communication in the commonplace sense. Here origin is transformed into a 'maelstrom' that forcefully 'tears the stuff of emergence into its rhythm'.[6] This land takes place for me as a film. It is the short dance film named *Reservaat* (Clara van Gool, Netherlands, 1988) during which two fur-clad dancers – but shall we call them 'women'? – tango across a bleak and wintry park or 'Reservation'. Far from nature, the reservation roots its dancers in a historical relation. Grafted from the stuff of these texts – philosophical, literary, cinematic and choreographic – the next step, setting off a whole sequence with myriad combinations is the risk of proposing a new and transitional name. This name – *Des Jeunes Nées* – is not the outcome of the contract of exchange but emerges from a poetic licence that solicits unfamiliar and unpredictable kinship beyond the gridlock of structuralism. And through the writing of this name these textual animals, the 'newly borns', spring forth as an unforeseen off-shoot of Hélène Cixous and Cathérine Clément's provocation *La Jeune Née*.

Breaking, then, with what has virtually become a commonplace for feminist theory, namely the exchange of women between men as the institution of culture, this chapter of *The Origins of Deconstruction* readdresses the ways in which questions concerning gender and sexuality can be posed, or rather, *posted*. For, when writing rather than communication is positioned as original the exchange-centred paradigm of gender begins to drift and, in this instance, the surprise of the queer feminine comes into view.

Speech marks

Does communication, then, communicate? To pose the question we assume that it does and that the meaning that it communicates is singular. We further assume that this communication, this *transportation* of communication, is carried by a medium or is itself a medium that carries that meaning without division, without degeneration. Need this be so? Perhaps, instead, the word 'communication' opens a field not limited to semantics or semiotics. So let's not accommodate any reservations we may have about the unique meaning of 'communication' by simply allowing for several meanings, according, for example, to context. The field opened up by but not limited to the semantics of communication acknowledges that 'one may [...] *communicate a movement*, or that a tremor, a shock, a displacement of force can be communicated'.[7] 'It is also said that different or distant places can communicate between each other by means of a given passageway or opening.'[8] In these cases communication cannot be limited to the transportation of 'phenomena of meaning or signification.'[9]

So, '... if women in general represent a certain category of signs, destined to a certain kind of communication...' can we rest assured that they will reach their destination?[10] That their carriage will remain on track? For the social contract of reciprocity to be fulfilled the answer to these questions must be in the affirmative. In that event, some guarantees might then be required in order to vouchsafe this exchange. One such guarantee might be to limit this communication through recourse to context, for example, kinship. However, what if context turns out to be structurally bound to failure? What if context can never become fully saturated or determined in advance? In this event the concept of context becomes inadequate and demands that the concept of writing should no longer be housed within our habitual category of communication.

If this should sound repetitively familiar, let me graft several contexts together and rephrase this displacement as that of the 'communication of women' by the writing, perhaps, of 'women'. Given this phrasing it may sound as if I am straightforwardly posing a shift in agency from one known group called 'men', who delimit the 'communication of women' toward another called 'women', who I hereby authorize to write themselves. This is only partially the case. Indeed, Luce Irigaray once critiqued Lévi-Strauss's attempt to ameliorate the functioning of women as gift by allowing that women, unlike words, also speak. She suggested that this so-called speech of women is in fact a 'prosopopeia' on the part of those who forget 'that matter can serve as a support for speculation but cannot itself speculate in any way'.[11] Moving towards the terrain of writing will, however, turn out to have other implications.

Following it step by step then, if writing is habitually supposed to extend the spatial range of communication beyond the moment of its production, this, again, depends upon the reliability of its transportation as well as its imagined similitude to the language of speech and gesture understood as directly representative of their objects. The necessity for writing, habitually thought, arises from the *absence* of the addressee, the presence of the addressor being provisionally assumed. In writing, the sender is separated from the communication which then, alone, even after the death of the sender, continues to produce effects. Although the absence of the sender, and of the recipient, in fact characterizes all writing, classically it is occulted and absence is made to serve as a supplement to presence: that which is absent is merely en route to being made safely present (again). In the course of this general displacement, however, absence becomes the necessary precondition for *any* specificity of *any* kind of sign. For writing to be legible it must be able to be 'repeatable–iterable–in the absolute absence of the addressee or of the empirically determinable set of addressees'.[12] Rooting writing in iteration renders the possibility of a truly secret code impossible: the marks comprising any communiqué in the process of their iteration can always be deciphered, the apparent enclosure of a private language is always breached by the structure upon which it depends. This breaching, 'this essential drifting' characterizes 'writing as an iterative structure cut off from all absolute responsibility, from *consciousness* as the authority of the last analysis...'[13] It also unties writing from a model of generation that purports, not incidentally, to be paternal. Displacing communication, all orders of 'signs', 'all languages in general' 'the entire field of what philosophy would call experience' come under the rubric of writing.[14] And writing, in Cixous's words, 'tears me apart, disturbs me, changes me, who? – a feminine one, a masculine one, some?'[15] And when Cixous writes 'some', I want to take her at her word.

Inextricable from the activity of iteration, and with the breaching of context, lies the generalized practice of performativity which, again, displaces communication since it does not ferry a meaning that lies prior to its utterance. Austin's illocutionary speech act that would bring about that which it names cannot be contained – exclusively contextualized – by an intentionality even though this is the ground upon which he distinguishes it from speech that is only, or apparently only, description. Since it operates through conventionality and not intentionality, the performative is left open both to failure and to a remainder. However rather than attempt to banish this failure, this threat to authority, iteration rewrites it as the condition of possibility for the success of any speech act. (Speech, hence is not opposed to writing, but is a variant of it.) Neither the destruction of success, nor the destruction of intentionality, this is rather the deposition of the latter as governor of the former. This condition of possibility is more specifically a *space* of possibility, and a disruptive, irruptive one at that.

There have been several attempts to clean the 'communication of women' so that Lévi-Strauss's analyses might serve a feminist purpose.[16] In her well-known article 'Woman as Sign', Elizabeth Cowie correctly identifies the pacifying nostalgia in his work that strives to retain some kind of value for women beyond or before their function in the circuit of exchange: 'their talent [...] for taking...part in a duet.'[17] Rather than attach his nostalgia to the desire for presence that is clearly flagged in the closing pages of *The Elementary Structures of Kinship*, Cowie frames it as a humanism inadmissible to structuralism's ambitions to investigate what happens here and now inside the set of relations particular to 'this' structure. Fundamental to her approach is a call for greater fidelity to structuralist theory: if Lévi-Strauss and feminist critics would concentrate on meaning produced relationally *within* the system and forget their attachment to a full presence exterior to that system which represents it with greater or lesser accuracy all would be well (Cowie is referring to Juliet Mitchell, Pam Cook and Claire Johnston). The implication is that if structuralism could be purified of ideological bias then its scientific ambitions would remain intact. I have no issue with Cowie's attempt to effect a paradigm shift in the feminist thinking of the 1970s away from a politics of representation more or less lodged in a pre-critical realism, away from a demand that film should better reflect the lives of real women and toward an analysis of film as a signifying system as itself productive of the category 'woman'. Yet, delays in the post notwithstanding, I would like to re-direct this shift towards the drift I have inferred.

Herself raising a concern with the word 'communication', Cowie suggests that we substitute 'signification' since, she says, 'what is crucial is the notion of a system which posits the sender as well as the receiver as *part of the system*, rather than as *operators* of the system'.[18] Ironically, in a subsequent reconsideration of the material of 'Woman as Sign' Cowie briefly indicates Derrida's critique of Saussurean linguistics.[19] However, rather than follow a deconstructive critique of the *transmission* of this system, her purpose remains to insist that the (formal) circuitry all works internally and efficiently without any exterior presence operating the levers. Recognizing that the operation of the system *orchestrates* not only the women but also the men – that it is a 'putting into place' of gender rather than a neutral transfer of terms – Cowie hovers on the brink of the *poststructuralism* of kinship. Misrecognizing deconstruction as a project concerning *signification* alone – rather than as also addressed to the interruptions of *force* – binds her to the sign and to semiotics as the transportation of presence and keeps her from interrupting the prescription of culture as heterosexual. Although Lévi-Strauss uses the term 'relation' and, although Cowie uses the term 'process', it is spacing, writing, iteration that more usefully theorize how the circuitry of exchange may misfire.

Spacing, writing, iteration: I want to insinuate these into the 'communication of women'. Writing of Antigone, Judith Butler remarks that:

> Kinship [becomes] not simply a situation that she is in but a set of practices that she also performs, relations that are reinstituted in time precisely through the practices of their repetition.[20]

I read this as a refusal of the appearance of a flattening permanence of the structuralist analysis of kinship – flattening in the sense of a self-perpetuating system ever repeating the same form. This performative reiteration as reinstitution precisely does not lose sight of the *institutional* pressure simultaneously articulated in and through the practice of kinship. The force of the institution, its possible success does not vanish. However, thought as performative, contingency is written into its every aspect.[21]

If we should instead pursue a written communication that posited the absence of the sender and receiver would the circulation of women then become derailed? If we no longer ignored the 'medium' within which these 'presents' are assumed to be carried? If we no longer assumed that an intentionality in the form of a consciousness present to itself governs their 'communication'? If the meaning ascribed to the circulation of these words that are women could not be exhausted or determined by a limited context? If 'the essential drifting' of language had infected these 'women' such that

they, too, drift beyond the moment of their production, rather than necessarily circulate in a system of exchange without remainder? If these words,
these women, carry not meaning but the force of breaking with 'their' context? The writing of, perhaps, 'women', to function as such, to be legible as
such, must be subject to iteration, to citation. Yet this performative iteration
holds no guarantees, certainly not that of perfect representation that communication would claim. *Iteration* subjects the words, subjects those whom
we call 'women', to *alteration*. Hence the women are not necessarily condemned to all be the Same, to be a repetition of the Same, perhaps even to
be 'women' since this circus revolves around the institution of gender.

The course of the choreographer

From *Reservaat*, dir. Clara van Gool,
Netherlands, 1998.

*Fragments of a vessel, in order to
be articulated together must follow
one another in the smallest detail,
although they need not be like one
another. So, instead of making itself
similar to the meaning, to the* Sinn
*of the original, the translation must
rather, lovingly and in detail, in its
own language, form itself according to the manner of meaning of
the original, to make both recognizable as the broken parts of the
greater language, just as fragments
are the broken parts of a vessel. For
this very reason translation must in
large measure refrain from wanting
to communicate...*

Walter Benjamin[22]

Moving on, in connection with another inference of the 'communication
of women', spelt out, the 'community' of women, I want also to invoke
the commonality between 'communication' as transportation, the sense of
metaphor, and translation. Yet, in the same breath as drawing on transportation and translation as analogies for each other, I want to draw in the
spacing opened up in and by translation in the hands of Walter Benjamin
who insists, according to Paul de Man's reading of 'The Task of the Translator', that 'metaphor is not a metaphor',[23] and that translation 'must in large
measure refrain from wanting to communicate.'

Publicity material for *Reservaat*, issued by its British distributor, Cinenova,
makes the claim that 'Removed from the rest of the world, the women are
free to express their desire'. The immediate framing of the reservation is thus
as *utopia*: the place of *freedom* where desire runs unfettered, and presence can

touch presence. I am not about to countersign that statement, whether in the form of a pre-critical assertion of identity or in the mistaken belief that deconstruction is, or is only, 'the narrative of the fully dispersed and decentred subject'.[24] Moreover both versions of 'freedom' can only bypass the kind of questions that the film actually enables. For, to frame the reservation as a space 'removed' from the 'rest of the world' is to forget the articulation of history and society and to place the women in an unconditioned 'outside' – free to vacate their former position of commodities. Such a utopian reading risks mistaking the degree of separation possible to occupy and forgets that 'one always inhabits, and all the more when one does not suspect it'.[25]

'Outside' in the reservation we are inside a dance. No diegetic music is indicated as the prompt for this dance, and only fragments of extradiegetic musical phrases dot the soundtrack. I do not take this dancing as the expression or indeed the communication of desire since the context that would encourage such an organicist reading of the tango, namely a *milonga* or dancehall, has been displaced. Rather it is its writing, or indeed, its choreography. Ironically the context that has occasioned this displacement could, at first glance, itself appear complicit with organicism, complicit with a return to nature and to uninterrupted, unimpeded, natural movement. That this context, the reservation, and this dance are plotted through the combination of camerawork, choice of black and white film, choice of shots, the framing, the visual and acoustic editing – all the rhetorical elements that choreograph this scene as cinematic – cannot, however, be disregarded. Yet this change of location allows for several alterations, most immediately that, with no other dancers to bump into and no social obligation to circulate anti-clockwise, the expanse of the park stretches out the dance. Like all good performance artists, the dancers 'use the space'. Their tango takes off on a tangent. Sometimes this means that their frequent and ludicrous extension of the most basic of tango steps – what is so lightly called 'walking', though it treats the ground as a 'tightrope' with the feet pushing across it before weight is transferred onto the heel – map out broad expanses of land and continue off camera.[26] Hence, either substantial segments of the dance remain out of sight or, as I prefer to think, the dance as it is translated cinematically includes holes or spaces within itself.

A very limited range of steps come into play in *Reservaat* – walking, the swivel of the *ochos*, the occasional embellishment, in sharp contrast to the furious demonstrations of Sally Potter's feature *The Tango Lesson* (UK, 1997). At the same time *Reservaat* makes full use of tango's capacity for invention: learn its steps; learn its language; re-articulate your body to inhabit its styles, forget that you have done this and begin a dance that can stop at any moment, even mid-figure, start out again at speed or incrementally. One point at which this dance's potential for inventing new steps can take place comes in the various ways that the relation between leading and following can be addressed. This might turn upon something as subtle as a tilt – a tilt in theoretical emphasis, or a tilt shifting the centre of gravity between the dancers, their manner of leaning, so to speak. In a sense tango *is* strongly led: sequences are propelled by the leader who effects shifts in the centre of gravity of the follower and hence leads, the slightest incline of a shoulder producing a forwards or backwards twist of the hip. One way of countering this theoretically would be to emphasize the structure of the dance and put the *figures* in control of both leader and follower who within this logic are now both castrated. Or, the two structural *positions* of leading and following could be granted with the proviso of an element of contingency admitted through suggesting that either of these two positions could be occupied by anyone, regardless of sex. Neither of these options work toward fraying the actual dynamic in hand, and the second still manages to retain a nature/culture, sex and sexual-position distinction. Assuming that there is no dynamic and the dance is of necessity more equal simply because in the instance of *Reservaat* it is empirically performed by women also misses the point, not least because it requires a series of inequalities to actually move along.

Rather than maintaining a state of separation, the performative iteration of every element of *Reservaat* involves the breaching of context upon context. Coursing through the carpet of dead leaves, the dancers pause to appropriate the picturesque fragments of fallen classical architecture as not a ground but a (dance) floor, a surface to spark more complex footwork; such complex steps that might more clearly demonstrate the intercourse of leading and following are persistently shot from the knee down where both dancers sport the same boots and hence appear the same; at the moment when the foregrounded change in leadership is ostentatiously marked and the follower temporarily leads the soft-focused reservation undergoes a radical spatial disturbance which is easily over-looked. Pivotally, the relation of ground to sky is inverted – trees grow out of the sky, branches become roots, and the framing cuts out any indication of the surface upon which the dancers move. The background in frame is the surface of the lake reflecting the park. If Derrida's generalized figure of dance 'changes place and above all changes *places*',[27] here in the translation of tango by film the reservation itself is shaken.

This sense of displacement recalls Benjamin's work on translation. In distinction from the work of the artist or poet when understood as animated by the desire to mean, to *communicate* in other words, the task of the translator in fact enjoys similarity with three less apparently related things. As philosophy is critical of the notion of itself as an imitation of the world, so is translation. As literary criticism generates an instability in the texts upon which it comments, ironically canonizing those texts in the ostensibly secondary order of criticism, so does translation. And, just as translation does not have a sensuous mimetic relation with its original, Benjamin affirms that history must not be understood from the point of view of nature.[28] History must not be made the analogy of nature, as that which inevitably, progressively and, hence, dialectically overcomes conflict through renewal. Instead, we must think these relations *in reverse*. Hence, in this reserve the original must be thought of in terms of the translation and nature must be thought of in terms of history. Communication, we might add, must be thought of in terms of writing. In so far as metaphor works through claiming natural resemblance it is this claim of metaphor that Benjamin refuses. Translation, thus, is not one. What links philosophy, literary criticism, history and translation is their intra-linguistic activity, their *textual* activity unbound to the printed matter of a book. They relate to the textuality of other texts, not to some notional extra-linguistic source of meaning. In this sense they relate to their various originals at the level of their *manner* of meaning. In situating a formal linguistic structure rather than an intention at the 'origin', the 'original' is destabilized or rather shown to have not been stable all along. This 'structure', however, has peculiar properties, not least the rendering of 'Origin' as historical through and through. And, in its German form, origin as *Ur-sprung* conveys more forcefully the instability of 'an offspring that springs from the alternation of becoming and passing away, of coming and going'.[29] This 'disclosure of the breach'[30] in the origin is what makes the origin historical, what makes history possible. And this double movement that attempts to repeat, or to restore – or, in this context, to reserve – but fails to do so perfectly, means that Benjamin's theory of history is like deconstruction.

As the reader has doubtless guessed, I want to move across, to course, even, from translation to choreography as a mode of criticism.[31] Choreography as the written notation of dancing itself functions as translation bound to a certain kind of failure. It also etymologically invokes the function of the chorus, of the embedding of critical commentary within a play.[32] Choreographic criticism then posits an original instability – linked to what I earlier referred to as performative iteration. Moreover, performative force – 'this force of breaking [with context that] is not an accidental predicate, but the very structure of [writing]' – resonates with the fissure in the *Ur-Sprung*.[33] How different is this 'story of origins' to the one closing *The Elementary Structures of Kinship*! The latter dreams the teleological dream of a world, nay a universe, since this is an emphatically universalizing discourse, spanning the Sumerian myth of a past golden age and the Andaman myth of a future one as evidence of the longing for a time when languages will not be confused, when words will not be common property, when the women will not be exchanged, 'communicated' or translated, but 'kept to oneself'![34] That the economy of reciprocity that exchange compels also in fact strives for the presents to be private property, to be 'kept to oneself' in so far as exchange functions according to the logic of communication without remainder 'where loss and expense are stuck in the commercial deal that always turns the gift into a gift-that-takes' should not pass unremarked.[35]

Des Jeunes Nées

From *Reservaat*, dir. Clara van Gool, Netherlands, 1998.

To write history also means to cite history. Implicit in the concept of citing, however, is that any particular historical object be ripped out of its context.

Walter Benjamin[36]

This complex pun doubles as an index of *Reservaat* and as a performative that grafts itself into an ensemble of other texts including, notably, one whose own punning style is concerned with the conjuration of a new feminine other in and through the queer name-sign of Jean Genet. Although the habitual English translation of *La Jeune Née* as *The Newly Born Woman* perhaps plays on the word born/e, it forfeits the elaborate puns suggested in French. In an effort to revivify the subtlety of Cixous' and Clément's disseminal textual practice I retain the French here. My repetition with an alteration of the singular to the plural renders the feminine specificity inaudible to speech, to the lure of presence, but marks it in the form of writing. This alteration gestures beyond both the singular, if internally riven, allegorical figure of *La Jeune Née* and beyond *Reservaat* since the plural remains an unspecified 'some' – in distinction to the apparent couple of the film.

The proper name of a book, *La Jeune Née*, divides itself, gives birth to herself: Là! Je une nais. Where? *Là!* Je n'est. Who? La Genet. What? La Gênet. Why stop here? I aid and abet this process. Why invoke this newly born woman as Genet, lover of prisons, thieving and sex, and keep her in isolation? Perhaps the sense of a gathering plurality that I invoke here is truer to the promiscuity of Genet. But Genet the man or Genet the name? I write also in the effort to be true to the promiscuity of writing – a promiscuity that traverses the man and the name without paying homage to the name-of-the-father. And I write a little tendentiously in the knowledge that the Cixous of *Sorties* makes a distinction between two bisexualities. The first kind she rightly rejects 'as a fantasy of a complete being [...] not made up of two genders but of two halves,' anticipating Butler's critique of Freudian bisexuality as *'the coincidence of two heterosexual desires within a single psyche'*.[37] The second kind that Cixous advocates 'does not annihilate differences but cheers them on, pursues them, adds more'.[38] Crucially the proliferating differences of this bisexuality are also located 'within oneself' unsettling fantasies of completion. Two questions: If differences are proliferating why call them to a halt at two ('bi-')? And, to what extent does the focus upon the libidinal play of (two) sexualities within a single body serve to elide bisexual sexual practices (for want of a better, or more sexy, phrase)?[39] The second question should not be understood as the swift assembly of a barrier between theory and practice – calling theory to account for practice – but the insistence that this binary cannot be substantiated. In my hands the chance of erotic contact is evoked through the plurality and the orality of this only minimally specified group, *Des Genets/Des Jeunes Nées*, which, in choosing *Des* rather than *Deux* multiplies its possibilities through the homonymic supplement of the common noun or verb, *déjeuner*, or, perhaps, *déjeunez*![40]

Des Jeunes Nées – the 'Jean Genets' – the prisoners of the reservation inhabit a structure that pre-exists them, indexed by the tango (at the least), a compulsory structure that there is no *easy* way to side-step. This is the double bind that would efface writing with communication. If kinship structures demand the promise of communication, if that contract must be entered into, let us not forget that while meaning, identity and authority may be promised there is no guarantee that such promises can be kept, best 'intentions' notwithstanding. Questions of inheritance, of fidelity to origin, of troping upon a reproductive logic, uproot themselves in the course of the dance. While this dance carries the traces of other contexts, other films, other instances of tango, the relation between these instances is as text to text, even those in the 'real' world, since what we call experience is also written. Following this course we can resist the temptation to view the dancers of *Reservaat* as *completely* 'free to express their desire' yet also theorize the way that choreography takes a hand in proliferating future configurations, future economies, of desire. Moreover, in reading this text by 'risking' 'getting a few fingers caught,' by adding 'a new thread' via the punning catachresis of the Genets/*Jeunes Nées*, I solicit this iteration of past contexts that yet translate into new ones. And now the outlaws make inlaws of unsuspecting objects.[41]

This dance, according to tango historian Marta Savigliano, contains no precedent for women dancing together. Regardless of whether her research remains ignorant of any lesbian clubs in Buenos Aires, for example, a case could easily be made for dominant tango narratives as exemplary of what Irigaray called 'hom(m)o-sexuality', especially as the dance became absorbed into European ballroom styles in and through the emphasis of a heterosexual, read 'hom(m)o-sexual', drama. Indeed, Savigliano convincingly argues that the familiar appeal to a 'natural' conflict between the sexes as 'expressed' in dance provided a foil for the class and ethnic fetishism also being, perhaps, *taught* during both tango's European ascension as well its rise to acceptability within Argentina's middle classes.[42] Just what is the course of a tango lesson anyway, we might ask. Certainly contemporary British lessons proper, along with their insistent distance from the pale imitation of ballroom style, frequently recite a narrative of origins dating from the brothels of Buenos Aires, bypassing any acknowledgement of all-male dance academies or the attempts to resist the corrupting influence of women within the dance at all.[43] Such lessons comprise endless reassurance that the man really is in control, while the lady, if she objects, can always lead. It is tacitly assumed that everybody really wants to lead, while the surety of the straight or, as I prefer to phrase it, *straightening*, classes depends upon following being positioned as not desirable. So far, so Freudian. The flattening *structure* of the lesson is, however, calculated to obscure the force required to step out of line. The proper circulation that it organises functions through the sharp and really very clever division of labour between leader and follower such that two leaders or two followers cannot *properly* dance together. It's a tangible, structural and legislative production of the hetero-sexual. If this circuit is in 'correct' use the leaders may only 'communicate' through the exchange of followers, the followers may not 'communicate' save as the prosopopeia of the leaders.[44]

This is only too 'successfully' dramatized in *The Tango Lesson* when Potter's sole conversation with another woman on the dancing circuit is a jealous spat with Pablo Veron's former dancing partner – *the one for whom she has been exchanged*.[45] And Potter, although she recognizes the power differential enacted in tango, appears to think that this can only be combatted through recourse to another structure, that of film-making. You teach me to dance and I will make a film about you, she says: this is the film's tightly knit organization. Exchanging tango for film-making in this way renders the two equivalent and keeps a very narrow model of power on track.

Yet, I would venture to suggest, something else may occur at the level of the force played out within the 'existing' structure of *a* tango lesson: in this place, where truly grammar and rhetoric collide, a student attempting to lead asked his teacher 'How can I control the lady?'[46] And in that impossible space, on that impossible evening, Readers, I was that 'lady'.

Something else again may occur if we consider the force of breaking from context characteristic of writing in light of *Reservaat* as well as the writing *in* light – the cinemato-graphy – that is *Reservaat*. Although it inherits a world of connotations, of contexts, the land of translation is not *bound* to reproduce them faithfully (while acknowledging that neither is it radically *boundless*). For, to rejoin an earlier citation:

> The movements of deconstruction do not destroy structures from the out-side. They are not possible and effective, nor can they take accurate aim, except by inhabiting those structures. Inhabiting them *in a certain way*, because one always inhabits, and all the more when one does not suspect it. Operating necessarily from the inside, borrowing all the strategic and economic resources of subversion from the old structure, borrowing them structurally...[47]

The newly born dancers of *Reservaat* are written in and by a technology that, through the syncopated spacing of both tango and film, interrupts the expected narrative sequencing of both. This syncopated spacing is the displaced site of kinship. Emphasizing metonymy, *Reservaat* poses the fragility of the question of community and of communication in terms of how signs (I use the word provisionally) succeed each other without that succession falling into a destiny foretold. Dancing across the *uncommon ground* of the reservation, the dancers do not form a community (of women). To posit the perfect 'communication of women' in Lévi-Strauss's sense would be to posit a totalized system with no remainder, nothing in reserve, no possibility of change. Like Butler I regard it as inadequate that the legacies of Lacanian psychoanalysis only admit familial contingency in the form of various inhabitants occupying symbolic positions while the positions themselves remain fixed.[48] However, to substitute the perfect, read immediate, community or communion of women exterior to their exchange between men, to assume their freedom ('And speech always presents itself as the best expression of liberty'[49]), would still be to subscribe to a nostalgic return to innocence.[50] The prospect of change is another name for the threat of alterity and this is what such nostalgia would hold at bay. Of course, alteration as intrinsic to the very fabric of writing as iteration is precisely what the text in hand welcomes: writing as the affirmative and promiscuous possibility of a repetition that is not repetition of same (more heterosexuality, unremarked, that is, more sexual difference understood as opposition, unremarked, together with its institutional privilege, unremarked) but opens on to the other (the possibility of a sexuality to come that is not simply the other of this binary). This also indicates that deconstruction does not remain locked within the reservation of linguistic immanence but breaches it.[51]

Furthermore, through displacing what is ostensibly of primary significance by what is apparently secondary, that is, displacing communication by writing, natural movement by choreography, nature by history, through thinking translation as the articulation of fragments that neither move from nor toward an organic whole but are re-articulated as fragments, through aligning translation with choreography, my reading of *Reservaat* interrupts 'the aestheticization of linguistic community or [...] the aestheticization of politics'.[52] The critique of community is not the destruction of a movement, far from it. Indeed it could easily be argued that the 'common' [*commun*], the 'as-one' [*comme-un*] is that which halts movement.[53] Denise Riley has argued that solidarity need not derive from resemblance, analogy, metaphor or identity, since the marshalling of such totalizing tropes marching as one and rooted in hostility to the other can always come unmoored through the incalculable force of irony.[54] In the terms of this paper this unmooring is that of a paradigm drift.

If we consider then, that part of 'the rest of the world' inherited within the reservation are the elementary structures of kinship but that these structures may be redrafted as performative or choreographic, then the iteration of the dance of *Reservaat* – the communication of these words that are 'women' – cannot be reserved *in advance* and *by definition* as heterosexual. If a communication can always not reach its destination, if this 'failure' conditions any possible 'success', what remains are nothing but the elementary ruins of kinship. Through the driftwoods of *Reservaat* the feminine comes unhooked from a presumed heterosexual relation that is also a humanism, and the choreography of this article produces kinship between foreign objects: a book, a proper name, a film, an animal... The contiguities lead on without arrest, if you catch my drift.

Notes

1. Walter Benjamin, *The Origin of German Tragic Drama*, trans. John Osborne (London: Verso, 1998), 95.
2. Claude Levi-Strauss, cited in Elizabeth Cowie, 'Woman as Sign', *M/F*, 1 (1978), 52.
3. Jacques Lacan, cited in Cowie, op. cit., 60.
4. I presented a related paper to this called 'The Kinshipping Forecast' focusing specifically on the derailment of structuralist kinship at *The Future Past of Visual Culture*, at Tate Britain in 2002. Both papers will be incorporated in my book *Machine-Events: Autobiographies of the Performative* (forthcoming).
5. Jacques Derrida, 'Signature Event Context', in *Margins of Philosophy*, trans. Alan Bass (Brighton: Harvester Press, 1982), 316.
6. Benjamin cited in – and vigorously translated by – Samuel Weber, 'Genealogy of Modernity: History, Myth & Allegory in Benjamin's *Origin of the German Mourning Play*.' *Modern Language Notes*, 106:3 (1991), 468.
7. Derrida, 'Signature Event Context', 309.
8. ibid.
9. ibid.
10. Claude Levi-Strauss, *The Elementary Structures of Kinship*, James Harle Bell and John Richard von Sturmer (eds), revised edition (London: Eyre & Spottiswoode, 1969), 496.
11. Luce Irigaray, *This Sex Which Is Not One*, trans. Catherine Porter (Ithaca and London: Cornell University Press, 1985), 177.
12. Derrida, 'Signature Event Context', 315.
13. ibid., 316, emphasis in original.
14. ibid., 317.
15. Hélène Cixous, 'Sorties', in Hélène Cixous and Catherine Clément, *The Newly Born Woman*, trans. Betsy Wing (Minneapolis: University of Minnesota Press, 1986), 85.
16. On the subject of the cleaning of theoretical tools, see Jacques Derrida, 'Structure, Sign and Play in the Discourse of the Human Sciences', in *Writing and Difference*, trans. Alan Bass (London: Routledge and Kegan Paul, 1978), 284.
17. Lévi-Strauss, 'Woman as Sign', 55.
18. ibid., 57.
19. Elizabeth Cowie, *Representing the Woman: Cinema and Psychoanalysis* (London: Macmillan, 1997), 18.
20. Judith Butler, *Antigone's Claim: Kinship between Life and Death* (New York: Columbia University Press, 2000), 58.

21. Such has been the formative influence of Lacanian psychoanalysis in shaping the discipline of feminism, especially regarding film theory, that existing critique of the structure of the exchange of women has struggled to find any leverage within it. Kaja Silverman basically accepts Lacan's premise of universal castration as the Law of Language but refuses kinship as coextensive with the name-of-the-father, insisting that this is the location of contingency. However, the very terms and logic of castration imply the phallus regardless of whether we insist that 'both sexes' are castrated, and the threat of castration is issued by the father. Silverman's project is directed towards obliging the man to recognize his castration and cease projecting it upon woman. It is thus driven by an idea of equality: if both are castrated the field will be levelled. She also consistently advocates 'withdrawal of belief' from the 'dominant fiction' (which includes misrecognizing the penis as the phallus, upon which hinges the circuitry of castration, the Law, etc.). Strange that a critic so conversant with psychoanalysis should miss the unpleasant resonance of 'withdrawal' with the 'withdrawal symptoms' associated with quitting an addiction, as well as with *coitus interruptus*. See her *Male Subjectivity at the Margins* (New York and London: Routledge, 1992), 35–42. Donna Haraway, meanwhile, has both questioned feminism's assumption of its own innocence in appropriating Lévi-Strauss for the sex/gender distinction (in terms of class and race interests as well as the historical contingency of the classification of 'gender') and, more recently, called for the necessity to theorize an 'unfamiliar unconscious'. See her *Simians, Cyborgs & Women: the Reinvention of Nature* (London: Free Association Books, 1991), and *Modest_Witness@Second_Millenium.FemaleMan©_Meets_OncoMouseTM* (New York and London: Routledge, 1997), 265.
22. Walter Benjamin cited in Paul de Man, *The Resistance to Theory* (Minneapolis: Minnesota University Press, 1993), 89. I have made use of de Man's remarks about both his own and Carol Jacobs's more 'germanized' translation of this passage.
23. De Man, *The Resistance to Theory*, 83.
24. Gayatri Spivak locates this mistake in the work of Jacqueline Rose. See Spivak's 'Feminism & Deconstruction Again: Negotiating with Unacknowledged Masculinism', in Teresa Brennan (ed.) *Between Feminism and Psychoanalysis* (London and New York: Routledge, 1989), 208.
25. Jacques Derrida, *Of Grammatology*, trans. Gayatri Chakravorty Spivak (Baltimore: Johns Hopkins University Press, 1976), 24.
26. I take the play on tight/rope from Paul Bowman, 'Between Responsibility and Irresponsibility: Cultural Studies and the Price of Fish.' Paper given in the Centre for Cultural Studies, University of Leeds, February 2001.
27. Jacques Derrida interviewed by Christie MacDonald, 'Choreographies'. *Points... interviews 1974–1994* (Stanford: Stanford University Press, 1995), 94.
28. I say *sensuous* here to contrast with Benjamin's discussion of nonsensuous similarity – the means by which different languages 'while often possessing not the slightest similarity to one another – are similar to what they signify at their center'. See Walter Benjamin, 'On the Mimetic Faculty', in *Reflections: Essays, Aphorisms, Autobiographical Writings*, trans. Edmund Jephcott (New York: Schocken Books, 1986), 335.
29. Weber, 'Genealogy of Modernity', 469.
30. Benjamin, cited in Weber, ibid., 474.

31. Elena Alexander makes a connection between translation (quoting Benjamin), choreography and writing but without drawing out any consequences thereof. How she comprehends the status of 'intention' in Benjamin also remains vague. See her edited collection *Footnotes: Six Choreographers Inscribe the Page* (Amsterdam: G&B Arts International, 1998), 1–2.

32. The combination of choreography and the critical role of the chorus is also deployed, although somewhat differently, by Marta Savigliano in her *Tango: the Political Economy of Passion* (Boulder and Oxford: Westview Press, 1995).

33. Derrida, 'Signature Event Context', 317.

34. See the final paragraph of Lévi-Strauss, 'Woman as Sign', 497.

35. Cixous, 'Sorties', 87.

36. Walter Benjamin, cited in Carol Jacobs, *In the Language of Walter Benjamin* (Baltimore: Johns Hopkins University Press, 1999), 131, n17, emphasis in original.

37. Cixous, 'Sorties', 84. Judith Butler, *Gender Trouble* (New York and London: Routledge, 1999), 77, emphasis in original.

38. Cixous, ibid., 85.

39. There is a very curious footnote to Cixous's later article 'Castration or Decapitation' supplied by its translator, Annette Kuhn, comprising a few sentences that Cixous apparently wished to delete yet Kuhn chose to restore, at least at the level of a footnote. The excised/restored text affirms that Cixous's theorization of bisexuality is not concerned with the practice of having sex with both men and women but with an unconscious relation. The curiosity lies in Kuhn's framing of this note. In claiming that these sentences were deleted since they express 'a position tangential to the central interest of her [Cixous's] work, which has to do with homosexuality', Kuhn thereby manages to make it thoroughly undecidable as to whether homosexuality is central or tangential to this work (*Signs: Journal of Women in Culture and Society*, 7:1 (1981), 54–5 n5). Cixous's sexual conservatism is, however, apparent in an interview with Verena Conley when, in declaring herself to be against artificial insemination, Cixous virtually says that families need fathers. See 'Voice 1', *Boundary*, 2 (1984), 66. In contrast I would argue that there are thousands of ways to articulate 'family' as yet unthought. I infinitely prefer the Cixous who wrote 'let's de-mater-paternalize', 'Sorties', 90.

40. I expand upon several other directions in which *Des Jeunes Nées* can turn in a paper focused upon the politics and erotics of the name in translation: '*Des Jeunes Nées*: for a Confusion of the Tongue, the Lip and the Rim', *Issues in Contemporary Culture & Aesthetics*, 13 (2004), 171–8.

41. To invoke Derrida's exquisite account of reading in *Dissemination*, trans. Barbara Johnson (London: The Athlone Press, 1981), 63.

42. This also describes the course of *The Tango Lesson*.

43. Savigliano indicates the highly problematic imagined alliance between blackness and machismo in Vicento Rossi's 1926 work *Cosas de Negros (Things of Blacks)*: 'Rossi's black *milongueros*, masters of *cortes* and *quebradas*, had, once upon a time, applied their innovations to all social dances. This technique, which at some point gave rise to the tango, had the remarkable capacity to enact "true" maleness (*virilidad*).' To complete this melancholy tale of degeneration she then wryly comments 'interest invested in women contaminated the milonga style'. Savigliano, *Tango...*, 40.

44. Savigliano certainly recognizes dominant tango narratives in these terms, commenting that 'women's eroticism is constituted as restricted to a heterosexual money economy'; ibid., 61.

45. This scene is one of several in which the Latin women in the film are crudely exoticised.
46. For a 'translation' of this question see Paul de Man's discussion of Yeats's line 'How can we know the dancer from the dance?' in his *Allegories of Reading: Figural Language in Rousseau, Nietzsche, Rilke and Proust* (New Haven and London: Yale University Press. 1979), 11.
47. Derrida, *Of Grammatology*, 24.
48. Butler, *Antigone's Claim*, 71.
49. Derrida, *Of Grammatology*, 168.
50. As is the case in Sally Potter's earlier feature *The Gold Diggers* (UK, 1983) in which, after the women escape from the circuit of exchange and the means of production which they do not control, they then become gold diggers themselves, endogamously owning and keeping the production of gold themselves. In refusing the risk to self that both Cixous and Derrida associate with the economy of the gift, Potter's film ends up retaining the Lacanian metaphoric equivalence of women and gold.
51. Ewa Płonowska Ziarek convincingly refutes this often-made charge in her *The Rhetoric of Failure: Deconstruction of Skepticism, Reinvention of Modernism* (Albany: SUNY Press, 1996), 93.
52. ibid., 131.
53. As Derrida points out in 'I Have a Taste for the Secret', in his *A Taste for the Secret* (Cambridge: Polity Press, 2001), 25.
54. Denise Riley, *The Words of Selves: Identification, Solidarity, Irony* (Stanford: Stanford University Press, 2000). See my review in *parallax*, 22 (2002).

3
Feminine Endings: Dido's Telephonic Body and the Originary Function of the Hymen[1]

Ika Willis

The relation of a political state to its physical territory – central to questions of immigration, border control, and the idea of a shared national culture in a tele-technicized world – is naturalized through myths of what Derrida refers to as 'autochthony' (the generation of citizens by the earth itself). Such myths, as well as other figures of the processes through which states carry on an existence in space and time, often rely on a metaphorics of penetration and reproduction which in turn relies on a particular figure of the female body in relation to marital norms (which regulate proper and improper forms of penetration and reproduction). This chapter uses an understanding of political bounding as the inscription of territory gleaned from Derrida's readings of Rousseau and Levi-Strauss in *Of Grammatology*, together with the Derridean figure of the hymen from 'The Double Session', to examine the ways in which gender operates in the construction and transmission of the myth of originary autochthony. It proceeds through a reading of the fourth book of Vergil's *Aeneid* in order to locate these theoretical concerns in the state of Rome, both as a specific political entity which was founded in Italy by a Trojan refugee, Aeneas (and which therefore has an uneasy relation to autochthony/immigration from the very beginning), and as the state which in the Western imaginary often provides a model for political foundation and expansion *per se*.[2]

Carl Schmitt's famous definition of the properly political existence of a state as the ability to distinguish friend and enemy[3] leaves open the question of how the state as political entity is related to its geographical territory. Michel Serres uses the Romulus myth to demonstrate how a territorial boundary is used to map the friend/enemy decision onto a determination of inside/outside:

> To define a space with precision, we trace its borders ... Whoever is inside is a friend; whoever is outside is an enemy – this is the distinct, precise,

well-defined law of war. The first one who closed off a territory and took it upon himself to say 'this is mine' killed the first one who crossed into his enclosure...If you are outside and you penetrate, you are dead. Thus Remus, the brother...underwent this precision, this decision.[4]

However, any attempt to think these relations deconstructively must take account of Derrida's insight that the origin of autochthony is a *delocalized* territorial drive.

[The] speed of motorization, and hence that of tele-technical automation, produces a break with autochthony. This rupture cuts the telluric roots characteristic...of the classical enemy...But also – and first of all – this means that this territorial drive has itself always been contradicted, tormented, displaced and delocalized. *And that this is the very experience of place*...telluric autochthony is *already a reactive response to a delocalization and to a form of tele-technology*, whatever the degree of elaboration, its power, or its speed.[5]

If one takes 'autochthony' as the figure of coincidence between the State as it is constituted and the State as it should be, as the natural(ized) right relation between the citizen body, the state's territory and the state's political constitution, it is – as has been amply demonstrated, especially in the Roman context – the female body (modelled as bearer of a vagina which articulates and differentiates inside and outside) that performs the naturalization of that coincidence.

At its most basic level, the female body stands for the physical territory of a State. Already, then, this metaphorical apprehension of political territory models geopolitical space as susceptible to the same determinations as the female body, and – crucially – vice versa. Thus, for example, Serres' reading of the story of Tarpeia in *Ab Urbe Condita (AUC)* I, following the insights of much recent Livy scholarship, explicitly equates the hymen with a political/territorial boundary:

Tarpeia introduces the enemy into the place; she opens a closed door, raises a veil, a hymen, whatever...She opened the gate, the town wall, just as Remus had stepped over the hymen, the limit, the border.

It is through Tarpeia, a Vestal virgin, that the Sabine army of men gains access to the Roman citadel: this figure of the woman's body privileges the hymen as determinant, configuring it as the border, the mechanism for differentiating inside from outside, enforcing separation between two entities[6] (the Sabine men enter Rome as invaders/foreign bodies, not – for example – as guests or husbands).

The female body is also implicated, however, in the creation of alliances between states and in the reproduction of a state through time. Livy's Tarpeia episode appears within a longer narrative arc (Livy, *AUC*, 1.9–13, the rape of the Sabine women): the hymen is the operator here, too, if we take this term in its archaic sense of 'marriage'. The initial problem is the reproducibility of the Roman state:

> The Roman state had now become so strong that it was a match for any of its neighbours in war, but its greatness threatened to last for only one generation, since through the absence of women there was no hope of offspring, and there was no right of intermarriage with their neighbours.

Romulus and his men therefore abduct women from the neighbouring states, particularly from the Sabines. A war results, which ends in this way:

> Running across the space between the two armies [the Sabine women] tried to stop any further fighting and calm the excited passions by appealing to their fathers in the one army and their husbands in the other ... 'If,' they cried, 'you are weary of these ties of kindred, these marriage-bonds, then turn your anger upon us ... Better for us to perish rather than live without one or the other of you, as widows or as orphans.'
>
> The armies and their leaders were alike moved by this appeal ... the generals advanced to arrange the terms of a treaty. It was not only peace that was made, the two nations were united into one State, the royal power was shared between them, and the seat of government for both nations was Rome. After thus doubling the City, a concession was made to the Sabines in the new appellation of Quirites, from their old capital of Cures.[7]

In the figure of the Sabine woman, autochthony and importation – inside and outside – shelter one another. That is, it is through the assimilation of the foreign Sabine women that a relation between the Roman citizen body and its political territory can be established and can be reproduced through time as if it were autochthonous.

This is the paradigmatic use of the female body in the production of political territory. The female body is modelled in a specific way, as hymeneal. The Tarpeian woman, on the one hand, stands for a particular topographical operation of determining the inside and outside of a territory through a metaphorics of penetration: the Sabine woman, on the other, operates not only to reproduce the Roman state, allowing its existence to continue through time, but also as a mechanism relating the state to its outside (either through war or through ties of kindred/alliance/fusion) and the citizen body to its territory. Together the hymeneal figures trace a topography and temporality through which both the female body and political territory (extension in space and time) are apprehended.

It is possible to read the story of the Sabine women and of Tarpeia according to the figure of the hymen which takes place between Derrida and Mallarmé in 'The Double Session'. Tarpeia's body functions as a switch between inside and outside, producing a fantasy of a state's territory as securely bounded (and hence as penetrable): the bodies of the Sabine women, on the other hand, articulate a relation between two states which, at its limit, is fusion ('It was not only peace that was made, the two nations were united into one State...thus doubling the City'). This is the hymen as an undecidability between virginity/boundedness and marriage/union.

> We are thus moving...to the logic of the hymen. The hymen, the consummation of differends, the continuity and confusion of the coitus, merges with what it seems to be derived from: the hymen as protective screen...the vaginal partition, the fine, invisible veil which, in front of the hystera, stands between the inside and the outside of a woman.[8]

The hymen thus functions for Derrida as a boundary between inside and outside, but indeterminably *also* as a sign of 'continuity and confusion'. He says:

> 'Hymen'...is...a sign of fusion, the consummation of a marriage, the identification of two beings, the confusion between them...But it does not follow, by virtue of this hymen of confusion, that there is now only one term, a single one of the differends...It is the difference between the two terms that is no longer functional.[9]

The hymen, then, can be understood as the term through which political boundaries, the alliances and fusions of citizen bodies and the reproducibility of a state are negotiated in their interrelation. The hymen is the mechanism through which, or the path along which, the spatial and temporal extension and bounding of the Roman state is effected. When taken as a means of transmission the specificity of the hymen's operation as dependent on a particular construction of the female body becomes invisible: as Avital Ronell says of the telephone,

> As part of the building site, possibly even preceding it, the way cables have to be fitted and ditches dug prior to any construction, the telephone is inserted too deeply within the oeuvre to be laid on the surface lines.[10]

In the second book of the *Georgics*, in a passage praising rural life, Vergil stages this invisibility of the function of the Sabine (reproductive) hymeneal body. It becomes clear that the woman's body appears only as the necessary condition of paternity, inserted too deeply into the functioning of the rural idyll to appear on the surface of the scene. The scene is a rustic festival, and Vergil tells us: *dulces pendent circum oscula nati,/casta pudicitiam servat domus* (*G.*2.523f: 'the sweet sons hang around kisses, and the chaste home preserves its fidelity'[11]): this, the only reference to any women in the familial scene, merges the woman with the house (*casta...domus*) so that the woman is brought into the scene as the guarantor of the paternity of the sons. Ten lines later we are told *hanc olim veteres vitam coluere Sabini,/hanc Remus et frater* (*G.*2.532f, 'the old Sabine men once led this life, and so did Remus and his brother'). The passage makes visible the invisibility of the hymen's operation in the reproduction of a family or citizen body, by alluding to the woman's body in decorporealized terms (*casta domus*) as nothing but the guarantor of paternal transmission, and by referring to Romulus and the Sabine men without mentioning the Sabine women, through and on whom the relations between Romulus and the Sabine men were played out.

Similarly in *Aeneid* 4 there is a moment which makes visible the invisibility of the hymen's operation in the bounding of political territory. When Jupiter dictates a message to Mercury, telling Aeneas to relocate to Italy (at that time the territory of the Lavinian tribe), he says: *qua spe inimica in gente moratur/nec...Lavinia respicit arva?* (*A.*4.235f., 'in the hope of what does he dally among an enemy race [*inimica gente*] and does not look upon the Lavinian fields?') The phrase *Lavinia arva* allows the name of Aeneas' fated spouse to appear in the line,[12] though the word *Lavinia* here is an adjective relating to ethnicity/territory and its 'a' marks it as neuter plural rather than feminine singular. The relation of woman to land here is one of identity on the level of the signifier, operated through the ambivalence of the 'a' which equivocates between neuter and feminine, allowing the word *Lavinia* to mean 'of a particular geographical location' although it is indistinguishable from a woman's name. It is almost as if it were a matter of indifference whether Jupiter is referring to Aeneas' future wife or his future kingdom, since the two are identical letter for letter.

This disappearing act seems to be a feature of the hymeneal body, as if the successful operation of the hymen in the inscription of political territory on geographical space and the reproduction of the citizen body through time were dependent on a certain invisibility or absence of the female body, its subordination to the hymeneal arrangement. Indeed, in 'The Double Session' we find that Derrida's understanding of the hymen as an undecidability between bounded self-identity and consummation as the abolition of difference is derived from a mime: that is, from the murder of Columbine by Pierrot as enacted on/by Pierrot's body alone. Derrida writes: 'At once page and quill, Pierrot is both passive and active, matter and form, the author, the means, and the raw material of his mimodrama.'[13] Although Derrida has claimed that in the hymen as consummation 'it does not follow that there is now only one term', it is striking that here *he* (Pierrot) is *both* page and quill: that is, that both terms – derived from the hymeneal operation – are now subsumed into the single (male) body which is present.

In fact, Derrida-Mallarmé relies on the absence of Columbine's body from the mime for his/their development of an understanding of the relationship between love and violence, autoeroticism and heteroeroticism: it is the Columbine's absence which allows her murder to be called 'this non-violent crime, this sort of masturbatory suicide'.[14] Following this trajectory, the hymen appears, in addition to relating love and violence, to articulate (masculine) autoeroticism and heteroeroticism in intercourse, as in Irigaray's critique of the hymeneal/vaginal configuration of the female body:

> If the vagina is to serve *also*, but *not only*, to take over for the little boy's hand in order to assure an articulation between autoeroticism and heteroeroticism in intercourse (the encounter with the totally other always signifying death)...will woman not be left with the impossible alternative between a defensive virginity, fiercely turned in upon itself, and a body open to penetration that no longer knows, in the 'hole' that constitutes its sex, the pleasure of its own touch?[15]

The hymeneal topography, that is, inscribes the female body according to a heterosexual economy of violence in which heterosexual intercourse is articulated with (masculine) autoeroticism, as in the mime which enacts heterosexual intercourse and the murder of Columbine on the man's body. Thus the hymeneal configuration deprives the female body of the possibility of autoeroticism (and, for that matter, homoeroticism) – and thus, perhaps, of access to writing?

In the fourth book of the *Aeneid*, the story of Dido and Aeneas, and in particular in the staging of Dido's suicide according to a hymeneal logic, Vergil reconstructs, element by element, the Derridean hymen which does not take place: the enactment on a single body of the 'act of violence that is (at the same time or somewhere between) love and murder'[16] and hence the articulation of heteroeroticism and autoeroticism as the effacement of homoeroticism and as the moment of writing. However, Dido's manipulation of the hymeneal codes allows these elements to be put into play differently, gesturing, perhaps, towards the potential for a less tragic outcome.

Vergil makes marriage central to the story of Aeneas and Dido. It is through their marriage/relation that the enmity or alliance between Carthage and Rome is to be determined. '*quo nunc certamine tanto?/quin potius pacem aeternam pactosque hymenaeos/ exercemus?*', Juno asks Venus at A.4.98–100, suggesting that, rather than continuing their enmity through differentiating Rome and Carthage (Dido's kingdom), the two goddesses should contrive to ally the two states by bringing Dido and Aeneas together: 'Where will our great rivalry lead us? Why don't we rather accomplish eternal peace and bounden hymeneals?' Venus, however, *sensit...simulata mente locutam,/ quo regnum Italiae Libycas averteret oras* (*A*.4.105/6, 'sensed that she spoke with feigned intent, in order to divert the kingdom of Italy to Libyan shores').

The choice as set up by the goddesses runs along familiar lines. Marriage is equated with political alliance, and a relation between a citizen body and a geographic location is given as the outcome of such a marriage/alliance. The alternatives are:

1. Aeneas and Dido marry, making the Trojan refugees co-citizens of Carthage and merging the two citizen bodies into a single term (Venus says: '*incerta...si Iuppiter unam/esse velit Tyriis urbem Troiaque profectis,/miscerive probet populos aut foedera iungi*' [*A*.4.110–2: 'I...do not know whether Jupiter would wish there to be one city for the Tyrians and those who have come from Troy or whether he would approve the merging of their peoples and their joining in alliance'[17]]); the kingdom of Italy is diverted to a new location in Libya.
2. The rivalry between Juno and Venus continues unlimited (and hence Carthage and Rome are in a relation of political enmity); the kingdom of Italy is founded in the correct location.

These alternatives seem to conform to the specific form of undecidability gathered under the Derridean term *hymen*, with the hymen functioning either/both to separate off one entity in fierce isolation or/and to merge two entities into an identity which abolishes difference. However, it is the function of the term *hymen* itself which is subjected to scrutiny throughout the story of Dido and Aeneas. So far from identifying Dido's and Aeneas's marital relations with the political relations of their peoples, Vergil is careful to make it clear, from the very beginning, that the marriage of the rulers is not a necessary condition for the possibility of alliance between Carthage and the Trojan refugees. In fact, Dido offers the Trojans co-citizenship in Carthage, in terms which resonate with Derrida's hymeneal abolition of difference, even before she has met Aeneas:

> *vultis et his mecum pariter considere regnis?*
> *urbem quod statuo, vestra est; subducite navis;*
> *Tros Tyriusque mihi nullo discrimine agetur.*
> [*A*.1.572–4: 'Do you wish to settle here with me on an equal footing, even here in this kingdom of Carthage? The city which I am founding is yours. Draw up your ships on the beach. Trojan and Tyrian shall be as one *(nullo discrimine agetur)* in my eyes.']*[18]

The contrast to Lavinia, merged letter for letter with the graph of her territory, is striking.[19] Indeed, despite the way the goddesses set up the situation as if Dido were a Sabine woman, functioning along hymeneal lines to articulate political relations on a corporeal level, she conspicuously fails to conform to this model. The hymeneal paradigm, of course, depends upon a determination of the female body as *either* virgin *or* married: yet it is crucial to Dido's situation, to the narrative development of the Dido-and-Aeneas plot, and hence to the history of Rome (since the narrative functions aetiologically to originate the historical enmity between Rome and Carthage) that she is neither. She is, in fact, only able to maintain her status as the single female ruler of a small state, despite pressure from neighbouring kings to marry them and join her territory to theirs, because they respect her desire to remain faithful to her dead first husband, Sychaeus: her relationship with Aeneas throws her delicate negotiation of her marital status into disarray and makes her situation far more vulnerable.[20]

Dido's complex and skilful manipulations of marital codes culminate, in *Aeneid* 4, in her suicide, staged (in the classical tradition of female suicides) according to hymeneal protocols. In contrast to the Livian-Derridean-Mallarmean hymen which articulates autoeroticism and heteroeroticism through the suppression of the female body from the scene of violence/love, Dido's staging of her suicide as a marriage in the conspicuous absence of the male body inverts the scene element by element, in a manner which also makes visible the hymeneal suppression of female-female homoeroticism and female autoeroticism (as access to writing) and which, further, intervenes in the hymeneal merging of the woman's body with the political body of the state.

At the end of *Aeneid* 4 Dido climbs to the top of the pyre she has built out of Aeneas' possessions, lies down on their [marital][21] bed beside an effigy of Aeneas and stabs herself with Aeneas' sword. In this single moment she reinscribes the hymen from the *pactos hymenaeos* intended by Juno to fuse Troy with Carthage, instead determining the relation between Troy and Carthage as one of mutual exclusivity, founding Troy as Rome and Carthage as not-Rome. The reinscription is all the more striking since Vergil has taken care to set up Carthage as a potential Rome, from the moment when Aeneas first arrives on the scene:

> *pars optare locum tecto et concludere sulco;*
> *iura magistratusque legunt sanctumque senatum*
> [*A*.1.425f: 'Others were choosing sites for building and marking them out with the plough; others were drawing up laws and electing magistrates and a senate whom they could revere.']²²

The procedures and terminologies are conspicuously Roman (*concludere sulco* refers to the Roman practice of marking out the boundaries of a city by ploughing a furrow; *magistratus* and *senatus* are Roman institutions).

Dido is presented as in a parallel situation to Aeneas, having lost a spouse and a city and being in the process of founding a new city in a new territory: Aeneas' reaction to the scene described above, his first glimpse of Carthage, is to cry out '*o fortunati, quorum iam moenia surgunt!*' (*A*.1.437: 'How fortunate they are! *Their* walls are already rising!'[23]) and the conversation between Juno and Venus raises the possibility of a Trojan-Carthaginian state being founded in place of Rome (*A*.4.106, quoted above). It is only at the point of Dido's suicide that the (future) relation between Carthage and Rome is finally determined not as parallel, fusion or alliance, but as enmity and as mutual exclusivity:

> *nullus amor populis nec foedera sunto...*
> *...litora litoribus contraria, fluctibus undas*
> *imprecor, arma armis: pugnent ipsique nepotesque.*
> [*A*.4.624, 628f: 'Let there be no love between our peoples and no treaties...I pray that we may stand opposed, shore against shore, sea against sea and sword against sword. Let there be war between the nations and between their sons for ever.'[24]]

Dido's action in stabbing herself draws on a traditional relation between breaching and founding, as both rely on a determination of inside and outside (the verb *condo* can be used for both breaching and founding, and is used to determine Aeneas' stabbing of Turnus at the very end of the *Aeneid* as an act foundational of Rome, determining a difference between two entities and hence identifying them as separate). No longer will Trojan and Tyrian be fused, treated *nullo discrimine*: the breach between them is inscribed on Dido's body as she produces two separate citizen bodies. In her lovesick frenzy of betrayal, Dido has been compared to

> *eumenidum...demens videt agmina Pentheus*
> *Et solem geminum et duplices se ostendere Thebas.*
> [*A*.4.469f: 'Pentheus in his frenzy when he was seeing columns of Furies and a double sun and two cities of Thebes.'[25]]

This Theban doubling reverses the Sabine doubling. There, Sabines and Romulans were fused into a single state (*urbe geminata*); here the single state of Carthage bifurcates and must be resolved into two separate states through the hymen, which functions here like a Schmittian political mechanism for distinguishing friend and enemy. The movement is the inverse of Livy's, going from the Sabine hymen to the Tarpeian: yet here it is Dido who is the agent who is both page and quill, foregrounding the relation between her body and the land and manipulating it through technology and through writing rather than through an autochthonic confusion of the two.

The foundational moment of breaching which occurs when Dido stabs herself with Aeneas's sword could be read as tragic, as if her use of Aeneas's sword doomed her to a phallic topography and deprived her of the possibility of autoeroticism. As noted, Dido's suicide restages Mallarmé's Pierrot's mime so that the autoeroticism of the agent who is both page and quill is played out on a female body, opening the question of the possibility of woman's autoeroticism. Irigaray insists that 'woman's autoeroticism is very different from man's':

> She touches herself in and of herself without any need for mediation, and before there is any way to distinguish activity from passivity. Woman 'touches herself' all the time, and moreover no one can forbid her to do so, for her genitals are formed of two lips in continuous contact...This autoeroticism is disrupted by a violent break-in: the brutal separation of the two lips by a violating penis, an intrusion that distracts and deflects the woman from this 'self-caressing'.[26]

By taking up the sword, that is, and by repeating the paradigmatic scene of penetration as the reinscription of boundaries, so that her body and the Carthaginian state metaphorically comprise one another through the hymen, Dido risks staging her autoeroticism – 'the experience of touching-touched [which] admits the world as a third party'[27] – as 'a violent break-in: the brutal separation of the two lips by a violating penis', or, as Derrida puts it, 'the introduction of a weapon, or letter opener, to mark the taking of possession' of 'the closed, feminine form of the book, protective of the secret of its hymen'.[28] Here penetration is understood as a violence of taking possession, enacted on (done to) the female body as inert matter.

For Derrida, the moment of writing-as-breaching inaugurates

> the space of reversibility and of repetition traced by the opening, the divergence from, and the violent spacing, of nature, of the natural, savage, salvage, forest. The *silva* is savage, the *via rupta* is written, discerned, and inscribed violently as difference, as form imposed on the *hyle*, in the forest, in wood as matter.[29]

Similarly in 'Freud and the Scene of Writing' he characterizes breaching as 'the tracing of a difference in a nature or a matter which are conceivable as such only in their *opposition* to writing'.[30] Writing under its configuration as breaching – like the opening of the book with the letter-opener – is an act of violent penetration which determines what has been breached as passive even as it opens a road, a *via rupta*.

However, here as in the territory of the Nambikwara from which Derrida derives his formulation of the *via rupta* as the violent inscription of difference, another line crosses the scene.

The territory of the Nambikwara is crossed by the line of an autochthonic picada. But also by another *line*, this time imported:

[An abandoned telephone line] obsolete from the day of its completion... (Sometimes the termites attack [it], and sometimes the Indians, who mistake the humming of the telegraph wires for the noise of bees on their way to the hive.)[31]

In the territory of the Romans, into which women had to be imported before an autochthonic relation to the land could be established, perhaps 'autochthonic' and 'imported' cannot be clearly demarcated. Dido's suicide intervenes in this binary also. Her determination of Carthage as the enemy of Rome is effected through two acts/speech acts: the breaching of her body by Aeneas' sword and her curse. It is through the curse, as a telephonic line crossing the Carthaginian territory, that she avoids falling into the Irigarayan-hymeneal trap of determining her body as inert 'matter' or 'nature' through the inscriptive moment of breaching/stabbing: further, this telephonic operation highlights the priority of tele-technology to autochthony, as in the passage of Derrida-on-Schmitt with which we began.

The curse reads, in part:

nullus amor populis nec foedera sunto.
exoriare aliquis nostris ex ossibus ultor...
[*A*.4.624–5: 'Let there be no love nor treaties for the peoples.
Some avenger will rise from our bones...']

The curse thus founds a space in which the break between Dido and Aeneas, Carthage and Troy, will be repeated as war through the *aliqius... ultor* ('some avenger': Hannibal, as we know from history). The phrasing and staging makes it clear that Dido is not fulfilling the Sabine function of reproducing the citizen body in time through the hymen as guarantor of generational chronology: Dido has informed both Aeneas and us that she is not pregnant (*A*.4.327–330), and the terms of the 'curse' with which she speaks[32] specifically exclude reproduction through pregnancy.

However, the specifically erotic/marital format of Dido's suicide and curse opens it to being (mis)read, as it is by Ovid and Freud, in terms of pregnancy as non-writing. A line from Dido's curse, *exoriare aliquis nostris ex ossibus ultor*, surfaces in *The Psychopathology of Everyday Life*.[33] Freud devotes the second chapter, 'The Forgetting of Foreign Words', to an analysis of a 'small incident' in which a young man, attempting to quote this line to Freud in conversation, forgets the word *aliquis*, 'someone else'. From this slip, via, to begin with, the progression aliquis-a-liquis-liquid (the deletion of/refusal to read the initial 'a', which is the very letter connoting *otherness*[34] and hence emphasizing that the *aliquis ultor* stands in no determinable genetic or kin relation to Dido), Freud is able to deduce that the young man is worried because his girlfriend's period is late. By figuring Dido as a generative body rather than as a performative voice, this version denies Dido access to writing, reading the scene as if menstruation and pregnancy were nature or speech and not writing.

Dido's suicide is, in fact, arranged around a similar constellation of pregnancy, resistance and misreading to that which produced the suicide of Bhubaneswari Bhaduri and its misreading, analysed by Spivak in 'Can the Subaltern Speak?' and again in *A Critique of Postcolonial Reason*.[35] For Bhubaneswari Bhaduri as for Dido, it is precisely the introduction of the term 'pregnancy' which allows a reductive misreading of female bodily strategies to take place: Bhaduri waited until she was menstruating before committing suicide in order 'to displace (not merely deny), in the physiological inscription of her body, its imprisonment within legitimate passion by a single male',[36] yet only a few years later her family remembered her as a woman who killed herself for love. Similarly, within a few years after the publication of the *Aeneid*, Ovid's *Letter from Dido* figures the death of Dido and the subsequent history of conflict between Rome/Carthage and Troy/Rome through pregnancy: *Heroides* 7.13–7, 'Perhaps, too, you are leaving behind a pregnant Dido, you wicked man, and part of you lurks shut up in my body... and together with his mother will perish Iulus's brother'. Such an understanding of the scene of Dido's suicide encloses it within the fraternal relation which haunts all Rome's wars in the figure of Romulus/Remus, making the enmity of Rome and Carthage a matter of kinship trouble and reading Dido's curse as mother-to-son transmission through the figure of pregnancy. In Vergil's version, however, and by contrast, since the curse is aetiological, there is no other path by which the *aliquis ultor* can rise from Dido's bones than the curse itself. Dido substitutes a voice which operates in time for the production of political space through the merging of the female body with the land: to subject her to Sabine protocols is to miss the specificity of her manipulations of the codes and to fail to hear her voice for the humming of the bees. In fact, Dido's manipulation of the hymeneal relation posits a telephonic female body: where Lavinia's hymeneals submerge her in geographical space, Dido's extend her sphere of action through time and space through a vocal transmission in the feminine gender, though the significance of this too has been missed by commentators who read according to the gendered protocols of Latin vocal transmission and who take the hymen as denying the possibility of a homoeroticism not organized around bodily presence.

The progress of *Aeneid* 4 can be seen as the progressive separation of Dido from same-sex affective relations and her subordination to a particular, tragic, form of heterosexuality. The book opens with an encounter between Dido and her 'sister of one soul with her' (*A.4.8: unanimam ... sororem*); her second speech to her sister, Anna, is an indirect address to Aeneas (*A.4.424*, 'go to him and say...'); her third (*A*.4.478–98) is a lie, deceiving Anna into helping Dido build the pyre on which she will die.

At the end of the book, Anna returns to Dido as she is dying and says, in part:

> ...*si quis super halitus errat,*
> *ore legam.*
> [*A*.4.684–85f '...if some last breath wanders above,/I shall gather it in my mouth.']

Servius' comment on this line is: 'I shall gather in my mouth (*ore legam*): womanishly (*muliebriter*), as if she could receive the soul of her sister and transfer it into herself.'[37] Transmission here is bodily and immediate, as if it could be not mediated by any form of *techne*, any denaturalized or legal processes. Servius' Vergil's *ore lego* fantasizes the metempsychotic direct communication or transference of soul to soul, presence to presence, from one entirely contingent body to another – and baldly states that this is *womanish*. Yet the meaning of *ore lego* cannot be exhausted by Servius' *muliebriter*: the womanish in Vergil is crossed by the line of the 'a' as neuter/feminine and cannot be as seamlessly self-identical and self-present as Servius tries to announce.

Transfer or reproduction through the *ore lego*, moreover, is not always already womanly-bodily, in Vergil or elsewhere. The phrase – which can mean not only 'gather in the mouth' but also 'read with the mouth' – articulates bodily reproduction with vocal/technological reproduction: it is used for pure autochthonic reproduction in a passage from the *Georgics* dealing with the reproduction of bees, fantasized as a similar structure of pure transmission to the Dido-Anna encounter, but this time figured as asexual-masculine affiliation:

> *quod neque concubitu indulgent nec corpora segnes*
> *in Venerem solvunt aut fetus nixibus edunt:*
> *verum ipsae e foliis natos, e suavibus herbis*
> *ore legunt, ipsae regem parvosque Quirites*
> *sufficient...*
> *ergo...*
> *...genus immortale manet multosque per annos*
> *stat fortuna domus et avi numerantur avorum.*
> [*G*.4.197–209: 'they neither indulge in bedding-together, nor undo their bodies slack in Venus or give forth fruit in pain; they gather newborns with their mouths (*ore legunt*) from the leaves, from the sweet grasses, they supply the king and the little Quirites...Therefore...the race remains immortal, and the fortune of the house stands through many years, and grandfathers' grandfathers are counted.']

Metempsychosis in the *Aeneid* is figured as womanly – that is, apolitical and purely bodily; at the other extreme, *ore lego* in the *Georgics* is a form of cloning Romans, purified of any risk of contamination through the intervention of bodies/women, though the term *Quirites* once more serves to make visible the invisibility of the Sabine hymeneal function in this fantasy (the term is a name for Roman citizens that memorializes the doubling of the city through its fusion with the Sabine people: *ita geminata urbe ut Sabinis tamen aliquid daretur Quirites a Curibus appellati* (Livy, *AUC*, 1.13.5, 'After thus doubling the City, a concession was made to the Sabines in the new appellation of Quirites, from their old capital of Cures' [Roberts' translation]).

In general the term *ore lego* posits the mouth as site of reproduction, in a tradition of vocal transmission inherited from the epitaph of Ennius. The *ore lego* therefore complicates all discussions of reproduction and boundaries in Rome through its telephonic configuration of time and space. This is writing not as the *via fracta* but as a technology of disembodiment, a line which crosses territory but which constitutes neither a boundary nor an available road through a *silva* determined through its opposition to writing.

Dido's suicide, properly read, thus hints at the possibility of a telephonic female body, one which is not reduced to inert/generative matter or territory but one which gives rise to a series of aberrant forms of transmission, including a homoerotic path of reproduction on the lips of women.[38] She is neither the originary buried virgin (Tarpeia, Antigone), foreclosed at the foundation of a political territory, nor the Lavinian-Sabine wife guaranteeing paternity and autochthony, nor yet the tragic anti-Sabine woman whose position outside the marital-reproductive norm leaves her no option but suicide (Ovid's Dido, Bhubaneswari Bhaduri). Dido rewrites these figures, as well as Mallarmé's Pierrot/Columbine, rendering visible all the tele-technics of gender which must be put in place *before* the origin myth of autochthony can be built.

Notes

1. This paper was written with the assistance of a grant from the AHRB (now the AHRC), which the author gratefully acknowledges.
2. See, for example, Duncan F. Kennedy, 'A Sense of Place: Rome, History and Empire Revisited', in Catharine Edwards (ed.) *Roman Presences: Receptions of Rome in European Culture, 1789–1945* (Cambridge: Cambridge University Press, 1999), 19–34, 26: 'Rome acts as a figure for whatever now represents this notion of empire... [including] secular formations which seek to describe themselves as "empires".'
3. 'As long as a people exists in the political sphere, this people must... determine by itself the distinction of friend and enemy. Therein resides the essence of its political existence.' Carl Schmitt, *Concept of the Political*, trans. George Schwab (New Brunswick: Rutgers University Press, 1976), 49.
4. Michel Serres, *Rome: The Book of Foundations*, trans. Felicia McCarren (Stanford: Stanford University Press, 1991), 149.

5. Jacques Derrida, *Politics of Friendship*, trans. George Collins (London and New York: Verso, 1997), 142–3.
6. This model of the hymen as an impermeable boundary does not take account, for example, of its permeability to menstrual blood: some things can pass through the hymen without breaking it, and it can be broken or stretched in other ways than through vaginal penetration. We should, therefore, already be aware of this use of the hymen as inaccurate and therefore interested (and therefore interesting).
7. Livy, *Ab Urbe Condita* 1.13.1–5, trans. Rev. Canon Roberts (available online at www.perseus.tufts.edu/cgi-bin/ptext?lookup=Liv.+1.13). Further citations marked *AUC* in text.
8. Jacques Derrida, 'The Double Session', in *Dissemination*, trans. Barbara Johnson (New York: Athlone Press, 1981), 212–13.
9. ibid., 209.
10. Avital Ronell, *The Telephone Book* (Lincoln: University of Nebraska Press, 1989), 199.
11. Except where otherwise stated, all translations from the *Georgics* and the *Aeneid* are my own.
12. We know from various prophecies in the *Aeneid* that Aeneas is fated to marry Lavinia, the daughter of the King of the Latins, and become king of the Lavinian territory.
13. Derrida, 'The Double Session', 198.
14. ibid., 201.
15. Luce Irigaray, *This Sex Which Is Not One*, trans. Catherine Porter with Carolyn Burke (Ithaca: Cornell University Press, 1985), 24.
16. Derrida, 'The Double Session', 213.
17. David West's translation (Vergil, *The Aeneid: A New Prose Translation*, trans. David West [Harmondsworth: Penguin, 1991]), slightly modified.
18. West's translation.
19. It is a commonplace of *Aeneid* scholarship that Lavinia – even when she appears as a character rather than as a piece of word-play – is barely characterized.
20. See the *Aeneid* (A.4.211–8) (a neighbouring king is speaking): 'This woman was wandering about our land and we allowed her at a price to found her little city. We gave her a piece of shore to plough and laid down the laws of the place for her and she has spurned our offer of marriage and taken Aeneas into her kingdom as lord and master, and now this second Paris, with eunuchs in attendance and hair dripping with perfume and Maeonian bonnet tied under his chin, is enjoying what he has stolen...' (West's translation).
21. In square brackets because the marital status of Aeneas and Dido is notoriously undecidable: the narrative suggests first that they are married (A.4.166–8, 'The sign was first given by Earth and by Juno as matron of honour... and the heavens were witness to the marriage'), and then that they are not (A.4.171f, 'Dido...no longer kept her love as a secret in her own heart, but called it marriage, using the word to cover her guilt'); Dido insists that they are married (A.4.316–9, 'I beg you by our union, by the marriage we have begun'); Aeneas insists that they are not (A.4.338f, 'Nor have I ever offered you marriage or entered into that contract with you'). (All West's translations.)
22. West's translation.
23. West's translation.
24. West's translation.

25. West's translation.
26. Irigaray, *This Sex Which Is Not One*, 24.
27. Jacques Derrida, *Of Grammatology*, trans. Gayatri Chakravorty Spivak (Baltimore and London: Johns Hopkins University Press, 1976), 165.
28. Derrida, 'The Double Session', 259.
29. Derrida, *Of Grammatology*, 107–8.
30. Jacques Derrida, 'Freud and the Scene of Writing', in *Writing and Difference*, trans. Alan Bass (London and Chicago: Routledge and Kegan Paul/University of Chicago Press, 1978), 214.
31. Derrida, *Of Grammatology*, 108: italics denote a quote from Levi-Strauss.
32. The idiomatic use of the word 'curse' as a euphemism for menstruation should be borne in mind here.
33. Sigmund Freud, 'The Forgetting of Foreign Words', Chapter 2 in *The Psychopathology of Everyday Life*, trans. Alan Tyson, ed. James Strachey (London: Ernest Benn, 1966), 8–14. My attention was drawn to this chapter by a mention – in a very different context – in Don Fowler, *Roman Constructions: Readings in Postmodern Latin* (Oxford: Oxford University Press, 2000), 201.
34. 'quis' means 'someone', 'aliquis' means 'someone else', on the model of 'ibi' (there/where) and 'alibi' (elsewhere).
35. I have used the account of Bhubaneswari Bhaduri's suicide given in Gayatri Chakravorty Spivak, *A Critique of Postcolonial Reason* (Massachussetts: Harvard University Press, 1999), 306–11.
36. ibid., 307.
37. Servius *ad loc.* (available online at www.perseus.tufts.edu/cgi-bin/ptext?lookup= Serv.+A.+4.685).
38. The Ennian tradition of vocal transmission is specifically in a masculine medium: *Volito vivos per ora virum* ('I fly, living, on the lips of men').

4

On Prejudice and Foretelling 2*

Thomas Docherty

And should I then presume?
And how should I begin?

T. S. Eliot, 1917[1]

Let us begin by going back to a beginning, in which the question of going back to a beginning is posed (but not for the first time). In 1967, Derrida wrote this:

> The displacing of the relationship with the mother, with nature, with being as the fundamental signified, such indeed is the origin of society and languages. But can one speak of origins after that? Is the concept of origin ... anything but a fiction?[2]

There is, thus, an original point – an origin of society and languages – identified as 'the displacing of the relationship with the mother', even if this point, once alluded to, destroys the very possibility of its own conceptualization in anything other than the terms of a necessary fiction. Yet the point stands that talk of origins remains possible. Thus it remains possible seriously to ask the question of 'how to begin', to ask 'where does a deconstruction come from?' or even 'where does deconstruction begin?' It is not satisfactory, in response to such questions, to offer the glib warning that deconstruction will always already have demonstrated that origins are inhabited by the derivations that owe their status to the origin as such, and that derivations in turn are marked by originality. Derrida's own gloss on the situation remains clear:

> There is a point in the system where the signifier can no longer be replaced by its signified, so that in consequence no signifier can be so replaced, purely and simply. For the point of nonreplacement is also the point of orientation for the entire system of signification. That point does

not exist, it is always elusive or, what comes to the same thing, always already inscribed in what it ought to escape or ought to have escaped... If culture is thus broached within its point of origin, then it is not possible to recognize any linear order, whether logical or chronological. In this broaching, what is initiated is already corrupted, thus returning to a place before the origin.[3]

The 'displacing of the relation with the mother' which is the origin of society and languages, thus, is an event that disrupts the purity of a logical/chronological order in which the present moment can be simply aligned with a 'prior' moment whose essential content determines – *predetermines* – the possibilities of the present.

Far from being a 'non-question', the question of the origins of deconstruction, and within that, the question of how a beginning might be possible, remains a significant problem and issue. Yet, in literary or cultural criticism, one does not simply 'decide' to 'do a deconstruction' with respect to any particular text or concept; one does not 'initiate' a deconstructive manoeuvre in a simple act of decision-making. As has been repeatedly pointed out by Derrida and others (but every repetition implies an origin that is being reiterated), deconstruction is not a 'method' to be 'applied'. In the relatively early days of the controversies surrounding deconstruction, Culler pointed out that even after we might deconstruct the ostensibly temporal logic of cause-and-effect, in which we disturb the neat linearity in which effects are thought to follow from causes (or, as I'll put it here – and this will become more significant – sons from mothers), this 'does not lead to the conclusion that the principle of causality is illegitimate and should be scrapped'.[4] Deconstructions must have their beginnings in some sense of that term; and it is this that will be the concern of the present essay; but put in the manner in which I raise the question above: 'Where does deconstruction come from?'

For de Man, deconstruction was, in a sense, always-already there. When he briefly works on a passage from Proust's *A la recherche du temps perdu* by way of introduction to *Allegories of Reading*, he is able to argue that: 'The deconstruction [in this instance of the relation between metaphor and metonymy] is not something we have added to the text but it constituted the text in the first place'.[5] In this sense, deconstruction involves an 'unveiling', an *aletheia*, whose point is to effect an intimacy between the act of reading and the consciousness that was required to make the text as a written document in the first place. As de Man glosses his argument:

> A literary text simultaneously asserts and denies the authority of its own rhetorical mode, and by reading the text [of Proust] as we did we were only trying to come closer to being as rigorous a reader as the author had to be in order to write the sentence in the first place.[6]

The criticism at work in deconstruction, then, is not a simple *aletheia* – a hermeneutic tearing away of veils – but also an act involving a temporal unveiling, a revelation of the *reading* carried out by the author *prior* to her or his *writing*. That temporal unveiling, with its seeming disturbance of chronological linearity, opens the necessary relation of non-coincidence between writer and reader, between writing and reading. In short, it opens the text to time itself which, in de Man's words, 'can be defined as 'precisely truth's inability to coincide with itself'.[7]

It can be seen, thus, that we have both *aletheia* and a temporality in which difference as such is established as the very condition of the revelation of a truth: these, combined, give a hint at what is at the core of deconstructive activity. That core, we might say in this beginning, can be characterized as a *failed confessing*. Confession promises revelation, and strives for a revelation that stems from the kernel of whatever we might identify as 'the self'; and further, it invokes a temporal predicament, for it confesses, in the present moment, now, a past, doing so in such a way as to establish not only a coincidental identity between past and present (I, who stole the ribbon, am the same I who now narrates the tale of that theft), but also a difference between the present and the past (in now revealing my self, I am different from the self who preferred to occlude the fact of my theft in the past: am now more honest, more truthful, more giving). Confession, in this regard, is marked by the kinds of temporal predicament explored by de Man in his famous 'Rhetoric of Temporality' essay, where he argues that:

> Irony divides the flow of temporal experience into a past that is pure mystification and a future that remains harassed forever by a relapse within the inauthentic. It can know this inauthenticity but can never overcome it.[8]

Confession, put in these terms, is related directly to the presiding problem governing modernity: autonomy. To ask 'where does a deconstruction come from?' is thus rather like asking 'where does a confession come from?'; and both are tantamount to asking whether it is possible ever to be *authentic*. Both confession and autonomy involve the question of origination, beginning; both involve finding some motivating or determining agency that initiates the act as such. Lyotard, in his posthumously published work-in-progress on Augustine's *Confessions*, indicates the double-temporality of the confessional order:

> *Les Confessions s'ecrivent sous le signe temporal de l'attente. L'attente, c'est le nom de la conscience du futur. Mais ici, parce qu'il s'agit non seulement de confesser la foi dans une fin 'en souffrance', mais de se confesser, d'exhiber la souffrance de ce qui a été fait, l'attente doit repasser par le passé, remonter vers sa source, vers la vie malheureuse, vers l'oeuvre qu'elle fut.*[9]

Waiting here is a waiting oriented at once towards the future and towards the past, thereby making the present moment a moment of a specific *conversion*. Confession is ostensibly the revelation of a truth that pre-exists the act of confessing; and yet, that truth *is* not unless and until it has been narrated or unless and until it *has the potential that it will be* narrated and revealed. The condition of autonomy is extremely similar: autonomy rests on the presumption that there is an originating, motivating self or a self-as-agent; while, simultaneously, the self is given only after the autonomous act identifiable as acts motivated from that self, originating in that self, will have been carried out.[10]

Given this abiding problem of origination, it is perhaps not surprising, then, that Derrida eventually made the turn towards a kind of confessing in his 'Circonfession'.[11] In what follows, I shall explore two related questions: first, what is at stake in deconstruction as a confession or *aletheia* (and this will be related to a complex meditation on suicide); secondly, can we be precise in finding a motivating instance for deconstruction, even dating it (and this will involve a question concerning politics, coloniality, and theology). The result will be one that allows me to relate deconstruction directly to foretelling and to prejudice, to 'telling' the future and judging it *in advance*.

On suicide

> who himself beginning knew?
>
> *John Milton*[12]

Lurking behind Milton's question is another, perhaps simpler, question: 'who knows his own mother?'

Derrida's 'Circonfession' is, through all its 59 'periods', in some ways the chronicle of a death foretold. The abiding concern all the way through it is the coming – foretold – death of Georgette Derrida, Jackie's mother; and the text is punctuated by a further concern about whether Jackie (who has just been diagnosed, at 59, with Lyme's disease, a condition whose symptoms approximate in some respects those of a stroke) might pre-decease his mother.[13] 'Circonfession' takes its place in a text whose pedagogical purpose is the conventional one, whereby Geoffrey Bennington will describe '*sinon la totalité de la pensée de J.D., du moins le système général de cette pensée*'.[14] The task of 'Circonfession' is to escape such systematicity, to 'surprise' Bennington (and all other readers). Paradoxically, thus, 'Circonfession' aims to contribute to the elucidation of 'Jacques Derrida' (and, by synecdochic extension, of deconstruction) while simultaneously obfuscating such elucidation: it will reveal and conceal at once, the concealment thereby requiring further elucidation in turn.

The 'confessional', elucidatory aspect of 'Circonfession' is driven by a tacit presumption that somehow, in the living self of Derrida – in the autobiography, the self-life-writing, the life that writes itself, the self that is lived as writing – we might find a source or origin for deconstruction, an explanatory 'cause' back to which the sophisticated work can all be referred, as a son might refer his identity back to his mother and to his formation at her hands; and yet, simultaneously, such a view is called into question by the text's relation to the 'Derridabase' of Bennington, circling above it, striving to be able to 'foretell' all that Derrida might ever write. Confession is here yoked to autobiography as a form of *aletheia*; but, simultaneously, there is nothing to be revealed, for nothing can surprise 'G.', sometimes 'Geo', ambiguously Geoffrey and Georgette, who, like blind Tiresias in whom two sexes meet, knows and foresuffers all.[15]

Derrida models his own beginnings here on those of his Algerian compatriot, St Augustine. For both men, the mother-son relation is determining; and, for both men, the death of the mother is felt as a crucial event, turning-point, or 'conversion'. Further, Augustine (rather belatedly in his text) opens his famous meditations on time by asking why he should confess to God when God already knows in advance the entire content of the confession that will have been made; and when Derrida begins his own text with an explicit allusion to this *cur confiteor* passage, the jocular analogy here is with the 'predictability' of deconstruction, as G., whose system (or 'programme'/*logiciel*) will reveal the predeterminability of all that Derrida can write, circles over and above Derrida's confessional text.

For Augustine, the confession is to stem from the core of his being, and it is to be truthful and communicable, but this raises problems:

> When [men] hear me speak about myself, how do they know whether I am telling the truth, since no one *knows a man's thoughts, except the man's own spirit that is within him?* ... What does it profit me, I ask, also to make known to men in your sight, through this book, not what I once was, but what I am now? I know what profit I gain by confessing my past ... But many people who know me, and others who do not know me but have heard of me or read my books, wish to hear what I am now, at this moment, as I set down my confessions. They cannot lay their ears to my heart, and yet it is in my heart that I am whatever I am.[16]

For Derrida, the confession stems not from the heart but rather from the mutilated penis: it is as if the foreskin, and most especially its cut, is what will foretell; or as if the core of the self – and indeed, the very motivating force or animating force of Derrida and his work – is in this mutilating cut, this attack on the very forefront of Derrida's infant body.

This cut is, of course, at the centre of the text of *Jacques Derrida*, as it is in many of Derrida's doubled/doubling texts (most famously and perhaps most extremely in *Glas*, the earlier text that already sounds a death-knell). Derrida *'privé d'avenir'* as he puts it,[17] ponders why it is that one might write *'quand on ne croit pas à sa propre survie...quand on écrit pour le présent mais un present qui n'est fait...que du retour sur soi de cette survie refusée'*.[18] Such a writing might be called *'une création sans lendemain'*; and, indeed, it was so called by another Algerian writer, whose presence haunts 'Circonfession': Camus.

The menacing, circumcising cut, carried out by a knife that was unseen by Derrida but graphically presented in the cut text of *Jacques Derrida*[19] echoes the presence of a knife seen elsewhere, when Meursault, his eyes blinded by tears and salt, confronts the Arab that he is about to kill. There are numerous parallels linking Derrida's text and that of Camus available in these pages; but two are most important.[20] Meursault describes the day's heat: *'C'était le même soleil que le jour ou j'avais enterré maman'*; and, further, when the Arab takes the knife from his pocket as Meursault advances, *'La lumière a giclé sur l'acier et c'etait comme une longue lame etincellante qui m'atteignait au front'*.[21] The decisive moment of the murder is the moment when *'tout a commencé'*, according to Meursault, when *'la mer a charrié un souffle épais et ardent'*.

It is difficult to ignore this kind of parallel, given that Derrida himself puns in his text between *'mer'* and *'mère'*, and when he wonders about the propriety of his being *'capable de publier sa fin, d'en exhiber les derniers souffles'*, publishing these last breaths for rather literary reasons, as if he is adding to the literary series of texts on *' "l'ecrivain et sa mere", sous-serie "la mort de la mere" '*.[22]

Camus, who opens *L'Etranger* with the death of a mother *'aujourd-hui...ou peut-être hier'*,[23] knew, like Augustine and Derrida, the importance attaching to the death of the mother. While for Augustine that moment reverberates with theological significance, for Camus it was always political. Rather reverentially disposed towards his mother, he always feared the fact that she remained in Algeria at times of crisis when there was the constant possibility of her being killed in the midst of the political battles in Algeria at any time between the passionate Communist struggles of the 1930s and the moment of decolonization for which Algeria was preparing when Camus died. Derrida's anxieties about pre-deceasing his mother were misplaced; Camus was the son who died, absurdly, before his own mother, with the unpublished confessional text of his beginnings, *The First Man*, in his briefcase.

To know one's own beginning is to know one's mother; but it is also to distance oneself from one's mother – to assert an autonomous identity – and thus, crucially, it is to know the death of the mother. Distancing such as this can be achieved, for Derrida, either through the death of the mother or through writing (broadly equivalent, as we should recall from the citation from *Of Grammatology* with which I opened the present piece):

j'attends l'interruption d'une course contre la montre entre l'écriture et sa vie, la sienne, la sienne seule, celle dont je m'eloigne a mésure que j'en parle, pour la trahir ou calomnier à chaque mot...[24]

That writing of a distance is a mode of asserting autonomy; and in it, Derrida demands pardon, as in a restorative or 'holy' confessional act. The question of excuses and pardon permeates the text of Camus, as it does that of Augustine. All three of these writers are thus linked, structurally and geo-politically.

Interestingly, all three have interesting things to say regarding suicide. For Augustine, it was unforgivable, 'monstrous'. It is not to be permitted even as a means of escaping from the commission of sins.[25] Camus, famously, describes suicide as the only serious philosophical problem, beside which everything else is mere frippery: '*Juger que la vie vaut ou ne vaut pas la peine d'être veçue, c'est répondre à la question fondamentale de la philosophie*'.[26] And here, also, in 'Circonfession', that spontaneous (*sua sponte*), responsible, self-confessing and self-denying (*suicidal*) text, Derrida writes that '*je me donne la mort*'.[27]

This last case requires a further gloss. In 'period' 34 of 'Circonfession', Derrida describes the 'conversation' between him and Georgette 'this 30 December 1989' in which his questions or conversational gambits to his mother are as words spoken to himself, for he knows that he will get no response from his mother. It is this situation, of course, that allows him to present the confession as a 'confession of/for others' ('*je ne me confesse pas, je confesse plutôt les autres*'[28]). This confession is not a straightforward *aletheia* in this sense; for the self that is confessed is not the self who speaks the confessional discourse. As argued above, that self is not only temporalized, but also displaced. More importantly here, though, this situation provokes an extremely telling response, in every sense of that phrase. When Derrida responds himself in the place of his mother, in period 34, he writes an intriguing phrase: '*nous nous euthanasions à demander ce qu'une vivante penserait si elle voyait la mort arriver*'.[29] This is Derrida and his mother, then, finding a happy death together, in this very writing or failed confession. The mother cannot confess (she is silent); the son cannot confess himself; yet the writing unites them in an initiating act of writing that both distances Derrida from his mother and, paradoxically, offers a most personal portrait of their extremely intimate relation at once.

When '*nous nous euthanasions*' returns, as '*je me donne la mort*' in period 53, it does so in a fashion that explicitly politicizes this happy death. In 53, Derrida considers the concept of heritage or inheritance, in the logic of which, citing Augustine, we have a paradoxical inversion of chronological time: '*ut* maior *seruiret* minori', 'that the *elder* will serve the *younger*'. This is taken from Book VII, Chapter 9 of Augustine's *Confessions*, and in that text, it is lifted directly from Paul's Epistle to the Romans (Romans, 9:12). That chapter in Paul is one in which Paul expresses pity for the Jews; but he does so in terms that call to mind the question of knowing one's own beginning. Paul argues here that salvation depends on God's mercy: 'it is not of him that willeth, nor of him that runneth, but of God that sheweth mercy' (Romans, 9:16); and, in this situation, who are we to question God:

> 18 Therefore hath he mercy on whom he will have mercy, and whom he will he hardeneth.
>
> 19 Thou wilt say then unto me, Why doth he yet find fault? For who hath resisted his will?
>
> 20 Nay but, O man, who art thou that repliest against God? Shall the thing formed say to him that formed it, Why hast thou made me thus?
>
> 21 Hath not the potter power over the clay, of the same lump to make one vessel unto honour, and another unto dishonour?

This chapter of Romans goes on to discuss the *conversion* of the Jews, which, according to Paul, will bring salvation, *survie*. Conversion, linked to the relation with the mother, is of the essence of Augustine's text; but in Derrida, the issue is not so explicitly theological. The relation between Jews and Christians is, in some ways, already integral to Derrida's biography, for he is, after all, a kind of *marrano* or 'Catholic Jew':

> *si je suis une sorte de marrane de la culture catholique française, et j'ai aussi mon corps chrêtien, hérité de sa en ligne plus ou moins tordue ... je suis de ces marranes qui ne se dissent même pas juifs dans le secret de leur Coeur, non pour être des marranes authentifiés de part ou d'autre de la frontière publique, mais parce qu'ils doutent de tout ...* [30]

In Derrida, the question becomes more explicitly a political question of inheritance, and specifically of his Algerian inheritance. In 53, the period in which he considers why one writes solely for the present, *'quand on ne croit pas à sa propre survie ni à la survie de quoi que ce soit'*, he remarks that his writing is necessarily in an inherited tongue:

> *je me donne ici la mort ne se dit qu'en une langue dont la colonisation de l'Algérie en 1830, un siècle avant moi, m'aura fait présent*, I don't take my life, *mais je me donne la mort.* [31]

Thus, giving oneself death, giving death to oneself, is explicitly related to a question of geo-political inheritance. Its origin lies exactly one century before Derrida's birth, in the colonization by France of Algeria.

Confession, we might say, requires sovereignty over the self. How can there be such sovereignty in a colonial situation and its legacies? This may well be the reason why '*une confession n'a rien à voir avec la verité*'.[32] For Derrida is frequently at pains in 'Circonfession' to claim a confession that is not *aletheia* at all, but rather a 'making' true, a *faire la verité*. That is an important distinction, whose politics I shall now try to reveal more explicitly, for it relates directly to the fraught fundamental Camusian question that is haunting 'Circonfession'. Is life worth being lived; should one attend to survival, to a 'living on', as Derrida expressed it in his contribution to Yale's *Deconstruction and Criticism*?

On prejudice

When Milton opened *Paradise Lost*, he was already blind; and when Derrida opened 'Circonfession', the text whose writing is done while he is frequently blinded by tears, he had just prepared the exhibition entitled *Memoires d'aveugle* for the Louvre. Milton will write 'Of Man's First disobedience, and the Fruit/Of that Forbidden Tree, whose mortal taste/Brought Death into the World'; and, in doing so, he will write (perhaps involuntarily) the narrative of how humanity can attain to a condition of sovereignty. Derrida is also writing a 'paradise lost' in a mode of '*nostalgerie*', a painful return homewards to Algeria. The fundamental question in both writings regards freedom, and how it is that humanity can assert sovereignty over life itself, over a living on. Both are related to vision; but to vision in the sense of the possibility not just of seeing with the eyes, nor of de Manian 'insight', but also of vision in the sense of what can be 'envisioned', or what can be foreseen, foretold.

Agamben has also recently considered this question, in relation to his fundamental thesis that modernity is marked by the politicization of what he calls 'bare life'. Agamben's contention is that in modernity, the distinction available between *zoe* (biological existing) and *bios* (the mode of living) has been effectively elided, and that politics (properly the domain of a *bios* distinguished from *zoe*) has fully entered 'bare life' itself. In a certain sense, we are all as Poor Tom in *King Lear*, a 'poor, bare, forked animal' (Act III, scene 4), but an animal whose 'unaccommodated' condition is not just a biological but also a political condition. In Agamben, this situation is one that begins to allow us to address what has happened to the Jews during the twentieth century.[33]

One particular aspect of Agamben's case is extremely relevant for this present essay. In *Homo Sacer*, he considers the question of suicide and its unpunishability in law. To do so, he begins from a 1920 text, *Die Freigabe der Vernichtung lebensunwerten Lebens* (or *Authorization for the Annihilation of Life Unworthy of Being Lived*), by Karl Binding and Alfred Hoche, both eminent professors of medicine. Agamben points out that 'in order to explain the unpunishability of suicide, Binding is led to conceive of suicide as the expression of man's sovereignty over his own existence'.[34] Such a conception, ostensibly one that dignifies the suicide and gives a (paradoxical) freedom to the being who kills herself or himself, brings problems in its wake, however. The explication of suicide in this manner allows for a similar conceptualization of the stakes of euthanasia, as an act that annihilates a 'life unworthy of being lived'. It is not difficult to see, from this ostensibly well-intentioned 1920 medical text, the gradual shift into the position of Nazism, just over a decade later, where Jews and other refugees were deemed to be living 'a life unworthy of being lived' and therefore killed – but killed in accordance with a philosophy that could not conceive of such killing as a 'crime' or a homicide in the normal ways. Suicide, seen as a limit-case of autonomy, becomes complicit with its opposite; in this case, the assertion of a freedom becomes complicit with the Holocaust.

This has its counterpart in Derrida's text. The confessional text is not concerned with crime, but with its theological counterpart, sin; or, as Derrida puts it, Augustine's *Confessions* are *'une forme de theologie comme autobiographie'*.[35]

When Augustine considers – and prohibits – suicide, in *City of God*, he does so in terms that are explicitly concerned with sin; but also, and more importantly for present purposes, in terms that relate to the issue of sovereign control over one's own body and life. He asks whether it might be permissible to kill oneself if the aim is to *forestall* sin. In particular, he thinks of those who have been or may become victims of sexual assault or rape during imperial wars. The argument is a sophisticated one, in which Augustine makes the point that if the victim is not party to the sin or violation, then she remains chaste:

> ... virtue, the condition of right living, holds command over the parts of the body from her throne in the mind, and ... the consecrated body is the instrument of the consecrated will; and if that will continues unshaken and steadfast, whatever anyone else does with the body or to the body, provided that it cannot be avoided without committing sin, involves no blame to the sufferer.[36]

Augustine then further agues that this holds good in all cases, so that there is no excuse for those women who kill themselves *in advance* of being violated, in order to try to *prevent* the very possibility of their becoming complicit with the rape and thus complicit with sin. The key question here, for our understanding of Derrida, is not just that pertaining to forestalling future sin, but also that pertaining to what might be done, or have been done, to the body (and particularly to its sexual parts) *without consent* or *complicity*. Such is Derrida's circumcision. By analogy with the Augustinian argument, thus, circumcision does not 'identify' Derrida, does not *bind* him, does not *determine* or *predetermine* what he is and does. In short, deconstruction *cannot* be seen to derive from a Judaic mentality or psychology.

The foreskin, cut from the body, is described as a wedding-ring, *une alliance*. Such a ring, such an alliance, ties Derrida to his mother in a most intimate fashion; but the text also plays explicitly on the multiple meanings of the *alliance*. In the first place, in 1943 and since, 'L'alliance' was above all the name not of a wedding-ring, but rather of the school that Derrida was supposed to attend, having been expelled from his previous school in El-Biar on account of his Jewishness. Derrida, however, confesses to playing truant from this school, and going instead to watch the file of Allied soldiers (soldiers in an *alliance*) going into the brothels, in an ostensibly legitimized form of that imperial sexual violation discussed by Augustine.[37] The foreskin, thus – and more particularly its violation – links sex to war and both to the position of the schoolboy (the *'petit juif très noir, très arabe'*) expelled.

For Augustine, then, suicide is forbidden even if its aim is to control one's final theological destiny, by preventing a future of sin and thus enabling the regaining of paradise. For Derrida, suicide is *impossible*, for there is no self to be killed in the first place. Yet suicide is still related to the question of sovereignty and futurity. The eradication of the self that is 'Circonfession', confession as the *'privation de soi'*, is a theological 'suicide' directed at trying to open the possibility of a futurity that is not predetermined. Derrida's wager, after all, is that he will be able to surprise Geoffrey, that he will take Geoffrey by surprise, that he will escape identification in Geoffrey's 'Derridabase'.

It is this that the confession fails to do; and it is in this respect that it is a failed confession. Bennington, in the 'Actes' section of *Jacques Derrida*, is able to write, in a parenthesis, that he is less surprised than Derrida might suppose by this exhibiting of Derrida's circumcision: *'depuis longtemps, il ne parle que d'elle, je pourrais le montrer citations a l'appui'*.[38]

It is thus the case that deconstruction, as a failed confessing, fails also to produce the possibility of surprise. That is to say: deconstruction fails to enable the possibility of a non-predetermined future; or, in other words, it fails to produce a freedom in the form of an autonomous sovereignty. To re-phrase that yet again, deconstruction is tied to predetermination, which calls into question the relation between deconstruction and foretelling a future, between deconstruction and prophecy (especially, of course, specifically the prophet Elijah), between deconstruction and pre-judgements or prejudice.

When I opened this section with my allusion to Milton, it was not simply to allow the alignments of various blindnesses. Milton struggles in *Paradise Lost* to maintain the claim that humanity is free with the Augustinian question of 'why confess'/*cur confiteor*. Milton's God *knows* that the first man and woman will fall; but Milton claims that such foreknowledge is not in itself prejudicial for man was made 'Sufficient to have stood, though free to fall', as God says:

> Freely they stood who stood, and fell who fell…
> … They therefore as to right belong'd
> So were created, nor can justly accuse
> Their maker, or their making, or their Fate;
> As if Predestination over-rul'd
> Their will, dispos'd by absolute Decree
> Or high foreknowledge; they themselves decreed
> Their own revolt, not I: if I foreknew,
> Foreknowledge had no influence on their fault,
> Which had no less prov'd certain unforeknown.[39]

This passage tries to reconcile freedom with prejudice; and the consequence is the rather shocking suggestion that God is no more or less in control of things than humanity itself. The choice of Adam and Eve would have been as it was, would have been 'certain', whether God knew it or not.

Likewise, deconstruction is *prejudicial*. Its practice is a constant struggle to reconcile *aletheia* (the confessing or revelation of what has been done: the past in all its *necessity*) with the *prophetic* (the 'making' of truth in all its *contingency*). The name for this struggle is nothing other than prejudice itself. Deconstruction's origin lies in a certain prejudice that bars Derrida from his schooling, certainly; but the originary and *motivating* source of deconstruction lies in this problematic issue of free autonomy, an autonomy whose enactments will always-already have been foreseen once they have been carried out. Predetermination is the stake.

For Derrida, that is also a political question. '*Qui suis-je?*' he asks his mother, on numerous occasions; but, as his mother remains silent, he is also asking himself. He is Jew, he is Arab, he is Catholic; he is Algerian, he is French. How can these be reconciled in J. D. (the initials, pronounced in French, approximate to the enunciation of another author whose ties to Algeria were profound and whose writings played a formative role in Derrida's literary education, Gide)? '*Qui suis-je*' is also a question that must not predetermine '*qui serai-je*', nor can it itself have been predetermined by the question '*qui étais-je*'. Foreskinning is not foretelling; and, it follows, one's inheritance or tradition (one's Jewishness or Christianity, say) can neither explain nor forgive/excuse one's actions: the subject is, of necessity, an ethical being whose freedom is determined in the act and *after the fact*. That is to say, freedom is not to be characterized as it would be in existentialism, say, by the subject making choices; rather, freedom is seen only *after the fact* or after the act has been committed.

This would align deconstruction with the politics of the absurd, that near-indigenous Algerian philosophy. The absurd is that point, in mathematics, beyond which it makes no sense to go: it is the origin of deconstruction.

Notes

*This was originally published as Chapter 1 of the author's *Aesthetic Democracy* (Standford University Press, 2007).

1. T. S. Eliot, 'The Love Song of J. Alfred Prufrock', in *Complete Poems and Plays* (London: Faber, 1969), 15.
2. Jacques Derrida, *Of Grammatology*, trans. Gayatri Chakravorty Spivak (Baltimore: Johns Hopkins University Press, 1976), 266. The year 1967 can be regarded as a kind of beginning for deconstruction, in that it was during that year that the impact of Derrida's writings began to be felt, for the first time in a major fashion, in the Anglophone and literary (i.e., non-philosophically specialist) world.
3. ibid., 266–7.
4. Jonathan Culler, *On Deconstruction* (London: Routledge and Kegan Paul, 1983), 87.
5. Paul de Man, *Allegories of Reading* (Cambridge MA: Yale University Press, 1979), 17.
6. ibid., 17
7. ibid., 78. In relation to this, see also Paul Ricoeur, *De l'interpretation* (Paris: Seuil, 1965), 35–6; and cf. my commentary on this in my study, *After Theory* (revised and expanded 2nd edition; Edinburgh University Press, Edinburgh, 1996), 43ff.
8. Paul de Man, *Blindness and Insight*, 2nd edition (London: Methuen, 1983), 222; but cf. my extended commentary on this essay in *After Theory*, 115–41.
9. Jean-Francois Lyotard, *La Confession d'Augustin* (Paris: Galilée, 1998), 96.
10. In much earlier work, I characterized this point of conversion as a 'revolutionary moment', in a mode that was perhaps over-excitedly political. This present essay is a more measured reading of autonomy or of beginnings, carried out in a less politicized fashion. For the earlier reading, see my *John Donne, Undone* (Methuen, 1986), *passim*. For a much more sustained inquiry into beginnings, of course, see Edward Said, *Beginnings* (New York: Columbia University Press, 1985).
11. Geoffrey Bennington and Jacques Derrida, *Jacques Derrida* (Paris: Seuil, 1991). It is structurally important that 'Circonfession' is 'presided over' by Bennington's own text, 'Derridabase', part of whose presumption is that there should be no surprise, that it is possible to construct a 'programme' that will have always already foretold what it is possible for Derrida to propose. Yet, surprises there are.
12. John Milton, *Paradise Lost*, ed. Christopher Ricks (Harmondsworth: Penguin, 1989), 182 (Book VIII, line 251).
13. In fact, Georgette Derrida outlasted the completion of 'Circonfession' by some eighteen months or so; and, as I write (today, on my birthday, 23 July 2001), Derrida has just passed, by one week, his seventy-first birthday (15 July 2001). Many happy returns.
14. Bennington and Derrida, *Jacques Derrida*, 3.
15. The fact that Tiresias 'unites' the two sexes is important here, for 'Circonfession' is, as is well known, largely about Derrida's penis and its mutilation through circumcision. That mutilation is one that can be related to symbolic castration, as in John D. Caputo's reading in *The Prayers and Tears of Jacques Derrida* (Bloomington and Indianapolis: Indiana University Press, 1997), esp. 239–40; but it also relates to Derrida's 'secret name', Elie or Elijah, the name of the prophet who faces down Jezebel in 1 Kings 18ff.

16. Augustine, *Confessions*, trans. R. S. Pine-Coffin (Harmondsworth: Penguin, 1961), 208–9.
17. Derrida, 'Circonfession', 30.
18. ibid., 263.
19. Bennington and Derrida, *Jacques Derrida*, 277: '*je ne voyais même pas mes yeux, pas plus que jadis la main qui leva le couteau sur moi*'; and cf. 67 for the image of just such a knife.
20. I shall leave aside, in what follows, a third parallel between the writers: their passion for playing football.
21. Albert Camus, *L'Etranger* (Paris: Gallimard, 1957), 89–90. On the importance of 'tears', another aspect of the parallels, see Caputo, *Prayers and Tears*.
22. Derrida, 'Circonfession', 38.
23. Camus, *L'Etranger*, 7.
24. Derrida, 'Circonfession', 155.
25. Augustine, *City of God*, trans. Henry Bettenson (Harmondsworth: Penguin, 1972), 38–9 (Book 1, ch. 27).
26. Camus, *Le Mythe de Sisyphe* (Paris: Gallimard, 1942), 15. Interestingly, his analysis of death itself resembles strikingly that of Wittgenstein in the *Tractatus Logico-Philosophicus*, proposition 6.4311. There Wittgenstein writes 'Death is not an event of life. Death is not lived through'; and cf. Camus in *Le Mythe*, 30: '*en realité, il n'y a pas d'experience de la mort. Au sens propre, n'est experimenté que ce qui a été veçu et rendu conscient*'.
27. Derrida, 'Circonfession', 263.
28. ibid., 175.
29. ibid., 167
30. ibid., 160. Derrida as a kind of doubting Thomas, therefore.
31. ibid., 263; cf. 39, ' "*j'ai envie de me tuer*" '.
32. ibid., 103; cf. 109 for the direct relation of this to 'the Jews'; and cf. 126 for its direct relation to circumcision.
33. For a fuller argument on this, see my essay on Agamben, 'Potential European Democracy', *Paragraph* (2002), special edition on Agamben, ed. Brian Dillon.
34. Giorgio Agamben, *Homo Sacer*, trans. Daniel Heller-Roazen (Stanford: Stanford University Press, 1998), 136.
35. Derrida, 'Circonfession', 84.
36. Augustine, *City of God*, 26 (Book 1, ch. 16).
37. Derrida, 'Circonfession', 66, 164.
38. Bennington and Derrida, *Jacques Derrida*, 301.
39. Milton, *Paradise Lost*, 60 (Book III, line 99, lines 103–119).

5
Extremes Meet

Jean-Michel Rabaté

> Comment c'est je cite avant Pim avec Pim après Pim comment c'est
> trois parties je le dis comme je l'entends.
>
> *Samuel Beckett*, Comment c'est, *1961*

Beckett chose the simplest solution when he translated his French title into
simple English: strict literalism, 'How It Is'. He knew he could not easily keep
the pun on *commencer/comment c'est*, and he chose not to be too Joycean
in these matters – as he could have by translating it as 'Big Innings', for
instance. Instead, a difficulty had already been signalled quite subtly in the
French text: *'je cite'*, easily translated by 'I quote', and *'comme je l'entends'*
both point to the double meaning of 'as I hear it' and 'as I understand it',
thus stressing the paradox of a beginning, a 'to begin' (*commencer*), that is
already a quotation. 'I quote' implies that the speaker is not starting from
scratch but repeating something that has been uttered or written, perhaps
a previous inscription, possibly by himself. Thus the text will find as many
versions of itself not only as there will be subsequent translations in other
languages (translations which will have to repeated, modified and constantly
updated whereas the 'original', we suppose, will remain itself) but also as
there will be performances of its textuality by the simple act of speaking or
reading. Or so one thinks. This somewhat convoluted preamble should aim
at highlighting the presence of a quote in my own title, a quote that most
readers will have recognized, and I will confirm that yes, I have been quoting Derrida quoting Joyce in the 'envoi' or finale concluding his extended
discussion of Levinas in 'Violence and Metaphysics':

> Are we Greeks? Are we Jews? But who, we? Are we (not a chronological,
> but a pre-logical question) *first* Jews or *first* Greeks? And does the strange
> dialogue between the Jew and the Greek, peace itself, have the form of
> the absolute, speculative logic of Hegel, the living logic which *reconciles*
> formal tautology and empirical heterology after having *thought* prophetic

discourse in the preface to the *Phenomenology of Spirit*? Or, on the contrary, does this peace have the form of the infinite separation and of the unthinkable, unsayable transcendence of the other? To what horizon of peace does the language which asks this question belong? From whence does it draw the energy of its question? Can it account for the historical *coupling* of Judaism and Hellenism? And what is the legitimacy, what is the meaning of the *copula* in this proposition from perhaps the most Hegelian of modern novelists: 'Jewgreek is greekjew. Extremes meet?'[1]

Extremes meet – we know (but who, we?) what they may be: Jew and Greek, man and woman, death and life, speech and writing, culture and anarchy, you can add whichever binary you like...How do they meet? Through fusion, copulation or war? It seems that the question of 'how to begin' is indissociable from that of *comment c'est*, how it is. To try and show 'how it is', I will have to postpone a direct discussion of the 'proposition itself', taken as it is out of context, a proposition put forward in fact not by one character but an object, Lynch's Cap, a cap that has been addressed by Stephen Dedalus and suddenly erupts into speech in an episode often called the Nighttown or the brothel section of *Ulysses* – just 'Circe':

> THE CAP (*with saturnine spleen*): Ba! It is because it is. Woman's reason. Jewgreek is greekjew. Extremes meet. Death is the highest form of life. Ba!'[2]

Without having to enter into a technical textual discussion of a very complex passage in *Ulysses*, what interests me here, first of all, is the way Joyce is seen as a Hegelian writer whose 'literature' should be able, in some way, to answer some of the aporias generated in the wake of Levinas's philosophy of the other. Besides, we have quite a number of narratives provided by Derrida about his own 'beginnings' as a philosopher; when working under the supervision of the Hegelian Jean Hyppolite, he devoted some time to 'structure and genesis' (a title that Hyppolite had used with respect to the *Phenomenology of Spirit*) in Husserl, or of Maurice de Candillac on the 'ideality of the literary object'; he was sent to Harvard for one year (1956–7), with the pretext of studying Husserl's manuscripts, but there he actually read much more Joyce in the Widener Library – and eventually got married in Boston. It is this 'marriage' of Joyce and Husserl that I would like to discuss here, a union achieved under the sign of the complementarity of opposites (itself a very Joycean notion). The first result of this active 'copula' was to find written expression in some pages of the Introduction to Husserl's *The Origin of Geometry*. Here is how Derrida reminisces in a 1994 roundtable extemporization with Caputo about this episode:

> I think that Joyce is a great landmark in the history of deconstruction...In my first book on Husserl I tried to compare the way Joyce treats

language and the way a classical philosopher such as Husserl treats language. Joyce wanted to make history, the resuming and the totalization of history, possible through the accumulation of metaphoricities, equivocalities, and tropes. Husserl, on the other hand, thought that historicity was made possible by the transparent univocity of language, that is, by a scientific, mathematical, pure language. There is no historicity without the transparency of the tradition, Husserl says, while Joyce says there is no historicity without this accumulation of equivocality in language. It is from the tension between the two interpretations of language that I tried to address the question of language.[3]

And to substantiate his life-long confrontation with Joyce, Derrida gives two examples of important motifs for him: paternity considered as a 'legal fiction', and the power of the 'yes' in *Ulysses*. Before reopening these recurrent themes, my interest in the archaeology of Derrida's reading of Joyce will force me to reopen the Introduction to Husserl's *Origin of Geometry*.

1   Begging the question of an Origin

After all, this is not be a bad place to start, if we wish to investigate the beginnings of deconstruction. This *is* a good place, even, if it can help us distinguish (or be 'critical' about) a series of gestures that are often thought of as identical or at least overlapping: founding a discipline, thinking about origins, beginning an inquiry, starting off on a reading, a journey, etc. If, as I am going to suggest by a radical apocope, a beginning is always less and more than itself, being both a beg – i.e., a begging of the question of origins – and an endless echoing of its -ing (there is no begin without an -ing, i.e., a process whose gerund may be actually infinite), then we need to reopen Derrida's confrontation with the beginnings and endings of phenomenology.

It is therefore important to assess how and why a 'beginning' is not identical with an 'origin', even though any beginning can later be taken as an origin, in a disjunction which entails a fresh reconsideration of transcendental history. This is why Derrida is alert to the style of Husserl's pages that he translates:

In effect these pages of Husserl, first written for himself, have the rhythm of a thought feeling its way [*d'une pensée qui se cherche*] rather than setting itself forth [*plus qu'elle ne s'expose*]. But here the apparent discontinuity also depends on an always regressive method, a method which chooses its interruptions and multiplies the returns toward its beginning in order to reach back and grasp it again each time in a recurrent light.[4]

This regressive method is inseparable from a practice of writing that can appear as paradigmatic: thinking would thus be from the start – and one can begin anywhere, obviously condemned to start *in medias res* – writing for oneself. Writing for himself in order to hear himself think, Husserl we know will then give these pages to others like Eugen Fink who will type them, and begin the long process of transmission when they are added to the huge corpus of the Husserliana – until, one day, they are translated into French and annotated.

I might then offer a first generalization as working hypothesis: deconstruction begins with Husserlian phenomenology seen as a 'method' of thinking or a 'style' of writing which takes origins as a theme of meditation; by its readiness to take risks (such as the wish to be open to literature, even Joyce's literature), phenomenology will end up providing a wholesale critique of classical Reason. For, indeed, the late piece (1936) entitled *The Origin of Geometry*, while contemporary with the *Crisis of European Sciences and Transcendental Phenomenology*, sends us back to one of Husserl's earliest philosophical essays, *The Philosophy of Mathematics* (1891). Both treatises address the function of mathematical or geometrical ideal unities (or idealities) by returning to their foundation in consciousness – hence opening a transcendental operation. To speak of a 'return' here may seem to beg the issue of the foundation, or simply of the beginning – but it is precisely a return to some point that is not an absolute beginning in the historical sense. Or rather, the main shift in Husserl's thought between the 1880s and the 1930s consists in a renewed consideration of the role of history. This reopening of the file of historical reason is based upon the awareness that the present is in a state of crisis, and that the road to transcendental idealism cannot be the same as before. The method followed will then have to be different from what traditional philosophical systems have done so far. Derrida points out a dangerous hesitation in this movement toward history: when 'history itself breaks though into phenomenology' (*fait irruption dans la phénoménologie*) it is more and more difficult to contain it or assign it to a well delimited space.

While constantly *practised* in the *Crisis* itself, this new access to history is never *made a problem*. At least not directly and as such. On the one hand, the consciousness of a crisis and the affirmation of a teleology of reason are *only* new paths or means for legitimizing transcendental idealism once again. On the other hand, to put the whole development of Western philosophy into perspective, to define the European *eidos* and the man of infinite tasks, and to recount the adventures and misadventures of the transcendental motif, concealed each time by the very gesture that uncovers it: all this would give credit to a kind of synoptic retrospection that no criticism of historic reason had explicitly justified from the start. Neither the structures of historicity in general ... nor the methods of the phenomenology of history were made the objects of specific, original questions. This confidence was supported by the system of apodeictic certainties of phenomenology itself, which could be considered as a criticism of reason in general. If this teleological reading of history could not be characterized in Husserl's eyes by the dogmatic impudence with which so many philosophers (from Aristotle to Hegel to Brunschvicg) perceive in the past only the laboured presentiment of their own thought, it is because this reading referred to the very idea of transcendental phenomenology – which is not a philosophical system.[5]

If we agree to identify Husserl's writing style and his a-systematicity we can foresee where Derrida's trajectory will carry him: towards a thinking of Difference as undermining from the start any possibility of founding phenomenology and hence all philosophy on an absolute origin, seen as the Nowness of a Living Present.[6] He will have in between to deal with an inevitable question (contained in the parenthesis I have skipped): is the historicity of science and philosophy the culmination of history or totally elsewhere, as a condition of possibility beyond history?

I wish I could continue quoting in its entirety this dense and remarkable passage of the *Introduction* to Husserl's essay on geometry. I will nevertheless choose a focus in the role of 'literature' – a theme used as a springboard for the issue of 'traces', for writing defined as the practice of difference which reappears more strongly with Joyce. All this could begin with the strange footnote in which, as he insists on the necessity to keep a record of scientific inventions through language, Husserl grants literature an apparently surprising pre-eminence:

> But geometrical existence is not psychic existence; it does not exist as something personal within the sphere of personal consciousness: it is the existence of what is objectively there for 'everyone'... And all forms newly produced by someone on the basis of pregiven forms immediately take on the same objectivity. This is, we note, an 'ideal' objectivity. It is proper to a whole class of spiritual products of the cultural world, to which not only all scientific constructions and the sciences themselves belong but also, for example, the constructions of fine literature.*
>
> *But the broadest concept of literature encompasses them all: that is, it belongs to their objective being that they be linguistically expressed and can be expressed again and again; or, more precisely, they have their objectivity, their existence-for-everyone, only as signification, as the meaning of speech. This is true in peculiar fashion in the case of the objective sciences: for them the difference between the original language of the work and its translation into other languages does not remove its identical accessibility or change it into an inauthentic, indirect accessibility.[7]

The remark about translation is crucial: Husserl is above all interested in the possibility of preserving a nucleus of meaning, this is why language is indispensable to geometry. But in fact, as Derrida stresses in his commentary, it is geometry which provides a model for literature on Husserl's view and not the reverse. 'Every linguistic dimension that would escape this absolute translatability would remain marked by the empirical subjectivity of an individual or society. For Husserl, the model of language is the objective language of science. A poetic language, whose signification would not be *objects*, will never have any transcendental value for him'.[8]

However, Joyce would not be dismayed by this thesis, since he opened his collection of stories *Dubliners* with a tantalizing hint that geometry was indeed the master science. In the famous opening paragraph of 'The Sisters' we hear of a *gnomon* ominously knotted with *simony* and *paralysis* and its source is acknowledged: Euclid's *Elements*. 'Every night as I gazed up at the window I said softly to myself the word *paralysis*; it had always sounded strangely in my ears, like the word *gnomon* in the Euclid and the word *simony* in the Catechism.'[9] Even if Joyce has in mind a very precise figure in which an identical parallelogram has been taken away from another bigger parallelogram, as if one corner was simply missing, it would be worth paralleling them with what Husserl has to say about Euclid, the first geometrician according to Greek tradition, who introduces a very early infinitization (which still needs mathematics to be dealt with) in the science of shapes. In this movement, the whole issue of technology will engulf itself – as Heidegger has well noted.

> Starting from this inaugural infinitization, mathematics cognizes new infinitizations, which are so many interior revolutions. For, if the primordial infinitization opens the mathematical field to infinite fecundities for the Greeks, it no less *first* limits the a priori system of that productivity. The very content of an infinite production will be confined within an a priori system which, for the Greeks, will always be *closed*. The guide here is Euclidean geometry, or rather the '*ideal Euclid*', according to Husserl's expression, which is restricted to sense, not historical fact.[10]

Indeed, as a confirmation of this insight, one can notice that a 'gnomon' was not only used as a geometrical figure (the carpenter's tee) but also in mathematical relations to mean any proportion between two numbers such that one will contain the other. By opening itself to geometry, Joyce's text suggests the first trap set for the reader (and of course his characters): the lure and prestige but also the endless aporias of textual infinitization.

What seems to bother Derrida in his commentary at this point is that Husserl's reliance on a strict model of translatability risks meeting intractable limits as soon as one wishes to address the constitution of subjectivity and its dependence on language, which is, let us not forget it, another part of the project of phenomenology. Here, Derrida seems ready to simply contradict

Husserl, especially when the latter seems to be seeking for a Nature which would provide an origin or a ground for all pre-cultural identities:

> But preculturally *pure Nature* is always buried. So, as the ultimate possibility for communication, it is a kind of inaccessible infra-ideal. Can we not say, then, just the opposite of what Husserl said? Are not non-communication and misunderstanding the very horizon of culture and language? Undoubtedly misunderstanding is always a factual horizon and the finite index of sound intelligence taken as infinite pole [sentence modified]. But although the latter is always announced so that language can begin, is not finitude the essential which we can never radically go beyond?[11]

In this revealing aside, in which Derrida seems to abandon the mask of the good pupil who carefully annotates and introduces the text he has translated, another tone can be heard – closer to Heidegger clearly, but also, such would be my contention, informed by Blanchot.

What is most telling there is the idea that the 'latter' pole of infinity is announced 'so that language can begin' – a notion not so far from the thesis of Roland Barthes in *Writing Degree Zero* (modern literature is purposely without any 'style' so as to let language speak by itself – such would be the main effort of the 'nouveau roman'). Husserl has nevertheless considered language in this essay: he takes the example of *Löwe* (lion) to conclude that such a word is both an 'ideal objectivity' (*eine ideale Gegenständlichkeit*) and something that is given a 'linguistic living body' (*Sprachleib*) in German – a language in which, moreover, it exists objectively 'only in virtue of ... two-levered repetitions and ultimately in virtue of sensibly embodying repetitions'.[12] Like Euclid's theorems, which remain the same in all its translations, *Löwe* belongs to a commonly shared universe for humanity. Civilization is the community of those who, by speaking, can not only name the world but share the world.[13] And writing makes this communication become virtual, anticipating the idea that language is sedimented, and that, in spite of the requirement of pure univocity without which a science would not be rigorous, words pile up on another, and any discovery will be made not only by avoiding the 'seduction of language'[14] but also by taking into account the specific 'passivity' that is implied by tradition. The rest of Husserl's essay is then devoted less to geometry than to problems posed by tradition and history.

Even if Husserl keeps attacking historicism and its fascination for unanalysed raw facts, and sees Hegel primarily as a historicist philosopher, Derrida is quite right when he points out similarities in Husserl's and Hegel's treatment of language. I will thus need to focus myopically on a revealing footnote in Derrida's *Introduction*. In the text, Derrida sums up Husserl's theses on the ideality of words:

> Thus, the word has an ideal Objectivity and identity, since it is not identical with any of its empirical, phonetic, or graphic materializations. It is always the *same* word which is meant and recognized through all possible linguistic gestures. Insofar as this ideal object confronts language as such, the latter supposes a spontaneous neutralization of the factual existence of the speaking subject, of words, and of the thing designated. Speech, then, is only the practice of an immediate eidetic.*
>
> *The linguistic neutralization of existence is an original idea only in the technical and thematic signification that phenomenology gives it. Is not this idea the favourite of Mallarmé and Valéry? Hegel above all had amply explored it. In the *Encyclopaedia* (one of the few Hegelian works that Husserl seems to have read), the lion already testifies to this neutralization as an exemplary martyr: 'Confronting the name – Lion – we no longer have either an intuition of such an animal or even an image, but the name (when we understand it) is its simple and imageless representation; in the name we think' (§462). (This passage is cited by Jean Hyppolite in his *Logique et Existence: Essai sur la Logique de Hegel*, p. 39, a work which, on many points, lets the profound convergence of Hegelian and Husserlian thought appear.)
>
> Hegel also writes: 'The first act, by which Adam is made master of the animals, was to impose on them a name, i.e., he annihilated them in their existence (as existents)' (System of 1803–1804). Cited by Maurice Blanchot in *La Part du Feu* ... p. 325.[15]

If Hegel and Husserl converge when affirming the idea that the word is the death of the thing, the dramatizing language of Hegel is foreign to the technicality of Husserl's idiom. Without being over-dramatic myself, I would like to pause here and salute the remarkable overlapping of two texts that have indeed marked a whole generation of French philosophers: both take their point of departure in Hegel but so as to break completely with the Hegelianism that had been marked by Kojève's neo-Marxist rendering of the *Phenomenology* in the years immediately preceding the Second World War.

Logic and Existence was published in 1953 and, by staging an apparent recantation of its author about the respective merits of Hegel's *Phenomenology* and his *Logic*, it significantly displaced previous anthropological readings of Hegel often identified with Kojève's thesis, for which everything would boil down to the confrontation between Napoléon and the Philosopher of Absolute Knowledge, or, in the dialectic of consciousnesses, to the interaction between the Master and the Slave. In 1953, Hyppolite's main focus was the loaded relationship between Hegel's logic, a 'logic of sense' or pure relations, and the phenomenology seen as an 'introduction' to the System. The new stress on logic and language eventually relegated the ontology of existence or essence to a previous horizon of thought. What mattered then was less ontological difference than the conditions by which sense could be made, as Deleuze would point out in his groundbreaking review of Hyppolite's new work. Philosophy thus becomes an ontology of sense – sense being defined as 'the absolute identity of being and difference'.[16] It is indeed obvious that the whole new generation that included Foucault, Derrida and Deleuze would take its bearing in this intelligent repositioning of Hegel's thought.

The reference to Blanchot belongs to a somewhat different world, closer by some aspects to Kojève and anthropological readings of Hegel. Derrida quotes the famous essay 'La Littérature et le droit à la mort', which closes *La Part du Feu*, a collection of essays dealing with Kafka, Mallarmé, Hölderlin, René Char, Rimbaud, Lautréamont, Valéry, Nietzsche and many other writers. This last piece provides the theoretical core of the book, and is largely based upon a reading of Hegel. Kojève is still felt to be an authority on Hegel (he is quoted as having shown how Marx and Hegel agree fundamentally and also as having demonstrated that 'understanding is the equivalent of a murder').[17] Blanchot also relies on Hyppolite's *Genesis and Structure* to point out that the main political discovery in Hegel is not based on the issue of slavery but on that of the Terror during the French Revolution. Marquis de Sade is presented as the writer who embodies Terror … but this is another story.[18]

Fundamentally, Blanchot starts from Hegel to explore all the paradoxes a Writer will have to face: and the first is, typically, the impossibility of really beginning.

> From his first step, as Hegel says more or less, the individual who wants to write is blocked by a contradiction: in order to write, he needs the talent to write. But in themselves, talents are nothing. So long as he has not sat at a table and written a work, the writer is not a writer and he does not know whether he has the ability to become one. He has talent only after he has written, but he needs talent to write.[19]

The writer then becomes, to follow another Hegelian phrase, a nothingness who works in and with nothingness.

Beyond these Hegelian references that seem to structure the argument, one sees another reference looming larger and larger in Blanchot's text: Levinas, who provides not so much a way out as another terminology to move out from the pathos of negativity.

> Literature, this blind vigilance which, wishing to escape from itself, falls deeper and deeper into its own obsession, is the only available translation of the obsession of existence, if the latter is the very impossibility to leave existence, being that is always thrown back to being, which, in the

depthless depth is already at the bottom, abyss which is still a foundation for the abyss, recourse without which there is no recourse.[20]

The new abyssal foundation is here not so much Hegel's 'night' but rather the 'there is' (*il y a*) of Levinas's *From existence to existent*. No need to expatiate here on the personal and tangled links that connected Blanchot, Levinas and Bataille; what matters is the sign that through a text Derrida read very closely – since he quotes Hegel through it – the impact of Levinas's thought is already perceptible. It may also be a mere coincidence of dates, but Derrida's *Introduction* to Husserl was written just a year after the publication of Levinas's *Totality and Infinity* (1961) – a superb philosophical novel in which the figure of Odysseus, who only aims at returning home, is taken as the paradigm of a purely Greek mode of thinking: phenomenology engages in 'purely imaginary adventures or undergone, as with Odysseus, only to go back home'.[21]

As Derrida writes in his turn: 'This historicity or traditionality is always presupposed by every Odyssean repetition of Joyce's type, as by all *philosophy of history* (in the current sense) and by every *phenomenology of spirit*. The essences of finite totalities and the typology of figures of the spirit will always be idealities that are bound to empirical history'.[22] One can sense why he needed a little more time to digest Levinas's conflation of all phenomenologies of spirit and of Greek philosophy as such – from the point of view of a radical Jewish sense of ethics that refuses the nostalgic return of Spirit to the site of the Same. His reply took two more years and was published in 1964 as 'Violence and Metaphysics'.

What Blanchot brings to Derrida is the strong awareness that any 'work' will surprise its writer – and the sense that writing is the name of a process by which I 'become other'.[23] Which is not far from the remark quoted in passing in the Introduction about the possibility of considering writing as a mere archive, or in the words of Jean Hyppolite, a 'subjectless transcendental field': 'Writing, as the place of absolutely permanent ideal objectivities and therefore of absolute Objectivity, certainly constitutes such a transcendental field'.[24] We are approaching the years of what was to become the inception of 'Structuralism' with the concept of a 'transcendental structure without a subject'. While, in a 1959 essay on 'Genesis and Structure and Phenomenology', Derrida makes the point that there is no antagonism between these two concepts for Husserl who always tries to reconcile a 'structuralist demand' and a 'genetic demand',[25] in his discussion of the *Origin of Geometry* Derrida seems reluctant to opt for this relatively easy way out that would consist in abandoning the subject and the structure of intentionality altogether. Let us not forget that for Derrida (as for Husserl, of course) transcendental intentionality is an 'original structure'[26] and the occlusion of this structure signifies non-sense. Husserl will have recourse to another kind of odyssey: if reason leads us to speech as auto-affection, hearing oneself speak, then one can conclude that writing is not only a necessary evil (like paternity for Joyce) but an unavoidable detour: 'In emerging from itself, hearing oneself speak constitutes itself as the history of reason through the detour of *writing. Thus it differs from itself in order to reappropriate itself'.*[27] Here, clearly, the 1959 essay points to *La Voix et le Phénomène* (curiously translated as 'Speech and Phenomena').

This phenomenological structuralism is of course essentially strategic; it allows one to point out the paradoxes and difficulties involved by the links between intentionality and its 'linguistic flesh' or 'graphic body' – in other words, writing:

> The possibility or necessity of being incarnated in a graphic sign is no longer simply extrinsic and factual in comparison with ideal Objectivity: it is the *sine qua non* condition of objectivity's internal completion...Therefore, the act of writing is the highest possibility of all 'constitution', a fact against which the transcendental depth of ideal Objectivity's historicity is measured.[28]

Another question remains: it is after having stressed the convergence of Husserl and Hegel in their idealizing strategies that Joyce, 'the most Hegelian of all writers' (let's add 'perhaps' as a saving modifier) is quoted as a radical alternative to phenomenology's idealizing gesture. Why not, instead of Joyce, allude to Heidegger as an internal questioning of phenomenology? Why is it that the name of a novelist, poet and polyglot mythologist is needed at this juncture?

In the *Introduction* to the *Origin of Geometry*, Joyce is called upon as much as the author of interconnected puns that make *Finnegans Wake* a perfect pastime for retired linguists as the launcher of an 'Odyssean repetition'.[29] However, Derrida is reluctant to identify Joyce's project with that of pure historicism, and notes that Stephen Dedalus's deepest wish is to wake up from 'the nightmare' constituted by history.

2 'Binding idealities' with Joyce

From that turning point in the *Introduction* to the *Origin of Geometry* Joyce acquires a monumental and emblematic stature. He seems to embody by himself a radical alternative to phenomenology – while Husserlian phenomenology condenses the fundamental desire of philosophy, a desire to reduce the equivocation of everyday speech to the univocity of a concept. As Derrida recalls it in a very condensed manner in 'Two Words for Joyce' – a talk presented twenty years after the *Introduction* – Joyce calls up for Derrida much more than a 'great novelist of the modern period' but sketches an entire philosophical programme:

> The other great paradigm would be the Joyce of *Finnegans Wake*. He repeats and mobilizes and babelizes the (asymptotic) totality of the equivocal, he makes this his theme and his operation, he tries to make outcrop, with the greatest possible synchrony [*faire affleurer à la plus grande synchronie*] at great speed, the greatest power of the meanings buried in each syllabic fragment, subjecting each atom of writing to fission in order to overload the unconscious with the whole memory of man: mythologies, religion, philosophies, sciences, psychoanalysis, literatures.[30]

A hyperbolic style is needed to dramatize the impact of a no less hyperbolic project. The admiration granted to the unheard-of idea – since Dante at least – of creating a new language from some seventy idioms calls up less Babel than the Flood. In this torrential downpour, Joyce the demiurge is replaced by an almost nightmarish version of a totality which is closer to Doctor Mabuse or to Roland Barthes's remarks on the 'monster of totality' in his own *Roland Barthes*.[31] Besides, Joyce does not limit his enterprise to 'mobilizing' the totality of culture, he both demobilizes and immobilizes (which is how Levinas described the effect Derrida has produced on him: he was compelled to go back to the time of the *drôle de guerre* when he was mobilized in the army with nothing to do, and then was demobilized soon after). What distinguishes Joyce is that he refuses the nuclei of meaning which for Husserl are necessary when a language is translated into another without, apparently, believing as Heidegger does that truth follows the tangled path of folk etymologies. 'This generalized equivocality of writing does not translate one language into another on the basis of common nuclei of meaning . . . it talks several languages at once, parasiting them'.[32] In 1962, as we have seen, Joyce was mentioned at the end of a series of other literary references: after Goethe's *Faust* already quoted by Husserl as an example of literary ideality, one also meets Valéry, Mallarmé and Blanchot.[33] This leads to an allusion to what Gaston Bachelard has called the 'bibliomenon': 'This "being of the book", this "instance of *printed* thought" whose "language is not natural", Gaston Bachelard calls a "*bibliomenon*".'[34] Husserl was aware that writing 'defines and completes the ambiguity of all language'.[35] In the long sequence of philosophical writers who bring literature to bear on thinking, Joyce brings to Husserl the counterweight of a writing not just bound in culture but also 'unbound' in the sense that its chains of links belong to a purely empirical system, from that of spelling to the empirical hazards of local myths, religions, and historical narratives:

> And, like Joyce, this endeavour would try to make the structural unity of all empirical culture appear in the generalized equivocation of a writing

that, no longer translating one language into another on the basis of their common cores of sense, circulates throughout all languages at once, accumulates their energies, actualizes their most secret consonances, discloses their furthermost common horizons, cultivates their associative syntheses instead of avoiding them, and rediscovers the poetic value of passivity. In short, rather than put it out of play with quotation marks, rather than 'reduce' it, this writing resolutely settles itself *within* the *labyrinthian* field of culture 'bound' by its own equivocations, in order to travel through and explore the vastest possible historical distance that is now at all possible.[36]

3   Tradition and the dividual latent

I would suggest that what is offered by Derrida here is not a philosophical reading of Joyce; such a reading remains to be done, and it would for instance develop the consequences of Joyce's Hegelianism or of his mediaevalism. Derrida seems at one point in his *Introduction* on the verge of beginning this, when he quotes Aristotle on colour and transparency:

> It is not by chance that there is no phenomenology of the Idea. The latter cannot be given in person, nor determined in an evidence, for it is only the possibility of evidence and the openness of 'seeing' itself; it is only *determinability* as the horizon for every intuition in general, the invisible milieu of seeing analogous to the diaphaneity of the Aristotelian Diaphanous, an elemental third, but the one source of the seen and the visible: 'by diaphanous I mean what is visible, and yet not visible in itself, but rather owing its visibility to the colour of something else'. It is thanks to this alone 'that the colour of a thing is seen' (*De Anima*, 418b).[37]

It looks as if Derrida were going to embark on a commentary of the most 'phenomenological' passage in *Ulysses*, Stephen's famous meditation on the act of seeing which quotes exactly the same passage from the *De Anima*:

> Ineluctable modality of the visible: at least that if no more, thought through my eyes... Snotgreen, bluesilver, rust: coloured signs. Limits of the diaphane. But he adds: in bodies. Then he was aware of them bodies before of them coloured. How? By knocking his sconce against them, sure. Go easy. Bald he was and a millionaire, *maestro di color che sanno*. Limit of the diaphane in. Why in? Diaphane, adiaphane.[38]

But this is not Derrida's aim, precisely because he needs to introduce Joyce into the field of philosophy as an exemplification of 'writing' in action. Joyce as an author of 'inventor of discursivity' names a kind of anti-philosophy traversing philosophy. His polyglottism and anti-historical historicism, his generalized equivocation and encyclopaedic hubris, are factors that Joyce may have condensed to a high degree but are also shared by most high-modernist poets and artists. The point here is not to establish a philosophical dialogue (as one sees on the same page of the *Introduction* in which Derrida notes that the 'dialogue between Husserl and Heidegger could go on indefinitely').[39] The reference to Joyce is more powerful because there is no way of grasping a concept behind the unleashing of the writing process.

I would like to insist on a shift which could be of interest to Joyce scholars: without changing the general thesis on Joyce, the 1962 reading places *Ulysses* and *Finnegans Wake* together, while in 1982, twenty years later, Derrida seems to differentiate sharply between the *Wake* (by then safely canonized as an archetype of the avant-garde textual production by his friends of the *Tel Quel* review) and *Ulysses* taken as the site of a personal and quasi-autobiographical exploration of several key themes: feminine affirmation of life as a redoubled yes-yes saying; male circumnavigations, periplums and perambulations – in short, odysseys. At any rate, safely coming back to Ris Orangis...In 1982, Derrida feels obliged to make the revealing qualification: 'The other great paradigm would be the Joyce of *Finnegans Wake*', as we have seen. Does this mean that one can forget the megalomania of a totalizing program of hypermnesic strategies because one comes closer to the riddle of femininity embodied by Molly Bloom? Or are the two novels still conceptually linked in Derrida's mind?

In order to progress along this investigation, it seems to me that the series of theses elaborated on Joyce from the *Introduction* to the *Origin of Geometry* to 'Ulysses' Gramophone' redouble enigmatically Eliot's thesis of the 'mythical method' – a thesis that underpins most modernist visions of literature. T. S. Eliot had claimed that *Ulysses* worked on two planes and presented a systematic parallel between classical antiquity and the 'present' of Dublin 1904. The handling of such a parallel would be for Eliot a way of controlling the uneasiness facing the 'chaos' observed in contemporary history. Joyce, like Einstein, would have produced a scientific discovery bridging the gap between a cultural or 'ideal' order and the irrelevance or confusion of present day events. Derrida's thesis about a Joyce seen as an anti-philosopher of writing can appear as a variation on Eliot's fundamental thesis about tradition and order. Eliot's 1923 article on 'Ulysses, Order and Myth' expands the theses launched in 'Tradition and the Individual Talent', an essay published in 1919 to define what constitutes the 'historical sense' and its links with a global tradition. Like Husserl in *The Origin of Geometry*, Eliot sees the consciousness of history in the present: 'What is historically primary in itself is our present'[40] Husserl says, while Eliot admits that culture builds a quasi-organic system which any new masterpiece, as soon as it introduced, will radically modify in all its relationships. Thus when *Ulysses* is introduced into the field of Western culture, it is the whole of Homer's works that change. For instance, we will read the *Odyssey* differently, we will be looking for puns differently, and will pay more attention to certain racial stereotypes, and so on...In the same way, the election of Joyce to the role of synthesis of universal culture and history will have important consequences for the creation of a new reader. This has been perceived by Derrida and expressed in an interview with a very competent Joyce scholar, Derek Attridge:

> *Ulysses* arrives like one novel among others that you place on your bookshelf and inscribe in a genealogy. It has its ancestry and its descendants. But Joyce dreamt of a special institution for his oeuvre, inaugurated by it like a new order. And hasn't he achieved this, to some extent? When I spoke of this as I did in 'Ulysses' Gramophone', I did indeed have to understand and share his dream too: not only share it in making it mine, in recognizing mine in it, but that I share it in *belonging to the dream* of Joyce, in *taking a part* in it, in walking around in *his* space. Aren't we, today, people or characters in part constituted (as readers, writers, critics, teachers) *in* and *through* Joyce's dream? Aren't we Joyce's dream, his dream readers, the ones he dreamed of and whom we dream of being in our turn?[41]

Going a little further than the main modernist writers who all dreamed of creating a new audience by a new writing, Derrida postulates the birth of a new subject in the wake of Joyce's works. The creation of a new subject is not a mere trope to talk about changes in habits of reading, it entails the constitution of a new ethical sense. This ethical sense can be defined as 'responsibility', less in the Kantian or Levinassian meanings than in the Husserlian sense. Husserl and Eliot seem to be working together at redefining an ethical relationship to tradition: 'To meditate on or investigate the sense [*besinnen*] of origins is at the same time to: make oneself responsible [*verantworten*] for the sense [*Sinn*] of science and philosophy, bring this sense to the clarity of its "fulfil(ment)", and put oneself in a position of *responsibility* for this sense starting from the total sense of our existence'.[42]

This, coupled with a feeling that one should feel an entire European tradition in one's 'bones' produces a programme to which Eliot would have entirely subscribed: 'the historical sense compels a man to write not merely with his own generation in his bones, but with a feeling that the whole of the literature of Europe from Homer and within it the whole literature of his own country has a simultaneous existence and composes a simultaneous order'.[43]

While Eliot supposed that the apparition of a new masterpiece always redistributes the aesthetic values of the past according to a logic of minimal differences (the *whole* ideal order of culture must be, 'if ever so slightly', altered each time something really new occurs in it[44]), Derrida posits that the totalizing masterpiece modifies not only our reading and writing habits but also creates a new subject: let us say that this subject will be us if and if only we accept to recognize ourselves as read in advance by the author, traversed by Joyce's reading. A double genitive is then at play, both objective and subjective, since this is the kind of hesitation that is inevitably produced by this new writing in us, without our being aware of its unconscious inscription. As we know, Stephen Dedalus spoke of Shakespeare as the father of his grandfather and his own grandson, presenting him as the paradigm of the self-generating artist who thereby constitutes a world we happen to be inhabiting too. Aware of this circularity, and also in awe of it, Derrida sees in Joyce's hypermnesic machine a powerful 'programme' that will also unleash a more terrifying danger.

One of the consequences of this programme is that no reading can become 'ideal' and thus will not contribute another ideality for the greater glory of culture as Husserl would have requested it. Reading cannot disentangle itself from either the materiality of an archive or from the living inheritance of actual families. We are aware of the curious fascination of Joyce scholars for manuscripts, drafts, first editions, autographs, holographs, letters, notebooks, all culled in the more than sixty volumes of the James Joyce Archive – with the constant addition of recently discovered proofs and unpublished manuscripts sold for a fortune at auctions. What may not be well-known is the no less curious fascination of Joyce's grandson for this scene: Stephen Joyce, heir and addressee of certain texts, still occupies today the position of moral guarantee in the Joyce industry, and intervenes regularly in the choice of translators, editors, and even texts that can be anthologized. This is why Derrida could not resist the pleasure of dedicating the first version of 'Ulysses' Gramophone' to Stephen Joyce. This spectral genealogy confirms that we are all 'Joyce's grandsons' – we are all caught up in the technological apparatus already announced by Bloom in *Ulysses* when he imagined that old men and women's voices should be recorded so as to keep a trace of their last wishes after their death...

It might then be possible to generalize this principle: no critical discourse can free itself from its family history, no chosen affiliation could allow one to forget one's more or less direct filiation. This is why I have tried to situate Derrida in that French scene of phenomenology in the 1960s, a scene dominated by the ghosts of Cavaillès and Kojève, and in which Gaston Bachelard, Tran Duc Thao and Jean Hyppolite are the 'masters', as much perhaps as Foucault, Althusser and Blanchot. In the same fashion, when we talk of modernism in North American universities, it is impossible to forget the role of people like Hugh Kenner or Harry Levin, who personally knew Joyce and Pound. With the modernism that took shape at the time of the European crisis in the sense of its own tradition, one cannot bracket off the agency of the creators themselves, all keenly aware of their active role in the dissemination of a tradition they partly created. Joyce for one chose a few important relays such as Valery Larbaud, Stuart Gilbert, Frank Budgen, Louis Gillet, Carlo Linati, Jacques Mercanton, Ernst Robert Curtius and a few others to ensure his own immortality – an immortality measured by the number of books and theses devoted to him. In that sense, as Nora Joyce herself expressed rather naively, there was only one other chap her husband had to get the better of – William Shakespeare. 'Ulysses' Gramophone' also echoes the somewhat unpleasant impression that nothing can be written on Joyce that would not have been manipulated or thought of in advance by the writer.

This is also because, as Derrida explains, the entire work of Joyce thinks itself in the secondarity of a double filiation, caught up as it is between self-generation (the myth being the infinitely self-generating texts as one sees with *Finnegans Wake*) and the responsibility to the whole of a European tradition that opens its ear to the other, since European becomes 'earopen'[45] in the Wake:

> *Finnegans Wake* is a little, a little what? a little son [there is here an untranslatable pun on 'petit-fils': *un petit, un tout petit-fils*] of Western culture in its circular, encyclopaedic, Ulyssean and more than Ulyssean totality. And then it is, simultaneously, much bigger than even this odyssey, it comprehends it, and this prevents it, dragging it outside itself in an entirely singular adventure, from closing in on itself and on this event. What is called writing is the paradox of such a topology.[46]

This paradox will take several figures in 'Ulysses' Gramophone' – some pointing to recurrent patterns like the signature, the postcards, the 'yes yes' needed by any performative gesture, the disjuncture between competence and performance, while new traits are taken from the network of Joycean associations and signifiers: various communication machines, telephones, gramophones, the fragrance of perfumes and flowers, behind the 'perfumative' the endless war of languages, the warring brothers, the name of Babel and He War...

4   Husserljoyce is Joycehusserl: Voyce and phenomena

A second consequence of this familial haunting is the opening up of the entire issue of competence, for instance, the competence that is requested if one wishes to call oneself a 'specialist of Joyce' or a 'Joycean'. Here is the point on which Derrida appears as the most 'deconstructive' facing Joyce, or rather the 'Joyce scholars' perceived as an intimidating body but also an institution that lacks a secure foundation. The 'International James Joyce Foundation' provides a concrete example of what Husserl has to say about culture and tradition. The so-called James Joyce Foundation is thus a misnomer because it needs the 'Sophist', the Stranger, who will authorize them from the outside. If there is indeed a Joycean family gathered around the author (Stephen Joyce's favourite tag is: 'I am a Joyce, not a Joycean') such a notion excludes any specific competence, understood as cultural capital. While Joyce scholars dispose of the 'totality of competence in the ency-clopaedic field of the *universitas*'[47] they are in need of the non-expertise of a foreigner who will both question their foundations and reassure them. The foreigner will declare:

> As a matter of fact, you do not exist, you are not founded to exist as a foundation, which is what Joyce's signature gives you to read. And you can call on strangers to come and tell you, as I am doing in replying to your invitation: you exist, you intimidate me, I recognize you, I recognize your paternal and grandpaternal authority, recognize me and give me a diploma in Joycean studies.[48]

Here the tone is clearly ironic, if not frankly satirical. Behind the Hegelian joke about 'recognition', there is nevertheless a Husserlian question: under what condition can the Joyce studies be seen as a 'rigorous science'? Derrida's foundational question is not to be understood in a Heideggerian sense (lead-ing us to the *Grund* as abyss or *Ungrund*) but in a Husserlian sense, since the issue is that of the condition of possibility of literary studies seen as a rigor-ous science . . . or not! This questioning not only defines a type of knowledge but also its ritual transmission, since it encompasses the whole of culture and history, that is to say precisely that the totality of what Husserl saw as the 'present' (more than the presence) of the consciousness safely embodied in a living tradition. The return of this question (the *Rückfrage*) in the field of the academic institution has important effects – and if I had more time, I would like to demonstrate how they affect any reading of *Finnegans Wake* in terms of competence and performance.

These questions would no doubt apply as pointedly to the field of decon-struction and to what has not yet been called the domain of 'Derrida studies'. Can one be a Derridean in a rigorous sense? As we know, answers will vary; Rorty would say No and would laugh at the preposterousness of the question, while Gasché would say Yes and demonstrate the very pos-sibility of founding anew such a critical field. While leaving this question open, I would like to stress that the purely deconstructive moment does not describe the whole intervention on Joyce. On the contrary, the general tone of 'Ulysses' Gramophone' is more assertive, ludic and autobiographical than political, questioning or debunking. Derrida's reading of Joyce appears almost Nietzschean or, if one can risk this, Deleuzian, especially when it cli-maxes in a poetic rhapsody on Molly's Yesses. However, Molly's final Yes has replaced the utopia of an absolute foundation as self-presence, the missing or impossible cornerstone of presence as voice – Joyce's voice – failing which Husserl's whole project founders.

Similarly, by selecting only two words from *Finnegans Wake*, Derrida grants a paradigmatic function to what might have been glossed as a simple bilingual pun – 'He war' unites and splices 'He was/Er war/War/He made war/wahr-heit'). This is taken from II, 1 – a passage dealing with the children at play in Chapelizod's pub: 'And shall not Babel be with Lebab? And he war. And he shall open his mouth and answer: I hear, O Ismael, how they laud is only as my loud is one'.[49] The undecidability between War and truth yields no 'truce', no peace yet, as Levinas would have it . . .

Have, then, extremes met? Husserl and Joyce, or Joycehusserl, yes: this cannot work as a fusion or an equalization of differences. In order to avoid pure indifference (Duchamp's main principle) one needs to continue the fight in the wood of words. Equivocation generates endless 'ambiviolences', to quote both Joyce and Stephen Heath. Joyce deconstructs Husserl, Husserl deconstructs Joyce. Because of Joyce, Derrida chooses to begin yet again with Husserl – half-way, as it were, between Hegel and Heidegger. In the course of some forty years of philosophical work, he has seemed to have moved at times closer to Heidegger (*Geschlecht*), at times closer to Hegel (*Glas*) but always with Joyce somewhere in the background. To begin with the 'again' hidden in *Finnegan* will be less to think the absence of any 'origin' than the strategic choice of a perpetually dedoubled origin.

Notes

1. Jacques Derrida, *Writing and Difference*, trans. Alan Bass (Chicago: University of Chicago Press, 1978), 153.
2. James Joyce, *Ulysses* (New York: Garland, 1984), 15: 2096–98 (reference by number of episode and line number).
3. John Caputo (ed.) *Deconstruction in a Nutshell: Conversation with Jacques Derrida* (New York: Fordham University Press, 1996), 26.
4. Edmund Husserl, *The Origin of Geometry with an Introduction by Jacques Derrida*, trans. John P. Leavey, Jr (Lincoln: University of Nebraska Press, 1989) – a translation of Edmund Husserl's *L'Origine de la Géométrie*, traduit par Jacques Derrida, avec une introduction (Paris: Presses Universitaires de France, 1962), 26 n2.
5. Husserl [Derrida], *The Origin of Geometry*, 29–30.
6. ibid., 153.
7. ibid., 160.
8. ibid., 82.
9. James Joyce, *Dubliners*, ed. Terence Brown (London and New York: Penguin, 1992), 1.
10. Husserl [Derrida], *The Origin of Geometry*, 127–8.
11. ibid., 81–82.
12. ibid., 161.
13. ibid., 162.
14. ibid., 165.
15. ibid., 67.
16. Jean Hyppolite, 'Appendix', in *Logic and Existence*, trans. Leonard Lawlor and Amit Sen (Albany: SUNY Press, 1997), 195.
17. Maurice Blanchot, *La Part du Feu* (Paris: Gallimard, 1949), 312.
18. ibid., 311.

19. ibid., 295.
20. ibid., 320.
21. Emmanuel Levinas, *Totalité et Infini, Essai sur l'extériorité*, deuxième édition (La Haye: Martinus Nijhoff, 1965), xv.
22. Husserl [Derrida], *The Origin of Geometry*, 103.
23. Blanchot, *La Part du Feu*, 305.
24. Husserl [Derrida], *The Origin of Geometry*, 88.
25. Derrida, *Writing and Difference*, 157.
26. ibid., 162.
27. ibid., 166.
28. Husserl [Derrida], *The Origin of Geometry*, 89.
29. ibid., 103.
30. Jacques Derrida, 'Two Words for Joyce', in Derek Attridge and Daniel Ferrer (eds), *Post-Structuralist Joyce* (Cambridge: Cambridge University Press, 1984), 149.
31. Roland Barthes, *Roland Barthes*, trans. Richard Howard (Berkeley: University of California Press, 1994), 179.
32. Derrida, 'Two Words for Joyce', 149.
33. Husserl [Derrida], *The Origin of Geometry*, 58 n1.
34. ibid., 91.
35. ibid., 92.
36. ibid., 102.
37. ibid., 138.
38. Joyce, *Ulysses*, 3:1–8.
39. Husserl [Derrida], *The Origin of Geometry*, 138 n164.
40. ibid., 176.
41. Jacques Derrida, *Acts of Literature*, ed. Derek Attridge (New York and London: Routledge, 1992), 74.
42. Husserl [Derrida], *The Origin of Geometry*, 31.
43. T. S. Eliot, 'Tradition and the Individual Talent', *The Sacred Wood* (London: Methuen, 1950), 49.
44. ibid., 50.
45. James Joyce, *Finnegans Wake* (London: Faber and Faber, 1939), 419:14.
46. Derrida, 'Two Words for Joyce', 149. NB: last sentence not translated into English: '*Ce qu'on appelle l'écriture, c'est le paradoxe d'une telle topologie*' (Jacques Derrida, *Ulysse Gramophone, Deux Mots pour Joyce* [Paris: Galilée, 1987], 26).
47. Derrida, *Acts of Literature*, 281.
48. ibid., 284.
49. Joyce, *Finnegans Wake*, 258:11–13.

Part II

Inauguration

6
The Opening to Infinity: Derrida's Quasi-transcendentals

Claire Colebrook

The beyond or the this-side which gives sense to all empirical genius and all factual profusion, that is perhaps what has always been said under the concept of *'transcendental'*, through the enigmatic history of its displacements. Difference would be transcendental. The pure and interminable disquietude of thought striving to 'reduce' Difference by going beyond factual infinity toward the infinity of sense and value, i.e., while maintaining Difference – that disquietude would be the transcendental, since it can look forward to the already announced *Telos* only by advancing on (or being in advance of) the Origin that indefinitely reserves itself. Such a certainty never had to learn that Thought would always be to come.[1]

This essay[2] locates Derrida's philosophy of deconstruction within the phenomenological tradition of transcendental philosophy. My main focus will be on Derrida's reading of Husserl. I will argue that it is Derrida's fidelity to the Husserlian concepts of 'intentionality' and 'reduction' which leads to the formulation of deconstruction as a procedure that begins with transcendental questions. But while Derrida regards transcendental questions as necessary and essential to philosophy, he also insists that such questions must always rely on 'quasi-transcendentals'. Such quasi-transcendentals themselves provoke 'deconstructive' questions regarding the limits of philosophy: these are questions of the empirical determinations of transcendental projects. I will conclude by arguing that Derrida's deconstruction provides a new way of thinking the relationship between philosophy and the human sciences. Derrida's extension of transcendental phenomenology into what he refers to as ' deconstruction' will be explored by way of the following five claims that are pertinent to all of Derrida's work but which will be examined here in his early work on Husserl. For it is in Husserl's late work on the relation between philosophy and the positive sciences that Derrida identifies a transcendental movement essential to metaphysics in general.

1. There is a transcendental imperative in the very structure of experience. We can recognize this structure when we consider the nature of language, but the implications extend beyond language to consciousness in general.
2. The thought or concept that we might form of this transcendental imperative always occurs from within experience or meaning, despite the fact that it refers to 'conditions' which are anterior to meaning.
3. In Western philosophy this *necessary* logic of the transcendental has always been understood in terms of time. However, this understanding of a transcendental temporality that is the condition for all appearances requires an empirical determination of space. A certain notion of space has tied the Western understanding of transcendental time to an ethics of activity as opposed to passivity.
4. The thought or representation of transcendental temporality always takes place from within a specific epoch. There is always a specific or determined way in which time 'in general' is abstracted from the worldly representations of time. Any articulation of transcendental logic can only be quasi-transcendental, for it borrows from the finite figures it seeks to explain. We therefore need to look at the etymological conditions that enable any language to theorize the possibility of language in general. (Philosophy is not just one language game among others, but its capacity to think the 'opening' of any language is itself an event of language.)
5. Transcendental questions are only possible with a non-empirical notion of history. We can only think of a specific epoch if we have some general sense of human history, which is then instantiated in any historical period. Any positive science requires a transcendental 'horizon'. But the condition for thinking this transcendental horizon is some concept of human life in general, or a concept of subjectivity that is different from its empirical or 'human' forms. Such a notion of the unity or horizon of subjectivity depends upon determined spatial conditions. This means that we can ask about the philological, historical and textual conditions that make transcendental questions possible. But this also means that we can ask about the conditions that enable the very project of 'human' sciences. (This was the project of Michel Foucault whose work, alongside Derrida's, can be read as a transcendental study of transcendental philosophy.)

The transcendental imperative

According to Derrida, who throughout this paper I will be reading through his work on Husserl, the transcendental project is 'announced' in experience.[3] (Experience is only possible, Husserl argues, if something like a transcendental Idea is already in operation.) Philosophy, in its transcendental forms, only brings to explicit articulation a structure that necessarily governs all experience or consciousness. This can be understood if we consider the Husserlian theory of intentionality, a theory to which Derrida rigorously adheres, both in his reading of Husserl and in his much later engagement with John Searle and speech-act theory.[4]

Consciousness is intentional because it is always consciousness-of. In fact, consciousness is nothing other than directedness towards some sense. The experience of a spatio-temporal object is coherent because of the sense-bestowing activity of consciousness. The various perspectives cohere only because experience aims at presenting the thing fully; some full presence must be anticipated in order to provide an idea of unity that organizes and renders experience the experience *of* what is other than itself. There is then, in all experience, an aiming for the fulfilment of presentation. If this were not so, no world or objectivity would be possible at all. There can only be a world or experienced empirical reality through intentionality. (Intentionality is not just apperception; it is not just the synthesis of perceptions, for it synthesizes perceptions through *sense*, which is reducible neither to the thing itself, nor its aspects, but is an anticipated fulfilment of perception.) This is disclosed in the 'eidetic reduction', the analysis of the very structure of experience if it is to be experience at all. (Derrida follows Husserl in seeing the eidetic reduction as distinct from, and prior to, the transcendental reduction. The eidetic reduction is *static* – describing the very structure of experience – while the transcendental reduction is *genetic* – accounting for the possibility of such a structure.) If we look at any experience and describe it faithfully then we recognize that all experience is guided by sense. Consciousness must intend or anticipate some object such that all its experiences may be experienced *as* experiences *of* some world. This 'telos' in experience applies even if the guiding sense undergoes modification, is initially vague, or remains unfulfilled or 'empty'.

The ideal object is, for Husserl according to Derrida, the privileged object from which this notion of experience will be explicated. For while a spatio-temporal object is essentially always open to further modifications, the sense of the ideal object is, properly, fully present to consciousness. We can manipulate mathematical and geometrical symbols in an empty or unfulfilled manner, mechanically combining the terms as if by rote. But it is the very essence of the ideal object to be capable of full presentation. A sense is strictly idealized or formalized only when it is 'freed' from any determination outside consciousness. We don't have the full sense of a truth of logic until we recognize its validity regardless of any of its specific instances. The mathematical ideal object is only *ideal* when it can be thought and presented as a *pure* sense; it is at once objective – not reducible to a psychological event – but nevertheless immanent to consciousness in general. Its meaning is essentially available to any possible consciousness, and this meaning can be fully presented. Regardless of the empirical origin and regardless of the signs or tokens used to convey its sense, once it is constituted within a formal language any consciousness whatever must be capable of retrieving the original sense of the ideal object. If this were not possible then we would merely be dealing with a local or 'factual' sense. The sense of the ideal object has freed itself from the facts and specific regions that are nevertheless required for its constitution.

The eidetic reduction takes the experience of an object – such as the ideal object of mathematics – and inquires into its structure and sense. In the case of the ideal object or ideal truth, its very *meaning* is that it is not reducible to consciousness or an event within the world. To say that a mathematical theorem is *true* is to say that it is valid for any possible history and for any possible culture: 'Pure truth or the pretension to pure truth is missed in its *meaning* as soon as one attempts ... to account for it from within a determined historical locality'.[5] Like the spatio-temporal object, the very experience of the ideal object already presupposes, or 'intends' the possible existence of other experiencing subjects, or what Derrida refers to as a 'transcendental community'.[6] Such a truth *would also* be valid in the future. The eidetic analysis of the spatio-temporal object, however, also reveals an entirely different mode of intentionality and sense; for such an object is always given as anticipated, as open to future revision *and* as part of a specific 'life-world' or horizon of meanings. Once the meaning of the intended object has revealed a certain structure, the transcendental reduction can question how such a sense is possible. The transcendental reduction, as opposed to the eidetic reduction, takes the experience of worldly being – the world given as a region of objects, both natural and ideal – and asks how being at all is possible. How is the intentional aiming for presence that is essential to all experience possible? According to Husserl and phenomenology, the transcendental reduction discloses the absolute status of consciousness, and this is where phenomenology distinguishes itself from Kantian transcendental idealism. Transcendental questions inquire into the conditions for possible experience. Kant demonstrated that any experience whatever required the *a priori* forms of time and space; it makes no sense to think of knowledge or experience outside such conditions. Phenomenology, on its own account, goes one (transcendental) step further. We cannot simply describe the *a priori* structures of experience; we need also to account for how such *a priori* structures are possible. (This is not just the demand to account for the very nature of consciousness; it is also a requirement to explain the possibility of the very *idea* of the *a priori*.[7] How is it that we ask the question of what must be valid for any possible consciousness? Where does this idea of consciousness in general come from? Derrida refers to this question as the 'opening to infinity'.[8]) If time is a necessary condition for experience, how is time possible, and what is its genesis?[9] Time is not just the form that knowledge must take; time is absolute life. Time is not the synthesis *by* the subject *of* intuited data; subject and object are constituted within the absolute flow of time that is also nothing other than the life of consciousness. Time is intentionality and, according to Derrida, meaning and sense. For, without the intentional aiming towards a world and presence there would be no connection of time into a *recognizable* unity. (Recognition or self-presentation is, for Derrida, the idea, telos and ethic of transcendental phenomenology.) It is the flow of consciousness itself which produces a 'world' as a unified horizon within which any single experience is possible, including the experience of the experiencing subject or 'ego'.

All experience is intentional; this can be demonstrated if we describe any experience with fidelity (as in the eidetic reduction). The spatio-temporal object 'intends' a future fulfilment of perspectival perceptions; the ideal object intends a truth and validity above and beyond any specific instance. Intentionality, as disclosed in the transcendental reduction, is nothing more than the *meaningful* flow of time, a time that is always directed towards the presentation of sense. The experience of any thing as present, existing, or as located within the world requires a transcendental horizon of the world in general.[10] The transcendental reduction reveals that any givenness presupposes a belief or positing of the world. (Such a 'belief' or acceptance is not a psychological event, but is required to think of *any* thing, including the 'psyche'.) This *sense* of the world is temporality: a unified order of appearances that aim at or are directed towards some presence while retaining previously intended appearances.

Derrida draws two interpretative consequences from this structure of intentionality. The first is that the Idea of presence is essential to the structure of experience.[11] *To a certain extent* Derrida's own quasi-transcendental method is critical of this Idea in so far as he both challenges what he refers to as the 'telos' of philosophy which establishes the full presence of sense as its ideal. (Why, for example, do philosophers of language take the successful act of communication as the norm, rather than considering the 'structural possibility' of non-presentation that resides in the very condition of language?) In his reading of Husserl Derrida argues that Husserl takes as his 'model' the ideal object of mathematics and geometry.[12] (Indeed, Husserl criticizes Descartes's dependence on geometry as a given set of rules or method, rather than seeing geometry as an ideal and intuitable *sense*.[13] Husserl, Derrida argues, must dismiss any merely empirical understanding of space in favour of a space that can be experienced by consciousness in general.[14]) Unlike the perspectivally given spatio-temporal object which, necessarily, always remains to some extent presumed, the mathematical object *can* be fully presented. Indeed, according to Derrida, it is this re-activation of ideal sense which governs the project and ethics of Husserl's phenomenology. Ideal objects are neither real nor psychological; their ideality requires that even though they have been constituted by some consciousness within history, their *sense* can always be re-presented.[15] If geometry is valid this is because its sense is not merely received; it is always possible to repeat the founding and justifying sense. Sciences may operate with constituted systems, but the ideal truths of science are only possible if the constituted system can be repeated and reactivated independent of its factual or empirical origin. Derrida refers to this as a transcendental history or historicity, which needs to be distinguished from empirical history and historicism.[16] He also identifies this phenomenological method of transcendental history with the transcendental project as such and with metaphysics. Truth, he insists, is nothing other than this 'telos' of pure presence, this requirement for that which will remain the same regardless of any 'worldly' event. Philosophy must be critical of any merely constituted, received or worldly sense: *once constituted* the sense of truth must transcend any of its constituting acts. If something is true then it must be capable of being validated, brought to presence and comprehended. The ideal of truth is the ideal of presence. But this philosophical ideal of truth is 'announced' in experience, for there is no experience of a world without this sense of a presence to be fulfilled and a world that is there for others. Philosophy, as phenomenology, is essentially transcendental. It does not accept the constituted facts of a science, system or language, but enquires into the sense or possibility of any worldly system. Philosophy must, then, have an Idea of truth that is not *within* any constituted language or system; such a truth must be and will have been available for representation from within any language whatever.[17]

This is why Derrida frequently uses the phrase 'in general'. Gathered from Kant, it performs a transcendental function in Derrida's work. The historian can describe the history of geometry or literature, listing various facts, but the philosopher – if she is really doing philosophy – must ask: what is geometry in general? (How is the ideal or formal character of space possible?) What is literature in general? (What, in all these cases, is the *concept*[18] of the literary that organizes a factual study?) More importantly, as in the transcendental reduction, the philosopher can ask: what is history in general? (The very fact that we can ask such a question demonstrates an Idea that intends some sense beyond any single fact.) For Derrida this question of history in general is *the* transcendental question precisely because being or any presence is only possible through history. Only if there is some *sense*, a meaning which remains the same through time, can there be a unified 'world'. More importantly, only with a *teleological* sense of history can there be truth. It is only if we imagine what would be the case for any possible epoch or culture that we can have the idea and project of strict scientific truth. The very *meaning* of a scientific proposition posited as true is that it must be capable of being restored to the full presentation of its original formulation. For Derrida, following Husserl, *if* we accept the intentional nature of all experience[19] – its aiming towards presence – then the philosophical commitment to pure truth is 'announced' in experience. Further, the phenomenological commitment to a transcendental reduction that reactivates the very sense of the world is the fulfilment of philosophy, for metaphysics is only possible as the idea of a truth above and beyond any factual or empirical history.

So, the first consequence of the intentional nature of consciousness is that the idea of presence governs meaningful experience, and this idea is also the telos of metaphysics. The second consequence that Derrida draws regarding the structure of intentionality concerns the nature of language, especially concepts. In his long-running debate with John Searle, Derrida reaffirmed his commitment to intentionality and did so through an argument regarding the relation between concepts and contexts. A concept only works or has meaning if it intends some sense. The condition for a context – you and I speaking together – is that we posit some sense which is not just what I want a word to mean but which must carry across a community of speakers. According to Searle this necessary expectation is best explained through context: what a word means depends upon the conventions of a context. Without such a context where conventions of exchange determine what we can and can't do with words, words would have no meaning at all. The mistake Derrida makes, Searle argues, is to think that because a concept has no necessary, essential and fully present sense that its meaning is then indeterminate. Nothing in the *concept* determines sense, admits Searle, but contexts have a determining function. It makes no sense to ask what a concept means in general, free of any particular context, for meaning is only possible through shared recognition, mutual exchange and convention (or a specific context). Transcendental questions – at least the sort employed by Derrida – rely on a misguided commitment to the *ideality* of concepts; they posit some sense independent of contexts and then fall into despair when no such sense is presented.[20]

According to Derrida, however, a concept can only work and there can only be contexts if concepts do *intend* (if not possess) such an ideality. Once a concept is articulated within a context it is possible for it to be repeated outside that context. Further, in order for us to recognize a context, such as a conversation, a lecture or a stage-play, we must already have some sense of just what such a context is. Derrida is quite prepared to admit the determining function of contexts. But he insists that such determinacy is only possible *because* concepts are undecidable. There can only be shared communication if meaning has been freed from any specific speaker and given a repeatable form or sense that allows it to be circulated throughout a context.[21] In order for what I say to be meaningful it must be possible for it to function in my absence.[22] And if this is *possible* then it's also possible that an utterance might detach itself from a context. It is possible to read Shakespeare according to the context of Elizabethan England, but this contextual location is only possible and recognizable because it's also possible to repeat Shakespeare in other contexts. We might argue that to do so is less valuable and that *Richard III* is a richer text when *not* read as a comment on Nazi Germany. But we would have to make an argument for such a contextual location; the context itself can't decide on what counts as a legitimate and illegitimate use. If something can be articulated and meaningful within a context then it bears all the features of repeatability that allow it to be repeated beyond that context.

A concept, Derrida insists, is meaningful only if it refers to a sense that transcends my specific or singular intention. It is always possible, therefore, that I might ask, 'What is justice in general?' or 'What does justice really mean?' Now it's true that this question of the ideal sense of a concept must begin from a determined context. (We can always choose not to ask such a question precisely because, like Searle, we will insist that such a disengaged or pure sense can never be presented. Or we can, like Derrida, say that the question itself, while never capable of presenting a concept's pure sense, can produce an Idea of a sense that *would* exceed any contextual determination.) If a concept works and can be repeated in a variety of conversations *within* a context, then it can also, necessarily, be questioned *as if* it were to apply to no particular context. Searle is quite right to maintain that there are no ideal meanings that are already there, only to be articulated within contexts. But Derrida contends that while no such ideal meaning may be *present*, and that concepts are always contextually located or 'decided', there is also a future sense or intention that transcends a context. This is a *possible* sense, the possibility of future repetitions that render a concept 'undecidable'. Indeed, a context can only determine or decide a concept because a concept is undecidable; if it did not have the *possibility* of being repeated with another sense that is not present and activated in this context then its exchange within the original context would also not be possible. This is intrinsic to the function of *any* concept: that it intends some *sense* above and beyond the specific instances of its use. In so-called 'normal' cases, of course, we *don't* ask about what a concept means *in general*, or what its essential sense or intention is independent of its uses. For Derrida, however, the *possibility* for a concept to be meaningful across contexts or to *not* be stabilized by a context tells us about the structure of language and the structure of experience.[23] There must be some idea of presence or a telos in any act of meaning. A language necessarily harbours the possibility of a transcendental question – of sense in general – but this is also the possibility of the non-presence or non-fulfilment of sense. It is only when a concept or sense has been formalized into some iterable sign that it can be meaningfully exchanged *and* corrupted or misused. It is only because a concept is not fully determined by its context, that it can be repeated in an 'empty', 'parasitic' or even unintended manner. (Analogously, Husserl argues that the ideal objects of geometry can only be transmitted in a meaningful history if they are inscribed in a system of signs, but this is *also* what allows for the 'fall' of science into empty repetition and the loss of foundations.) In the debate with Searle this 'structural possibility' of concepts means that any pragmatic commitment to remaining within contexts and *not* asking transcendental questions depends upon a prior decision that privileges the successful speech act over the always possible unfulfilled use of a concept.

This is a privilege that both characterizes the transcendental project (which aims to bring the conditions of sense to presence and comprehension) and which is also undone by the transcendental project. It is always possible to appeal to the sense of a concept beyond its contextual determination. However, while Derrida follows Husserl in arguing that there is an Idea, ideal or telos of sense in experience and language, and that this Idea is recognized in the transcendental inquiry into the very structures of meaning in general, Derrida also asks how the Idea of the transcendental itself is possible. Much of his own work is a transcendental investigation into the Idea of presence or sense which operates as the telos of philosophy, language and meaningful experience.

Quasi-transcendentals

It is often noted that Derrida's deconstruction operates by a 'double method'. Like Kant and Husserl, Derrida does not see metaphysical striving as an activity imposed by philosophers on everyday experience and language. Reason has a structure which necessarily 'opens to infinity'. The very synthesis of the world into an ordered unity requires the Idea of presence. In *Limited Inc* Derrida stresses this necessary opening of contexts. Ethical questions can never be answered from within contexts precisely because it is always possible to ask the question of a concept's sense above and beyond any contextual determination. It is because concepts have a necessary 'undecidability' or because concepts are necessarily capable of freeing themselves from their ground or origin that we must attend to, and be responsible for, the *decision* of concepts. In the absence of any foundation for language, responsibility for the determination of language is heightened. Any appeal to contexts as that which decides or contains the force of a concept is Derrida suggests, a moralism that evades the always-possible transcendental question. The transcendental question expands responsibility in two directions, and these are brought out in the double method of deconstruction. First, it is always possible to ask the sense of a concept – for example, what justice is in general – above and beyond any of its contextual instances. We might say, as Derrida has done, that there is a 'justice-to-come' or a 'democracy-to-come': the Idea of a justice or democracy which is promised by the concept but which is also belied by any of the concept's given determinations. The very Idea of justice, for example, is that which would remain above and beyond any empirical determination of justice, always capable of being appealed to in a dispute or dialogue about justice. We may only have determined cases of justice that are always *decided*. But there is also a necessary undecidability of a concept that promises a justice of the future.

On the other hand, and this is the other 'side' of the double method, the transcendental question can also operate in the other direction: not towards the sense of a concept in general, or to the Idea of the concept, but to the conditions for the possibility of the concept. This brings us to Derrida's notion of iterability or quasi-transcendentals. (He also refers to 'aconceptual' concepts or non-concepts.) A concept only works if there is an intended sense that can be repeated and reactivated or appealed to through time and across contexts. This repeatability requires some recognizable system of differences as its support, such as the phonemes, inscriptive marks or signifiers of a language. (For Derrida the 'trace', strictly speaking, is the event of inscription or marking which allows for, or produces, identifiable marks, and so the trace remains absent from the system it conditions.[24]) Thought is only possible after the tracing of a system, and so the trace itself must remain *unthought*.[25] Conceptuality or sense – while intentionally directed towards a fulfilment or presence – relies upon a system of *differential* marks. Thought is conditioned by a system: a system whose terms are produced through difference or relation. The structure of an iterable system is not determined by what each mark *is* but by its differential relation to all other marks. The letters of an alphabet or the phonemic differences of a language are never meaningful in themselves but only through reference to each other; nor is their differentiation or tracing an event whose sense can be retrieved or comprehended. The iterable mark is 'created' (or, rather, effected) through opposition and is therefore anterior to sense, intention and presentation. Iterability is itself never capable of being presented; it is what allows the intentional structure of presence and presentation to operate. Intentionality – the process of a meaningful connection of experiences into an ordered unity – necessarily relies on absent differential or iterable differences. Derrida argues that there will always be some graphic 'remainder' in the production of sense. However, any attempt to think or conceptualize this differential process that allows the conscious synthesis of sense to emerge can only do so by 'borrowing' from an already determined system.[26] There may be a transcendental imperative to think the very emergence of sense and meaning, but we can only do so from within meaning, supported by a system or 'syntax' prior to all meaning. There are two responses we might make to this circularity or inability for the transcendental question to be fully self-grounding. The first would be the Heideggerian notion of the circle. We use the word 'being', necessarily, because we live in a world to which we are always directed as something other than ourselves. We can ask, *from our position within the world and beings*, what *Being* is: a Being not to be ostensibly defined by any single being. It would be a mistake to think that this question is like any other and might be presented with an objective answer, such as 'Being is ... God, mind, matter, spirit or consciousness'. Rather, such a question can only disclose the *meaning* of Being, the sense of Being that enabled us to have beings, a sense that we never really brought to light. From our natural or everyday understanding of beings we ask a transcendental question – what is Being? – and are brought back to where we were all along. The meaning of being, what is hidden in all our articulations of being, is time. For in order to say that anything *is*, that it remains *present*, we are already deploying projections and retentions of time. The question of Being does not take us outside our world of sense and presence; it interprets the very meaning of presence.[27]

Derrida's quasi-transcendentals are an attempt to break this circularity, a circularity that he identifies with time and meaning. Beyond the *meaning* of being – the concept or sense from which our world is given – there are forces, traces or differences which effect meaning but which are not comprehended by meaning. We can use a term within meaning to try to think that which is not brought to presence, meaningful or presentable. Derrida refers to these as aconceptual concepts or non-concepts or remarks that *'différance'* is 'not a concept' and that it 'is not'.[28] The minute we have named or referred to transcendental *'différance'* or 'tracing' it has been returned to repeatability and sense. We cannot *name* those unintended, singular, lost or 'anarchic' differential movements that produce and disrupt sense, for to name a singular event is to conceptualize it, refer it beyond itself and include it within temporal comprehension and relation. Derrida agrees with Heidegger that any attempt to think what is other than time – say, as condition, *a priori* or what lies before time – must both use temporal concepts *and* rely on temporal synthesis in order to *mean* anything at all. The challenge to the circle of time lies, for Derrida, in a method that is quasi-transcendental. Time may be the limit of thought as sense and meaning, but the capacity to *think* this limit is derived from spatial events. (Such events can be named *quasi*-transcendentally as spatial because metaphysics has defined time as inner sense and the synthesis of unity, in opposition to outer sense, simultaneity and dispersion of spatial points. The points of time are always points of 'now' or 'presence': points *from which* the past and future are projected and retained. They are only 'points' in so far as they have been separated from the prior unity of time as an unpunctuated flow. Metaphysics has always, Derrida insists, defined itself against spatial concepts of time, and this is because space has been understood as outside the comprehension of sense and meaning. A quasi-transcendental method can only think the other of time and sense from within the figures of time and sense. The first step is to demonstrate the figures through which the transcendental has been thought; the second is to destabilize those figures by demonstrating their limit.

Far from the transcendental critique returning to the meaning or sense from which the unity of the world is possible, Derrida's quasi-transcendentals attempt to name forces at work in language which do not emerge from consciousness, intention or presence. According to Derrida there are ethical as well as formally rigorous reasons for a transcendental project which can only yield quasi-transcendental and non-final 'answers'. Derrida's 'aconceptual concepts', such as the trace, *'différance'*, writing or *grammé*, are attempts to disrupt what he interprets as a Western ethics of recognition and onto-theology: an ethics that bases decisions on some ground of being outside the decision. If time forms a transcendental horizon, and time is the active self-synthesis and recognition of consciousness, then a certain privilege or decision is granted to the active and self-comprehending modes of *human* life as opposed to those of passivity, affect and loss. The idea that all being emerges from the temporal synthesis of sense posits a consciousness or humanity in general which functions as the world's transcendental or retrievable horizon.[29] The idea of a time, which differs from itself in order to produce concepts or a meaning which allow it to return to sense and recognition, brings with it a specific notion of ethical and political agency.[30] There is a privileging of a self-determining, active and non-affected subjectivity:

> in spite of all the themes of receptive or intuitive intentionality and passive genesis, the concept of intentionality remains caught up in the tradition of voluntaristic metaphysics – that is, perhaps, in metaphysics *as such*. The explicit teleology that commands the whole of transcendental phenomenology would be at bottom nothing but a transcendental voluntarism.[31]

By contrast, Derrida's own work looks at all the passive forces in language and philosophy which have an ethical force and for which we may need to bear responsibility. Our concepts may operate in ways that we do not intend, or may have a force that is not reducible to contextual origin or pragmatics.[32] To think forces beyond those of active comprehension and temporal self-genesis is both a more rigorous transcendentalism and a way of thinking ethics and politics beyond decision and agency.

The Western epoch

It is in his reading of Husserl, especially Husserl's *Origin of Geometry*, that Derrida demonstrates how the transcendental project of phenomenology is made possible through a specific determination of space. To begin with, Derrida draws attention to Husserl's transcendental criticisms of Descartes and Kant. Descartes correctly begins philosophy by doubting all received opinions regarding the being of the world and attends only to appearances. However, according to Husserl, Descartes locates appearance within a worldly region (*res cogitans*) and assumes that the subject is a different type of worldly thing or substance. Transcendental phenomenology, by contrast, suspends or brackets all claims to the status of being and asks how any being or region comes to appear, including the being of the subject and the 'immanent' region of consciousness. An inquiry is only rigorously transcendental, then, if it frees itself from any specific region of being, especially the being of man or the subject. This is also what separates phenomenology from Kantian criticism, for the latter stops at the region of the understanding and the a priori without investigating the sense and genesis of the a priori.[33] The task of phenomenology, in contrast with a critical or Kantian transcendentalism that describes necessary conditions, is to explain the 'opening to infinity' or the 'passage to the limit': how an empirical and factual experience of space can yield an ideal spatiality (geometry) that is not attached to any specific region:

> the culture of truth is itself only the possibility of a *reduction* of empirical culture and is manifested to itself only through such a reduction, a reduction which has become possible by an irruption of the infinite as a revolution within empirical culture.[34]

The difficulty of the phenomenological project, according to Derrida, lies in this extremely rigorous transcendentalism. Husserl refuses to halt the transcendental question at any specific region – such as the subject or understanding – in order to account for the emergence of regionality in general *and* the philosophical question of this pure region. Husserlian phenomenology is, for Derrida, the fulfilment of the circular telos of all metaphysics. Philosophical or scientific truth begins with the Idea of a truth of the world in general: that is, what is true not just for this or that epoch or culture, but true for the very epoch of human life. Science posits this truth in a naïve or unreflected manner; it searches for universal truths. Philosophy is capable, even in its Greek infancy, of bringing this Idea of truth to articulation; philosophy defines the ideal of truth as that which must remain the same or true for any epoch or subjectivity. In phenomenology, however, Husserl accounts for the genesis of the Idea of the world in general, or truth, and does so from within the concrete life of the world. He does this, Derrida argues, by producing a distinction between an empirical or factual history and a transcendental or ideal history. And it is no accident, Derrida insists, that Husserl's privileged example is geometry.[35] For the very idea of the transcendental must posit something like a world *horizon*, or a unified space within which all concrete life and empirical experiences of space are possible.[36] While the ancient Greek inauguration of science and geometry is a factual origin – there must have been some in-worldly inscription of geometrical axioms – these axioms enable, and require the idea of, space in general. On the one hand, inscription and factual origins – specific geometers within an epoch – are required to constitute the sense of this ideal region. On the other hand, the very sense of these ideal objects is such that their meaning can operate even when all *actual* traces of the origin are erased. We may well never actually know the psychological empirical history of Euclidean geometry; but the very *sense* of the axioms referring to any space whatever can always be reactivated in an ideal or transcendental history. Seeing an axiom *as valid* is nothing other than a capacity to reformulate its sense. It must always be possible in any positive science – if it is a *science* – to retrieve the genesis of sense. Now, according to Derrida, it is this Idea of science or an ideal history that is crucial to the Western epoch of time as meaning and meaning as time. The very project of transcendental reactivation and comprehension, the project of returning to the opening of the Idea of the unity of the *world in general*, rests upon an idea of the Western epoch. For it is only in the self-representation[37] of Western science and through the Greek 'opening to infinity' that there is an idea of truth freed from any given region. Husserl takes all experience of specific beings 'back' to the very sense of a 'world' or unified horizon, which is there for me, for others, has been there for the past and will be there for the future. Even the non-comprehension or untranslatability of other cultures requires the recognition of them *as cultures* and therefore as within the same 'life-world'. Husserl's inclusion of time, being and sense within the general horizon of concrete life is, according to Derrida, *the* ethic of a necessarily transcendental tradition of philosophy. It is only with the notion of life in general, freed from any determined image of man, that there can be a) the ideality of mathematics and geometry and b) the transcendental phenomenology that accounts for how such ideal objects are constituted. For Derrida, though, this transcendental horizon of absolute consciousness as the history of all sense, or the transcendental history, which thinks of a truth in general, must always bear the traces of a determined, empirical, factual or singular space.

This has two broad consequences for Derrida's own philosophy of deconstruction, a 'method' that can be seen to extend the transcendental claims of phenomenology beyond phenomenology. If the transcendental/metaphysical question is only possible with the idea of a region or community in general,[38] what are the singular forces that allow for the production of this idea? (This is the etymological dimension of deconstruction, which I will explore in the next section.) Second, and finally, how do we think the historical and geographical emergence of the notion of this *Ur-region* of transcendental inquiry? (This is the philological dimension of deconstruction, which will be the focus of the conclusion.)

The etymological reduction

The transcendental reduction describes the appearance of any region – such as natural objects, other persons, my own conscious life, the ideal objects of science – and then asks about the sense, meaning or intention which enables such a region to appear. Ultimately, there must be the Idea of presence or sense in general which grounds the world, the idea of a unified horizon that is there for any consciousness whatsoever. However, according to Derrida, Husserl never asked the question of the genesis of this sense of the living present. He brought the telos of philosophy to self-recognition but never inquired how this logos or life in general produced the sense of the present upon which its own recognition depends. In order for Husserl to posit a transcendental horizon within which life comes to presence he must differentiate between the world as experienced and the genesis of that world; but this transcendental soul or life, if it is to be truly transcendental, must not be represented as a substantial thing. We use the language of consciousness, soul or 'man' but these terms must be disengaged from their everyday use, employed only as analogies or metaphors. *Without* this function of metaphor or analogy we would always remain within our determined language and life-world. We must think consciousness as *other than* any of its determined figures, but also not as another thing. Its difference from the world must not be an actual or spatial separation but a transcendental determination. According to Derrida,

> If the world needs the *supplement of a soul*, the soul, which is in the world, needs the *supplementary nothing* which is the transcendental and without which no world would appear. [...] We must, if we are attentive to Husserl's renewal of the notion of 'transcendental', refrain from attributing any reality to this distance, substantializing this nonconsistency or making it be, even merely analogically, some thing or some moment of the world. If language never escapes analogy, if it is indeed analogy through and through, it ought, having arrived at this point, at this stage, freely to assume its own destruction and cast metaphor against metaphor...
>
> It is at the price of this war of language against itself that the sense and the question of its origin will be thinkable. This war is obviously not one among others. A polemic for the possibility of sense and world, it takes place in this *difference*, which, we have seen cannot reside in the world but only in language, in the transcendental disquietude of language. Indeed, far from only living in language, this war is also the origin and residue of language. Language preserves the difference that preserves language.[39]

There can only be sense if it is *other than* the concrete or empirical signs of a language; but this difference from language, this sense *of* the world, is only possible through language. For Derrida, Husserl never questioned the linguistic support or medium of the philosophical logos. Such a question would go beyond the linguistic systems within which concepts are articulated to consider the transcendental conditions of language, conditions that are 'spatial' in so far as they lie outside the self-genesis of consciousness and the comprehension of sense.[40] Derrida contrasts deconstruction with the hermeneutic circle of temporality. The privileging of time as sense or as the way in which life differs from itself in order to synthesize itself through history, and then know itself *as time*, relies on a prior, unstated and ethical distinction between two types of space and two types of line.

Derrida frequently refers to a 'decision' which inaugurates the very idea of philosophy as transcendental self-comprehension but which philosophy itself cannot master (precisely because philosophy always begins from an idea of active self-mastery). It is in his early essay on Heidegger that he draws attention to two notions of the line or *grammé*. Aristotle, no less than Heidegger, distinguishes the line that we might use as an analogy for time from the line of space. Time can only be thought as a line *by analogy* because a spatial or mathematical line has simultaneous points. It's possible to occupy a point in space while other points are present, simultaneous, different and unrelated to each other, not present to each other. The 'nows' of time, by contrast, are always present; any other 'now' can only be thought from the present now and as another now. The nows of time are not strung indifferently together and alongside each other in simple relations of presence and absence; the now is the present through which all past and future 'nows' will flow. The 'line' of time is not a series of points, dispersed beyond the point of the present but is only thinkable from the present as a series of past nows and future nows. This is, Derrida concludes, a privileging of self-presence and self-comprehension that places time as a transcendental origin beyond any of its determined or punctuated figures, for time is a flow and a unity and must not be confused with any of its synthesized constitutions. The philosopher must rigorously point out that the line of time is *only analogous* to the line of space.

Derrida draws two points from this. First, the transcendental is produced through this function of analogy. Second, the function or 'distance' of analogy must itself be thought through analogies and metaphors. (The transcendental subject is not to be confused with the psychological subject; time is not to be confused with the spatial images we have of it; sense must be distinguished from any of its tokens; transcendental history or the genesis of meaning lies before any empirical history; and the horizon of the 'world' must strictly separated from the 'earth' as a natural object.) Derrida is not simply critical of the transcendental as analogous to the empirical but strictly separate from it. Indeed, he regards this capacity for metaphor and analogy as the very 'opening' of philosophy. But it does mean that the transcendental is marked by its point of departure and that we would do well to recognize the determined figures from which the transcendental is effected: including the figures of 'distance', 'passage', 'transport' and 'exchange' which we use to think metaphor and analogy (the analogies of analogy or the metaphors of metaphor).

This leads to the second point regarding the privileging of a certain notion of line in Aristotle. The analogy of the line of time as a circle that traces itself in order to return to and comprehend itself is not an innocent metaphor or analogy but privileges, or rests upon, the hierarchy of *energeia* over *dynamis* (that is, an 'energy' that realizes and actively expresses itself, as opposed to a movement or power without sense).[41] The mathematical points of space are dispersed through the line and are not comprehended by a single point. If we were to think time in this 'mathematical' way then time would not be the flow of self-constituting becoming and sense within a single unity. It would be marked by absence, discontinuity, non-comprehension and affect from without (points beyond inclusion or active relation).

This, indeed, is how Derrida wants to think the history of philosophy and transcendental questions. Despite its self-definition, philosophy is not the active passage of self-comprehension through time that can turn back and recognize its origin in the production of meaning. Philosophy has been determined from without by 'factical', contingent, undecidable and errant figures from which its positing of transcendental justification is launched. This claim distinguishes Derrida's etymological emphases from Heideggerian *Destruktion*, although Derrida also recognizes that Heidegger at times thought that we might think beyond the epoch of the *meaning* of Being towards that which effects Being. A Heideggerian etymology, following on from Husserl's phenomenology, insists upon the possible reactivation of sense. 'Logos', for example, originally referred to a 'saying-gathering'. Before we constituted some simply self-present system of 'logic' there was an active and purposeful relation to the world. Logos was not an imposed formal system but a discourse of the world dynamically produced through exchange, disclosure and meaningful action.[42] Derrida, by contrast, does not approach etymology or the textual basis of philosophy to bring 'us' back to an earlier sense.[43] On the contrary, it is often the case that a 'trace' or *grammé* produces a difference upon which philosophy rests but which cannot be justified from within a philosophy. In his essay on Heidegger's critique of the tradition of time Derrida shows how Aristotle must rely on the *aporia* of the word *hama*: without this figure that refers both to spatial and temporal simultaneity the very analogy that Aristotle draws to *differentiate* time from space would not be possible.[44] Furthermore, and more importantly, we can only think analogy and metaphor because of certain figures. What would the idea of metaphor be without the reference to exchange, substitution, carrying-over, vehicle or transport? What would analogy be without the spatial figures of difference, distance, or being alongside? More specifically, what would the notion of sense or meaning be without a certain figure of the *voice*? If we cannot think of an intelligible sense or intention 'behind' the signifier – if we don't have the signifier of *meaning* – then no single mark could be read as intended or meaningful. The question, for Derrida, is the linguistic and material/empirical production of those figures which enable us to think the intelligible and the transcendental. For Husserl it is the figure of the living voice that enables a difference between any given signifier and its prior sense, but Derrida also looks at the figure of the mouth in Kant,[45] the word '*Geist*' in Heidegger[46] and the word 'communication' in speech-act theory.[47] There must always be some word or 'supplement' that is used, within a text, to signify the ground or origin of the text. Without such a supplement, without the production of an origin of sense, the text could not produce the depth of meaning or intention that is essential to all 'saying'.

Philology of philosophy

Derrida is largely in agreement with the Husserlian transcendental project. We are presented with the experience of ideality, the sense of space in general, number in general or truth in general. Phenomenological responsibility lies in accounting for the genesis of this sense. We need to explain the very possibility of the metaphysical question. How is it that we can think consciousness in general, irreducible to any of its determined, psychological or empirical figures? Such a project, Derrida argues, requires the thought of a unity: a human consciousness in general capable of recognizing itself in the Greek 'opening' of the idea of science and of fulfilling this project in the phenomenology of absolute consciousness. A transcendental intersubjectivity that allows for the very thought of different cultures and relative epochs itself relies on the general horizon of a 'world': a unity within which 'we' are variously located and which allows for the possibility of translation, understanding and even the recognition of misunderstanding or difference. It demands a 'pure and precultural *we*'.[48]

Like his near contemporary, Michel Foucault, Derrida can be seen as following in the tradition of Nietzsche's philological approach to philosophy's emergence. Nietzsche had provided an explicitly moral account of the genesis of philosophical truth. It is only those who lack the strength to deal with the forces of chaos and life who invent a higher world of truths and justifications that will enslave the power of this world.[49] But Derrida is more Kantian than Nietzsche. Whatever the lowly origin of the transcendental question and the thought of the supersensible, once I *can ask* about truth in general, or once I *can think the possibility* of what is not reducible to the empirically given, then this produces and demonstrates an Idea of freedom. It is the *sense* of what is not reducible to context that 'opens' philosophy. Derrida's own project affirmed *both* the necessary possibility of transcendental questions *and* their philological or 'geological' emergence (their locality, determination or 'decision'.)

This opens up a new relation between the human sciences and philosophy. First, we can always ask how – from certain historical, philological or ethnographic sources – it becomes possible to think human life as a general unity. How does the transcendental tradition of philosophy and its self-realization become possible? This would issue in a history of philosophy that is not so much a history of ideas as a history of what Foucault referred to as the 'middle region' or 'historical *a priori*'.[50] If philosophical or transcendental questions require the unity of thought in general, how is the medium or milieu of this unity produced in the various forms of subjectivity, culture, spirit, consciousness, language or 'man'? In the eighteenth century it was various projects in the positive sciences that enabled both the notion of human life in general and a unified human history.[51] The idea of 'man', as both Foucault and Derrida have argued, has been crucial to the transcendental project *and* to the critique of the transcendental project. For it is always possible to find a residual 'anthropologism' in determinations of the transcendental subject. 'Man' is just that being who is capable of thinking his existence as *other than* any determined image of man, but this empirical-transcendental understanding always risks being normalized into yet one more moral image of humanism. So, on the one hand, philosophy can be interrogated from a philological perspective, looking at the ways in which transcendental questions are opened from specific figures and regions. Foucault wrote a history of how 'man' was formed from the general space of 'life', language and labour enabled by the disciplines of biology, linguistics and economics. Secondly, and at the same time, there can also be a transcendental critique of the human sciences. For all claims to examine human life in its relative contexts of 'history', 'culture', 'discourse', 'signification' or 'context' can only do so through an already decided general space or horizon. In this case it is always possible to ask, say, 'what is culture in general?' or 'what is history in general?' (The latter is precisely the question Derrida directs to Foucault's 'history of reason': the very idea of a history of reason must be buttressed by some already determined rational unity *within which* the specific determinations of reason might be described and criticized.) Derrida suggests, on some occasions, that the metaphysics of presence are inescapable and that we can only interrogate its determined figures. For the very project of meaning or sense will necessarily presuppose some unified horizon within which difference can be understood:

> Horizon is the always-already-there of a future which keeps the indetermination of its infinite openness intact (even though this future was announced to consciousness). As the structural determination of every material indeterminacy, a horizon is always virtually present in every experience; for it is at once the unity and the incompletion for that experience – the anticipated unity in every completion.[52]

In so far as we speak and think we do so with the necessary telos, or intentionality, of a shared horizon of sense and a present world that is there to be disclosed. On the other hand, Derrida no less frequently also suggests that new modes of writing might enable us to think beyond a self-recognizing community of philosophy to a politics that focuses on the errant, non-meaningful and passive forces at work in thinking: 'A writing exceeding everything that the history of metaphysics has comprehended.'[53] His own work has sustained both sides of the transcendental question and project: a recognition of the essential possibility of thinking a sense that lies beyond any empirical instance *and* an interrogation into the non-sensical conditions for such thinking.[54]

Notes

1. Jacques Derrida, *Edmund Husserl's Origin of Geometry: An Introduction by Jacques Derrida*, trans. John P. Leavey (Lincoln: University of Nebraska Press, 1989), 153.
2. An earlier version of this paper appeared in *From Kant to Davidson: Philosophy and the Idea of the Transcendental*, ed. Jeff Malpas (London: Routledge, 2005).
3. Derrida claims that deconstruction is not a 'method', but he is able to make this claim precisely because his work usually begins by reading a philosopher faithfully in order to follow their own arguments to a point of decision: a point where the meaningful arguments of the text rely upon some unargued and received distinction. Derrida's point is not to criticize such gaps in the argument, but to demonstrate a necessary structure of all metaphysical arguments. His procedure is to follow an argument through in order to show its necessary dependence *and* its necessary attempt to free itself from such dependence. In the case of Husserl, the fact that there is a movement of reason 'announced' in experience is an idea Derrida finds *both* in Husserl and in Western metaphysics. By following Husserl's specific understanding of reason we can understand the structure of any possible articulation of reason. Most of what Derrida says in his work on Husserl is written by adopting the voice or position of Husserl, only to show the way in which Husserl ultimately partakes in the very structure of metaphysical arguments as transcendental arguments which he had sought to explain.
4. It could be argued that Derrida's adherence to intentionality and the premises of phenomenology is in fact more rigid than Husserl's own. There has been much recent work on Husserl that would insist that his late work on time-consciousness and meaning challenges the earlier definitions of intentionality as a direction of consciousness aiming at full sense and presence. (Merleau-Ponty had, early on, argued that Husserl's concept of intentionality leads out of metaphysics and the primacy of consciousness to a sensible understanding of the world. See, especially, Maurice Merleau-Ponty, *Signs*, trans. Richard C. McCleary (Evanston: Northwestern University Press, 1964). More recently, and with a far more challenging re-reading of Husserl, Donn Welton has explained the origins of meaning, from intentionality, without the privilege to full presentation which Derrida regards as the hallmark of Husserl's philosophy. See *The Origins of Meaning: A Critical Study of the Thresholds of Husserlian Phenomenology* (The Hague: Martinus Nijhoff, 1983). Throughout this essay I will be considering *Derrida's* reading of Husserl. According to Derrida it is the strict commitment of intentionality that is the very essence, not just of transcendental phenomenology, but of any possible metaphysics.
5. Jacques Derrida, ' "Genesis and Structure" and Phenomenology', in *Writing and Difference*, trans. Alan Bass (London: Routledge and Kegan Paul, 1981), 154–68, 160.
6. Derrida, *An Introduction*, 92.
7. ibid., 117.
8. ibid., 131.
9. In his reading of Husserl Derrida makes much of Husserl's requirement for an explanation at the levels of structure *and* genesis. On the one hand, as opposed to psychologism or historicism, there are universal structures of logic and validity. On the other hand, as opposed to the Platonizing gestures of a Frege, such

structures must have their genesis within conscious life, and must come to recognition in the history of consciousness even if they transcend any specific historical epoch.

10. Derrida, *An Introduction*, 83.

11. Derrida continually refers to Husserl's essential dependence on the Idea in the Kantian sense: we require a concept of full presence that structures experience but which is not presented within experience: 'It is not by chance that there is no phenomenology of the Idea. [...] If there is nothing to say about the Idea *itself*, it is because the idea is that starting from which something in general can be said' (Derrida, *An Introduction*, 138–9). Derrida also, however, regards the key difficulty of phenomenology to lie in the dependence on this Kantian notion. While the Idea, for Kant, is a feature of a transcendental subject who provides the limit of what can be known, the Husserlian project seeks to explain and account for the being and possibility of the subject, and therefore of the Idea (Derrida, *An Introduction*, 42).

12. Derrida, *An Introduction*, 27.

13. ibid., 33.

14. 'The world, therefore, is essentially determined by the dative and horizontal dimension of being perceived [*l'être-perçu*] in a gaze whose object must always be able to be a *theorem*' (Derrida, *An Introduction*, 83).

15. 'The ultimate form of ideality, the ideality of ideality, that in which the last instance one may anticipate or recall all repetition, is the *living present*, the self presence of transcendental life.' Jacques Derrida, *Speech and Phenomena and Other Essays on Husserl's Theory of Signs*, trans. David B. Allison (Evanston: Northwestern University Press, 1973), 6.

16. Derrida, *An Introduction*, 87.

17. ibid., 77.

18. Derrida, in his debate with Searle which I will examine further on, insists on the ideality of concepts: a concept can only be meaningful if it intends some general sense and cannot just be a generalization from already given cases.

19. Much of Derrida's own work challenges this conditional. In his later work, especially, he suggests that there are forms of 'experience' or life that are not structured by the aims of intentionality; such events of non-fulfilment occur in art, literature, error, chance, corruption, death (literally and metaphorically) and passive affect. At this stage, though, Derrida is following through the premises and requirements of Husserl's philosophy. He will always remain committed to the idea that metaphysics is necessarily a commitment to truth as presence *and* that there is a structure to thought (as meaningful) that ties experience to the goal of presence. What he will continue to question is whether we might think or write outside the epoch of presence.

20. John Searle, 'Literary Theory and its Discontents', *New Literary History* 25:3 (Summer 1994), 637–67.

21. Jacques Derrida, *Limited Inc* (Evanston: Northwestern University Press, 1988), 119.

22. Derrida, *Speech and Phenomena*, 54.

23. Derrida's emphasis upon transcendental possibility is both an extension and a critique of Heidegger's critique of the metaphysics of presence. Heidegger had argued that (initially and inauthentically) we tend to think of the world as something present and *then* that certain things are possible. But the reverse is the case; possibility conditions the actual world. Our present world depends on possibility, or what is *not yet* present: I can only experience this world as existing if I

have some project of meanings and a future that will be given. The object before me is experienced as a thing in so far as I can approach it, use it and place it meaningfully within the life that I am always directed towards. Derrida shifts the emphasis, however, away from a possibility of activity and actualization to a possibility of loss, non-fulfilment and even death (Derrida, *Speech and Phenomena*, 54). This will be explored more fully further on in Derrida's remarks on time.

24. 'There may be a difference still more unthought than the difference between Being and beings. We certainly can go further toward naming it in our language. Beyond Being and beings, this difference, ceaselessly differing from and deferring (itself), would trace (itself) (by itself) – this *différance* would be the first or last trace if one could still speak, here, or origin and end [...] Such a *différance* would at once, again, give us to think a writing without presence and without absence, without history, without cause, without *archia*, without *telos*, a writing that absolutely upsets all dialectics, all theology, all teleology, all ontology.' Jacques Derrida, *Margins of Philosophy*, trans. Alan Bass (Brighton: Harvester, 1982), 67.

25. This assumes, of course, that thought here refers to meaningful thought. As far as Derrida is concerned metaphysics has never defined thought or consciousness in any other way than as meaningful, or as capable of representing and repeating its own sense to itself.

26. This is already admitted within the Husserlian project. We can think transcendental subjectivity and sense only in its difference from empirical subjectivity. We must use the same 'worldly' language in order to refer to the very origin of the world. 'This ambiguity concerns the unavoidable expressions: "belief in the world", "acceptance", and so forth, which originally possess a psychological meaning but which nevertheless enter into the theory of the reduction as transcendental concepts. These terms must therefore not be taken in their usual sense, but first take on their integral philosophical meaning from the performance of the reduction itself. This ambiguity, which encumbers every one of the phenomenological *epoché*'s self-interpretations, is caused by the unavoidable "falsity" of its point of departure within the natural attitude. The countless misunderstandings which Husserl's philosophy had to suffer are caused by the fact that one retains and works with primarily "psychological" concepts within the familiar ease of their worldly meaning, thus failing to participate in their decisive modification by performing the reduction.' Eugen Fink, 'The Phenomenological Philosophy of Edmund Husserl and Contemporary Criticism', in R. O. Elveton (ed.), *The Phenomenology of Husserl: Selected Critical Readings* (Chicago: Quadrangle Books, 1970), 73–147, 117.

27. Martin Heidegger, *Being and Time*, trans. Joan Stambaugh (Albany: SUNY Press, 1996).

28. Derrida, *Margins*, 3, 6.

29. Both Heidegger and Husserl try to define Da-Sein or consciousness against any normative notion of human life. Consciousness must not be confused with any in-worldly anthropologism. But it's this transcendental manoeuvre which is just the issue for Derrida: the securing of a ground of consciousness in general that is other than any empirical notion of 'man' will always be supported by, or derived from, a figure of the human. It could be argued that Heidegger's move away from Da-Sein and the meaning of Being to Being as Time anticipates Derrida's own criticism. (Indeed, in his book on Heidegger's politics Derrida suggests that Heidegger also criticizes a history of self-comprehension, suggesting a way out of

the Greek epoch of presence.) Even in *Being and Time* Heidegger had argued that there is no time in general; the syntheses of time or existence are 'equiprimordial' with located (and therefore spatial) syntheses.

30. Many writers have regarded this connection between transcendental recognition and ethical activity as a *good* thing. If we realize that there is no foundation for our decisions other than ourselves then we have to be responsible for our decisions; we can no longer posit a law outside ourselves. Derrida is critical of this phenomenological ethic of responsibility precisely because he believes that responsibility can go further: if we acknowledge the role that unintended events have on thought – such as, but not exclusively, the textual events of a language – then we may need to consider forces or 'decisions' that are not ours but which nevertheless structure our thinking.

31. Derrida, *Speech and Phenomena*, 34.

32. Both deconstruction and, perhaps more explicitly, feminist criticism have looked at the ethical consequences of the errancy of concepts. No one, or at least not everyone, may have intended to use the concept of reason to institute a sexual hierarchy. (Interesting cases for feminist theory are not really those of conscious oppression or prejudice but concern all those 'oppressions' within the language we speak and the structure of our thought.) The concept of reason has an inscriptive history which no speaker or writer can fully control. 'Reason' translates the Latin 'ratio' which describes some grounding logic or order through which the world is given. And this concept relies on certain figures – of a world that possesses its own order awaiting representation in consciousness. This also gives certain norms for thinking: of an active subject who is rational insofar as he reflects and uncovers a world that is not in itself capable of giving forth its own sense. According to Luce Irigaray, it is just this 'scene' of thinking which both produces the normative notion of the active, rational subject alongside a passive and mute world; and this scene is contaminated with the force of a sexual hierarchy or 'scenography' (Luce Irigaray, *Speculum of the Other Woman*, trans. Gillian C. Gill, Ithaca: Cornell University Press, 1985). Derrida undertakes a similar analysis of many concepts to see whether they can, with all the efforts philosophers make, be disengaged from certain metaphysical determinations that are not autonomously intended or decided. In *Limited Inc* he argues that the concept of 'communication', for example, is intertwined with the concept of metaphor, and that both concepts determine a certain order of thought: 'because the value of displacement, of transport, etc., is precisely constitutive of the concept of metaphor with which one claims to comprehend the semantic displacement that is brought about from communication as a semio-linguistic phenomenon' (Derrida, *Limited Inc*, 2).

33. 'The inaugural mutation which interests Kant *hands over* geometry rather than creates it. [...] Kant's indifference to empirical history is only legitimated from the moment that a more profound history has already created nonempirical objects. This history remains hidden for Kant' (Derrida, *An Introduction*, 39–42).

34. Derrida, *An Introduction*, 59.

35. Much of the critical force of deconstruction is directed towards the function of 'exemplarity', or the ways in which certain cases (such as the successful speech-act, formal languages or conscious intention) provide the ground for explaining consciousness and language in general. The task of quasi-transcendentalism is to show how the marginalized case (writing, error and misinterpretation) is an essential possibility that structures the original. There could be no successful speech,

for example, if there were not a system of signs that also opened the possibility for speech to be misunderstood.

36. For Derrida, 'the privileged position of the protentional dimension of intentionality and that of the future in the constitution of space in general must be acknowledged'. Derrida, *An Introduction*, 135.

37. This is not to say that other cultures have no truth or science. But, for Derrida's Husserl, it is the Western idea of truth that is also tied to a certain self-understanding of Western history, for it is in the West that the idea of human life in general is explicitly thematized.

38. 'Only a communal subjectivity can produce the historical system of truth and be wholly responsible for it' (Derrida, *An Introduction*, 60).

39. Derrida, *Speech and Phenomena*, 13–14.

40. 'It is rather significant that every critical enterprise, juridical or transcendental, is made vulnerable by the irreducible factuality and natural naiveté of its language' (Derrida, *An Introduction*, 69–70).

41. Derrida, *Margins*, 51.

42. Heidegger, *Being and Time*, 30–1.

43. Indeed, he refers to such a determination of origins as 'etymologism': an activity that asserts the continuity of sense rather than its necessary unreliability. Derrida regards his own attention to etymology as prior to phenomenology (and therefore prior to sense and experience). He repeatedly refers to 'the need for a certain renewed and rigorous philological or "etymological" thematic, which would precede the discourse of phenomenology' (Derrida, *An Introduction*, 69).

44. Derrida, *Margins*, 56.

45. Jacques Derrida, 'Economimesis', trans. R. Klein, *Diacritics* 11:2 (Summer 1981), 3–25, 4.

46. Jacques Derrida, *Of Spirit: Heidegger and the Question*, trans. Geoffrey Bennington and Rachel Bowlby (Chicago: University of Chicago Press, 1989).

47. Derrida, 'Signature Event Context', in *Limited Inc*, 1.

48. Derrida, *An Introduction*, 81.

49. Friedrich Nietzsche, *On the Genealogy of Morals and Ecce Homo*, trans. Walter Kaufmann and R. J. Hollingdale, ed. Walter Kaufmann (New York: Vintage, 1967).

50. Michel Foucault, *The Order of Things* (London: Tavistock, 1970).

51. André Leroi-Gourhan, *Gesture and Speech*, trans. Anna Bostock Berger (Cambridge, MA: MIT Press, 1993), 4–19.

52. Derrida, *An Introduction*, 117.

53. Derrida, *Margins*, 67.

54. In response to Richard Rorty's question, 'Is Derrida a Transcendental Philosopher?', I would argue that it's not, as Rorty suggests, a possibility of two competing readings of Derrida. There's not a transcendental Derrida and a pragmatic Derrida; his transcendentalism and his pragmatism depend upon the specific determinations of each other. Derrida's 'pragmatics' no longer refer to human and conscious intent, and his transcendentalism no longer refers to a general *a priori* that can be thought outside any of its determined figures. See Richard Rorty, 'Is Derrida a Transcendental Philosopher?' *Essays on Heidegger and Others: Philosophical Papers, Volume Two* (Cambridge: Cambridge University Press, 1991), 125.

7
Splitting the Origin: Writing and Responsibility

Margret Grebowicz

In the well-known interview with Henri Ronse, approximately a decade after the publication of his *Edmund Husserl's 'Origin of Geometry': An Introduction*, Derrida offers an account of the beginning of deconstruction. He states: 'In a classic philosophical architecture, *Speech and Phenomena* would come first.' Although the *Introduction* was actually published five years prior to *Speech and Phenomena*, the latter poses the question of the relationship of speech and writing to the history of metaphysics, specifically to 'metaphysics in its most modern, critical, and vigilant form: Husserl's transcendental phenomenology', and is thus the best point of entry.

Of course, the question of the beginning is not merely one question among others for Derrida. Somewhat mysteriously, he adds that *Speech and Phenomena* may be read as 'the other side' of another work, namely the *Introduction*, in which 'the problematic of writing was already in place as such, bound to the irreducible structure of "deferral" in its relationship to consciousness, presence, science, history, and the history of science, the disappearance or delay of the origin, etc'.[1] His amendment suggests that to relate *Speech and Phenomena* to the *Introduction* in this way is to understand the beginning of deconstruction outside of the constraints of a 'classic philosophical architecture'. Derrida's reply takes the form of the metaphysical displacements, or 'interventions', symptomatic of deconstruction: the beginning subject to the logic of supplementarity, of the supplement which makes the origin possible, and thus, of the 'disappearance or delay of the origin'.

Interestingly, in spite of this provocation, his commentators continue, in a classically philosophical fashion, to treat *Speech and Phenomena* as the authoritative expression of Derrida's engagement of Husserl – and to treat this engagement as the most classic and complete example of deconstruction's critique of the 'metaphysics of presence', of philosophy's history of 'logocentrism'. For Derrida himself, and for his critics, deconstruction begins, properly speaking, with the critique of phenomenology from a linguistic, or semiotic, perspective, and with an interrogation of the history of

143

philosophy from the vantage point of that critique.[2] This location of the beginning of deconstruction in the analysis of the sign allows us certain hermeneutical comforts. First of all, it allows us to place Derrida's early work in relationship to poststructuralism in general, as a response to structuralist linguistics and its manifestations in literary theory. Secondly, we can locate the analysis of Husserl within the semiotic context of *Of Grammatology*, Derrida's landmark work of the same year. In other words, the problem of signs offers a certain consistency to the moment of deconstruction's beginning, a more or less fixed location within the 'historical, political, philosophical, and phantasmatic structures' of the time.[3]

On the other hand, what would it mean to take seriously Derrida's provocation and to consider his engagement of Husserl as an originary moment subject to deconstruction's 'logic of the supplement' – an 'origin' which was never one, never simple, always already split, doubled, supplemented? John Leavey attempts this in the preface to his translation of the *Introduction*, citing Derrida's reference (in Henri Ronse's interview) to the 1962 work as 'further justification for a close reading of Derrida's first major published essay'. Writing in 1976, Leavey points out that this early engagement of Husserl not only introduces us to Derrida's early work, but also 'furnishes a basic part of the framework for his later, present work'. That framework, Leavey tells us, is phenomenology, insofar as 'Derrida has found in and *at the limits* precisely where phenomenology fails (i.e., where it becomes the modern, exemplary recapitulation of Western metaphysics) a fertile ground for cultivating questions about the non-philosophical *per se* (the limits or 'margins' of philosophy), about writing, origins and history, and différance'.[4] Like Derrida himself, Leavey emphasizes the overlap between the *Introduction* and Derrida's later work, offering the 1962 engagement of Husserl as an early articulation of those themes which propel deconstruction long after Husserl is no longer invoked by name.

Over a decade later, in another one of the noticeably few essays devoted specifically to the *Introduction*, Rudolf Bernet continues the attempt to understand the text in terms of the themes we now take to be constitutive of Derrida's early work. Bernet begins by pointing out that 'the legitimate desire of the contemporary reader to discover intimations of Derrida's own later work in his interpretation of Husserl contributes much to the reader's almost despairing sense of feeling at a loss before this text'. He attributes to this despair the neglect which the *Introduction* has suffered at the hands of Husserl scholars and Derrida scholars alike. His reading is devoted to alleviating some of this despair – unfortunately, with the help of the mysterious notion of 'influence'. Writing from the vantage point of 'the question of the extent to which Husserl's text on the origin of geometry has exercised a decisive influence upon Derrida's own thought', Bernet traces back some major themes found in *Speech and Phenomena* and in *Of Grammatology* to the analysis of Husserl in the *Introduction*.[5]

Both Leavey and Bernet attempt to take the *Introduction* seriously, on its own terms, and thus take up Derrida's challenge to read the beginning of deconstruction as an instance of the supplement constitutive of the origin. Their readings offer the opportunity to explore the degrees of success with which these attempts, and Derrida's challenge itself, truly avoid the blueprint of a 'classical philosophical architecture'. If we justify, as they do, turning to the 1962 text with the claim that the problematic of the 1967 text is already in place there, are we attending sufficiently to the difference between them, the difference that would split the mythic origin of deconstruction? As for the inclination to describe as 'legitimate' the desire to 'discover intimations of Derrida's own later work in his interpretation of Husserl', does it not fail to take note of those aspects of the *Introduction* which make it significantly different than Derrida's other work on Husserl? Contrary to Derrida's suggestion that the *Introduction* is relevant because of the concerns it shares with *Speech and Phenomena*, should we not rather attend to those concerns and analyses which the *Introduction* does *not* share with Derrida's other works on Husserl, in order to problematize, in a robust sense, the beginning, and thus to evade the 'classical' reading of Derrida's corpus?

This is the task of the present study: to address those aspects of the *Introduction* which distinguish it from *Speech and Phenomena*, in order to remain 'true' to what deconstruction has taught us about origins. The most striking difference is that Derrida engages in an extensive reading of Husserl's analysis of responsibility in the *Introduction*, but this set of concerns is entirely absent from *Speech and Phenomena*. The absence, the break in what we now wish to see as the continuous flow of thought from the earlier work to the later, would not be so conspicuous, were it the case that discursive responsibility, the responsibility for one's words, were simply not that important for the analysis of language in early deconstruction.

In the course of the same interview, however, in an attempt to distinguish his early work from the 'death of metaphysics' talk, which was in fashion at the beginning of his career, Derrida indicates that responsibility is a significant issue. Dissociating his notion of the 'closure of metaphysics' from a straightforward rejection of, or from an attempt at reform of, philosophy, he states: 'The limit of the philosophical is singular; its apprehension is always accompanied, for me, by a certain unconditional reaffirmation. If one cannot call it directly ethical or political, it is nevertheless a matter of the conditions of an ethics or a politics, and of a responsibility of "thought", if you will'.[6] Thus, the apprehension of the 'closure of metaphysics' or of 'the limit of the philosophical' does not relieve us of philosophy, or provide an escape to the non-philosophical. Instead, it results in something Derrida calls 'a responsibility of thought'. The limit of the philosophical somehow renders thought responsible.

Responsible: what might this word mean in the context of deconstruction, of apprehending the limit of the philosophical? Deconstruction's most classic, rigorous manifestation, the notion of the 'general field of writing', may be read as a radical critique of the notion of responsibility. In Derrida's analysis, the conjunction of difference and repetition, 'iterability', results in two incommensurable effects. Iterability makes possible all effects of identity and property – i.e., that my proper name stands for me, that my signature is mine and mine alone, that when I 'give my word', I have a promise to keep, that when I testify under oath, I tell the truth, and so on. At the same time, iterability makes possible the breakdown, or crisis, of identity and property – i.e., that there is another person in the phone book with 'my' name, that my signature can be forged, that promises are broken, that I perjure myself in court, and so on. Derrida's notion of iterability does not imply that we are not responsible, but it does mean that the notion of responsibility at work in our world is conditioned by the possibility of a crisis of responsibility. The critique Derrida offers of the speech/writing relationship, as tradition-ally understood, is nothing less than a critique of the notion of a responsible agent, as traditionally understood. It begins with the radical undermining of the possibility of responsibility for one's words. Derrida even thematizes this, for example, describing writing as 'an iterative structure cut off from all absolute responsibility, from consciousness as the authority of the last anal-ysis'.[7] Elsewhere, this time approaching the notion of language not with the structure of iterability, but with another now-famous structure, that of dis-semination, he writes: 'Responsibility and individuality are values that can no longer predominate here: that is the first effect of dissemination.'[8]

Thus, Derrida's appeal to the notion of responsibility in his description of the apprehension of the limit of the philosophical poses a problem. In a recent essay, concerning the notion of 'response' at work in the concept of responsibility, he wonders 'what could be the responsibility, the quality or the virtue of responsibility, of a consistent discourse which claimed to show that no responsibility could ever be taken without equivocation and without contradiction?'[9] How could such a discourse be a 'responsibility of thought'? The *Introduction* shows that these questions, contemporary as they may sound, are already in place in Husserl. This, I suggest, is why Derrida found himself 'seduced', as he puts it, by Husserl's descriptions of writing.[10] Simultaneously the condition of the possibility of objectivity and the con-dition of the possibility of a crisis of meaning, writing is an ethical problem in Husserl's work, and the connections between Husserl and Derrida in this regard indicate the possibility of reading a consistent ethical concern in the inquiries of early, 'classic' deconstruction.

'The Origin of Geometry' begins as an epistemological inquiry concern-ing the connection between objective existence and what takes place in the first geometer's mind: 'how does geometrical ideality (just like that of all sci-ences) proceed from its primary intrapersonal origin, where it is a structure within the conscious space of the first inventor's soul, to its ideal objectiv-ity?'[11] Husserl begins his answer by turning to language, which functions as a condition of intersubjectivity, and of the experience of intersubjectivity, in general. Language causes humans to experience the world as something they have in common. His relatively uncritical focus on language as what humans have 'in common' reaches a climactic expression in this essay, as Husserl describes the 'community of empathy and of language':

> In the contact of reciprocal linguistic understanding, the original production and the product of one subject can be *actively* understood by others. In this full understanding of what is produced by the other, as in the case of recollection, a present coaccomplishment on one's own part of the presentified activity necessarily takes place.

Language, understood first of all as speech, is so faithful a communication of mental contents that one actually produces a 'mental structure' identical to the one in the interlocutor's mind. This identity is experienced as such, as a 'self-evident consciousness of the identity of the mental structure in the productions of both the receiver of the communication and the communicator'. The result is a perfect, intersubjective manifestation of the object which was once present only in the mind of the first geometer: 'In the unity of the community of communication among several persons the repeatedly produced structure becomes an object of consciousness, not as a likeness, but as the one structure common to all'.[12] Language makes possible the philosophy-as-community Husserl describes in the 'Vienna Lecture' – as the ideal structures of the theoretical attitude are 'concurrently lived through and taken over without any difficulty by others', even by 'outsiders', who enter into *theoria* 'through sympathetic understanding'.[13]

At this stage, the geometrical object's existence is no longer dependent on its awakening in the original geometer's mind – however, insofar as it exists as something common to the speaker's community, it does not yet enjoy fully objective status. 'What is lacking' from this schema 'is the *persisting existence* of the "ideal objects" even during periods in which the inventor and his fellows are no longer alive … their continuing-to-be even when no one has [consciously] realized them in self-evidence.' Writing allows the geometrical object freedom from any conscious realization whatsoever, a freedom that 'lifts' the 'communalization of man' to a 'different level'. As it extends the possibility of 'communication' over greater spans of time and space, writing allows the 'community' of man to span both time and space far greater than the circle of speakers present to each other in spoken discourse. Writing 'is, so to speak, communication become virtual' – it is the possibility that communication takes place in the empirical absence of the speaker or hearer. As Derrida puts it in *Of Grammatology*, 'when the local community is dislocated to the point where individuals no longer appear to one another, become capable of being imperceptible, the age of writing begins'.[14] This absence, on which Husserl bases the difference between spoken and written language, is the necessary condition of objectivity.

'The Origin of Geometry' is one of the few places where Husserl actually analyses writing as distinct from language in general, but how important a role does this distinction play? In other words, as opposed to Derrida's extensive attention to the concept of writing in particular, is Husserl's attention to writing not simply a subset of his general interest in the role of language in the constitution of ideal objects? And, in the end, should we not attribute Derrida's interest in writing to the notion of *écriture* fashionable in his own intellectual context, rather than to his interest in this period of Husserl's thought? The analysis of writing in the 'Origin' shows that the notion of writing is of decisive importance for phenomenology – first of all, because it plays such a central role in what is perhaps transcendental phenomenology's greatest challenge: the epistemology of objective knowledge. Objectivity is not merely one problem among others for Husserl. Arguably, transcendental phenomenology's extensive study of the nature of subjectivity is ultimately an account of the constitution of the objective world, an attempt to answer the question, 'How is any object in general possible?', in line with the Kantian inquiry. The study of subjectivity is the means by which Husserl distinguishes phenomenology, as an account of objective nature, from the accounts of nature we find in the physical sciences. With his notion of a 'science of pure possibilities', Husserl makes the study of subjectivity – as constitutive of the objective world – serve as a foundation for the 'factual' sciences of nature, like physics, as when he writes that 'the study of subjectivity is unconditionally required for a full clarification of the sense and structure of physical nature'.[15]

Perhaps it could be argued that 'writing' is a much more technical term in deconstruction than it is for Husserl. We learn from Derrida that writing is the structural possibility of the 'death' of the subject – it introduces the possibility that my words be read, received, after my death. At the same time, the posthumous text is precisely not 'mine', but subject to endless interpretation, without the possibility of grounding in an 'origin' that is the living present of its producer. Writing inaugurates a 'we will never know what he/she really meant'. This, however, is precisely the problem to which Husserl himself points to when describing writing as the condition of the crisis of the sciences – that science as we know it 'excludes precisely the questions which man, given over in our unhappy times to the most portentous upheavals, finds the most burning: questions of the meaning or meaninglessness of the whole of this human existence'.[16]

As opposed to the active coaccomplishment he describes in the case of intersubjective linguistic understanding, Husserl describes the 'awakening' of mental structures by writing as 'passive', like a 'more or less clear memory'. In the first phase of awakening, writing actually 'effects a transformation of the original mode of being of the meaning-structure [...] It becomes sedimented, so to speak'. The passively awakened object can then, in principle, be actively awakened: 'this is the capacity for reactivation that belongs originally to every human being as a speaking being.' In addition to the capacity for reactivation, however, another capacity belongs to every speaking being: the capacity to fall 'victim', as Husserl puts it, 'to the *seduction of language*', and engage in 'a thinking in terms of things that have been taken up merely receptively, passively, which deals with significations only passively understood and taken over, without any of the self-evidence of original activity'. In addition, then, to the absence of one's interlocutor, writing functions by means of another kind of absence, or of absence understood in a different, but related, way – the absence of the original idea, in its fullness and activity. The danger of this possibility is that 'greater and greater segments of this life lapse into a kind of talking and reading that is dominated purely by association' instead of the kind of reciprocal reactivation of full meaning which takes place in 'the community of empathy and of language'.[17]

The absence proper to the notion of writing, that which makes writing a particular type of linguistic communication, is at once what makes objectivity possible, and what sends the objective sciences into crisis. Because of the possibility of radical detachment from the moment of its production, the geometrical idea can be handed down is this associative manner, which 'forgets' the subjective dimension at the core of the idea's truth. Writing allows the ideal object to be awakened less and less fully, until its original meaning – the meaning present in the original geometer's mind at the moment of the idea's production – is lost, and we end up performing manipulations with the object which fail to take this original meaning into account.

Ultimately, it is to this *'sort* of objectivity' that Husserl ascribes the failure of the positive sciences to truly describe the world – the world of subjects of experience.[18] Truth – the 'sort of' truth Husserl has in mind when he describes science as 'thinking directed towards the attainment of truths and the avoidance of falsehood' – involves a connection with the living present of the original geometer's idea. Science can claim to be true only by maintaining the original, subjective dimension. Since it is the 'seduction of language' which endangers the access to the subjective dimension of objective discourse, Husserl calls for a commitment on the part of the scientist to avoid this seduction, and to 'put a stop to the freeplay of associative constructions'. The danger of linguistic sedimentation can be avoided 'only when one has a view to the univocity of linguistic expression and to securing, by means of the most painstaking formation of the relevant words, propositions, and complexes of propositions, the results which are to be univocally expressed'. Husserl thus describes univocal expression, or the 'securing' of one's original meaning in the expression one then offers up to interlocution, as the scientist's responsibility: 'This must be done by the individual scientist... by every scientist as a member of the scientific community', a community Husserl describes as 'a community of knowledge living in the unity of a common responsibility'.[19] In contrast to most philosophies of science, which attempt to demarcate science as a particular kind of knowledge, Husserl's analysis demarcates 'science', or the 'thinking directed towards the attainment of truths and the avoidance of falsehood', as a particular kind of commitment to language, and to communication. In the essay's most Cartesian moment, he describes this commitment to univocity as 'a matter of a firm direction of the will, which the scientist establishes in himself, aimed at the certain capacity for reactivation'.[20] Science is a sort of will-to-univocity, to the absolute transparency of language, and to the possibility of retaining the originary, subjective, pre-scientific moment as constitutive of the truth of the objective idea.

Husserl's analysis, especially in his discussion of the responsibility of scientists, does not treat language as simply a secondary moment in science, the moment, which comes *after* knowledge. Instead, 'meaning' is a sort of simultaneity of language and knowledge. Univocal expression guarantees scientists the 'personal certainty that everything they put into scientific assertions has been said "once and for all", that it "stands fast", forever identically repeatable with self-evidence and usable for further theoretical or practical ends – as indubitably reactivatable with the identity of its actual meaning'. Language, used 'properly', guarantees reactivation, self-evidence, and the integrity of the scientific knowledge transmitted throughout the tradition. The footnote which concludes the discussion of responsibility underlines this connection: since the sedimentation of meaning is, Husserl tells us, 'unavoidable', 'the goal of reactivatability can only be relatively fulfilled', and perfectly univocal expression remains a sort of regulative ideal. Accordingly, 'Ultimately, objective, absolutely firm knowledge of truth is an infinite idea'.[21] Thus, the 'firm direction of the will', the commitment to communication as a perfect conductivity of ideas, is a commitment to the absolute achievement of something, which can be achieved only relatively.

'The Origin of Geometry' thus introduces two unexpected issues into the discussion of science and the epistemology of objectivity. First, Husserl's approach to the question, 'How are ideal objects possible?', introduces an ethical dimension – relying on notions like commitment, community, responsibility and the will. Second, Husserl's discussion of the language of science ultimately focuses on the inexactitude of 'natural'[22] language, on the necessity of sedimentation and misunderstanding, instead of the Leibnizian fantasy of universal language. His claim that absolute knowledge is an infinite idea, or an 'Idea in the Kantian sense', is not the straightforwardly Kantian claim it appears to be – here, the practical impossibility of absolute knowledge is due not to the limits of reason, but specifically to the limits of language.

The latter point is, of course, where Husserl and Derrida intersect explicitly. The majority of Part I of *Of Grammatology* is devoted to the relationship between language, or signification in general, and what Derrida calls 'theory', or 'what unites philosophy and science in the *epistémè*'.[23] Theoretical discourse performs a kind of repression of its own written status, or, as Derrida puts it, 'the philosophical text, although it is in fact always written, includes, precisely as its philosophical specificity, the project of effacing itself in the face of the signified content which it transports and in general teaches'.[24] More generally, the discourses of the *epistémè*, although they in fact take place in natural language, and so have no way of escaping the possible corruption of 'truth' at the hands of natural language, must avoid acknowledging their linguistic embodiment, in order to emphasize content, and to give the illusion of exactitude, transmission, absolute translatability. The illusion is of translatability not only among the languages of different nations, but also from 'languages' like mathematics to natural language, from sets of computer data to natural language, from observational to theoretical terms, and so on.

Of Grammatology famously attempts to expose just that – the illusion from which the discourse of the *epistémè* suffers. Deconstruction shows that the possibility of corruption is present not only in natural language, but is a condition of signification in general: the moment the sign comes into play, 'truth' is jeopardized. The allegedly non-phonetic notational systems of science are no less subject to this jeopardy. The notion of sign entails substitution, re-presentation, secondariness, absence, and thus the loss of the origin, of the presence of the thing-as-such at some mythic moment 'before' the sign. In Derrida's classic analysis, the absence proper to writing, according to the traditional understanding of the speech/writing binary, is a condition of signification in general, rendering all language, even spoken language, a moment in what Derrida calls 'the general field of writing'. This means that writing is not a species of language – it is language which is a species of writing, insofar as all signification depends on absence, and the possibility of 'extraction and grafting'.[25]

Not so famously, even somewhat surprisingly, 'The Origin of Geometry' echoes these gestures step by step. Husserl begins by addressing the way in which language functions, the details of how communication takes place and makes intersubjectivity possible. He then turns his attention to the power of writing – whose function is unimpeded by the absence of either interlocutor – distinguishing writing as a species of language, and pointing out that it is specifically this power which makes objective knowledge possible. His next move, however, appears to reverse the genus/species relationship. Sedimentation, which Husserl has introduced as an unfortunate, potential result of writing, is in fact the unfortunate, potential result of language as such. He states explicitly that 'the capacity for reactivation belongs originally to every human being as a speaking being', but his reading also shows that the capacity for mere 'passivity' and for 'a kind of talking and reading that is dominated purely by association', belongs to every human being as a writing being, and finally, as a subject of language.

Derrida acknowledges Husserl's innovative discussion of writing by indicating that his appeal to univocity is not as conservative and traditionally scientistic as it may at first seem. Rodolphe Gasché's essay, 'On Responding Responsibly', addresses the *Introduction* in detail, but misses several crucial things: Gasché fails to discuss Husserl's use of the notion of responsibility, and furthermore underestimates the degree to which Derrida reads Husserl as a revolutionary thinker. Gasché focuses on Derrida's contrast between Husserl and Joyce – the former standing for the regulative ideal of univocity, the latter for the regulative ideal of total equivocity. To his credit, he formulates a thorough response to the position that deconstruction is an uncritical celebration of equivocation, and that its author's performance of the infinite possibilities of citation and grafting means that Derrida, like Joyce, points to 'a language that could equalize the greatest possible synchrony with the greatest potential for buried, accumulated, and interwoven intentions within each linguistic atom, each vocable, each word'.[26] On the contrary, Gasché points out, deconstruction shows us that the fantasy of total equivocity depends upon univocity as its horizon, and 'Joyce's project depends upon the Husserlian project'.[27] Since both Husserl and Joyce embark upon totalizing projects, Gasché concludes, 'Derrida operates from a position which is neither that of Husserl, nor that of Joyce, nor, for that matter, philosophical or literary'.[28]

Gasché's reading of the relationship between Joyce and Husserl, however, wishes to maintain the symmetry of their projects, a symmetry that Derrida explicitly rejects in the *Introduction*. Husserl's position is, in a sense, much less naïve than Joyce's dream of language as pure equivocity – it sees, first of all, that even as 'univocity corresponds to the very vocation of science', equivocity is irreducible, and the identity of sense cannot be guaranteed in language. Sense is 'always inscribed within a mobile system of relations and takes its source in an infinitely open project of acquisition. Even if those relations are, within a science, relations of pure idealities and "truths", they do not therein give rise any less to some singular placings in perspective, some multiple interconnections of sense, and therefore some mediate and potential aims'. If we take seriously the notion of intentionality, we must distinguish between sense and object, and allow that even ideal objects are experienced on the level of sense, and so are subject to what we might generally describe as 'mediation'.

> If, in fact, equivocity is always irreducible, that is because words and language in general are not and can never be absolute objects. They do not possess any resistant and permanent identity that is absolutely their own. They have their being from an intention which traverses them as mediations.[29]

The irreducibility of mediation in the constitution of meaning is precisely at work in Derrida's notion of iterability – the simultaneous identity and difference constitutive of the repetition, which makes a code possible. He appears to describe Husserl's position in the same terms: 'The "same" word is always "other" according to the always different intentional acts which thereby make a word significative. There is a sort of *pure* equivocity here, which grows in the very rhythm of science.' Thus, Husserl's position accepts iterability as the condition of the possibility of meaning, and the pure possibility of equivocity as the condition for the possibility of science – and, finally, as we have seen, that 'the scientific statement, without being questioned again as to its truth, always remains provisional'.[30] Thus, if Gasché is correct that Derrida's adventures in grammatology are not philosophical, then, possibly, neither are Husserl's. In other words, either Derrida is not really 'between' Husserl and Joyce (since they do not represent opposite poles), or Husserl's text itself occupies that same between-space.

In *Of Grammatology*, Derrida performs and thematizes the possibility of two simultaneous and inconsistent readings – or of one reading, which indicates two simultaneous and inconsistent moments in a single 'position'. The possibility of these simultaneous (but inconsistent) readings is itself an effect of the general field of writing, of the infinite 'citationality' and 'grafting' which makes meaning possible. Because writing irrevocably corrupts the possibility of 'proper' meaning, 'the writer writes *in* a language and *in* a logic whose proper system, laws, and life his discourse by definition cannot dominate absolutely'.[31] Furthermore, a deconstruction, a grammatological reading, a reading which attends to the general field of writing, 'must always aim at a certain relationship, unperceived by the writer, between what he commands and what he does not command of the patterns of language that he uses'.[32] In this respect, the *Introduction* appears to prefigure the kind of reading we find fully developed in *Of Grammatology*, the reading which operates according to the logic of the hinge – '*la brisure*'[33] – illuminating not similarities, but connections taking place at (as?) points of difference. Perhaps the *Introduction* is the site of such an intersection between Husserl and Derrida, or between a traditional Husserl, a closeted metaphysician concerned with epistemology, and Derrida's more progressive Husserl, a self-described failure of a metaphysician whose only remaining questions concern ethics. Perhaps we are witnessing the encounter between the anethical Derrida concerned solely with the formal nature of language and the Derrida always already turning his eye toward problems of responsibility. In any case, we can be sure that reading the *Introduction* as an 'origin of deconstruction' is not a simple question of literary history, of decoding meanings and attributing motives, of reading anyone, anything 'correctly'.

Derrida's reading of Husserl in the *Introduction* shows that Husserl's position is 'essentially' split, that 'The Origin of Geometry' always performs more than one gesture. He reminds us that this is 'the difficulty we are striving to illuminate here': writing is 'sense gathered into a sign,' Derrida writes, which is why Husserl describes it as external, sensible, *and* 'as the *intrinsic possibility* and *intrinsic condition* of acts of objective cognition'.[34] In fact, the problem of the transcendental itself is the problem of the general field of writing – of the intervention of exteriority in the integrity of an interior. If writing raises the question of 'the possibility of truth's disappearance', the other side of the question turns out to be at the heart of phenomenology: 'what is the sense of its appearing?'[35] Underlining the parallel between the inquiries, and thus emphasizing the import of the problem of writing for phenomenology, Derrida writes that

> since transcendental consciousness can always and with complete free-dom modify or suspend the thesis of *each* (therefore of *all*) contingent existence and of *each* (therefore of *all*) transcendence, its very sense is *de jure* and absolutely independent of the whole world. The situa-tion of truth, particularly, of geometrical truth, is analogous. It therefore provokes the same questions.[36]

Derrida thus shows that the problem of the general field of writing is at stake at the heart of the phenomenological project, and that the transcendental itself is always already the problem of the possibility of responsibility.

And yet, this responsibility suffers from its own equivocations. As Derrida points out, 'only *freedom* can let itself be threatened this way'. The concept of responsibility on which Husserl relies entails the assumption that 'we are always free to reawaken any passively received sense'.[37] Husserl explicitly states this in his claim that the capacity for full reactivation belongs to us as subjects of language. In Derrida's reading, reactivation and responsibility are identical – reactivation is a responsibility for sense. 'Responsibility here means shouldering a word one hears spoken, as well as taking on oneself the transfer of sense, in order to look after its advance' – a task required of both parties who come into contact with sense, 'the one who receives, but also and first of all the one who creates and then expresses the sense'.[38] On the other hand, and at the same time, Husserl insists that sedimentation is an inescapable condition of language, which implies that it is precisely as subjects of language that we are not free to reactivate all received sense, or to consistently look after the transfer of sense by means of univocal expression.

Unlike the Leibnizian fantasy of a 'universal characteristic', Husserl's demand for scientists to take on the responsibility of sense is truly a post-Kantian demand. However, this is not the Kantian tradition to which phenomenology appears to belong more or less unproblematically – the tradition of transcendental philosophy, teetering on the brink of idealism. Instead, Husserl invokes the Kant of the antinomies and of the second *Critique*, focusing on the limits of reason and their ethical consequences. He calls absolute univocity an 'Idea in the Kantian sense', the sense of a regulative ideal. As Derrida's reading reminds us, however, 'it is not by chance that there is no phenomenology of the Idea'.[39] Phenomenology relies on the notion of evidence and givenness to such a degree that the notion of a regulative ideal appears to be a part of the Kantian legacy which Husserl cannot legitimately inherit: 'the certainty of what can never immediately and as such present itself in an intuition should pose some serious problems for phenomenology (problems similar to those, for example, of the constitution of the alter ego by an irreducibly mediate intentionality)'.[40] Derrida does not imply that the Idea in the Kantian sense has no possibility of appearing at all, but that the appearing of the regulative is of a different sort than what Husserl demands in the 'principle of principles', which would be 'the immediate presence of the thing itself "in person" '.[41] In contrast, the evidence proper to the Idea 'cannot depend on a phenomenological type of evidence'.[42] The regulative is a sort of limit to phenomenology (just as the other, whose invocation at this juncture can hardly be an accident, poses a limit to phenomenology).

Thus, in the *Introduction*, Derrida draws attention to those aspects of Husserl's work which are not anchored in the metaphysics of presence, but which make him confront the limits of his own discourse. Responsibility is not given in consciousness. In Husserl's conclusion that rigorous science is the responsibility to univocal expression, or the responsibility for sense, Derrida faces a mental-level problematic akin to the one he will later indicate for the grammatological (insofar as it is a 'science' of writing) project: 'phenomenology cannot be grounded as such in itself, nor can it *itself* indicate its own proper limits'.[43] He here focuses on not only the metaphysics at work in Husserl's 'principle of principles', but also on the way in which Husserl's notion of responsibility undoes that metaphysics, leaving phenomenology '*stretched* between the *finitizing* consciousness of its *principle* and the *infinitizing* consciousness of its final *institution*, the *Endstiftung* indefinitely deferred in its content but always evident in its regulative value'.[44] Again, the evidence proper to the *Endstiftung* – 'phenomenology's ultimate critical legitimation' – is 'announced', not given, in consciousness. Responsibility is announced as something yet to be fulfilled. 'Husserl's phenomenology starts from this *lived anticipation* as a radical responsibility (something which, when considered literally, does not seem to be the case with the Kantian critique)'.[45] Indeed, Kant's philosophy, in which reason itself is able to delineate its own limits, seems to neutralize any 'lived anticipation' of the Ideas. Husserl's thought, in contrast, suffers from the problem of its own right to speak: if the possibility of rigour is the responsibility to univocal expression, then Husserl's thought itself is infused with this responsibility. Thus, Husserl's gesture is like Derrida's precisely insofar as it does not mirror Kant's project. Geoffrey Bennington is correct to remind us that 'grammatology is always already impossible in a more radical manner than an Idea of Reason', and so, Derrida seems to say, is the notion of phenomenology that Husserl faces at the end of his career.[46]

If we take seriously Derrida's claim that the apprehension of the limits of philosophy provokes a responsibility of thought, then we must also take seriously the lesson of the *Introduction*, which shows that Husserl's work, his thought, suffers from a significantly similar responsibility. Like Derrida, Husserl does not merely repeat the Kantian gesture. Derrida's reading shows us that Husserl's imperative to univocal expression is also more radical than an Idea of Reason, because phenomenology, with its principle of principles, cannot account for the regulative. Bennington writes, 'If we are right to suggest that Derrida interrupts the movement toward the Idea, and paradoxically plunges us back into the "present" and the "empirical", then clearly our ethics and politics are changed too. The free community of rational beings can no longer simply be invoked, even regulatively, to orient our ethical and political judgment, nor can its various surrogates'.[47] Husserl's discourse does precisely this: it interrupts the movement toward the Idea, plunges us back into the empirical, into the evidence of experience – which is why the Idea in phenomenology is more radically impossible than the Idea in Kant. The 'free community of rational beings' thus cannot 'simply be invoked', even by Husserl, who performs this invocation obsessively in his call to univocal expression. Derrida's reading indicates that already in the text of Husserl, this community is a fantasy, and this invocation an indeterminate address. Finally, and possibly first of all, it indicates (once again, but, of course, first of all) that the encounter with the empirical and transcendental event of writing is precisely what begins, irreversibly, to change 'our ethics and politics'.

Notes

1. Jacques Derrida, 'Implications', in *Positions*, trans. Alan Bass (Chicago: University of Chicago Press, 1981), 5.
2. According to Newton Garver, 'the core of Derrida's analysis, or "deconstruction" [is] a sustained argument against the possibility of anything pure and simple which can serve as the foundation for the meaning of signs', an argument which, he claims, 'strikes at the very idea of a transcendental phenomenology'. Newton Garver, 'Preface', in Jacques Derrida, *Speech and Phenomena*, trans. David B. Allison and Newton Garver (Evanston: Northwestern University Press, 1973), 9, 22.
3. Geoffrey Bennington and Jacques Derrida, *Jacques Derrida* (Chicago: University of Chicago Press, 1993), 20–2.
4. John P. Leavey, 'Introduction', in Jacques Derrida, *Edmund Husserl's 'Origin of Geometry': An Introduction*, trans. John P. Leavey Jr (Lincoln: University of Nebraska Press, 1989), 8. Author's emphasis.
5. Rudolf Bernet, 'On Derrida's "Introduction" to Husserl's *Origin of Geometry*', in H. J. Silverman (ed.), *Derrida and Deconstruction* (New York: Routledge, 1989), 139–40.

6. Jacques Derrida, 'The Almost Nothing of the Unpresentable', in Elisabeth Weber (ed.) *Points...Interviews 1974–1994* (Stanford: Stanford University Press, 1995), 80.

7. Jacques Derrida, 'Signature Event Context', in *Margins of Philosophy*, trans. Alan Bass (Chicago: University of Chicago Press, 1981), 316.

8. Jacques Derrida, 'Outwork', in *Dissemination*, trans. Barbara Johnson (Chicago: University of Chicago Press, 1981), 5.

9. Jacques Derrida, 'Passions', in *On the Name*, ed. Thomas Dutoit (Stanford: Stanford University Press, 1995), 9.

10. Derrida, 'Almost Nothing', 78–9.

11. Edmund Husserl, 'The Origin of Geometry', in Derrida, *Edmund Husserl's 'Origin of Geometry': An Introduction*, 161.

12. Husserl, 'Origin', 163–4. Author's emphasis.

13. Edmund Husserl, 'The Vienna Lecture', in *The Crisis of European Sciences and Transcendental Phenomenology*, trans. David Carr (Evanston: Northwestern University Press, 1970), 285. In fact, there are no real 'outsiders' in the era of *theoria*: 'Unlike all other cultural works, philosophy is not a movement of interest which is bound to the soil of the national tradition. Aliens, too, learn to understand it and generally take part in the immense cultural transformation which radiates out from philosophy.'

14. Jacques Derrida, *Of Grammatology*, trans. Gayatri Chakravorty Spivak (Baltimore: Johns Hopkins University Press, 1976), 282.

15. Edmund Husserl, *Ideas Pertaining to a Pure Phenomenology and a Phenomenological Philosophy, Second Book*, trans. Richard Rojcewicz and Andre Schuwer (The Hague: Kluwer Academic Publishers, 1993), 95.

16. Husserl, *The Crisis of European Sciences*, 6.

17. Husserl, 'Origin', 164–5. Author's emphasis.

18. Husserl, *The Crisis of European Sciences*, 7. Author's emphasis.

19. Husserl, 'Origin', 165.

20. Husserl, 'Origin', 166. See note.

21. Husserl, 'Origin', 165, 166 (note).

22. A designation I will not question here, but which is precisely at the heart of the problem of writing. As *Of Grammatology* shows, Saussure's insight concerning the arbitrariness of signs turns the sign into an opportunity for questions concerning nature and the institution.

23. Derrida, *Of Grammatology*, 92.

24. Husserl, 'Origin', 160.

25. See Derrida, 'Signature Event Context'.

26. Derrida, *Introduction*, 102.

27. Rodolphe Gasché, 'On Responding Responsibly', in *Inventions of Difference* (Cambridge MA: Harvard University Press, 1994), 232.

28. Gasché, 'On Responding Responsibly', 233.

29. Derrida, *Introduction*, 104.

30. ibid. Author's emphasis.

31. Derrida, *Of Grammatology*, 158. Author's emphasis.

32. ibid.

33. See Derrida, *Of Grammatology*, 65–9.

34. Derrida, *Introduction*, 92, note. Author's emphasis.

35. ibid., 93.

36. ibid., 96. Author's emphasis.

37. ibid., 99. Author's emphasis.
38. ibid., 149, 100.
39. ibid., 138.
40. ibid., 106.
41. ibid., 137–8.
42. ibid., 139.
43. ibid., 140. Author's emphasis.
44. ibid., 138. Author's emphasis.
45. ibid., 141. Author's emphasis.
46. Geoffrey Bennington, 'Deconstruction and the Philosophers', in *Legislations: The Politics of Deconstruction* (London: Verso, 1994), 41.
47. ibid.

8

Derridean Beginning and Deleuzian Becoming*

Paul Patton

Poststructuralist philosophers are especially fond of the paradoxes that surround the idea and the event of beginning, where this is understood as a singular, identifiable moment of transition from one situation or state of affairs to another: a moment ago this talk had not yet begun, now it has – or has it? One thinks of Foucault's anxiety about beginning his Inaugural Lecture at the Collège de France, in which he imagines himself slipping surreptitiously into a discourse that has already begun, so that 'there would be no beginning', and so that he would initiate nothing as he begins to speak of an intellectual project that he has already begun.[1] As though repeating Foucault's expression of a desire not to have to begin, Derrida often plays with the form of an address which defers its own commencement, for example by repeatedly announcing his intention to begin, as he does in his response to John Searle, or by pointing out, as he does in *Politics of Friendship*, that by beginning with a quotation he has not yet said anything, or at least said anything in his own name. These are all performative ways of problematizing our understanding of beginning as an identifiable moment in time at which 'something happens'.

But Derrida and Deleuze also provide conceptual challenges to the idea of an event, or a beginning, as a singular identifiable moment in time. Derrida, for example, in his discussion of the ghosts that haunt the opening scene of Shakespeare's *Hamlet* and the beginning of Marx and Engels' *Communist Manifesto*, reminds us that a beginning or a first time is only possible on the assumption that it will be followed by other times in the same series. As such, a beginning or first time anticipates its own repetition in the series of other times which make it a first time, even as its unique position in that series make it also a last time: 'Repetition *and* first time, but also repetition *and* last time, since the singularity of any *first time* makes of it also a last time'.[2] It is difficult not to hear in Derrida's comments an echo of the concept of differential repetition which Deleuze outlines in *Difference and Repetition*.[3]

More generally, a concern with 'the event' or with the nature and logic of events in general is a theme which is common to the work of both Derrida and Deleuze, as it is to other postructuralist philosophers. Derrida's 'spectral' analysis of events as a kind of insubstantial or virtual presence is antici-pated in Foucault's suggestion in *The Order of Discourse* that events do not belong to the order of bodies yet are not something immaterial either. They are rather a peculiar kind of being that needs to be understood in the para-doxical terms of a 'materialism of the incorporeal'. Both are anticipated in Deleuze's analysis of events in *The Logic of Sense*, where he draws upon the Stoic conception of events as incorporeal entities expressed in language and attributed to bodies and states of affairs. Derrida offers a similar account of particular events, such as the event of my signing a document, as the actu-alization or instantiation of what he calls 'the pure reproducibility of a pure event'.[4] My signature is itself a pure event which is not reducible to any par-ticular act or series of acts of signing. Understood in these terms, events are never present but always differential phenomena which participate in the iterable structure of writing or any other instituted trace. What makes a par-ticular occurrence an event of a certain kind is the fact that it actualizes an incorporeal or pure event. In this sense, for Derrida as for Deleuze, events involve a kind of incorporeal doubling of material occurrences in virtue of which they become events of a certain kind.

Similarities such as this between Deleuze and Derrida form part of the background of this chapter. I have long held the view that the appreciation of the philosophy of both of these philosophers of difference, of differen-tial repetition and iterability, would benefit from comparative study of their work, especially their early works published around 1968 and 1969: *Writing and Difference, Speech and Phenomena, Of Grammatology; The Logic of Sense* and *Difference and Repetition*. Such comparative study holds out the promise of a deeper understanding of their philosophical positions, freed from the con-straints of their idiosyncratic styles and particular vocabularies. However, what I want to focus on here are the parallel ways in which they compli-cate the idea of beginning by drawing out its connections with becoming, as this is expressed in their respective concepts of repetition and iterability. In addition, I want to show how this concept of becoming is developed in Deleuze and Guattari's overtly political concept of minoritarian becoming in *A Thousand Plateaus*. Finally, I want to test this concept of minoritarian becoming by reference to the particular kind of becoming-animal portrayed in J. M. Coetzee's novel *Disgrace*.

I suggested a moment ago that Derrida and Deleuze both seek to problema-tize the idea of an event, or a beginning, as a singular identifiable moment in time. When we think of beginnings as moments of rupture or decision in which something new emerges, what emerges always has the structure of an institution. Thus, in his essay 'Critique of Violence', and in relation to the institution of the law, Walter Benjamin distinguishes the founding violence that institutes and positions law ('law-making violence') from the violence that conserves and maintains the law ('law-preserving violence'). In 'Force of Law: the "Mystical Foundation of Authority"', Derrida deconstructs this distinction between an inaugural or founding moment and the subsequent moments in which what has begun is preserved or maintained, thereby undermining the basis of the understanding of beginning as a moment distinct from the institution or process which it inaugurates. The difference between the violence of foundation and the violence of conservation can be generalized to encompass any distinction between the acts or events of foundation of an institution and the acts or events through which it is maintained. It is an unsustainable difference, Derrida argues, in so far as any act or event of foundation or inauguration anticipates the conservation of what it founds: 'It belongs to the structure of fundamental violence that it calls for the repetition of itself and founds what ought to be conserved, conservable, promised to heritage and tradition, to be shared'. Conversely, 'conservation in its turn refounds, so that it can conserve what it claims to found'. As a result, there is no 'rigorous opposition' between foundation and conservation but only what Derrida calls a 'différentielle contamination' between the two.[5] Ultimately, it is the logic of iterability which ensures the mutual and differential contamination of acts of foundation and conservation by each other. For Derrida, the structure of events is that of the trace or the structure of iterability which he outlines in detail with respect to the institution of writing in general. It 'inscribes the possibility of repetition at the heart of the originary',[6] thereby threatening the rigour of the distinction between acts of foundation and those of conservation: 'Iterability requires the origin to repeat itself originarily, to alter itself so as to have the value of origin, that is to conserve itself [...] This iterability inscribes conservation in the essential structure of foundation'.[7]

Deleuze mounts another kind of challenge to the understanding of events as simple identifiable moments in time by developing an ontology of processes of becoming. The connection between his understanding of events and his ontology of becoming is most explicit in *The Logic of Sense*, where he appeals to the peculiar temporality of events in order to argue for a distinction between the ordinary historical time in which events occur (*Chronos*) and the time of the event itself (*Aion*) which is irreducible to the former time. Consider a time before the event and a time after: the infinite divisibility of the series of moments implies that there are two converging series on either side of the event, but no point in time at which these series meet. Thus, from the perspective of ordinary historical time, the event is 'eternally that which has just happened or that which is about to happen'.[8] This is not yet an argument for another kind of time or another dimension within time. In his discussion of Lewis Carroll in the first paragraph of *The Logic of Sense*, Deleuze offers a further argument which points to the paradoxical nature, from the perspective of ordinary time, of events themselves. When we say that Alice grew (she became taller) this implies that she became taller than she was before. By the same token, however, she also became shorter than she is now (assuming that she continued to grow). The realm of becoming thus admits contradictory predicates (becoming taller, becoming shorter) in a manner inconceivable within linear time. Although she is not taller and shorter at the same time, she becomes taller and shorter at the same time: 'this is the simultaneity of a becoming whose characteristic is to elude the present.'[9] It follows that events are coextensive with 'becomings'. Moreover, events have their own inner complexity and structure that are often imperceptible from the point of view of ordinary time.[10]

Derrida also draws attention to the paradoxical time of events. For example, in his discussion of the aporia of decision he points out that 'there is no moment at which a decision can be called presently and fully just',[11] since its justice depends on both its relation to prior rules and protocols and on it not being simply the application of such rules. If the decision has already been taken, then if it is a just decision it has followed or reinvented a rule and is therefore no longer presently or fully just. If the decision has not yet been taken we cannot say whether or not it conforms to any rule, or whether it is arbitrary, and so we cannot call it just either. Derrida's point is that it is only the decision that is just or unjust, and the moment of decision is an evanescent point which cannot be identified within the linear temporal order of experience. A just decision therefore has the temporal structure of the future anterior: it will have been just. The moment of decision or justice, like the moment of foundation or inauguration, 'always takes place and never takes place in a presence'.[12]

This paradox with regard to the justice of a decision is itself only a special case of the paradox with regard to the temporality of a decision or indeed any event: at what moment does the event take place? Its occurrence, like its justice, is eternally either in the future or in the past. A decision, like any other event, involves what Derrida calls here 'the undecidable', the moment or event of decision which cannot be captured within the order of the calculable or the linear time of experience but which remains 'caught, lodged, at least as a ghost – but an essential ghost – in every decision, in every event of decision'.[13] Derrida's 'undecidable', like the figure of aporia of the 'experience of the impossible' which bears the burden of his affirmative deconstructive analyses of invention, justice, hospitality and forgiveness, resembles Deleuze's concept of the event. This experience of the undecidable is also an experience of the event, or an experience of that which is necessary in order for there to be an event. Derrida's distinction between particular occurrences and the 'pure reproducibility of the pure event' is mirrored in Deleuze and Guattari's distinction between historical events as these are incarnated in bodies and states of affairs and pure events or incorporeal becomings which are only imperfectly actualized in the linear time of history: 'what History grasps of the event is its effectuation in states of affairs or in lived experience, but the event in its becoming, in its specific consistency, in its self-positing concept, escapes History.'[14]

Consider the phenomenon of colonization as an example of an event which exhibits the kind of internal structure attributed to events by Deleuze, and as an institution which exhibits the kind of differential contamination described by Derrida. The colonization of an already inhabited country is a very particular kind of beginning. Considered as an isolated act occurring at a singular moment in time, such as the proclamation, in 1788, on a coastal outcrop off the northern tip of Cape York, of the sovereignty of British Crown over half the continent of Australia, such an event is absurd. Like the Declaration of Independence, it only makes sense and draws what legitimacy it has in anticipation of the process and the institution which follows. In the colonial case, this is the process of settlement which brings with it a multitude of ways in which the founding act of the imposition of a new sovereign is repeated and reinforced by the imposition of a new law, new culture and new forms of government on the territory and its indigenous inhabitants. The subsequent policies and actions of colonial governors, magistrates, police and the settlers under their protection reproduce and reinforce the initial act of foundation. The policies of 'aboriginal protection' and assimilation lead to the marginalization, disempowerment and incarceration of much of the indigenous population. They continue the work of colonization which was only nominally carried out by the initial acts of settlement and the assertion of sovereignty. Understood in this manner, change is never as abrupt or as assured as is suggested by the concept of singular beginning. Partial decolonization may occur, but a colonial society is a complex system of institutional, discursive and affective relations which cannot easily be removed.

None of this precludes the possibility of resistance, both internal and external, to such colonial regimes. On the contrary, the fact that the violence of colonization is institutionalized in the form of law means that the colonial institutions themselves are open to reinvestment by other forces and reintepretation to other ends. This is what enables institutions such as the law to be transformed even as they are maintained and reproduced. I suggested earlier that, for Derrida, it is the structure of iterability that undermines any absolute distinction between foundation and conservation in favour of regarding these as differential moments of an ongoing process of repetition and alteration. We should not forget that, at the same time, iterability also inscribes foundation in the essential structure of conservation. Although in his discussion of Benjamin in 'Force of Law' Derrida draws on one side of the logic of iterability in order to point out the contamination of foundation by conservation, in other contexts he is no less concerned to deploy the logic of iterability to point out the contamination of conservation by foundation. Iterability implies not only the repetition or refounding of what was established but also the possibility of its alteration. The possibility of separating a mark or trace from any given context and its repetition in a new context implies new possibilities for interpretation. Writing, for example, is both the permanent possibility of communication of meaning but also the impossibility of stable or secure communication, at least of a single meaning. The other side of the logic of iterability therefore implies the possibility of transformation, proliferation and dissemination alongside that of conservation.[15]

In *A Thousand Plateaus*, Deleuze and Guattari describe a similar process of 'continual variation' or deterritorialization in which novelty emerges in the course of the repetition of established acts and events under different circumstances or in different contexts. This monumental work develops another version of Deleuze's ontology of becoming in the form of a theory of machinic assemblages, where these are defined not by their forms of conservation but by their forms of modification or metamorphosis, by their 'cutting edges of deterritorialization'.[16] Ultimately, these assemblages or abstract machines are a kind of open or evolving multiplicity which is itself a process of becoming other: 'becoming and multiplicity are the same thing.'[17] In these terms, Deleuze and Guattari argue that societies are defined by their lines of flight or deterritorialization, by which they mean that there is no society that is not conserving or maintaining itself on one level, while simultaneously being transformed into something else on another level. In other words, fundamental social change happens all the time. Sometimes it happens by degrees, as we have seen with the steady erosion of myths and prejudices about sexual difference and its implications for social and political institutions under the impact of feminism thoughout the twentieth century. But sometimes fundamental social change occurs through the sudden eruption of events which inaugurate a new field of social, political or legal possibilities. These are turning points in history after which some things will never be the same as before, but they are not necessarily violent or bloody events. They are examples, Deleuze suggests, of 'a becoming breaking through into history'.[18]

An example of an historical event of this kind, which I discuss in *Deleuze and the Political*, is the emergence, in a series of decisions by superior courts, of a body of law which recognizes and protects a form of Aboriginal or native title to land in common law countries such as Australia or Canada. In the final chapter of the book, I suggest that the emergence of native title jurisprudence amounts to a transformation of the institutional form of the colonial capture of native land, in so far as it undermines the legal doctrine of terra nullius and its consequences for the law of property within each jurisdiction. I also suggest that the emergence of this body of law might usefully be understood as a process of deterritorialization, with all the potential and all the dangers identified by Deleuze and Guattari's analysis of deterritorialization. Everything depends on the kinds of deterritorialization and reterritorialization at work in a given context. At the end of *A Thousand Plateaus*, Deleuze and Guattari outline a normative typology of processes of deterritorialization which distinguishes a number of distinct types. First, deterritorialization is either relative or absolute. It is relative in so far as it concerns only movements within the actual – as opposed to the virtual – order of things. Deterritorialization is absolute in so far as it concerns the virtual – as opposed to the actual – order of things. Absolute deterritorialization is not a further stage that comes after relative deterritorialization. It is an order of things which is manifest only in and through relative deterritorialization, but an order in which things are in a state of becoming. It is a qualitatively different order of being which is both immanent and transcendent to the actual order of relative deterritorialization and reterritorialization. Second, relative deterriorialization can take either a negative or a positive form. It is negative when the deterritorialized element is immediately subjected to forms of reterritorialization which enclose or obstruct its line of flight. It is positive when the line of flight prevails over secondary reterritorializations and above all when deterritorialized elements reconnect in mutually supportive and productive ways. In this sense, Deleuze and Guattari suggest absolute deterritorialization will be expressed in positive form when there is construction of 'revolutionary connections' between different kinds of deterritorialized element or between different processes of deterritorialization.[19]

To return to the issue of comparison between Deleuze and Derrida, there are a number of similarities at this point between the respective ways in which they conceive of events and the possibility of change on the basis of a logic or an ontology of becoming. In *Deconstruction in a Nutshell*, John Caputo aptly comments that deconstruction is not conventionalist but 'inventionalist' in the sense that it is 'interested in the new, unpredictable, unforeseeable, unprogrammable "effects" that are forth-coming, incoming, in-ventable within a currently prevailing set of conventions'.[20] For Derrida, it is the undecidability which inhabits every event that in turn guarantees the deconstructibility of present institutions and the permanent possibility of fundamental change. And it is the iterability of all institutions that sustains Derrida's insistence on the permanent possibility of the deconstruction of existing states of affairs, or his insistence that deconstruction can assist in opening up the present in order to 'let the other come'. This deconstructive 'invention' of the future, however, is not invention in the ordinary sense since it concerns the advent of the absolute or entirely other. This is of course an impossible task, which is why the affirmative gesture of deconstruction 'can consist only in opening, uncloseting, destabilizing foreclusionary structures so as to allow for the passage towards the other'.[21]

In a kind of distant proximity with Deleuze and Guattari's distinction between absolute and relative deterritorialization, Derrida distinguishes between a relative and an absolute future, where the latter is the future which remains irreducible 'to-come' (*à-venir*). In a manner which parallels Deleuze and Guattari's suggestion that there is 'a perpetual immanence of absolute deterritorialization within relative deterritorialization',[22] this absolute other and absolute future are at once both transcendent and immanent conditions of things becoming other than they are.[23] Deleuze and Guattari's characterization in *What is Philosophy?* of the events that are expressed in philosophical concepts as the contour of events 'to come' is mirrored by Derrida's concept of the 'to come' as 'the space opened in order for there to be an event, the to-come, so that the coming be that of the other'.[24] Finally, just as for Deleuze and Guattari, absolute deterritorialization contributes to the creation of 'a new earth and a new people', so the kind of invention which concerns deconstruction is not the work of 'the identifiable "we" of a community of human subjects'. Rather it is the invention of another 'we' which is only constituted as such by the advent of something other, an invention of another world 'which invents *us*'.[25]

None of these formulae tell us much about the conditions under which fundamental change can occur. The texts of Deleuze and Guattari and those of Derrida both provide a set of formal criteria, but little in the way of content which might enable judgement in particular situations. Up to this point, I have pointed to the similarities between the Deleuzian and Derridean understandings of events in terms of becoming. At this point, however, a significant difference between them emerges with respect to the peculiar 'inventionalism' of Deleuze and Guattari's project. As they specify in *What is Philosophy?*, their conception and practice of philosophy is that of a process of inventing concepts, and in *A Thousand Plateaus* they invent a great many concepts, including a politically charged concept of becoming. In general terms, Deleuze and Guattari understand by 'becoming' precisely what Derrida understands by the process of iteration, namely 'the action by which something or someone continues to become other (while continuing to be what it is)'.[26] But whereas Derrida does not go beyond the analysis of particular structures of iterability and the to-come which remain an immanent transcendent condition of the possibility (and impossibility) of change, Deleuze and Guattari proceed to describe a series of more specific ways in which something or someone becomes other. In *A Thousand Plateaus*, the becomings which interest them are not simply becomings-other but minoritarian becomings. The concept of becoming is therefore intimately linked to the concept of the minoritarian, and through this to the processes of deterritorialization which define a given qualitative multiplicity. They distinguish between minorities conceived as subsystems or determinate elements within a given majority and the process of becoming minor or minoritarian which refers to the potential of every element to deviate from the standard or norm which defines that majority. In these terms, to become-minoritarian is to embark upon a process of deterritorialization or divergence from the norm, while at the same time there is no such thing as becoming-majoritarian: 'all becoming is minoritarian'.[27]

In other words, for Deleuze and Guattari the important question becomes that of the conditions under which minoritarian becoming occurs. What kinds of becoming are capable of sustaining an absolute line of flight? In relation to what other elements or agencies does deterritorialization become absolute and positive? In so far as the subject of modern European society and political community, the subject of rights, duties and moral obligations, is human, adult and overwhelmingly masculine and white, then animals, children, women and people of colour are minorities, and as a result becoming-animal, becoming-child, becoming-woman and becoming-coloured or becoming-indigenous are potential paths of deterritorialization of the majority. For example, we learn from anthropology, myth and folktales that human beings have propensities for a variety of becomings-animal. These are not a matter of literally becoming the animal, Deleuze and Guattari suggest, but rather of enhancing the powers one has or acquiring new powers by entering into a proximity to the animal. It is question of forming a trans-individual assemblage with the real or imagined powers of the animal in question. They point out that, from an historical point of view, these processes of becoming-animal are usually related to marginal social groups or movements, so that there is 'an entire politics of becomings-animal, as well as a politics of sorcery, which is elaborated in assemblages that are neither those of the family nor of religion nor of the State. Instead they express minoritarian groups, or groups that are oppressed, prohibited, in revolt, or always on the fringe of recognized institutions...'.[28]

An important feature of these minoritarian becomings-animal is that they always involve a relation to a pack or multiplicity of some kind, and to an anomalous figure who stands not only on the border of the multiplicity in question, but who represents a limit beyond which everything changes. Melville's *Moby-Dick* provides an example of such a becoming-animal. Ahab's becoming is a line of flight which takes him beyond life itself. The white whale stands for all those figures with whom we enter into a pact in order to pass beyond a given state of life or being. He is an anomalous figure in the sense that he represents 'the unequal, the coarse, the rough, the cutting edge of deterritorialization'.[29] Through his relentless pursuit of the white whale, Ahab enters into a becoming-whale while at the same time the object of his pursuit becomes the white wall of human weakness and finitude through which he desires to pass: 'How can the prisoner reach outside except by thrusting through the wall? To me, the white whale is that wall, shoved near to me. Sometimes I think there's naught beyond. But 'tis enough'.[30]

Ultimately, Deleuze and Guattari's practice of philosophical invention must be judged by reference to the particular concepts that they have invented (although perhaps not only by these concepts). The pragmatism of their conception of philosophy must be taken seriously, which implies that the only appropriate test of the concepts they invent consists in attempting to make them function in new contexts. For this reason, and for the remainder of this chapter, I propose to examine the usefulness of their approach to the politics and process of becoming in relation to another textual test case, J. M. Coetzee's 1999 Booker Prize-winning novel, *Disgrace*. This is a particularly good terrain on which to test these concepts because of the ways in which the history and current transformation of South Africa in the post-apartheid era are implicated in the events and the lives of the characters. The dismantling of the apartheid regime is another example of an historical event which might be understood in Deleuzian terms as the deterritorialization of a system of colonial capture, and the novel shows clearly how the institutional forms of this system are deeply embedded in the social, linguistic and psychic structures of South African social life. It is not obvious how iteration can lead to alteration in this case, or by what means inherited structures of temperament and language can be transformed. But in Coetzee's novel the beginnings of transformation unfold in a manner consistent with the Deleuzian concept of becoming because of the role played by a form of becoming-animal in the lives of its central characters.

The novel tells the story of David Lurie, an aging male professor of English literature who enters into an abusive sexual relationship with a young student. He is subsequently charged and found guilty of sexual harassment; however, he refuses any form of contrition or apology and is eventually forced to resign from the university. He goes to visit his daughter Lucy who lives on a small farm in the country where she makes a modest living growing produce and flowers and operating a boarding kennel for guard dogs used by the beneficiaries of the colonial regime: 'Dobermanns, German Shepherds, ridgebacks, bull terriers, Rottweilers. Watchdogs, all of them, she says.'[31] David Lurie helps out with the dogs, and later works at an animal refuge where he helps another woman, Bev Shaw, to dispose of unwanted strays. The dogs are animals out of place in the new South Africa just as he is out of place in the new university and in the new social relations emerging between men and women, white and black. He begins to care for the unwanted and abandoned former guard dogs of the apartheid regime out of sympathy: he and they are both part of the debris of history. The novel ends with his sacrifice of a young partly crippled dog for which he has developed a particular fondness. But through this series of affective alliances with animals (including two sheep), he regains a capacity to love and care for others, including the daughter he does not understand. In this sense, it is plausible to suggest that he embarks upon a becoming-animal which is also a form of minoritarian becoming in Deleuze and Guattari's sense of the term, a line of flight or deterritorialization along which this particular majoritarian subject begins to change.

Or so it seems. There is much in the novel which presents a bleak picture of social relations in the new South Africa and some commentators take a more critical view. David Lurie is in many ways an unredeemed character who remains unrepentant about his rape of the student, uncomprehending of the social changes taking place around him and unwilling to change. He often fails to comprehend the motive of others, especially those of his student and his daughter, and those of Lucy's African neighbour and sometime helper Petrus. Salman Rushdie, in a widely circulated review of *Disgrace*, takes the mutual incomprehension of the characters in the novel to encapsulate its vision of post-apartheid politics: 'The whites don't understand the blacks and the blacks aren't interested in understanding the whites [...] Petrus comes closest, but his motives remain enigmatic and his presence grows more menacing as the novel proceeds.'[32] Through incidents such as the attack on Lucy's farm in which she is raped and David is set alight, through the transformation of her African neighbour Petrus from 'dog-man' to farmer and landowner, it can be argued that Coetzee depicts a South Africa in which the roles of white and black are simply reversed rather than transformed. A rearrangement of positions rather than a genuine deterritorialization of oppressive social relations takes place. On this reading, there is no minoritarian becoming and no new beginning. I believe it underestimates the amount of change which is portrayed in the central characters.

David Lurie is no doubt a character in full deterritorialization mode as his personal, social, professional and intellectual world collapses around him. He is in every respect a figure of the old world who no longer fits in. But, in Deleuzian terms, and in relation to the historical and political changes occurring around him, his story appears to be one of *negative* rather than positive deterritorialization. He has no place in the society slowly and painfully emerging from the ruins of apartheid and accordingly, at the end of the novel, spends most of his time with the stray dogs while remaining a spectator to the changes in the lives of his daughter and others actively engaged in the coming-to-be of the new South Africa.

Yet if David Lurie's story is indeed a story of disempowerment and disgrace, it is not only that. It is also the story of a man coming to terms with ageing and with the approach of his own death. Bev Shaw, the woman who administers death to the dogs, says to him at one point: 'I don't think we are ready to die, any of us, not without being escorted.'[33] His role with the dogs in this refuge of last resort is precisely that of escort and what he shares with them is disgrace, in particular what Coetzee describes as 'the disgrace of dying'.[34] It is this disgrace which forms the zone of indiscernibility in which he becomes-animal. It is a disgrace more threatening than the one associated with his dismissal from the university and the social death associated with that event which sets him on the path of deterritorialization. It is true that there is only minoritarian-becoming in the Deleuzian sense if there is some movement or transformation in the assemblage concerned. In the end, despite his repeated protestations that he is too old to learn new tricks, Lurie does become a different person. He learns to accept his daughter's independence and her right to make choices in relation to her own life in the new South Africa, choices of which he would be incapable (she chooses to stay when he offers her the possibility of flight to Holland). At the end, in the act of giving up his favoured dog, he learns to accept the inevitability of death and the finitude of life, 'the only life there is. Which we share with animals'.[35] This is a thoroughly secular novel in which Lurie learns to live with disgrace as 'a way of being'. He thereby finds a form of ironic redemption from the 'disgrace' of dying by accepting life itself as a state of disgrace.

Moreover, Coetzee's novel offers other stories about the affective and social transformations under way in South Africa besides that of David Lurie. There are in fact several different kinds of disgrace in the novel, all of them associated with different kinds of becoming-dog. As well as Lurie's social disgrace and the disgrace of dying which he shares with the dogs at the refuge, there is the disgrace of his daughter at the hands of her African attackers and her own becoming-dog in response to the attack and the danger of continuing to live alone in the country. She chooses not to speak to the police about her rape, she chooses to stay rather than leave, she accepts the transformation in her relations with Petrus – the former helper and 'dog man' become neighbour, landowner and patriarch. Her response to the attack on her is to accept that in the end she will have to rely on the protection of Petrus rather than the police or the armed white neighbour. She will surrender her land in exchange for a place within his extended family and accept what her father can only perceive as humiliation: 'Perhaps that is what I must learn to accept. To start at ground level. With nothing. Not with nothing but. With nothing. No cards, no weapons, no property, no rights, no dignity.' 'Like a dog.' 'Yes, like a dog.'[36]

Throughout the novel, Lucy is far more conscious of the historical changes under way than her father, and far more deliberate in her responses to them: 'forward looking'[37] as Petrus describes her. If anything in the novel points toward the possibility of a positive deterritorialization of the old social and affective structures of the apartheid era, it is Lucy's willingness to embark upon a becoming-African by transferring her land to Petrus and eventually accepting his protection. There are undoubtedly further issues raised by the fact that Coetzee chooses to represent the beginnings of the micropolitical dismantling of apartheid through the story of this woman (and indeed by the bleak treatment of relations between men and women throughout the novel). But let me conclude by commenting on two features of the novel which accord with Deleuze and Guattari's concept of minoritarian becoming. First, becoming is always complex and tends to occur in combination with other processes which form a 'bloc' of becoming. Thus, David Lurie's becoming-animal is bound up with an increasingly critical awareness of his masculinity and a corresponding movement of becoming-woman as he acquires new levels of sensitivity toward others, learns to cry, and so on. At the same time, his becoming-animal and becoming-woman is bound up with Lucy's becoming-African. Second, as we saw in the example of Melville's Ahab, becomings typically take place in relation to some form of qualitative multiplicity and are mediated by an anomalous figure at the border of the multiplicity who represents the threshold of absolute deterritorialization.

In *Disgrace*, it is Petrus who plays this role in relation to Lucy's becoming-African. We are only given glimpses of Petrus's own story and then largely through the eyes of his white interlocutors. African people and social relations are mysterious, sometimes threatening, but always other. But Petrus is the sole point of ethical contact between Lucy and her father and the largely undifferentiated indigenous African population. It is through her relationship to Petrus and her refusal to dictate the terms of this relation or to give it up after the attack on her that Lucy's becoming-dog is bound up with her becoming-African. Hers is a painful but also a more positive micropolitical story of the deterritorialization of the social relations which were both products and supports of the colonial regime. The kind of becoming-African which it portrays is not and cannot be the kind of new beginning which breaks suddenly and completely from the past, but is perhaps the only possible form of transition to a truly post-colonial society.

Notes

*This chapter is based on the author's 'Becoming Animal and Pure Life in Coetzee's *Disgrace*', *Ariel: A Review of English Literature*, 35: 1–2, 2006.

1. Michel Foucault, 'The Order of Discourse', in *Language and Politics*, ed. Michael J. Shapiro, trans. Ian McLeod (Oxford: Blackwell, 1984), 108.
2. Jacques Derrida, *Specters of Marx*, trans. Peggy Kamuf (London and New York: Routledge, 1994), 10.
3. At the beginning of this book, he suggests that repetition should not be understood in terms of a series of interchangeable or equivalent phenomena but rather in terms of the recurrence of a unique or singular phenomenon which has no equivalent. In this sense, following Péguy, he suggests that, in a celebration or commemoration such as Bastille Day, it is not the subsequent occasions which commemorate or represent the fall of the Bastille, but the fall of the Bastille which celebrates and repeats in advance all the Bastille Days. Gilles Deleuze, *Difference and Repetition*, trans. Paul Patton (London and New York: Continuum, 1994), 1.
4. Jacques Derrida, 'Signature Event Context', in *Margins of Philosophy*, trans. Alan Bass (Chicago: University of Chicago Press, 1981), 328.
5. Derrida, 'Force of Law: the "Mystical Foundation of Authority"', in Drucilla Cornell, Michael Rosenfeld and David Gray Carlson (eds), *Deconstruction and the Possibility of Justice* (London and New York: Routledge, 1993), 38.
6. Derrida, 'Force of Law', 38.
7. ibid., 43.
8. Gilles Deleuze, *The Logic of Sense* (London: Continuum, 1990), 8.
9. ibid., 1.
10. Deleuze cites the following passage from Péguy's *Clio*: 'Suddenly, we felt that we were no longer the same convicts. Nothing had happened. Yet a problem in which a whole world collided, a problem without issue, in which no end could be seen, suddenly ceased to exist and we asked ourselves what we had been talking about. Instead of an ordinary solution, a found solution, this problem, this difficulty, this impossibility had just passed what seemed like a physical point of resolution. A crisis point. At the same time, the whole world had passed what seemed like a physical crisis point. There are critical points of the event just as there

are critical points of temperature: points of fusion, freezing and boiling points, points of coagulation and crystallization. There are even in the case of events states of superfusion which are precipitated, crystallized or determined only by the introduction of a fragment of some future event' (Deleuze, *Difference and Repetition*, 189).

11. Derrida, 'Force of Law', 24.
12. ibid., 36.
13. ibid., 24.
14. Gilles Deleuze and Félix Guattari, *What is Philosophy?*, trans. Graham Burchill and Hugh Tomlinson (London: Verso, 1994), 110.
15. It is this dimension of iterability which enables Judith Butler to see the performativity of gender as a condition of possible transformation as well as conservation: 'it is also by virtue of this reiteration that gaps and fissures are opened up as the constitutive instabilities in such constructions, as that which cannot be wholly defined or fixed by the repetitive labor of that norm. This instability is the deconstituting possibility in the very process of repetition...' Butler, *Bodies That Matter: On the Discursive Limits of 'Sex'* (London and New York: Routledge, 1993), 10.
16. Gilles Deleuze and Félix Guattari, *A Thousand Plateaus* (London: Continuum, 1988), 88.
17. ibid., 249.
18. Gilles Deleuze, *Negotiations 1972–1990*, trans. Martin Joughin (New York: Columbia University Press, 1995), 153.
19. Deleuze and Guattari, *A Thousand Plateaus*, 473.
20. John Caputo, *Deconstruction in a Nutshell: Conversation with Jacques Derrida* (New York: Fordham University Press, 1996), 103.
21. Jacques Derrida, 'Politics and Friendship', in *Negotiations 1972–1990*, 182.
22. Deleuze and Guattari, *A Thousand Plateaus*, 56.
23. Compare Derrida's analysis of the immanent transcendence of the law in Kafka's 'Before the Law': 'the inaccessible transcendence of the law before which and prior to which "man" stands fast only appears infinitely transcendent and thus theological to the extent that, so near to him, it depends only on him, on the performative act by which he institutes it... the law is transcendent and theological, and so always to come, always promised, because it is immanent, finite and so already past' (Derrida, 'Force of Law', 36).
24. Jacques Derrida, *Politics of Friendship*, trans. George Collins (London: Verso, 1997), 216.
25. *Psyché*, 342.
26. Deleuze and Guattari, *What is Philosophy?*, 177 (translation modified).
27. Deleuze and Guattari, *A Thousand Plateaus*, 106, 291.
28. ibid., 247.
29. ibid., 244.
30. Herman Melville, *Moby-Dick* (Standard edition, London, 1922–1924), 167.
31. J. M. Coetzee, *Disgrace* (London: Vintage, 2000), 61.
32. Salman Rushdie, 'Light on Coetzee', *Sydney Morning Herald*, 6 October 2000, A7ff. Reprinted in Salman Rushdie, *Step Across This Line: Collected Nonfiction 1992–2002* (New York: Random House, 2002), 297–8.
33. Coetzee, *Disgrace*, 84.
34. ibid., 143.
35. ibid., 74.
36. ibid., 205.
37. ibid., 136.

9
'Words of Air': On Breath and Inspiration[1]

Claudia Baracchi

> I begin with words of air, but pleasant to hear.
>
> *Sappho, fragment 1a*[2]

> You see, I really do not myself know, yet, but wherever the discourse, like a wind, tends, there we must go.
>
> *Plato*, Republic, *394d*

The present essay is oriented to and by concerns that, while no doubt interwoven, may be clearly discerned and enumerated:

1) First among them is the question of divine inspiration which, in this context, is transfigured and addressed in its environmental dimension. In other words, divine inspiration comes literally to mean 'environmental inspiration'. Intimated here is the insufficiency of all reflection on the divine and the natural which would fail to interrogate these categories precisely in their convergence and concurrence, indeed, in their being (at) one. Not less importantly, the discussion of inspiration by reference to the environment or *physis* announces a thinking of the environmental which, far from being a matter of 'applied philosophy', requires the careful reconfiguration of fundamental metaphysical (or, to be more precise, *radically physical*) categories.

The reading of Plato's *Phaedrus* here proposed progressively illuminates the commonality (the universality, if you wish) of body, materiality, or what will have been called the elemental. Accordingly, the physical or elemental comes to be thought as condition – not only the human condition, but the condition of all that is, moves and lives in its being, moving and living. (The question whether or not to consider such condition transcendental is secondary and subordinated to the comprehension of condition in elemental terms.) The element of air and the concomitant dynamics of respiration, inspiration, osmotic exchange and interpenetration appear to be particularly crucial in the unfolding of the dialogue. Air, that which is shared in common, which crosses boundaries, permeates and gathers, which grants communication as well as circulation, ends up being revealed as the unifying element of this allegedly fragmented text. For, indeed, it is the medium of the propagation of *eros* as well as *logos*, of love as well as discursive articulation. Hence, it provides cohesiveness (however evanescent) to a conversation ranging from the mystery of desire to the analysis of rhetoric and writing.[3]

2) The theme of inspiration, in its divine or elemental character, necessarily raises further questions concerning the status of inspired utterance, that is to say, in this case, of philosophical discourse itself. This approach to the *Phaedrus* should be complemented by reference to other Platonic dialogues, most notably *Ion*, where the poet is said to be 'a light and winged thing' (534b). Indeed, in light of the phenomenon of inspiration, the connection should be explored between the figures of the philosopher, of the poet, and of the diviner who, while irreducible to one another, appear to be moved and sustained in their comportment by *theia moira*, divine gift or allotment.[4] Poetic singing and intellectual articulation similarly stem from an undergoing, a 'divine *pathos*' (*Phaedrus* 238c). It is also worth recalling, if only because of the ubiquitous references to the art of medicine in the *Phaedrus*, that in the Hippocratic *corpus* thinking is crucially associated with air and the respiratory function.[5]

3) The themes introduced so far finally point to a third, central question, that is, the question of the subject or, more precisely, of the speaking and writing subject. In the *Phaedrus* one witnesses the emergence and articulation of *something like* a subject. It is important to be cautious with the language of subjectivity, for what emerges here should rather be called a *configuration of singularity*, which, unlike the modern subject, is neither purely active nor free, but crucially marked by passivity. One observes such a configuration unfolding in an osmotic relation with the environment; the individual is *animated by the surrounding*. One is therefore led to wonder about the physical-physiological (*physis*-related) origin of utterances, to hear them as responses to what is breathed in, as originary translations or repetitions of what is taken in. Words may not originate 'within'. Indeed, the demarcation between interiority (subjective inwardness) and exteriority (environing nature) presents itself as ultimately improbable. The singular shines forth as a figure, an appearance, as the play and ethereal glow of surfaces – as a resounding apparition scribing itself upon and as the sensuous.

Taken up in this way, the *Phaedrus* clearly offers more than a few occasions to discern broader ramifications in the Platonic *corpus* and to reconsider, maybe even twist free of, various 'articles of faith' still prevalent in Platonic interpretation and yet, in the final analysis, unwarranted. It also lends itself to a dialogue with contemporary discourses which proves more surprising than one is usually ready to acknowledge.

Lest its scope appear disproportionately ambitious, I should point out that the reading here delineated undertakes to address the above concerns and systematic issues in a most preliminary fashion and often by indirection. What is at stake here is beginning to disclose the possibility of reading Plato in an altogether other register and *simultaneously* to hear the Platonic text elaborate on questions that haunt and besiege us, today, with undiminished vitality and increasing urgency. Such an inceptive reading and such a hearing manifestly implicate each other. The point is therefore not so much, or not simply, approaching the Platonic text according to a contemporary sensibility or 'style', but rather receiving the Platonic text as never exhausted and archived, as exquisitely contemporary in its preoccupations – indeed, as yet to come. The present essay should be seen as an attempt, however merely preparatory, at exploring this temporal chiasm that simultaneously hinges upon and constitutes us.

*   *   *

As is well known, near the threshold of Plato's *Phaedrus* one finds a reference to the Delphic inscription (*gramma*): know thyself. Socrates, walking on the countryside with Phaedrus (Athens already behind them), says that it is this knowledge that he is pursuing and not yet able to grasp (229e–230a). The dialogue ends with the equally well-known critique of writing – a critique based on the contraposition of the practice of writing to vocal articulation, to the occurrence of vocalization in the immediacy of its living presence, in its ability to respond and correspond to circumstance. What follows is an attempt at illuminating the connection between the 'garden of letters [*en grammasi*]', concerning which Socrates manifests evident hesitation, and the emergence of the subject: a subject perplexed about itself in its very constitution, coming to itself as an enigma, in fact constituted precisely in broaching the question concerning itself; a subject, furthermore (let this be anticipated), surfacing not quite as an individual, as *individuum*, but quite divisible, indeed, dispersed and airy, speaking in and as many voices.

It should be noticed already that Socrates' position with respect to writing may not be reduced to simple condemnation. After all, writing is already essentially implicated in the possibility of the Apollonian prescription itself, which, far from resounding without any further mediation, presents itself through written letter, indeed, *as* written letter. Thus, it will be necessary to consider more closely the Socratic critique, to delimit and clarify its context, to show it in its crucially strategic function.

*   *   *

Towards the end of the dialogue, Socrates examines the *praxis* of writing by reference to an ancient story, a story he heard and offers to tell, though only the predecessors would know if it happens to be true (274c). Socrates begins to narrate as though letting the voices of the predecessors speak through him; and yet, it is precisely in the loss of such voices, in the irretrievability of their truth, that Socrates speaks. In a certain sense, the story is told for the first time ('Socrates, you easily make up stories about the Egyptians or anyone else you will,' remarks Phaedrus after listening [275b]).[6]

According to the *logos*, Theuth, the Egyptian god, invented the written letters (*grammata*). Such an invention, however, far from healing and sharpening memory, poisons it. Such is the logic of the *pharmakon*. Initiated to the practice of writing, the many will entrust to external evidence what they should, instead, retain in and by themselves. Therefore, they will progressively be invaded by oblivion, their interiority becoming a hollow, barren receptacle. What should live in the *psychê* (the aliveness and wakefulness of the *psychê* in its vitality) is released into the written letter and here comes to die. At most, Plato makes Socrates say, what is written may serve as a reminder, recalling for those who know what they already know. However, the written discourse in no way replaces the teaching that may occur only through the involvement and reciprocal commitment of teacher and student, through the provocation inherent in dialogue or, in general, in conversation.

The written text knows neither how to speak nor how to be silent, cannot tell when it may be opportune, worthwhile or appropriate to share and when not. Furthermore, it does not know how to respond to the specific demands of a given context – it disseminates itself indiscriminately, indifferently. If interrogated in the absence of the paternal authority of the author, the written discourse replies always in the same way, repeating itself, bound to the ineluctability of quotation. Developing the implications of this remarkable hermeneutical caricature, Socrates affirms that the one who knows, 'when he is serious [*spoudêi*]', does not write what he knows 'in ink, using a pen to sow speeches that are unable to defend themselves in speech and unable to teach the truth effectively'. Rather, the one who knows

> will sow his gardens of letters for amusement, it seems, and will write, when he does write, to store up reminders for himself, and for all who follow in the same track, against the forgetfulness [*lêthê*] that may come with old age, and he'll enjoy watching their tender shoots grow. While others resort to other kinds of play, refreshing themselves with drinking parties and whatever is related to these, this person, it seems, instead of indulging in these kinds of play, will engage in those I'm speaking of (276c–d).

Socrates will insist further on this point, emphasizing 'that there is necessarily a lot that's playful in a written speech on any topic, and that no speech whether in verse or in prose has ever been written that is worthy of much serious consideration' (277e). We read these words attributed to Socrates, and in so doing we find ourselves smiling, for it almost seems to us to catch a glimpse, between the lines (in the midst of those signs declared to be inert matter), of the smile of Plato himself – of Plato spending his days playing, that is to say, writing and simultaneously undermining the seriousness of his endeavour. But let us, for the moment, postpone these observations.

Such concluding remarks on writing are anything but surprising. They had been announced and rigorously pursued from the beginning of the dialogue. The text, let it be briefly recalled, opens with Phaedrus who, thanks to the promise of a discourse written by Lysias on love, attracts Socrates outside the city walls. In reading the written speech to Socrates, Phaedrus will expect to stir up wonder and admiration in him. It is the discourse of a man attempting to win the favours of a boy, by presenting himself not in the name of love, but as a partner advantageous and reliable precisely because not in love, free from the delirious sickness of desire and hence fully self-possessed, in control of his own faculties.

To articulate this thesis convincingly would indeed seem to require the skills of a great sophist. Lysias' gifts will, however, fail to conquer Socrates. The latter, who repeatedly describes himself in erotic terms (in terms of desire and rapture), appears bewildered already in hearing Phaedrus announce Lysias' position, according to which one should accord one's favours to someone who is not in love. This is Socrates' immediate reply:

O, the noble one! If only he would write that one should gratify someone poor rather than rich, and older rather than younger, and so on for the many other things that are characteristic of me and of most of us. Then his speeches would indeed be urbane and beneficial to the general public (227c–d).

From this point on, even before Lysias' text is read, Socrates manifestly endeavours to subvert the logic informing rhetorical-sophistical production, to undo such logic by calling into question its constitutive elements.

Among the essential aspects of the sophistical *ethos* must be recognized, first of all, a view of writing in merely technical-instrumental terms. Secondly, in connection with this one should notice the denial of discourse as an embodied and temporal practice that belongs in the unfolding of the world; rather, discourse comes to be understood as composed (written, in fact) in a protected isolation, aside from the engagement with the surroundings; such a discourse will only later on find a connection with (impose itself on) the environment, coming into the world, as it were, from the outside (by being read, reproduced).[7] As Phaedrus readily observes, the expedient of writing allows the virtuoso in the art of oratory to obtain results of a sophistication and persuasive force unthinkable in a conversation or speech not formally prepared: 'Do you expect an amateur like me,' Phaedrus asks, 'to recite from memory, and without disgracing Lysias, what that cleverest of current writers composed at leisure over a long period of time?' (228a). Thirdly, one should emphasize the sophistical projection of an autonomous subject, free from *pathos* (from passion and affection), master of himself and hence of the word as well as the world, subject only to his own deliberation.[8] 'If you accept my proposal,' Phaedrus reads from Lysias' speech, 'my primary concern in associating with you will not be present pleasure, but future benefit, since I am not the slave of love but my own master' (233b–c). The sophistical strategies of self-assertion and struggle for power delineate the subject in his claim to autarchic determination.

On the ground of these presuppositions, the sophist speaks and says what he wants, regardless of the truth, believing to be able to turn to the surrounding environment (in its singularity, each time) only in order to make his own speaking more persuasive, without genuinely frequenting the circumstance and remaining affected by it. Such is the predatory, manipulative practice of the sophist, he who wants to seduce without himself undergoing the experience of seduction, who acts as if free from bonds of reciprocal dependence – or aspiring to be such. The critical treatment of writing at the conclusion of the dialogue should be understood within this framework, that is, in its ethical and political valences, as the result of the analysis of a certain mode of writing, of a certain configuration of human comportment here exemplified by Lysias. Considered aside from these preoccupations, such a critique remains formal and abstract. Ultimately it is Socrates himself who, shortly before his final reflections on the written word, observes that there is nothing per se inappropriate (shameful, *aiskhron*) in writing speeches. It all depends on the posture assumed in facing this task and how the task is carried out (258d).

*   *   *

It is important to notice that the Socratic response seems to stem not so much from an autonomous determination, but rather from Socrates' permeability to the suggestiveness of the surrounding. The Socratic response to the sophistical practice originates from an eclipse of subjective structures, from a dispersal (or recovery) of the subject *in* the other than itself; it is a response, indeed, a responsiveness out of a certain passivity. The *pathos* of human belonging in the world becomes manifest in its asymmetry with respect to the sophistical logic of the 'a-pathic' and sovereign subject, the citizen who wants himself free from worldly ties and presumes to entertain a preeminently instrumental relation to the world. The sophist and the philosopher are not two subjects who encounter and oppose each other, while sharing analogous presuppositions albeit defending contrary positions. Their encounter is infinitely oblique, *if* one can still speak of encounter here. Before the subject mastering himself and the circumstance (the subject starkly silhouetted against the circumstance, reducing it to his own background), the philosopher presents himself in his tendency to disappear, that is, to *become* the surroundings.

Socrates, then, does not formulate his critique of writing in the name of a subjectivity to be safeguarded in its fullness and integrity. He does so for the love of a living irreducible to inner life, to the insularity of a self-enclosed subject. This is a rather curious finding, starkly at odds with those interpretations that *want* to see the Socratic discourse as striving to overcome the assertory force of sophistry, as conquering and transfiguring sophistical assertion, reestablishing it on a transcendent level. But these statements must be examined in further detail and by reference to the Platonic letter.

The figure of an other manifesting itself through Socrates, speaking with Socrates' voice (so, at least, he says), is ubiquitous in the Platonic dialogue. One will recall how Socrates, in *Republic* VIII, lends his voice to the Muses, whose revelation irremediably overwhelms his own programmatic construction of the just city; or the way in which, in *Symposium*, Socrates evokes Diotima's dialectical procedure and teachings concerning Eros. In particular, one should recall the Socratic references to Apollo disseminated in the dialogues, especially in the *Apology*, where the confrontation with Apollo seems to constitute the *arkhê* of the insuppressible philosophical passion – where, thus, the philosopher says to be sent by the god. As has been pointed out, Socrates is indeed he who ironically dissimulates himself, repeating: 'the word doesn't belong to me', but to the god.[9] What is striking in the *Phaedrus*, however, is the multiplicity of sources of the Socratic word – or, if you will, the multiplicity of the shapes and guises of the god. The word doesn't belong to me, but to who, or what, whispers it to me and speaks through me: Socrates seems to suggest this, in his readiness to give voice to the solicitations and energies manifesting themselves in the surrounding scene. His posture here bespeaks availability to an intimate relation with the *physical* locus of the dialogue, an acknowledgment of *topos* not as abstract space but as unrepeatable (literally irreplaceable) receptacle of the present.

In being there, Socrates is present *in* and *to the place* – not *in* or *to himself*, but present *outside himself*, ecstatically. Such a dedication, attention or presence to place (and here presence, the word 'presence', is strained to its limit and begins to drift away from itself, or at least from its usual semantic range) makes possible a symbiotic bond with that which at once pervades, surrounds and indeterminately exceeds the human – a bond with nature, both in its sensible dimension and in its proliferation of invisible animation. It is from this experience that the human emerges as *suspension* in the other, as osmotically bound and belonging to the other.

Since the beginning the *Phaedrus* (which, let us remember, is the only Platonic dialogue unfolding outside the city walls) presents the figure of Socrates unusually exposed to the environs, its voices, the moods and registers of the living – a figure exhibiting a subtle receptivity, seeming to absorb the hum of the place, becoming its interpreter, almost spellbound, unable to ignore the unique qualities of phenomena all around and the inspirations transpiring from them. The plane-tree 'wide-spreading and tall', the *agnos* in bloom, the fragrant air, the cool spring flowing from under the plane-tree, the figurines and statues placed there, as if to designate a place sacred to the Nymphs and to Achelous the river god, the fresh and sweet breezes (literally, 'the breath of the place', *'to eupnoun tou topou'*), the reverberating chorus of the cicadas and the grassy slope – all this stirs up in Socrates such a wonder that Phaedrus treats him as if he were new to that locale (230b–d). But Socrates knows the site better than does Phaedrus himself, as is demonstrated by the fact that he knows of an altar, 'further along, where we cross over to the district of Agra', dedicated to Boreas, the wind from the North (229c). The attention he devotes to the place is, therefore, not due to its utter novelty. And, despite his assertion that countryside and trees won't teach him (a lover of learning) anything, in the course of the dialogue Socrates will often and conspicuously attribute his inspired speaking to the influence of the surrounding elements. He will say, for instance, to be possessed by the deities of that spot (238c–d). And he will make Phaedrus notice that the cicadas are inviting them to continue their conversation with renewed passion (258e–259c):

> ...as the cicadas above our heads sing and converse with each other in the summer heat, they also seem to me to be watching us. If they should see us not conversing but drowsily dozing under their spell like most people at midday, they'd justly laugh at us, thinking we were a couple of slaves visiting their retreat by the spring for a noontime nap, like sheep. If, however, they see us conversing and sailing by them without falling under their Siren-like spell, then in admiration they may grant us the gift they have from the gods to give to human beings (259a–b).

This reference to the cicadas subsequently receives a particularly significant elaboration, casting light on what the general orientation of the dialogue already suggested more than once, but only implicitly.

Socrates proceeds to establish a privileged relation between the cicadas and the Muses, acknowledging these insects, which love only to sing and converse, needing nothing else in the course of their brief existence, as emissaries (*angeloi*) of the divine:

> It's said that before the Muses existed, these cicadas were human beings, but after the Muses were born and singing made its appearance, some people in those days were so overwhelmed by the pleasure of it that they were caught up in singing and forgot to eat or drink and died before they realized what was happening. The race of the cicadas then developed

from them and they received from the Muses this gift of not needing any food from their birth, so that they sing continuously without eating or drinking until they die. Afterwards they go and report to the Muses who among those here honours each of them (259b–c).

It is, then, a certain unity of divinity and nature that is revealed with increasing clarity. That which is other than human, the inhuman exceeding and yet suffusing the human, is configured both in divine and physical terms. It is, indeed, within the embrace of nature that the divine dwells and, indiscernible from nature, emits (sends) signs. Such a sense of a palpitating and echoing nature, whose astonishing presence is called divine, is emphasized again shortly afterwards, in yet another gesture of Socratic self-dissimulation: 'I myself, Phaedrus, credit the gods of this place, and perhaps those representatives [prophêtai] of the Muses singing overhead who may have inspired [epipepneukotes] us with this gift. I myself certainly don't share in any art of speaking' (262d). A moment later Socrates again attributes the logoi he spoke to 'the Nymphs, who are daughters of Achelous, and Pan, the son of Hermes' (263d). This gesturing towards physis as divine dwelling is later brought into further focus: in order to situate his own resorting to myths and images, Socrates refers that the first oracular speeches (logous … mantikous) were those of an oak at the temple of Zeus at Dodona. In those times, he adds, 'since they weren't wise the way you young people are today, people were content in their simplicity to listen to an oak tree or a rock, if it spoke the truth' (275b).

It is in the context of such interpenetration with nature, then, that in the *Phaedrus* one can notice further episodes of Socratic rapture, of an abandonment to other voices – to the voices of 'wise men and women' of old, like Sappho and Anacreon (235b–c); to the peremptory call of the *daimonion* (242b–c); to the Dionysian chant of the choral leader (Stesichorus, 244a); to the influence of Phaedrus himself (242d, 244a). Ultimately, it is to this context that we should trace back the inspired 'praise of folly' woven by Socrates as a tribute to Eros, in order appropriately to honour the god – a praise not only declaimed but undergone, itself the fruit of a certain madness, of an openness to suggestions not fully comprehensible and uncontrolled (244a–257b). It is in this way that the philosopher poses himself towards Eros, the deity of love, whose presence becomes manifest in an enrapturing movement and demands the loss of oneself.[10]

*   *   *

Socrates, permeable, in a certain sense defenceless in that place outside the political walls, there were/there are no humans who could teach him, but only trees and streams, the breeze and noon heat, the Nymphs and others imperceptibly crowding the solitary summer landscape – Socrates becomes almost a mask, the place of the resonance of vocalizations not always ascribable to his subjective, sovereign deliberation. In fact, what comes to be manifest in and as Socrates is a kind of emptying, the loss of integrity of such sovereignty: the person as a place of transition between discontinuous dimensions, as empty form pervaded by the other than itself – an other crossing the hollow profile that delimits 'the individual', transgressing 'individual' boundaries, transiting from the hither side of such a profile, beyond it, inside out; an other which, *in* the individual, yet resoundingly overflows *outside* the individual . . . and back.

Socrates shows himself, then, as *persona*, as surface and appearing *through* which voice *resounds*. It is as though, in his being, Socrates would emerge as the locus of such a crossing, as readiness to affirm, in the void space of a certain non-being, of a certain being nothing, what presents itself and, at once, demands articulation. (Far from indicating neutral or indifferent extension, the emptiness of 'a certain non-being' would have to be understood as the locus of the inflection and deflection of what comes to pass, that is, as the condition of hospitality.) The subject thus manifest in the *persona* of Socrates, far from the figure of the individual who founds himself by and on himself, is revealed as a giving place (making room) and giving voice; as a giving oneself to the other, to an other always already inhabiting the movement of such giving. Such would be the nascent dynamic of the *pathos* then called philosophical. In this dawning manifestation of the 'subject' (and here the word is obviously employed equivocally, in a way that cannot be reduced to the conceptions developed subsequently in the venture of Western thought), the non-being, the mystery from which the subject ultimately originates and by which it is sustained is not covered over. Socrates' comportment, paradigmatically in the *Phaedrus*, allows, if not the conception of non-being as such, the divining of its interstices.

In this way is evidenced, among other things, the fact that Socrates does not limit himself to formulating a critique of sophistical writing and of the subjective autarchy on which such practice rests. That of Socrates is not a critique merely enunciated, released by a subject who, in turn, would operate as *fons et origo*, untouched by the implications of his own enunciation, hence reproducing in himself precisely those problematic traits he tries critically to address. What is at stake, instead, is a critique enunciated by a subject who undergoes his own speaking, who attunes himself to his own saying – or, more precisely, by a subject who has always already undergone an other speaking, the speaking of another, and whose speaking stems from such radical undergoing (from the lying-under that, even if by now illegible, radically defines, even underlies, the *hypokeimenon* as well as the *subjectum* and *substantia*). The Socratic critique, then, occurs as the practice of what is enunciated, that is, a fading away of the subject – a practice prior even to enunciation, rooted in a listening. In proposing such a critique, Socrates practises what he says, even before having fully said it; so much so that his speaking is configured *in* belonging to the practice, which in turn is informed by a *pathos*, an affection, a hearing – by listening to an other saying. Socrates, the one who gives himself as spacing and listening, who allows for the surfacing of voices through himself, *is himself* the critique *in deed*, in *ergon*, from which the critique in *logos* comes to be. (It goes without saying that the term 'critique', too, begins here to function equivocally, acquiring a valence clearly at odds with its modern, Kantian meaning.) Speaking infused with listening, listening pregnant with response: in this way, too, could the Socratic 'critique' be characterized.

It should be noticed that, in the entire dialogue, the only moment in which Socrates unquestioningly embraces the sophistical *ethos* coincides exactly with a gesture of his meant to suspend his involvement with the other than himself and in himself. When, initially, he seems to accept the logic of rhetoric and proceeds to compete with Lysias on the latter's terrain, Socrates pronounces his discourse with his face covered. This is his first discourse, in which he accepts the thesis defended by Lysias, that it is better to yield to someone who knows what he's doing rather than to someone madly in love. Here it is simply the matter of showing mastery of the topic and an argumentative clarity superior to that exhibited by Lysias – who repeats himself, does not expose his points in an orderly fashion, is not as irresistible an orator after all. In brief, Socrates at this initial stage resists Lysias. He opposes Lysias directly and, taken by a sort of competitiveness, plays according to the rules of the adversary, without preliminarily questioning them. As he himself says, he covers his face, isolating himself from what surrounds him, precisely in order not to fall into *aporia*, to avoid the confusion caused by a certain shame (237a).

In this case, Socrates no longer *is* a mask, but *wears* a mask, literally – a mask allowing him to play the game of authoritativeness, of technical virtuoso display – which does not require an intimate correspondence or self-interrogation. There behind the screen, entrenched in his isolation, avoiding the exposure to Phaedrus' seductive face and to the life surrounding them in its manifoldness, Socrates speaks as well as, even better than Lysias – analogously to Lysias, strong with an unconquerable interiority that neither opens to nor mingles with the world. However, as soon as he uncovers himself, Socrates finds the impossibility of speaking that way. Again he recognizes himself as invaded by a speaking he hardly understands, of which he becomes the spokesman (the prophet, literally – but always in the ironic-theatrical vein of someone professing to be 'barely literate' [242c]). At this point, it is the *daimonion*'s injunction that resounds within and without Socrates, that orders him to stop, not to cross the stream and return to Athens, but to remain and wash the impiety just committed. Someone else seems to have spoken through Socrates, Socrates now says, during that attempt to defeat Lysias in the rhetorical competition. Someone else who was not me – maybe it was you, Phaedrus, who led me astray and bewitched me with that speech you read. But now I will speak differently, I will make amends, purify myself from the offence against love – I will speak praising love, thus giving myself up to it (and would urge Lysias, too, to do the same as soon as possible).

And yet, even now, as he prepares to offer his second speech, it is not exactly Socrates that speaks. His speaking, stemming from the daimonic prescription, is readily attributed to Stesichorus, the archaic poet or choric leader. Socratic theatre (not so much the pretences, the veils and shrouds Socrates deliberately chooses, but the theatre that Socrates himself *is*) gives itself as the locus of the encounter, of the intertwinement of daimonic compulsion and the song that occurs in response to it – as the space of a certain dialogue. Rigorously speaking, Socrates is never truly the one who speaks, but it is always someone, something else, from an elsewhere which is not simply external to Socrates but rather constitutes him – an elsewhere to be understood, above all, as *a-topic*. The unfathomability of the one who hears oneself speak and, in thus hearing, *is* and simultaneously *is not* the one speaking, reveals a subject that is *of* the world in the double sense of the genitive – a subject encompassing the world while belonging to it, a subject constituted in the simultaneous interiorization and exteriorization of the world; as has been suggested, a subject *of* the world who is subject *to* the world and who, in its unfolding as the exiguous thread of vocalization, can appropriate neither himself nor the world.

The Socratic word is, then, *inspired* word, word that flows like another's breath, afflatus, the almost-nothing of a rustling breeze becoming a suggestion – word infused with *enthousiasmos*, that is, with the presence, or rather the excess, of the god. A saying that develops from the experience of being carried away (like Oreithuia by Boreas), of *ek-stasis*, of loss of control – no longer, or not simply, a speaking in which one says anything (if anything was ever said), but in which one is being said. In this speaking Socrates will now proceed to honour love and the madness accompanying it – to praise madness as divine gift, in its versions as poetic furore, prophetic vision, ritual purification and, in the end, as that love that is the philosophical *pathos*. Once again, we can see how what Socrates says is in accord with the *ethos* of his saying, to the how and the practice of his saying. Even more precisely, his saying and what it says spring from (are somewhat anticipated by) the *ethos*, the comportment of a subject dispersed but not annihilated, empty and therefore present to what presents itself – open, available, hospitable. Socrates says what he has always already en-acted.

It is easier now to understand the degree to which such a saying and such enacting may be incompatible with a practice like that of the rhetoricians – writing in order to read, mechanically reproduce. Those who strictly adhere to this practice have virtually no access to the possibility disclosed to Socrates – the possibility of reconsidering, perhaps even reversing one's position. Indeed, such a reversal becomes genuinely possible thanks to the vulnerability inherent in exposing oneself to the surrounding suggestions. But for those continuing to read with their faces covered, on the hither side of an insulating and protective screen, according to the programme pre-established prior to the moment in which life gathers and unfolds, this option is unthinkable. In this sense it is possible to see, among other things, how the critique of writing with which Socrates concludes the dialogue is not so much a quintessentially metaphysical attempt, as if in a proto-Husserlian vein, to subordinate the sign and its sensible exteriority to the primacy of the voice, incorporeal cipher of the interiority of meaning in its pure presence (as Derrida, more wilfully and better than others, has argued).[11] According to what was said so far, the Socratic critique seems rather to give itself as perplexity before a practice of writing that abstracts itself from life and is unable to respond and correspond to it. What is critically assessed seems to be writing as a tyrannical instrumentalization that, from its alleged atemporality, would impose itself on silence without encountering it. Nor should we without any further ado, reduce the primacy of the voice ('phonocentrism') to the exercise of logical-paternal authority (of authority in general). The voice privileged in the *Phaedrus* is not the phenomenological voice (the supersensible voice of interiority, the prerogative of a self-enclosed subject), but instead the symptom of an uncontrollable, irreducible, thoroughly sensible poly-phony, of an ek-static dispersion in the other.[12] It is precisely this that the rhetorical practice of writing would make impossible.

*   *   *

And yet. And yet, at this point it also opportune, indeed, necessary, to call into question the disarming stereotype of Socrates who, as Nietzsche put it, 'does not write'. In a way, Socrates does write, undeniably. Socrates writes, for not only what has heretofore been discussed as his 'saying' is indeed written (the writing of Plato), but also his writing is prior even to that of Plato, indeed dictates the latter, makes it necessary – in other words, pre-scribes it.

It prescribes it, let this be said in passing, just as the vocal articulation already prescribes alphabetic writing (that is to say, phonetic transcription), and as the latter, in turn, already prescribes a certain exercise of reason (of which the Western philosophical tradition is as exemplary as the technological dimension of our culture). Not by chance, in Greek the word *logos*, alone, covers the semantic range extending from the 'spoken word' to the law of signification underlying it (reason, in sum). As also Aristotle observes, in its primordial dimension (and primordial here does not indicate mere chronological anteriority), *logos* manifests itself in a certain freedom of the voice, in the excess of the voice with respect to unqualified emission of sound. Voice (as human voice shows, and we will not take up the question here as to whether this may be its exclusive prerogative) can articulate phonemes in composite units. Through such acoustic articulations, which are made possible by a certain physiological apparatus, something is indicated, gestured towards, intended, that is, *meant*. However, unlike the relation between images and things imaginally signified, the relation between sound and meaning remains elusive, or at any rate is not immediately imitative. The relation to the visible referent is in this case more tenuous, first of all because the word does not limit itself to signifying the visible (it could be argued that even the image, at the limit, does not signify only the visible); secondly, because, even when the referent is visible, the word does not evoke its morphology. Albeit not marking *tout simplement* an alienation from the sensible (sound still belongs in the sensible), the order of sound involves a more inscrutable relation between meaning and the materiality of the signifier. Aside from the kind of notation concretely utilized in various cultures, the fact itself that signification gives itself fundamentally through vocalization, that is, orally, already discloses in principle the possibility of a writing not offering a pictographic or ideogrammatic parallel of oral practices, but focusing on redoubling their features, undertaking to imitate and reproduce them, to transcribe them in order to fathom their most recondite potentiality. Such a writing strives to capture the utterance in its resonance, breaking it down and analysing it into its most basic components.

It has been observed that Socrates, despite his avoidance of writing, is not 'a man of orality' – that, on the contrary, his practice is pregnant already with a logic that will find its highest achievement in the practice of alphabetic writing and in the discourses structured by it. One can speak, then, of Socratic writing, in the sense of philosophical destination, of the destiny of a practice inaugurally incarnated in the figure of Socrates. Socrates does write, and his writing takes the form of a dissimulation of writing, of a certain privilege accorded to the voice, to the apparent immediacy of its invisible presence. Such a writing of the voice will always already have pre(in)scribed both the alphabetic-scriptural threshold (which presents itself as transcription of vocal temporality) and, subsequently, a certain progressive divergence from appearing and appearances (due to the phonetico-sonorous dimension of writing, to a certain freedom it displays with respect to the visible). More pointedly still, Socrates' comportment is informed by writing: as is clearly shown in the *Phaedrus*, he practises analysis in the way in which a reader practices it, a way that is orally impracticable as well as unthinkable.[13] Socrates writes, because he reads.

Socrates writes – so much so that Plato (and the others after him) will eventually succumb to the imperative of writing. He will have had to write, as if Socrates would write through him, as if he were but a prosthesis, an extension of the teacher. Or he will write as if reaching out towards the teacher (the beloved) now missing, as if bringing to completion the saying, the very being of Socrates. And so their relation itself becomes a figure of Socratic writing, a stretching out beyond oneself, an extending beyond one's limits and boundaries, even though this should entail (as it does entail) a loss of control and logical coherence, a renunciation of the exercise of paternal rights and authority over the work whose author one is, a going astray, despite oneself. As was seen above, such drifting is not less clamorous in the *ethos* of vocal primacy, that is, in the exuberant logic of ecstatic rapture. The an-archic vocality which above was called 'Socratic theatre', the locus in which a certain vocal resounding is brought to visibility in the form of Socrates' practice or enactment, is the writing that Platonic writing imitates – the writing of which Plato's writing is the *mimêsis*. Platonic writing is, then, the writing *of Socrates*, again, in the double sense of the genitive: Socrates himself writing, Socrates being written – Socrates subject *of* and *to* writing.

Plato's writing shows itself as a further aspect of Socratic excess or, better, as its doubling – and there is no way, not for us, ultimately to distinguish Socratic writing from its double. There is no Socratic theatre without the ulterior *mise en scène* of the Platonic dialogue. But, just as there no imitation without the occultation both of the imitator and the imitated (this is what Plato makes Socrates say in *Republic* III and X), so there is no staging of Socrates by Plato without a more or less spectacular disappearance of both. 'The word does not belong to me, but to Socrates and all the other characters.' In a certain sense, Socratic writing in Plato's transcription, this theatre within the theatre, is writing as we know it – and not only in the sense of philosophical writing as an autonomous genre. Bridging the gap(s) between Greek dramatic writing and the modern novel, as Nietzsche also said, Plato remains the inaccessible author of (the thoughts of) others who remain, in turn, inaccessible – the figure itself (if it is still a figure) of the evanescence of author and authority, the dramatization of the insubstantiality of *substantia*, of the exiguity of what is called 'subject', especially that subject that is the philosopher.

It is in this way that Socrates writes, makes himself written, demands that one write. His practice already implicitly circumscribes this possibility and is, therefore, such an exhortation: in virtue of its being liminally perceptible as such, the possible becomes necessary; as possible, it must be explored, it transmits itself as task – or compulsion. In such writing, though, Socrates writes through another, and makes him say that writing is something neither serious nor reliable. He writes, then, under erasure; writes and, in so doing, undermines himself; speaks, but his speaking is no simple assertion positing itself and becoming thesis or position. His writing is a trace. It is a saying without position, without designated and permanent place, *a-topos*; a saying that, if at all posing itself, poses itself in question.

The teacher discredits the making of the disciple, that making in a way assigned by the teacher himself. The teacher speaks through the disciple, and yet undoes the latter's speaking *qua* writing. On the other hand, it is only through the saying (the writing, making) of the disciple that the teacher has a voice at all. It is, then, the disciple who undoes his own saying, and who, furthermore, defies and transgresses the teacher's teaching, treating it impertinently precisely in the moment he proposes it, forcing the teacher to speak in writing. The relation between Plato and Socrates, this complex play of refractions which is a figure of writing itself, is moreover a cipher of the originary speaking of philosophy – a questioning, a saying without full legitimacy, indeed pervaded and sustained by an emptiness.[14]

*   *   *

Let us return, to conclude, to the critique of writing with which the dialogue comes to a close. In the course of the present analysis two modes of writing have surfaced (and thus the term 'writing', too, is in the end revealed as equivocal): in the first place, the abstracting and instrumental practice of sophistical writing with respect to which, as we have seen, remarkable reservations are expressed; secondly, the Socratic-Platonic practice of writing which, precisely in tracing itself as event, calls attention to sophistical writing and subjects it to critical scrutiny. These two modes of writing turn out to be irreducible, albeit not fully discernible from one another (if only because the former essentially becomes accessible to reflection within the horizon of the latter). Hence, while we notice a certain refusal of writing as an instrument of communication estranged from the world (as if somehow emancipated from it), we cannot ignore an affirmation of writing inherent in the very Platonic conduct. This writing unsays itself, says of itself that it is the pastime of an author no longer young. Writing becomes a certain way of playing with permanence, the relative permanence of the sensible, or better, of the visible – of the written letter over against the spoken word (which is still heard, and thus sensible, but ethereal and more fleeting).[15] As *mimêsis* of the Socratic theatre, and analogously to it, Plato's writing situates itself at the heart of the sensible or, more precisely, in the chiasm between the sensible and the sonorous that, invisible, in various ways inhabits it.

It is, indeed, only by being opposed to the assumption of an ultrasensible domain that the sensible may be construed as merely transitory. But in the *Phaedrus, pace* the venerable tradition attributing to Plato the dualism of sublunar realm and hyperuranian ideal, it seems that for humans the sensible constitutes a screen of stability and continuity, however qualified. Through writing, both oral articulation and intuition (which are fleeting, even dazzling in their rapid succession) are anchored to the order of the visible. Here they come to rest and are preserved for a while. When transposed into a written form, what is thought or said becomes accessible in a different temporal order. In writing, that is, one can capture flashing insights, bring them into an outline, and in this way it becomes possible to discern and elaborate their implications, to unfold what is enfolded within them, and bring into relief what may not otherwise come to light with such refinement. It is writing, more than fugitive speaking, that lends itself to analysis. And it is writing that discloses the horizon of the art of argumentation. The *praxis* of writing, precisely in its sensible, extrinsic and worldly character, offers the relative fixity necessary to argument and, in general, to research. As has been recalled already, Phaedrus notices this since the beginning (228a). Even Socrates is well aware of it, as is demonstrated when, well into the dialogue, he asks Phaedrus to read again the beginning of Lysias' discourse: if the dilated temporality of writing has allowed Lysias to elaborate his speech so much more effectively, this same temporality will now permit Socrates to read and dismantle such speech at leisure, repeatedly turning to the written page.[16] Although, as Socrates insists in the end, writing should not be taken that seriously, and although true knowledge can neither be transmitted nor learned through written discourses, the fact remains that the entire dialogue, in its modalities as well as in its themes, would be unthinkable outside the domain of such a practice. The presumption of autarchic thought imposing itself on life, as it were, from above or outside, then, is a lie. Rather, what emerges is a thought sustained, brought to be what it is, by life[17] – a mode of thinking which, through and thanks to the sensible, finds the shapes it finds, the ways of its unfolding and of its writing.

And yet, one could still object that it is only the thought one indulges in as a pastime which is interwoven with life in such a way. One could say that, even though in Plato the written articulation is but an image (which, as such, belongs in the order of the worldly), intellection (*noein*) abides, gathered in an ineffable interiority, not contaminated by writing, perhaps not even by the spoken word, hence independent from worldly contingency and absolutely still. This is not a slight question, for the decisions made with respect to Plato, more decisively than those regarding other philosophers, determine one's posture *vis-à-vis* the Western philosophical tradition referring to Plato as its inaugural event. That is to say, they determine the way in which such a tradition is construed. And calling into question the decisions and interpretive strategies constituting this tradition means not hastily accepting their necessity, but rather insinuating their arbitrary character. Such a complex question would have to be addressed by systematic and in-depth reference to other pertinent Platonic texts, from *Republic* to *Letter VII*. Here, in the margins, I will limit myself to a couple of indications (the barest gestures) concerning the *Phaedrus*. In the first place, it should be noticed that, according to Socrates, what is guarded in interiority is itself always already *written*. Referring to 'the living and ensouled speech [*logon . . . zônta kai empsukhon*] of the one who knows', Socrates says that it is 'written along with knowledge [*met' epistêmês graphetai*] in the soul' (276a). Secondly, it would be necessary to study the treatment of the soul (*psykhê*, the principle of life) as permanently in motion and metamorphosis (245c–246a). Far from being immutable and fixed (as that which is inanimate), the soul, ever living, 'never stops moving [*kinoumenon*]' (245c). It is immortal precisely by virtue of its never being the same; it endures, but is never self-identical.[18] It is writing alone that provides a qualified stability – however wandering and errant, as we saw, because of its indiscriminate dissemination.

*   *   *

In the end, those who live take leave – of one another and of the circumstances which gather(ed) them in delight (279b–c). In the end, they acknowledge at once their coming (having come) together and their being sundered (from one another, from themselves, from all else). Before departing, they invoke 'those there', 'Pan, my friend, and the other gods of this place' resounding with voices. They share the invocation, as though speaking in unison. Then, when the invocation has reached its perfect measure, the bond begins to dissolve. The receptacle of the dialogue is undone. 'Let's go.'

Notes

1. An early version of parts of the present essay appeared in 'La scrittura di Socrate', in *Intersezioni* XIX:3 (1999), 421–35. I wish to thank J. Taylor – for our quiet conversation. It was also published under this title in *Epoché*, 11:1 (Fall 2006), 29–51.
2. Trans. J. M. Edmonds.
3. In *Eros the Bittersweet* (Normal: Dalkey Archive, 1998), Anne Carson speaks of 'an ancient analogy between language and love, implicit in the conception of breath as universal conductor of seductive influences and of persuasive speech' (55).
4. In *Ion* the poet is said to be impelled to sing by *theia moira* (534c) or *theia dunamis* (533d). The poet is who s/he is precisely to the extent that s/he is literally out of his or her mind, *ekphrôn* (534b), abandoned by *nous* (534b, d). Just as is the case with the soothsayer, the poet does not him- or herself speak, but through him or her the divine presents itself (534d). This characterization is echoed in the *Phaedrus* (245a–b), yet in the latter context it is broadened to include the speaking of the philosopher. Prophetic utterance, healing prayers, poetry and philosophical discourse alike are shown to proceed from out of madness, which is a divine gift (*theia dosis*, 244a, *theia moira*, 244c). In *Apology*, Socrates speaks of *theia moira* as that which ordered him to practice philosophy throughout his life (33c). See also *Letter VII* (326b) and *Meno* (99e).
5. Allusions to the Hippocratic art are indeed numerous and often crucial in this dialogue that begins with the reference to two physicians, Acumenus and Herodicus (227a, d), and is marked by an encompassing concern with health. Acumenus is mentioned again, along with his son and colleague Eryximachus, at 268a. A description of Hippocratic method is laid out at 270c–e. In the Hippocratic treatise *On the Sacred Disease*, one finds the statement that it is the air (*aêr*) that supplies intelligence (*phronesis*) to that which is in the head. Of this gift the organ in the head is an interpreter and messenger (*hermêneus* and *angelos*) to us (XIX, XX). In marked contrast with Empedocles, who associates thinking with heart and the circulation of blood (to which, to be sure, breathing is essential), the author of this treatise states that the air drawn in reaches the brain first and leaves the gift of intelligence there, unscathed by the humours of flesh and blood, which would only diminish it (XIX).

6. Though not without occasional divergences, I refer to W. S. Cobb's translation of the *Phaedrus* in *The* Symposium *and the* Phaedrus: *Plato's Erotic Dialogues* (Albany: SUNY Press, 1993).

7. Here can be discerned what will have been called the quintessentially logo- or anthropocentric posture of Western humanism: removed from dialogical engagement/exposure, study or inquiry in its many modes occurs through and as objectification.

8. It is for essential reasons that, in this context, I will use the masculine pronoun.

9. See Carlo Sini, *Teoria e pratica del foglio-mondo. La scrittura filosofica* (Bari: Laterza, 1997), 17 and *passim*.

10. While a close analysis of Socrates' second speech exceeds the scope of the present discussion, it may be appropriate to point out that the imaginal discourse on love, madness and the soul's journeys and tribulations seems to be informed by the physical/divine exposure here hypothesized. Let us simply recall, besides the vivid descriptions of the soul's chariot perilously drawn by its two horses around the celestial circuit (248a–b), the psycho-physiology of the experience of love: the soul undergoing 'goose bumps', 'unusual warmth and sweating', the softening of the follicles allowing the growth of feathers 'from their roots over the entire form of the soul', the 'excitement' analogous to the 'itching and irritation that occur around the gums when the teeth are just coming through', the feathers pushing and pulsating 'like throbbing arteries', the 'pressures and pangs', the 'tickling and prickling' (251a–e, 254a).

11. See 'Plato's Pharmacy', in *Dissemination*, trans. Barbara Johnson (Chicago: University of Chicago Press, 1981), 61–171. Willfulness: one wonders about it, when texts or bodies of work are forced to fit given programmatic or systematic needs. While Derrida has in many ways and places elucidated a certain inevitability of violence in the labour of reading, one still wonders about the strategic, empowering function of wilful or truncated reading. In Derrida, for instance (but this is the case in Heidegger as well), one may be especially perplexed by the vigorous gesture bringing two millennia and a half of philosophical wonder, in a given geographical district, under the heading of Western metaphysics – a gesture that allows a projective (that is, reductive) approach to the Platonic problematic as pre-Husserlian and, hence, constitutes a powerful rhetorical device magnifying the movement and scope of deconstruction. But is this, again, the logic of patricide at work in philosophical generation? Is such logic, along with the ambivalent love it entails, truly necessary to generativity, philosophical or otherwise?

12. In J.-L. Nancy's *Le Partage des voix* (Paris: Galilée, 1982), the multiple and decentred phenomenon of vocalization points to phenomenal becoming and the dispersion of subjective structures – a function that in Derrida's discourse is attributed to the figure of writing.

13. But see also *Apology* 26d–e.

14. Derrida's 'Envois', in *The Postcard*, trans. Alan Bass (Chicago: University of Chicago Press, 1987), can be read as a sustained, if fragmented, meditation on (this) relation.

15. In *Letter VII* the problems raised concerning verbal articulation are not restricted to writing but refer to all manner of words. Being relatively more stable or immovable, that is, more impervious to the becoming of life, the written word only makes the shortcomings of verbalization more perspicuous. It is on this difficulty that is based, among other things, the incipient critique of legality (of laws as

written 'political statements') intimated in the *Phaedrus* with reference to Solon (278b–d). (In *Timaeus* the law-giver appears again in the context of the intersection of writing and matters Egyptian.) Aristotle will develop the *aporia* of law and the irreducibility of justice to juridical norms in Book E of *Nicomachean Ethics*. At any rate, what is crucial to heed in the *Phaedrus* is the suggestion that, far from having left the *polis* behind and found solace in the purely non-political sphere of *physis*, Socrates and Phaedrus bring the city, its speeches and preoccupations, with themselves in their walk into the countryside. The city is brought outside itself, face to face with *physis* – with that which is both other to the *polis* and the *polis'* (however non-political) condition.

16. 'Read me the beginning of Lysias' speech' (262d). And again: 'But tell me this also, since because of my inspired state at the time I don't remember at all, did I define love at the beginning of my speech?' 'You did, by Zeus, quite emphatically.' 'Ah! So you claim that the Nymphs, who are the daughters of Achelous, and Pan, the son of Hermes, are much more artful in making speeches than is Lysias, son of Cephalus. Or am I speaking nonsense? Did Lysias also at the beginning of his erotic speech compel us to take love as one definite thing, which he had a conception of, and then proceed to finish his speech, arranging everything to fit with this? Do you want us to read the beginning of his speech again?' 'If you think we should, but what you're looking for isn't in it.' 'Speak, please, so that I can hear the man himself' (263d–e).

17. Like everything living, thought may be more or less long-lived: it may come to pass as a sudden flash, as ephemeral as a cicada, or stabilize itself as if in a mineralized concretion, and endure for the time allotted to books, or again reside in some other manner and configuration.

18. On the soul *vis-à-vis* immortality and change, see *Symposium* 207d–208b.

Part III
Installation

10
Illegibility: On the Spirit of Origins

John P. Leavey Jr

1   Hypothesis: or, on having begged the question

If reading were what might be designated as phenolegocentric, as the gathering of sense 'booked', according to the insightful translation of Barbara Johnson of *livré*, in a present accessible to the first glance of a decipherment, of a retrieval of information, of the matter at hand, then nothing follows and everything is demonstrable: *this is that*. If reading, however, were to founder on such legibility, if reading were only eventual, eventual to illegibility – *eventuality* – then everything follows and nothing is demonstrable. A demonstration of reading would not be possible, only eventual, hence the illegibility up against which any phenolegocentrism founders in the addition of reading. All of which is to say, reading could not demonstrate itself except as illegible. Its secondariness, at best, can be amassed in an eventual demonstration that founders on the disjointure of its rhythm. And so we can add that reading is but the politics of reading.

2   Eventualities: on etymologies and the commonsensicals

Reading, beginning to weave, ordering (starting from the first row of the loom), joint, arm, fitted, art: an etymology of 'read' reads between the lines. And so there appears to be no place for illegibility except as error, fault, mistake, difficulty, the result of encryption, lack of insight for deciphering, and perhaps intent: for example, invisible ink.

AR and ER are the Indo-European roots for reading and origin (see *The American Heritage Dictionary of the English Language*), and in an etymological four-flushing of phenolegocentrism, send us running from one to the other in constructing any argument of the origin. The commonsensicals of illegibility appear to refer to the materiality of the readable; those of unreadability appear to refer to the potentiality of the readable. The material for illegibility appears to be under erasure, smudged, faded, invisible, indecipherable in its matter. The (un)readable is indecipherable, even inscrutable, and the origin unknown, unrecognized.

That set of sentences appears to sum up too quickly and insufficiently the commonsensicals of reading and its origin. Both terms appear inclusive of too much and too little, which would make any question of readability impossible to decide. And so we continue to read, to be read, to read one another's minds as the absolute basis for the commonsensical of reading in the spectographics of reading.

3   Topics

The topic that runs us together here is the origin(s) of deconstruction. After some thirty years, reflection back upon the 'beginning' moments of what came to be designated as 'deconstruction', even if that designation raises as many questions as it solves, seems appropriate, to the point, perhaps nostalgic, even retrograde. At times readable and unreadable at once, at times simply illegible, according to the ethics of the discussion. Rorty asked for more time on this.

4   Methods

This piece is composed of *eventualities*. I use this term in order to stress both the futurity (which refuses the despair of *futility*) and the event of any discussion of origins, especially of 'deconstruction', should such a thing exist. Each eventuality can only be reread, even in a first reading. Even in the dream of the perfect technics of memory, of the trace without any forgetfulness as constitutive of its memory, eventuality is that radical illegibility that cannot be remembered in order to be forgotten.

5   Redemption

I want to begin with a finale, with the last of the fragments of Adorno's *Minima Moralia: Reflections from Damaged Life*. The last reflection concerns redemption *Zum Ende*, as Adorno writes. If it were possible to escape thinking, there would be no need for redemption. Only perspectives that recognize the inescapability of thought are redemptive, not in the sense of redeeming from a damaged life, although these reflections are responsible to despair, but in the sense of redemption from totalization and escape.

> To gain such perspectives without velleity or violence, entirely from felt contact with its objects – this alone is the task of thought. It is the simplest of all things, because the situation calls imperatively for such knowledge, indeed because consummate negativity, once squarely faced, delineates the mirror-image of its opposite. But it is also the utterly impossible

thing, because it presupposes a standpoint removed, even though by a hair's breadth, from the scope of existence, whereas we well know that any possible knowledge must not only be first wrested from what is, if it shall hold good, but is also marked, for this very reason, by the same distortion and indigence which it seeks to escape. The more passionately thought denies its conditionality for the sake of the unconditional, the more unconsciously, and so calamitously, it is delivered up to the world. Even its own impossibility it must at last comprehend for the sake of the possible. But beside the demand thus placed on thought, the question of the reality or unreality of redemption itself hardly matters.[1]

The illegibility of redemption is its secondariness, 'even though by a hair's breadth', which means that this secondariness is 'before' the primacy of the real and reading. Derrida will eventually call this secondariness 'radical illegibility' in his reading of Jabès.

6   Shandy and Cubas

How is one to read the marbled pages? The blank but titled chapters? The physical move back and forth of asterisks, dashes and spaces? The reproduction of the narrative lines. The punctuation marks alone. In the writings of two narrators neither dead nor alive, living on, of the birth and the death, of Tristam Shandy and Brás Cubas, what is it to read? Are such devices unreadable? Illegible? What would it mean to decide this question that sees and hears from the other side, whether that be the side of the room or death?

7   Second read

For Benjamin, around 1917 or earlier, there is fragment 16, whose title entices, much like the book that is encompassed in fragment 177, with the constellation 'Perception Is Reading'.[2] These unpublished fragments on perception from 1917 contain the enigmatic phrase that 'Perception is reading', which is the title of one fragment (no. 16) and the opening line of another (no. 17). In fragment 177, reading is the second read. In fragment 17, the readable is in the realm of appearances. Gershom Scholem comments in *Walter Benjamin: The Story of a Friendship*, and this is quoted in the notes to the fragments in the sixth volume of *Gesammelte Schriften*:

> Even then he occupied himself with ideas about perception as a reading in the configurations of the surface, which is the way prehistoric man perceived the world around him, particularly the sky. This was the genesis of the reflections he made many years later in his notes 'Lehre vom Ähnlichen' [Doctrine of similar things]. The origin of the constellations as configurations on the sky surface was, so he asserted, the beginning

of reading and writing, and this coincided with the development of
the mythic age. The constellations were for the mythic world what the
revelation of Holy Writ was to be later.[3]

The piece of writing to which Scholem refers concludes on the matter of the
tempo of reading. After what could be called a history of speech and writing
and after differentiating profane and magical senses of reading, Benjamin
ends with 'fleeting'-ness of reading:

> So tempo, that swiftness in reading or writing which can scarcely be sep-
> arated from this process [from the clairvoyance of reading the heavens
> to the clairvoyance of reading writing, from reading entrails to reading
> runes], would then become, as it were, the effort, or gift, or mind to partic-
> ipate in that measure of time in which similarities flash up fleetingly out
> of the stream of things only in order to sink down once more. Thus, even
> profane reading, if it is not to forsake understanding altogether, shares
> this with magical reading: that it is subject to a necessary tempo, or rather
> a critical moment, which the reader must not forget at any cost lest he go
> away empty-handed.[4]

8   Second read 2

> Un texte n'est un texte que s'il cache au premier regard, au premier venu,
> la loi de sa composition et la règle de son jeu. Un texte reste d'ailleurs tou-
> jours imperceptible. La loi et la règle ne s'abritent pas dans l'inaccessible
> d'un secret, simplement elles ne se livrent jamais, au *présent*, à rien qu'on
> puisse rigoureusement nommer une perception.[5] [A text is not a text
> unless it hides from the first comer, from the first glance, the law of its
> composition and the rules of its game. A text remains, moreover, forever
> imperceptible. Its law and its rules are not, however, harbored in the inac-
> cessibility of a secret; it is simply that they can never be booked, in the
> *present*, into anything that could rigorously be called a perception.][6]

No perception – there is no such thing as a perception. The first comer must
be second in order to read, because the text is imperceptible, not subject
to perception, hence illegible, should legibility be perceptual. The second
glance reads. So reading is the recognition of the illegibility of the text, of
the origin as textual.

The reading of Plato's pharmacy is analysed in Gasché's *The Wild Card of
Reading: on Paul de Man*. Gasché explores a difference in reading between
Derrida and de Man, both arguing that reading is double. The difference:
de Man refers reading to language, Derrida to text, with the doubling of
the two thinkers breaking upon the knowledge, however small, of what
it read.[7] In another shorthand, Derrida reads undecidability to a decision;
de Man reads undecidability as the end of reading. And yet, allegories of

reading – I say this without returning to the texts themselves – are always additive. Even if the end of reading, the eventuality of that reading is eventual, not final. And here de Man and Derrida agree.

Derrida's text ends on a conjecture of a difference of another eventuality:

> – But maybe it's just a residue [*un reste*], a dream, a bit of dream left over, an echo of the night ... that other theater, those knocks from without ...[8]

9 In between

To begin with, the end of the beginning and of the end, as a warning of a reactive phase of thought. In 1985, Gilles Deleuze remarks about the problem of the origin:

> If things aren't going too well in contemporary thought, it's because there's a return under the name of 'modernism' to abstractions, back to the problem of origins, all that sort of thing [...] Any analysis in terms of movements, vectors, is blocked. We're in a very weak phase, a period of reaction. Yet philosophy thought it had done with the problem of origins. It was no longer a question of starting or finishing. The question was rather, what happens 'in between'?[9]

We've been warned to think carefully about any quest for origins. The quest(ion) is the happening between, always an eventuality.

10 Origin(s) of deconstruction

The topic is the origin(s) of deconstruction. Reading such a phrase, whether singular or plural, can lead to any number of approaches at first glance. Even leaving aside the genitivity of the phrase, there is in these approaches the assumption that there is such a thing as deconstruction, some thing called 'deconstruction', whose limits can be delimited or are to be delimited.

1) The origin is dated, and what is to be dated is the beginning of what is called 'deconstruction'. That date can be a signature, an event, the first use of the term, the beginning of its sense. For example, the Johns Hopkins Humanities Center symposium funded by the Ford Foundation in 1966 (18–21 October) on 'The Languages of Criticism and the Sciences of Man'.[10] Or perhaps the tracing out of the 'undecidables' summarized in *Positions* in 1972.[11]
2) The origin is deconstruction's. For example, in the term's possible precursors, for instance, in Husserl's *Abbau* and Heidegger's *Destruktion*. Or how the term has been used, conceived, modified, transformed, translated, 'deconstructed' by deconstruction, if such is the case. As in the occurrence of the word 'de-construction' with a hyphen in the 1967 *Of*

Grammatology,[12] and its attendant histories throughout other Derridean texts, other authors such as de Man, and then in the popular press, from *Newsweek* or *Time* to newspapers. Or in the elliptical definition given by Derrida in *Memoires: for Paul de Man* before a discussion of his refusal to agree to talk about 'deconstruction in America' and before proposing that it might need to be modified to the more hypothetical 'America is deconstruction':

> If I had to risk a single definition of deconstruction, one as brief, ellip-
> tical, and economical as a password, I would say simply and without
> overstatement: *plus d'une langue* – both more than a language and no
> more of *a* language.[13]

3) The origin is conceptual, as evidenced by such statements as 'The origin of deconstruction is translation' or 'The origin of deconstruction is the kiss'. There is the history to such statements, which would also have to be taken into account.
4) An origin, whatever one's approach, is legible, down to the facts. It is the 'what happened'. Even in the absence of the word itself.

11   Things – if there were such a thing – come about – illegible

The intonations and scansions of such a statement – if it were such – could preoccupy us even without any determination of its validity, usefulness or felicity. Grammatically, one might expect several other possibilities. In other words, the statement could be read as without grammar, a mistake, on the verge of losing any sense, almost illegible, almost unreadable, if these two words might be the same sense from the vantage of two different languages.

12   Scansion 1: there is nothing to say

I have nothing to say except that the origin is illegible, which means that I have nothing to say about the origin. And yet, if something comes about, even illegibly, is there some effect by which that origin is recognized or read, even in its illegibility? And why would the predicate of illegibility apply, be applicable to the origin? Why would the readability of an origin, even the sense of origin, be readable? What is the force pushing this readability?

13   Scansion 2

Perhaps one ought not to scan such outlandish statements. The unread-ability of the illegible is not only effective, hence pedagogical, but also the origin's origin. The origin claims readability, makes claims of readability in its illegibility, in its 'origin'. The origin of the origin is the readability that is illegible.

14   Commencement redux

If the topic here today and elsewhere is the origins of deconstruction, I want to propose a simple beginning. Against the unreadability of the illegible, I want to propose the reading of writing and difference of that origin, that illegibility that the origin is as origin. And by the example of the historicity of the writing and difference before *différance*, a less than artful reading, a mere reading here, of *Writing and Difference*, to specify one of the almost illegible effects of the origin of deconstruction.

15   Firstness

I do not wish to repeat here the complications of the reading of the 'first' books of Derrida, the first on the 'Origin of Geometry', most recently superseded by the appearance of the earlier work on Husserl that appears to give its title to one of the pieces in *Writing and Difference*. The other two are those works published in 1967, *Speech and Phenomena* and *Of Grammatology*. I have arbitrarily chosen this volume of essays because of the piece on Jabès and subsequently the essays on the origins. A subtitle could be given to the collection: On the origin of origins.

16

But I am not being clear. The question of the origin and of its spacing from itself is the interrogation of reading. The stake of the legibility and illegibility of the origin and of reading is the origin of reading. Phenolegocentrism might describe this long-established radical of reading and origin in the Western tradition. From France to Greece, in the geography of this piece as a deferred reading of 'Plato's Pharmacy'.

17

The eventualities hasten precipitously; the illegibility of the origin is quickly absorbed in its readability, the legibility of its appearance, its coming about.

18

19

Of Grammatology has the exorbitant method, *Speech and Phenomena* has the supplement of the origin. The origin of deconstruction reads the origin of the origin. And yet, there is nothing from which it may orient or originate itself.

20   On parle français

The origin of deconstruction, even in its illegibility, is French. Which solves nothing. See 'French Kissing' about the difficulties of national philosophy.[14]

21   Precursors

The origins of deconstruction can also be parsed as the origins that deconstruction brings about or concerns itself with or makes possible or legible. Not the origin of deconstruction as deconstruction, but the origins within the nonmethod of deconstruction. The illegibility here might be a simple mistake. The origins are quite legible. We read and reread, find within those origins much of the early work of deconstruction. And then there is the work of the precursors. Except where, when, and how to draw the difference of these two: precursor and deconstruction. A perhaps theoretical question, drawing this line defers reading: an eventual illegibility that (re)marks the discussions about deconstruction not with the Rortian 'not yet' (not yet, please, not yet, because the ironic arriving too early means the end of the interest in deconstruction), not with the de Manian rhetoricity against an aesthetic ideology, but with radicalness of a tempo before any before and after, with then a secondariness always in danger of 'being definitively lost'.[15]

22

There is the book, and there is the question. And so there is legibility, for which illegibility is always its absence. But what if there isn't first the book and the legible. What of all the rest? What, as Derrida asks, if the 'radical illegibility' is not cut from the page of the book, but is the very possibility of the book:

> The radical illegibility of which we are speaking is not irrationality, is not despair provoking non-sense, is not everything within the domains of the incomprehensible and the illogical that is anguishing. Such an interpretation – or determination – of the illegible already belongs to the book, is enveloped within the possibility of the volume. Original illegibility is not simply a moment interior to the book, to reason or to logos; nor is it any more their opposite, having no relationship of symmetry to this, being incommensurable with them. Prior to the book (in the nonchronological sense), original illegibility is there the very possibility of the book and, within it, of the ulterior and eventual opposition of 'rationalism' and 'irrationalism'.[16]

23

And what of writing? Derrida is insistent that Jabès is not at fault for not raising these questions. Writing cannot affirm the origin except as forgetfulness.

24 Benjamin 2

While *The Origin of German Tragic Drama* exemplifies a method regarding the duality of insight regarding the original (restoration and development in history, reestablishment as incomplete, otherwise not original[17]), and while this is supported in *The Arcades Project* as the movement of the origin from nature to history, from the 'pagan context of nature' to the 'Jewish contexts of history',[18] in *The Arcades Project* the constellated image, the dialectical image, is bound up with the disjointure of time and reading:

> What distinguishes images from the 'essences' of phenomenology is their historical index. (Heidegger seeks in vain to rescue history for phenomenology abstractly through 'historicity'.) These images are to be thought of entirely apart from the categories of the 'human sciences', from the so-called habitus, from style, and the like. For the historical index of the images not only says that they belong to a particular time; it says, above all, that they attain to legibility only at a particular time. And, indeed, this acceding 'to legibility' constitutes a specific critical point in the movement in their interior. Every present day is determined by the images that are synchronic with it: each 'now' is the now of a particular recognizability. In it, truth is charged to the bursting point with time. (This point of explosion, and nothing else, is the death of the *intentio*, which thus coincides with the birth of authentic historical time, the time of truth.) It is not that what is past casts its light on what is present, or what is present its light on what is past; rather, image is that wherein what has been comes together in a flash with the now to form a constellation. In other words: image is dialectics at a standstill. For while the relation of the present to the past is purely temporal, the relation of what-has-been to the now is dialectical: not temporal in nature but figural [*bildlich*]. Only dialectical images are genuinely historical – that is, not archaic – images. The image that is read – which is to say, the image in the now of its recognizability – bears to the highest degree the imprint of the perilous critical moment on which all reading is founded.[19]

Citations could, and probably should, continue of *The Arcades Project*, in which the relation of reading and the image is explored in relation to the dream: image to be read is the dream image that calls the historian to the task of dream interpretation;[20] the real can be read like a text;[21] all the entries and fragments on the awakening and the relation to dreams. The one I want to turn to for just a moment concerns illegibility, the relation of the materiality of the illegibility as the origin for the basis of citation, which is the writing of history:

> The events surrounding the historian, and in which he himself takes part, will underlie his presentation in the form of a text written in invisible ink. The history which he lays before the reader comprises, as it were, the citations occurring in this text, and it is only these citations that occur in a manner legible to all. To write history thus means to *cite* history. It belongs to the concept of citation, however, that the historical object in each case is torn from its context.[22]

The eventuality of reading for Benjamin is critical with the hope of a particular time for reading. The illegibility of history acts as both the foundation for its legibility and for its recognizability. As in *The Origin of German Tragic Drama*, the dual insight of restoration and incompletion is reading the origin, the original, as secondary, as the citation of what cannot be read. This tearing from context occurs at a hoped-for particular time, the eventuality of its reading. Eventuality suggests that the relation between the particular time and its reading underlies the need of Benjamin to 'pay...heed over many years to every casual citation, every fleeting mention of a book',[23] to blast ruins (not into ruins, as if there were some totality, some thing, suddenly fragmented), such that ' "Construction" presupposes "destruction" '.[24]

And there is, as Derrida points out in *Fichus*, the later letter to Gretel Adorno on reading, on the dream with the motif of reading and fabric, dated 12 October 1939. The unreadability within the dream extends to all but the top of the letter 'd' and of the pattern of the sheets surreptitiously revealed by the woman in a kind of surreal 'perception' – 'The sheet must have had imagery similar to the kind I had probably "written" years ago to give to Dausse.'[25]

25   Reading tempos

Eventualities of reading are always intercalated with another. Each eventuality of reading intercalates with another. *Coup de calendrier*. Sometimes over centuries, sometimes less, even within one book.

26   On the illegibility of Calvino

'*O Fates! come, come: Cut thred and thrum*'.

Thrum:

crowd...Magnificence...Each of the ends of the warp-threads left unwoven and remaining attached to the loom when the web is cut off...fringe...To compress, condense...to fringe...[26]

Kairos:

> The right measure . . . [Lat. *modus*] . . . the right point of time . . . the right point, right spot . . . thrums on the beam of the loom . . .[27]

The task of the reader is to reckon with the thrums.

One pedagogy of reading radical illegibility would make the reader's reckoning opportune: the chance and turn of the thrum – a fringe, an ornament, the fabric frame on the loom from which is cut the opportunity of the web's weave.

The opportunism of the reader could be traced in Barthes's fragment and conventional, hence anti-chance, alphabet:

> The alphabetical order erases everything, banishes every origin. Perhaps in places, certain fragments seem to follow one another by some affinity; but the important thing is that these little networks not be connected, that they not slide into a single enormous network which would be the structure of the book, its meaning. It is in order to halt, to deflect, to divide this descent of discourse toward a destiny of the subject, that at certain moments the alphabet calls you to order (to disorder) and says: *Cut! Resume the story in another way* (but also, sometimes, for the same reason, you must break up the alphabet).[28]

Or in Derrida's destinerrance (the chance of chance):

> PS I forgot, you are completely right: one of the paradoxes of destination, is that if you wanted *to demonstrate*, for someone, that something never arrives at its destination, it's all over. The demonstration, once it had reached its end, would have proved what it was not supposed to demonstrate. But this is why, dear friend, I always say 'a letter *can* always *not* arrive at its destination, etc'. This is a chance . . . PS Finally a chance, if you will, if you yourself can, and if you have it, the chance (*tukhê*, fortune, this is what I mean, good fortune, good fate: us). The mischance (the mis-address) of this chance is that in order *to be able* not to arrive, it must bear within itself a force and a structure, a straying of the destination, such that it *must* also not arrive in any way. Even in arriving (always to some 'subject'), the letter takes itself away *from the arrival at arrival*. It arrives elsewhere, always several times.[29]

Or the rhizome of Deleuze and Guattari: 'The rhizome is an antigenealogy. It is a short-term memory, or antimemory'.[30]

But I want to remain on the fringe of things, on, for literature, the title and the play of a particular title in order to explore a legibility and illegibility that are structurally doubled:

Se una notte d'inverno un viaggiatore[31]
If on a winter's night a traveler[32]

Literature can suggest the completion of the link, that in fact the web never allows for the cut away project: 'You are about to begin reading Italo Calvino's new novel, *If on a winter's night a traveler*…And you say, "Just a moment, I've almost finished *If on a winter's night a traveler* by Italo Calvino" ' (first and last lines of said novel). And it is often read according to that suggestion, you say.

This frame can also hide its displacement.

The schematics of the matter appear simple enough. The frame of the opening and closing sentences sets in motion and brings to a stop a hyper-novel: a novel on/of the novel. Two readers, male and female (*Lettore* and *Lettrice*), begin to read a book, included in this book, but are interrupted (printing errors, binding errors, counterfeit authors and translators, etc.). They continue to read and search for the book they originally took up, and we readers read the 'novels' right along with the two 'readers'. In addition, there is the interrupted beginning of a story spaced throughout the novel in the titles of the included novels themselves. So 'we' have read *If on a winter's night a traveler* by the time we have finished the last sentence. The frame delimits the boundaries clearly, the citational play ('If on a winter's night…' is the title of the novel, the title of a novel included in the novel, the opening line of the beginning of a novel of titles) is well controlled, no matter how much a translator or an author want it otherwise.

And yet, you are told that you are about to begin reading Calvino's new novel. You surmise that this statement occurs in the preface, separated from the book, and that you will begin to read it in a moment, in the next few pages. You turn to the section within the novel with that title (is this the beginning postponed by the prefatory fringe of that first section?) and are interrupted shortly after starting by repeated signatures. There is only the beginning of the novel. You return to the bookstore for the correct copy, meet the woman reader you will search and read with, love and marry. And you conclude that the bindery is involved with two errors: the signatures repeat and the books got mixed up: Calvino's and Bazakbal's. 'Then the book you began reading with such involvement wasn't the book you thought but was a Polish novel instead. That is the book you are now so anxious to procure.'[33] You begin reading, but 'realize that the novel you are holding has nothing to do with the one you were reading yesterday'.[34]

And yet, within the novel there is the diary of the author, who 'anticipates' our venture.

> I have had the idea of writing a novel composed only of beginnings of novels. The protagonist could be a Reader who is continually interrupted. The Reader buys the new novel A by the author Z. But it is a defective copy, he can't go beyond the beginning […] He returns to the bookshop to have the volume exchanged…

I could write it all in the second person: you, Reader...I could also introduce a young lady, the Other Reader, and a counterfeiter-translator, and an old writer who keeps a diary like this diary...[35]

The schematics of the titles and this hypernovel structure could be indicated following Flannery's suggestion as follows:

A by Z is really B by Y, but B by Y isn't. It's C by X. Etc. **All within 'A by Z'.**

Perhaps I should indicate this structure as the reverse:

'A by Z' (or "A' by 'Z") is really 'B by Y', but 'B by Y' isn't. It's 'C by X'. Etc. **All within A by Z.**

On the loom, follow the threads, you can't get lost. There is no fringe but the loom itself: A by Z. The author-title secures the threads to itself. But then there is the cut: threads and thrums, and the title is the fringe, even tied off. And so what one reads isn't what one reads. This structure could be indicated as the eventuality of illegibility itself. There is no frame that isn't displaced: A by Z (with or without quotation marks) can only indicate the structure of being in danger of definitive loss. No tempo of reading can escape that structure.

'*Se una notte d'inverno un viaggiatore*' (the title in italic, underlined, and within quotation marks) cannot solve the dilemma: no agreement can prevent the further play (addition or subtraction) of the quotation marks. The borders of the text continually fold in on themselves.

27 A by Z

The discussion of Calvino can be extended and intercalated from numerous directions: the death of the author, the signature, the intentional and affective fallacies, intertextuality, dialogics and heteroglossia, to name some without any specific order, all of which attempt to investigate and establish the lines of literature, delimit literature and rules for reading, for legibility, for establishing the kinds of certainty of A by Z. In *Glas* this signature eventuality brings us back to the illegibility of the text. If the signature no longer signifies, is outside the order of signification or signifying, it is not by that illegible for Derrida. The illegibility is of the proper name, if such a thing exists, and is that without which there is no signification or text.

The *seing* does not suffer to be illegible in this respect. If, at least, reading means (to say) to decipher a sense or to refer to something. But this illegibility that takes form by falling (from my hand, for example), that scrambles and broaches signification, is that without which there would not be any text. A text 'exists', resists, consists, represses, lets itself be read or written only if it is worked (over) by the illegibility of a proper name. I have not – not yet – said that the proper name exists, or that it becomes illegible when it falls (to the tomb) in the signature. The proper name resounds, losing itself at once, only in the instant of its *debris*, when it is broken, scrambled, jammed, while touching, tampering with the *seing*.[36]

The first comer or first glance is certainly not the author's. The radical illegibility 'before' the book here meets up with the *a tergo* illegibility of the author:

> everything is always attacked *de dos, from the back*, written, described from behind. *A tergo*. I am *already* (dead) signifies that I am *behind*. Absolutely behind, the *Derrière* that will have never been seen from the front, the *Déjà* that nothing will have proceeded, which therefore conceived and gave birth to itself, but as a cadaver or glorious body. To be behind is to be before all – in a rupture of symmetry. I cut myself off, I entrench myself – behind – I bleed [*je saigne*] at the bottom of my text. 'The author of a beautiful poem is always dead' (*Miracle of the Rose*).
>
> At the same time, by cutting myself off, by entrenching myself, by withdrawing my presence, by dying, I escape the blows in advance. The Behind and the Already, the *Derrière* and the *Déjà*, protect me, make me illegible, shelter me on the text's verso. I am accessible, legible, visible only in a rearview mirror.[37]

In danger of definitive loss – the eventuality of any reading – the text is read out of and in the tempo of illegibility, not its illegibility, as if to imply prior possession or decline, not in the reading scenes of recognition, but in the recognition that the definitive loss always already occurs in the diremption of the 'redemptive'. To speak then of the origin(s) of deconstruction is to speak of, to seek out, to write and read this displacement of reading and writing in general textuality. Perhaps only a hair's breadth, but with a certain absolute seism absolutely imperceptible.

Notes

1. Theodor Adorno, *Minima Moralia: Reflections from Damaged Life*, trans. E. F. N. Jephcott (London: New Left Books, 1974), 247 (# 153 of Part Three, 1946–47).
2. Walter Benjamin, *Gesammelte Schriften: Band VI: Fragmente vermischten Inhalts, Autobiographische Schriften*, ed. Rolf Tiedemann and Hermann Schweppenhäuser (Frankfurt am Main: Suhrkamp 1985), 32 and 205; see *Selected Writings: Volume 1: 1913–1926*, ed. Marcus Bullock and Michael W. Jennings (Cambridge MA: Belknap Press of Harvard University Press, 1996), 92 for fragment 16.

3. Gershom Scholem, *Walter Benjamin: The Story of a Friendship*, trans. Harry Zohn (New York: Schocken, 1981), 61; quoted in Benjamin, *Gesammelte Schriften: Band VI*, 655.
4. Walter Benjamin, *Selected Writings: Volume 2: 1927–1934*, trans. Rodney Livingstone et al. (Cambridge MA: Belknap Press of Harvard University Press, 1999), 697–8.
5. Jacques Derrida, 'La pharmacic de Platon', in *La dissémination* (Paris: Seuil, 1972), 71.
6. Jacques Derrida, 'Plato's Pharmacy', in *Dissemination*, trans. Barbara Johnson (Chicago: University of Chicago Press, 1981), 63.
7. Rodolphe Gasché, *The Wild Card of Reading: on Paul de Man* (Cambridge MA: Harvard University Press, 1998), 176–81.
8. Derrida, 'Plato's Pharmacy', 171.
9. Gilles Deleuze, *Negotiations: 1972–1990*, trans. Martin Joughin (New York: Columbia University Press, 1995), 121.
10. See Richard Macksey and Eugenio Donato (eds), *The Structuralist Controversy* or *The Languages of Criticism and the Sciences of Man* (Baltimore: Johns Hopkins University Press, 1970, 1972).
11. Jacques Derrida, *Positions*, trans. Alan Bass (Chicago: University of Chicago Press, 1981).
12. Jacques Derrida, *Of Grammatology*, trans. Gayatri Chakravorty Spivak (Baltimore: Johns Hopkins University Press, 1974, 1976, 1997), 10.
13. Jacques Derrida, *Memoires: for Paul de Man*, trans. Cecile Lindsay et al. (New York: Columbia University Press, 1986, 1989), 15.
14. 'French Kissing', in Julian Wolfreys et al. (eds), *French Connections: Exploring the Literary and National Contexts of Derridean Discourse* (Albany: SUNY Press, 1999), 149–63.
15. Derrida, 'Plato's Pharmacy', 63.
16. Jacques Derrida, 'Edmond Jabes and the Questions of the Book', in *Writing and Difference*, trans. Alan Bass (Chicago: University of Chicago Press, 1978), 77.
17. Walter Benjamin, *The Origin of German Tragic Drama*, trans. John Osborne (London: Verso, 1977), 45–6.
18. Walter Benjamin, *The Arcades Project*, trans. Howard Eiland and Kevin McLaughlin (Cambridge MA: Belknap Press of Harvard University Press, 1999), 462.
19. ibid., 462–63 [N3, 1].
20. ibid., 464.
21. ibid., 464 [N4, 2].
22. ibid., 476 [N11, 3].
23. ibid., 470 [N7, 4].
24. ibid., 470 [N7, 6].
25. Walter Benjamin, *The Correspondence of Walter Benjamin, 1910-1940*, ed. Gershom Scholem and Theodor W. Adorno, trans. Manfred R. Jacobson and Evelyn M. Jacobson (Chicago: University of Chicago Press, 1994), 614–16.
26. *Oxford English Dictionary*.
27. Liddell and Scott Greek Lexicon.
28. Roland Barthes, *Roland Barthes*, trans. Richard Howard (New York: Hill and Wang, 1977), 148.
29. Jacques Derrida, *The Post Card*, trans. Alan Bass (Chicago: University of Chicago Press, 1987), 123.
30. Gilles Deleuze and Félix Guattari, *A Thousand Plateaus*, trans. Brian Massumi (Minneapolis: University of Minnesota Press, 1987), 21.

31. Italo Calvino, *Se una notte d'inverno un viaggiatore* (Torino: Einaudi, 1979).
32. Italo Calvino, *If on a Winter's Night a Traveler*, trans. William Weaver (New York: Harcourt, 1981).
33. ibid., 28.
34. ibid., 33.
35. ibid., 197–8. Entry from Silas Flannery's diary.
36. Jacques Derrida, *Glas*, trans. John Leavey and Richard Rand (Lincoln: University of Nebraska Press, 1986), 32b–33b.
37. ibid., 84b.

11
Origins of Deconstruction? Deconstruction, That Which Arrives (If It Arrives)

Julian Wolfreys

> A (metaphysical) thought, which begins by searching for origins or foundations and proceeds to a reconstruction in order, infallibly finds that things have not happened as they ought [...] The more naïve believe in a paradise lost, the more cunning restore order by claiming to think, in order, the absence or loss of order. For Derrida, as for Heidegger... one is constructing things on an unquestioned value: *presence*.
>
> *Geoffrey Bennington*[1]

> ...(but what is more problematic than this concept of an original base for a fictional work?)...
>
> *J. Hillis Miller*[2]

> Men can do nothing without the make-believe of a beginning. Even science, the strict measurer, is obliged to start with a make-believe unit, and must fix a point in the stars' unceasing journey when his sidereal clock shall pretend that time is set at Nought. His less accurate grandmother Poetry has always understood to start in the middle; but on reflection it appears that her proceeding is not very different from his; since Science, too, reckons backwards as well as forwards, divides his unit into billions, and with his clock-finger at Nought really sets off *in medias res*. No retrospect will take us to the true beginning.
>
> *George Eliot*[3]

What does this phrase, *origins of deconstruction*, imply, name, state or identify? In whose interests is such a remark? What, in its articulation, remains either silenced and unread or otherwise remains to be said? Does it give us to read a disabling and impossible temporality in the same place as the desire for an identity? Who is interested in pursuing 'the origins of deconstruction'? What haunts the structure of this expression? Does it amount to an idiom or axiom? Of what order are the motifs of this phrase? What 'concepts' does anyone believe to be mobilized in whatever this phrase stages? What is going on *between* 'origins' and 'deconstruction'?

Everything takes place between

To hypothesize or otherwise to inquire into the 'origins of deconstruction' is to repeat, whether intentionally or otherwise, the age-old metaphysical demand or desire for foundation, for Logos and, from such a location, discernible order or progression as the historicity of that founding, originary site or concept. Accompanying such an inquiry for an ideality, at once 'supratemporal and omnitemporal',[4] would be the assumption or search for an absent presence or identity, which, in itself, is comprehended as complete, undifferentiated, homogeneous, full, simple and self-sufficient. Yet, as Michel Foucault has it, in a 'response' from 1968 to the Paris Epistemology Circle, 'analysis of discourse [is always]...a quest for and repetition of an origin that escapes all determination of origin'.[5] Still, one behaves as though there were both beginnings *and* a traceable continuity between those beginnings and the point at which any such inquiry begins with the injunction to turn back, as though one could offer, in Jacques Derrida's words, the reconstitution of 'the pure tradition of a primordial Logos toward a polar Telos'.[6] Indeed, as Foucault in the article already cited points out, such behaviour is, if not a manifestation of institutional power, then the institution, the singular *inauguration*, of a power the purpose of which is to effect a kind of self-reflective, self-interested discursive maintenance of that very continuity. It is, in turn, the function of the metaphysical demand to delineate that continuity, thereby maintaining the very same continuity. Such a gesture 'function[s] to guarantee the infinite continuity of discourse and its secret presence to itself in the action of an absence that is always one stage further back'.[7] As Foucault's remarks make plain, the processes in question are, of course, not restricted either to the immediate or previous interests in a supposed 'history', 'historicity', or 'genealogy' of 'deconstruction' (which I place in quotation marks in order to suspend the possibility of a ready assumption of meaning, value or identity for this word), which concentration serves to orientate the various essays in the present volume. It is, instead, the work of a certain procedural thinking, as is explicit in Foucault's comments, and as already addressed at the beginning of this paragraph; and, again, before that particular starting point, in the initial epigraph to this essay.[8]

Yet, as is well known, Jacques Derrida in a number of places addresses the logic of this search, and, equally, its fruitlessness. It is tempting to suggest that this 'major concern of Derrida's analysis', as Arkady Plotnitsky sums it up,[9] has been with Derrida from the beginning of his published works in 1962, with the *Introduction to* 'The Origin of Geometry'. 'The Time before First' offers another example.[10] While the motif of 'origin' or 'origins' (and the plural, at least, initially, does nothing in any drastic manner to 'origin-singular', at least not unless we call into question the concept and thinking of 'origin') as starting points appear to promise a beginning in being called to our attention, such a gesture only ' "begins" by following a certain vestige. *i.e.* a certain repetition or text'.[11] In 'Qual Quelle',[12] the impossibility of assigning either origin or source is also considered, as Derrida responds to these motifs in relation to questions of identity and consciousness in Paul Valéry. The source, we read, 'cannot be reassembled into its originary unity'.[13] In addition, we learn it is the philosopher, as exemplary representative of the laws of the institutional search outlined above, who (according to Valéry), always in search of the origin, of an originary voice or presence, voice as the guarantee of presence, reproduces what Derrida calls the 'crisis of the origin'[14] (a crisis acknowledged in Bennington's remarks, above) in the very act of writing on such a theme, whereby there is to be perceived 'discontinuity, delay, heterogeneity, and alterity...a system of differential traces'[15] that get the origin going.

The procedures by which the search for origin get underway and by which crisis comes to be reproduced take place around the name of 'deconstruction' also. Whether within the limits of an institutionalized programme of analysis, proceeding by all the protocols that such a programme prescribes or, more generally, in posing the question of determining 'deconstruction' and, specifically, 'origins of deconstruction', as though the terms and the concepts they appear to name are taken as understood, is to have comprehended nothing that has been said, for example, by Derrida and others concerning 'deconstruction'. As Derrida has remarked,

> deconstruction, in the singular, is not 'inherently' anything at all...the logic of essence...is precisely what all deconstruction has *from the start* called into question...Deconstruction does not exist somewhere, pure, proper, self-identical, outside of its inscriptions in conflictual and differentiated contexts; it 'is' only what it does and what is done with it, there where *it takes place*...[emphases added][16]

That 'deconstruction' only 'is', that it only has some momentary, provisional 'being' or 'identity' where and whenever it takes place, if it takes place, suggests that it is impossible to speak of 'deconstruction' 'in the singular', as is well known. This also suggests, furthermore, that because 'deconstruction' can only be discerned where it takes place, and because every instance will necessarily be perceived as differing from every other in the various 'conflictual and differentiated contexts', 'deconstruction-in-the-singular' cannot be assigned origins other than the 'origin', if we can use this term in this fashion, of its taking place on every occasion. Moreover, that 'it' can only be reflected on 'in the singular' as an event both inappropriate to and unappropriable for any 'univocal definition'[17] or totalizing determination signals that fact of 'its' instability. Certainly, in the light of this, it would be an act of misrecognition or misappropriation to attempt to gather together the work of various deconstructions, if in such a gathering there took place the erasure of differences between them (regardless, for the moment of the 'system of differential traces' making up any 'deconstruction') in order to produce the 'univocal definition'.

Several contiguous remarks need to be made: 1) whatever goes by the name 'deconstruction' simultaneously *exceeds* and *lacks* any ontological or metaphysical determination; 2) 'deconstruction' is irreducible to any statement or formula beginning 'deconstruction is...' or 'deconstruction is not...' (i.e., any modality producing identification as stabilization); 3) deconstruction (and here I will abandon the quotation marks), if it *is* anything, is that which necessarily *takes place* within any manifestation of structure *as* necessary to and yet which is radically incommensurable with or irreducible to that structure's identity or meaning. As Derrida remarks of deconstruction, it is '*firstly* this destabilization on the move in, if one could speak thus, "the things themselves"; but it is not negative' (emphasis added).[18] It is thus provisionally figurable as the non-identity *of* and *within* yet also other than any identity, where 'non-identity' is comprehended not as negation or dialectical opposite, but as the sign of *différance*. Deconstruction thus provides a provisional 'name' for the trace of an alterity by which the perception of identity is made possible even as otherness remains invisible, unacknowledged. If it is anything at all, it does not in fact require or await a subject's cognition or consciousness (as Derrida remarks in 'Letter to a Japanese Friend'[19]) to determine what is called deconstruction by assigning an undifferentiated or universal meaning to, or identity for, a 'singular event', for want of a better phrase.

One of the problems, then, surrounding the misunderstanding and misappropriation of deconstruction, so called, is ontological specifically, as well as being more generally metaphysical. If we turn to Martin Heidegger briefly, on the problem of determining Being, the procedures by which deconstruction as a term is made to operate in some quarters comes into focus. To recall a point just made, it appears as if deconstruction functions as a name, yet what it names is not this precarious trait but something determinate and delimitable; it is, therefore, a name used to identify a 'certain sameness in differentiation'. The phrase is Heidegger's, and he employs it to determine particular ontological approaches to the apprehension of Being: 'we understand being... in such a way that it expresses a certain sameness in differentiation, even though we are unable to grasp it'.[20] From this awareness, Heidegger concludes that, with regard to Being, 'there is no genus in itself'.[21] The same can, of course, be said of deconstruction.[22] This is insufficient, however. The definition of genus must, necessarily, be raised. Heidegger asks (and answers) thus:

> What is a genus? That which is universal and common to the many and can be differentiated and organized into species by the addition of specific differences. Genus is inherently related to species. Genus is inherently related to species and thus to species-constituting differentiation.[23]

It is instructive to watch Heidegger construct a circular logic here. In admitting to differentiation, he determines genus according to a range of species comprising differences that are relational rather than of the order of radical, heterogeneous difference. Being relational, such differences are also subordinate, in accordance, and of a piece, with the notion of genus. Thus the analysis of genus, proceeding by the acknowledgement of differentiation according to which the architectonic is delineated, makes a gesture by which it can fold back on itself, whereby 'species-constituting differentiation' is the connective fibre that allows us to know or assume genus. Such 'species-constituting differentiation' is only that belonging to the order of the same: that which constitutes the species and, from that gesture of folding back, to the implicitly circular reconstitution of the genus as an identity comprising so many genus-constituting species. In turn, the genus then becomes of the order of the self-same called the universal: 'the universal, comprehended and defined as species-enabling genus, is usually called "concept".'[24] However,

> [i]f being is not a genus, then it cannot be comprehended as a concept, nor can it be conceptualized ... If the delimitation of a concept ... is called definition, then this means that all definitional determinations of being must on principle fail.[25]

Quite simply, all misunderstanding concerning deconstruction arises from an ontological imperative, as it were, towards conceptualization. Being is not available to ontological inquiry, it is not a category or entity like others, and can only be known, as Heidegger makes clear in *Being and Time*, through beings and through a recognition of the irreducible difference *between* beings, which in turn allows for the thinking of being to arise. Similarly, deconstruction. Irreducible to either concept or origin (whether singular or multiple), deconstruction can only be known, if it can be known at all, as that which is already underway, already at work and within, ontological inquiry and conceptualization.

In the face of these statements concerning this peculiar name 'deconstruction' and the potential itineraries for reading that they might be imagined as generating, it has to be said that there are no 'origins of deconstruction' as such.

Such a response must give the reader pause, however. For, even though this statement situates itself in relation to the question or demand concerning origins-of-deconstruction and it does so, moreover, by pointing out the ways in which such a question might be construed as being articulated within and by wholly conventional parameters, its articulation is made possible only by those same conventions. It is given according to the very programme identified as the limit of the question itself. Responses, therefore, apparently in opposition, announce a role already assigned in the structure of iden-tification described as speculative dialectics. Situated in opposition to and subordinated by the instituting violence of the demand, the assumption in this response is that the question (or demand) with reference to origins-of-deconstruction is to be read in an entirely predictable way, and that this is the only reading available for that which calls this and other essays into being, a title which is not posed as a question as such but, instead, is simply stated: origins of deconstruction. The banal conventionality of the retort is clearly apparent in its resistance to the assumptions seeming to motivate the phrase in question. Furthermore, the reply – and this clearly is a reply, even if no question or statement were present, given a reading of the conventions of its various remarks – is markedly unoriginal, in all senses of that word. For not only does it say nothing that has not been said before, many times in a number of different ways, it presents nothing 'original', it has nothing of an 'origin' about it. It belongs to the predictable academic gesture or genre, the response or remark or, rather, re-mark, this being the re-statement, the re-situation of more or less established, if not canonical, positions or loca-tions within some manifestation of that dialectical structure, repeated again and again, without the adequate or necessary consideration of the concepts, motifs, tropes or terms herein employed.

So, let's begin again

Supposing the impossible. This is what is called for in the issuing of a request or command to write on 'the origins of deconstruction': a speculation on the possibility of the impossible, specifically in the guise of mapping or deter-mining so-called 'origins'. At the same time what is required in at least one reading of the injunction that causes this essay to be written is a gradual delimitation of the proper, of what is or might be proper allegedly to so-called deconstruction 'in the humanities', 'in the university today', 'in the history of Western thought'. What is demanded in effect is a response involv-ing the work of cartography. It is necessary to recognize, though, that such labour would have to proceed in the face of the unmappable, as though the inscription of every topographical co-ordinate invoked or implied countless others, in a constellation that, far from being exhaustible, would moreover enervate in the face of its own generative powers. Before – such a fantasy! – the location of any origin as such there would take place inevitably and inescapably multiplicity and multiplication, a fraying even as one seeks to tie together loose ends. One has, therefore, to turn back, to define the starting place of this essay not as a starting point at all, but instead as a necessary response, a reaction, to the impossible injunction and the impossibility that the injunction addresses and proliferates. Doubtless, there is more to say about this imaginary scenario.

The impossible attempt to consider the concept of origins, the origin, the very idea of an origin or origins *for* or *of* the notion of the origin (*an* origin, *some* origin) or, in fact, considering origins in all their impossibility clearly becomes even more impossible when the question concerning the location of origins is linked to this strange word, deconstruction. It appears then that I am asked to think with supposition and with speculation, supposing for the moment supposition or speculation to be modalities of thinking rather than the suspension of thought narrowly conceived in favour of some process of projection or conception, and asking for some impossible answer. The answer is impossible, strictly speaking, because the very idea of an answer implicitly assumes a moment of finality. There is implicit, often all the more marked for being so tacit, in the idea of an answer the assumption of speculation, projection and conception as modalities of thought that are perhaps related to but not wholly consonant with the rigorous thinking of a concept. There is furthermore in the assumption of the speculative project the idea that its problems can come to rest so that, teleologically or hermeneutically, where one ends is the origin itself, unfolded and refolded onto itself, a supplementary doubling of what had been there all along. As though the end were the beginning, as though destination were origin. The logic of circularity and the circularity of logic here inscribed are clearly haunted. And what haunts the effect of closing the circle is this phantom or phantasm of the origin, an origin, from the very elusiveness of which one must start all over again, fulfilling the promise of the Foucauldian assessment. What disturbs therefore, to return to where I began, is a barely submerged desire, all the more compulsive for being so caught up with the impossible and masquerading as some institutionally authorized archaeological or archival retrospect. Believing one can begin at all reveals in any such inaugural gesture the call of the institution, and the subjection of subjection interpellated by that call.

The very idea of the origin is thus that which arises inevitably and the search for the origin or origins belongs to a question or family of questions impossible to answer – what if? What if there were origins for deconstruction, what if there were an origin or origins of deconstruction? This is the starting point, the illusion of a beginning, and, it has to be added, *a beginning all over again*. Such a start, such an 'origin', begins and can only begin then as a response to a response.[26] Such circularity concerning origin is observed by Heidegger, in 'The Origin of the Work of Art'.[27] At the very beginning of the essay, Heidegger, stating that the 'question concerning the origin of the work of art asks about the source of its nature', offers the predictable answer – 'the usual view' – to that question: the artist.[28] Immediately after, however, the question and answer are folded back on themselves, as Heidegger continues by pointing out that the determination of the artist as artist only arises as a result of the work: 'The artist is the origin of the work. The work is the origin of the artist.'[29] Thus, 'origin here means that from and by which something is what it is and as it is'.[30] On this understanding, no absolute origin is either possible or conceivable, given the enfolding and regenerative reciprocity of the structural schema proposed by Heidegger; a schema, I would add, which propels itself in a double act: that of a doubling of any singular locatable place of origin outside or before any event, and also a dismantling, not only of the traditional conceptualization of origin, but also of the stabilizing separatism of the binary calculation: artist/work. Interestingly, Heidegger's gesture also disturbs the temporal priority on which any notion of origin is founded. More than this, however, there is in Heidegger's instituting complication a performative element. Clearly displacing itself as a response to a question arriving from some other place, Heidegger's beginning, in Dennis J. Schmidt's words, 'must not be taken as an excuse for an awkward or misfired beginning to the text but as a comment on the character of the beginning as such'.[31] However, I would argue for risking a stronger reading than Schmidt's: as just stated, Heidegger's gambit works so startlingly precisely because he does not merely *comment on*, as would the philosopher on the source, issuing what he or she believes to be a constative statement. Rather, the performative dimension has to be insisted on here. It is precisely this performativity which destabilizes logical calculation from within, radicalizing the thinking of origin from the start. And yet, of course, it is not so simple to decide on whether Heidegger's argument and the way in which he states it are simply *either* performative *or* constative. For, similar to Heidegger's scandalous assertions concerning a disseminative reciprocity between artist and work (or work and artist), so too, before any determination, his own discourse materially suspends the possibility of identification through its redoublings and divisions, especially in the first page, but also, arguably, throughout the entire essay. As J. Hillis Miller remarks apropos this suspension between the constative and performative, 'the tension between the two functions means that the performative aspect of the text makes it produce deceptive, illusory knowledge, or the illusion of knowledge'.[32]

But this is merely an illustration and a detour. If I attempt to imagine an origin or more than one origin, or even no more origins either for or of deconstruction, deconstructions, my response is then not a beginning as such (but this is already announced and is hardly original). I find myself entering into or, perhaps more accurately, locating myself within and in relation to a self-reflexive circularity which disrupts the certainty of the metaphysical demand, while engaging with the possibility that such an encircling 'opens up its own conditions'. Reflexive engagement clearly identifies itself as a response to the call, the demand, the injunction to speculate. In turn, such an injunction arrives or arises and comes to be seen as not itself an instituting formulation but, rather, a response in itself, to the other in itself, to that speculative 'what if'. Speculation hides itself and yet returns in, thereby exceeding the violence and logic (the violent logic) of institution and demand. This is where we are.

Imagine though for the moment the impossible, imagine that this is the place to begin: that it is possible start to speak of 'origins of deconstruction'. One might start, cautiously and conventionally enough, with a quotation.

> Necessarily, since it [deconstruction] is neither a philosophy, nor a doctrine, nor a knowledge, nor a method, nor a discipline, not even a determinate concept, only what happens if it happens [*ce qui arrive si ça arrive*].[33]

It is perhaps noticeable that the bracketed French – and it seems that, if there is a history or even an origin, or origins of deconstruction, one is always enjoined, silently, invisibly, or otherwise, to bracket the French, to demarcate some boundary, some location or idiom – appears in other words in my title. As one beginning, I have let go the more normative, more conventional translation (what happens if it happens) in the title, in order to emphasize arrival, a certain unexpected, yet inevitable, insistence, a certain idiomatic interruption or eruption of arrival, as though arrival and, specifically, the *arrival of an origin*, never happened only once, for the first time, but could take place, over and over again, and in a manner moreover irreducible to, uncontrollable by, any taxonomy or conceptualization of arrival. Which, of course, takes place already in the name of deconstruction. (A parenthesis: it is not going too far perhaps to suggest another translation, one redolent, inadvertently or not, with what might be called a 'biblical' resonance: that which comes to pass [if it comes to pass]. Such a phrase appears to acknowledge, to comment on, a simple event – *and it came to pass*. However, it might more appropriately be considered a performative statement the rhythms of which are pertinent to the present consideration. The articulation or inscription of the line, whether in the present, past or infinitive forms – it comes to pass, it came to pass, to come to pass – delineates a movement, the first part of which, coming toward a location or point of reference (such as the subject) and arriving from a future, the second part, departing from the point of reference, traversing it, and moving into a past. Writing or speaking this phrase traces materially – performs – that on which it is the purpose of the phrase to comment. Such a motion in the materiality of the letter marks and is marked by a disorientation of spatial and temporal assurances, announcing as it does a 'destabilization on the move'.) The spectral figure of an unanticipatable arrival, the ghostly arrival of such

a figure, might be said to figure – possibility of the impossible – origins-
of-deconstruction. That which cannot be anticipated concerning the arrival
thereby speaks of the undecidability of deconstruction/s, if I can say this, and
therefore, perhaps, of 'deconstruction's origins' (do deconstructions 'originate'? Do deconstructions cause origins to arrive, to happen or to come to
pass? Are deconstructions original?) even as origin takes place, in the chance
of deconstructions. How do we do justice to this?

In the face of the experience of the undecidable which the idea of the
'origin' names, it has to be recognized and stressed, again and again, that the
very idea is enigmatic, *auto-occlusive* perhaps; all the more mystifying even,
precisely because these names, *origin, origins*, are all too often deployed as
though what was being named were blatant, all too obvious and self-evident,
as though nothing could be clearer than the possibility of the origin. And
also hieratic and encrypted. For the mere sign of an origin or origins blares
the promise, the illusion, of a secret. And it is in such illusory certainty, a
rhetoric, if not a hegemony, of certainty,[34] that one encounters precisely the
obscurity that is situated at the obscure heart of any notion of origin. Take
the example and notion of tradition, as Foucault suggests:

> ... it is intended to give a special temporal status to a group of phenom-
> ena that are both successive and identical (or at least similar); it makes it
> possible to rethink the dispersion of history in the form of the same; it
> allows *a reduction of the difference proper to every beginning*, in order to pur-
> sue without discontinuity the endless search for origin [...] Then there
> is the notion of influence, which provides a support... which refers to an
> apparently causal process... [in which there is to be seen] the phenomena
> of resemblance and repetition [...] There are the notions of development
> and evolution: they make it possible to... link [events] to one and the
> same organizing principle... to discover already at work in each begin-
> ning, a principle of coherence and the outline of a future unity, to master
> time through a perpetually reversible relation *between an origin and a term
> that are never given*, but which are always at work.[35]

Tradition both authorizes and is authorized by origin. The one-and-only
time of origin is what tradition (or racial purity or the destiny of a nation)
both needs and is the means by which it keeps up the game. Influence, identity, succession, causality, resemblance, repetition, development, evolution:
in short, the delineation of that which amounts to a genetic purity. This
is the secret, a secret out in the open, promised by the idea of origin and
yet also hidden by that very idea, which obscurity justifies the inquiry into
origin, and which deconstruction arrives, if it arrives at all, to interrupt.

So, to return to the question of what happens, what arrives, what comes
to pass, what takes place, what passes (if it passes), what arrives (if it arrives
at all) *and also* what also cannot pass or come to pass, before which I am

immobilized, in the face of the impossible, impossibility itself: the demand, the call of the title, this impossible title, *origins of deconstruction*. This title arrived, as such things often do these days, in email, a demand and a request, an invitation from a friend, at one and the same time, then, both friendly *and* threatening. Its arrival recalled a question concerning arrival, concerning that strange figure of the *arrivant*, asked by Derrida: 'What is the *arrivant* that makes the event arrive?'[36] Derrida continues:

> The new *arrivant*, this word can, indeed, mean the neutrality of *that which* arrives, but also the singularity of *who* arrives, he or she who comes, coming to be where s/he was not expected, where one was awaiting him or her without waiting for him or her, without expecting *it* [*s'y attendre*], without knowing what or whom to expect, what or whom I am waiting for – such is hospitality itself, hospitality toward the event.[37]

Neutrality *and* singularity. Bearing this in mind – and returning to the first citation of Derrida, above, the one appearing, it should be noted, after the title (both titles, that which arrived via email, unexpectedly, and my own) and yet being one source, though not the only origin, for my title – it is no doubt possible, however reckless, to suggest different titles for this essay, if only so as to disrupt any sense of priority or origin: *deconstruction, that which arrives or happens (if it arrives or happens at all)* and *deconstruction, who arrives (if s/he arrives) or happens (if s/he happens at all)*. Whatever, or whoever, arrives unexpectedly causes to happen an event and, in anticipation of this originating arrival, I must wait without expectation; what is wholly, radically, original or, perhaps, ab-original, here is that which takes place *between* the *arrivant* and the subject. It is here, if anywhere, smallest of chances, that deconstructions, origins will, therefore, have occurred. *Origins-of-deconstruction come to pass in between*.

A note of caution. Everything takes place in 'between' (between beings, for example, or between the artist and the work of art). Yet, in the words of Jean-Luc Nancy, 'this "between", as its name suggests, has neither a consistency nor continuity of its own. It does not lead from one to the other; it constitutes no connective tissue [...] From one singular to another, there is contiguity but not continuity'.[38] It therefore follows that one cannot speak even of an origin (as such) *of* or *for* whatever chances to present itself *in* or *as* the figure of *between*, let alone *of* or *for* whatever one thinks one means when one speaks of *deconstruction*. *Between*, therefore, a motif without motive, the name of in-difference, intimate proximity *and* unbridgeable spacing – deconstruction, in other words, at the origin (one is tempted to say) of any search for origins or foundations, as Geoffrey Bennington has it.[39]

This is still to be too precipitate, however. Forestalling the illusion either of a beginning or any supposedly 'original' starting point as the beginnings of a tracing, consider the following consideration of Nancy's on the subject of origins:

> Meaning can only be right at [*à même*] existence [...] It is the indefinite plurality of origins and their coexistence... we do not gain access to the origin: access is refused by the origin's concealing itself in its multiplicity [...] The alterity of the other is its being-origin. Conversely, the originarity of the origin is its being-other, but it is a being-other *than* every being *for* and *in crossing through* [*à travers*] all being. Thus, the originarity of the origin is not a property that would distinguish a being from all others, because this being would then have to be something other than itself in order to have its origin in its own turn [...] the being-other of the origin is not the alterity of an 'other-than-the-world'. It is not a question of an Other... *than* the world; it is a question of the alterity or alteration *of* the world.[40]

Alterity, inaccessibility. There is inscribed here a response to and recognition of the priority and primordiality of alterities, heterogeneous and illimitable, irreducible to a negative theology governing the concept of an other. Such a determination would still imply an origin or source 'beyond' or 'other than', as the extract makes clear. If origin is an other, to place for the moment Stéphane Mallarmé's tongue in Jean-Luc Nancy's head, this is to comprehend origin radically as *différance* rather than source. Origin, therefore, nowhere as such, has always already returned not as itself but as a trace within any being as the non-identity of beings. There is, then, never the possibility either of an hypostasized Origin, or even multiple Origins, if by such a figure (and 'Origins' still is the name of figure-singular, if it is understood as indicating so many 'species' belonging to a genus aspiring to the universal concept of 'Origin') there is implied merely the polyvalent possibility of several sources for deconstruction. Rather, it is necessary to stress, in order to conclude this 'make-believe of a beginning', and following Nancy, that the idea of origin is incorrectly assumed if by this notion one believes one can identify or locate that to which deconstruction can be traced and yet which is separable from deconstruction, and thereby delimitable. At the same time, and to turn back to the beginning of this essay, it is also incorrect to assume that 'deconstruction' is a given, that the meaning of this word has been resolved epistemologically, which the presumption of origins would appear to announce. Indeed, one might risk the proposal that, if origin *is* an other and is only perceived through the trace of *différance*, *as* that irreducible disjunction and 'what makes every identity at once itself and different from itself',[41] is it not the case that deconstruction*s*, having to do with traces, 'with the logic of the "nonpresent remainder"', as Nicholas Royle puts it,[42] are the crossings-through that sign the being-other of origin, an origin, origins; or, to put this in another's words, in other words 'what emerges is in fact the very "origin" of [deconstructions], the material trace or the material inscription that would be the condition of possibility and the condition of impossibility'[43] of *origins*. And this can and does only take place, repeatedly, between.

Notes

1. Geoffrey Bennington, 'Derridabase', in Geoffrey Bennington and Jacques Derrida, *Jacques Derrida* (1991), trans. Geoffrey Bennington (Chicago: University of Chicago Press, 1993), 15–16.
2. J. Hillis Miller, 'Joseph Conrad: Should We Read *Heart of Darkness?*', in *Others* (Princeton: Princeton University Press, 2001), 135 n2.
3. George Eliot, *Daniel Deronda* ([1876] Oxford World's Classics, 1998), 1.
4. Jacques Derrida, *Edmund Husserl's 'Origin of Geometry': An Introduction* (1962) trans. (with Preface and Afterword) John P. Leavey Jr (Lincoln: University of Nebraska Press, 1989), 148.
5. Michel Foucault, 'On the Archaeology of the Sciences: Response to the Epistemology Circle', in Michel Foucault, *Aesthetics, Method, and Epistemology: Essential Works of Michel Foucault 1954–1984 Volume Two*, ed. James D. Faubion, trans. Robert Hurley et al. (New York: The New Press, 1998), 297–334, 306.
6. Derrida, *Introduction*, 149.
7. Foucault, 'Archeology', 306.
8. See Note 1.
9. Arkady Plotnitsky, *In the Shadow of Hegel: Complimentarity, History, and the Unconscious* (Gainesville: University Press of Florida, 1993), 238.
10. 'The Time before First', in Jacques Derrida, *Dissemination* (1972) trans. Barbara Johnson (Chicago: University of Chicago Press, 1981), 330–40.
11. Derrida, 'The Time before First', 330.
12. Jacques Derrida, 'Qual Quelle', in *Margins of Philosophy*, (1972) trans. Alan Bass (Chicago: University of Chicago Press, 1981), 273–306.
13. ibid., 279.
14. ibid., 291.
15. ibid.
16. Jacques Derrida, 'Afterword: Toward an Ethic of Discussion', trans. Samuel Weber, in *Limited Inc* (Evanston: Northwestern University Press, 1988), 141.
17. ibid., 141.
18. ibid., 147.
19. Jacques Derrida, 'Letter to a Japanese Friend', trans. David Wood and Andrew Benjamin, in David Wood and Robert Bernasconi (eds), *Derrida and Différance* (1985) (Evanston: Northwestern University Press, 1988), 4.
20. Martin Heidegger, *Aristotle's Metaphysics Θ 1–3: On the Essence and Actuality of Force* (1981). Second edition, trans. Walter Brogan and Peter Warnek (Bloomington: Indiana University Press, 1995), 28.
21. Heidegger, *Aristotle's Metaphysics*, 29.
22. An obvious, though instructive, difference being that Being has been subject to inquiry, speculation, and attempted definition for far longer than deconstruction. What is instructive, however, is that approaches to the absolute or universal determination of deconstruction are 'contaminated' by the same logic, the logic

which makes the demand 'What is…?', and which also, sooner or later, desires to pursue the matter of origins.

23. Heidegger, *Aristotle's Metaphysics*, 29.
24. ibid., 30.
25. ibid.
26. Arguably, the relentless structure I am describing can be seen in the situation of Foucault's comments cited at the beginning of this essay, which belong to a response to a demand on the part of the Paris Epistemology Circle, a demand to define 'the critical propositions on which the possibility of his theory and the implications of his method are *founded*' (Foucault, 'Archeology', 297; emphasis added), coming as the Circle's response to *Madness and Civilization*, *Birth of the Clinic* and *The Order of Things*. The words quoted here are those of the Circle, not Foucault's interpretation.
27. Martin Heidegger, 'The Origin of the Work of Art', in *Poetry, Language, Thought*, trans. and introduced by Albert Hofstadter (New York: Harper and Row, 1971), 15–89.
28. ibid., 17.
29. ibid.
30. ibid.
31. Dennis J. Schmidt, *The Ubiquity of the Finite: Hegel, Heidegger, and the Entitlements of Philosophy* (Cambridge MA: MIT Press, 1988), 102. Schmidt's reading continues in the same passage by pointing out how Heidegger opposes the figure of circularity to the 'traditional metaphysical admiration for…syllogistic straight lines'. Such straight lines, such unbroken linearity in general are, doubtless, those that would trace the continuity between a discourse, subject, or concept, and its origin.
32. J. Hillis Miller, *Speech Acts in Literature* (Stanford: Stanford University Press, 2001), 153.
33. Jacques Derrida, 'Et Cetera… (and so on, und so weiter, and so forth, et ainsi de suite, und so überall, etc.)', trans. Geoffrey Bennington, in Nicholas Royle (ed.), *Deconstructions: A User's Guide* (Basingstoke: Palgrave, 2000), 288.
34. Not to sound too certain about this, but it is perhaps a feature of many 'discussions' of or, more accurately, polemics concerning origins (let us say, for example, those on the part of particular fundamentalist Christian constituencies) that certainty is hegemonic inasmuch as there is no place available for the possibility of discussion, debate, challenge, uncertainty, scepticism, speculation or, indeed, any form of discourse, dialectical or otherwise, which would be able, according to the laws and rules of the discourse on origin, to question or call into question any article of faith. Nothing perhaps is more certain about a discourse which asserts certainty when nothing could be less certain than origin, an origin, origins.
35. Michel Foucault, *The Archaeology of Knowledge* (1969) trans. A. M. Sheridan Smith (London: Tavistock, 1972), 22, emphasis added.
36. Jacques Derrida, 'Finis', in *Aporias* (1993) trans. Thomas Dutoit (Stanford: Stanford University Press, 1993), 33.
37. Derrida, 'Finis', 33.
38. Jean-Luc Nancy, *Being Singular Plural* (1996) trans. Robert D. Richardson and Anne E. O'Byrne (Stanford: Stanford University Press, 2000), 10.
39. Bennington, 'Derridabase', 15.
40. Nancy, *Being Singular Plural*, 10–11.
41. Nicholas Royle, 'What is Deconstruction?', in Nicholas Royle (ed.) *Deconstructions: A User's Guide* (Basingstoke: Palgrave, 2000), 1–13, 11.

42. Royle, 'What is Deconstruction?', 7.
43. Andrzej Warminski, ' "As the Poets Do It": On the Material Sublime', in Tom Cohen, Barbara Cohen, J. Hillis Miller and Andrzej Warminski (eds), *Material Events: Paul de Man and the Afterlife of Theory* (Minneapolis: University of Minnesota Press, 2001), 28.

12
Philosophy of Cinders and Cinders of Philosophy: A Commentary on the Origins of Deconstruction and the Holocaust*

Robert Eaglestone

> We must begin wherever we are and the thought of the trace, which cannot not take the scent into account, has already taught us that it was impossible to justify a point of departure absolutely. Wherever we are: in a text where we already believe ourselves to be.
>
> Jacques Derrida, *Of Grammatology*[1]

> The thought of the incineration of the holocaust, of cinders, runs through all my texts [...] What is the thought of the trace, in fact, without which there would be no deconstruction? [...] The thought of the trace, without which there would be no deconstruction, is a thought about cinders and the advent of an event, a date, a memory. But I have no wish to demonstrate this here, the more so, since, in effect, 'Auschwitz' has obsessed everything that I have ever been able to think, a fact that is not especially original. Least of all does it prove I have ever had anything original or certain to say about it.
>
> Jacques Derrida, 'Canons and Metonymies...'[2]

> I do not find in *any* discourse *whatsoever* anything illuminating enough for this period [the twentieth century].
>
> Jacques Derrida, 'On Reading Heidegger...'[3]

Those who reflect on the Holocaust – including historians and philosophers – 'often begin by stating that the Holocaust signals the downfall of western civilisation and culture, and then go on to write about it with terms, methods, and implied beliefs unquestioningly inherited from that civilisation and culture'.[4] This is not the case with Derrida's work: its origins are precisely in the events of the Holocaust, and his reflections come from its cinders. However, since there is no new discourse, no new philosophical language or terms or methods or implied beliefs, only the ones inherited from the past, he writes about these and uses these, questioningly. To write about deconstruction and the Holocaust is not to write about a relationship between two separate things. Derrida's work begins in the Holocaust as a philosophy of the cinder (that stems from the cinder, that is about the cinder).

This 'beginning in Cinders' makes it very hard to argue that 'the origin of deconstruction is in the Holocaust'. It cannot be an argument of the 'what does A tell us about B' or 'applied' type ('what do Russian historians tell us about the retreat from Moscow?' or 'what does deconstruction tell us about the Holocaust?'). Nor can it be an 'if A is the case, then B follows' type (for example, 'all men are mortal and Prince Andrei is a man, so he will die') because here 'A' – the Holocaust – is always already implicated in 'B' – deconstruction. The two cannot be disentangled. I cannot *argue* that 'the origin of deconstruction is in the Holocaust': I can only show how it is, or describe it ('history is important in *War and Peace*'). So: this is a commentary.[5]

1   The cinders of philosophy

a) The task of reading

There is a remark of Derrida's – often cited – about commentary and opening a reading that has troubled me since I first came across it (uncomprehendingly, as an undergraduate – my biographical origins of deconstruction).[6] However, coming to an understanding of that remark – *an* understanding – has seemed to illustrate to me the relation between deconstruction and the Holocaust better than my previous attempts to follow his meditations on the Holocaust through his work.[7] The aim of the first part of this chapter is to follow this remark.

In *Of Grammatology*, in the section called 'The Exorbitant. Question of Method', Derrida discusses what a critical reading should produce, and, in explaining this, he writes that he would have to 'initiate a justification of my principles of reading... entirely negative, outlining by exclusion a space of reading that I shall not fill here: a task of reading'.[8] This 'task of reading' (deconstruction?) cannot be the 'doubling' of commentary, which – as it were – simply repeats the text. However, this

> moment of doubling commentary should no doubt have its place in a critical reading. To recognize and respect all the instruments of its classical exigencies is not easy and requites all the instruments of traditional criticism. Without this recognition and respect, critical production would risk developing in any direction at all and authorize itself to say almost anything. But this indispensable guardrail has always only protected, it has never opened, a reading.[9]

Opening clearly has Heideggerian connotations: the work of art 'opens up in its own way the Being of beings' for example.[10] It has Levinasian overtones, too – opening to the other. Perhaps, opening a reading is both: a poetic and/or existential revealing and a shaping or being shaped; and a responsible opening to the other. What this opening involves, however, is, as Derrida writes, defined negatively. It is not reading a text in the light of a referent (not, for example, in relation to an author's psychobiography) but instead it is 'intrinsic and remain[s] within the text'.[11] It does have aims, however. These aims are 'exorbitant': the negative definition of the 'opening' is the exorbitant, 'the point of a certain exteriority to the totality of the age of logocentrism. Starting from this point of exteriority...a certain deconstruction of that totality which is also a traced path...might be broached'.[12] Exorbitant: that which is outside the orbit or the orb (eye) of Western philosophy. To open a work to the 'exorbitant' is to rewrite it in a way that questions or reframes the framework in which the work appears. All this is well known.

The question then, is *why* one might want – as Derrida says in an interview elsewhere – to find 'a non-site, or a non-philosophical site, from which to question philosophy'.[13] There would seem to be a number of answers to this: because of certain sorts of fundamental religious beliefs, for example, for which reason and Western philosophy would be an enemy; or because of a sort of drunken, destructive creative madness (the urge to destroy is a creative urge after all – an urge to shape and so to reveal); or because philosophy – some sort of philosophy, at least – questions ultimate goals and premises, and, *contra* this, the way that totalitarian states work, according to Hannah Arendt, is to presume certain grounds (for example, 'the party cannot be wrong') and then to follow out the logic of these grounds. A philosophy that questioned these grounds would be an enemy to this, too. However, the answer in *Of Grammatology*, announced right at the beginning, is that this exorbitant position from which to question philosophy is sought because of a desire to 'focus attention on the *ethnocentrism* which, everywhere and always, had controlled the concept of writing'.[14] It is an attempt to expose this exclusion of that (and those) other to Western thought, outside its orbit. It is an ethical motivation. In his essay 'Force of Law: The "Mystical Foundation of Authority"' – and in response to demands that he discuss explicitly the ethics of deconstruction – Derrida argues, famously, that 'Deconstruction is justice'.[15] That (any particular) law can be deconstructed and that justice can't creates the gap in which deconstruction occurs. This is the motivation which underlies his work: 'justice as the possibility of deconstruction...the law, the foundation or the self-authorization of the law as the possibility of the exercise of deconstruction'.[16] *Of Grammatology*'s target, ethnocentrism – as a rule – has to be deconstructed because it is against justice. (Why ethnocentrism, in particular? As the epigraph above: '[W]e must begin wherever we are and the thought of the trace, which cannot not take the scent into account, has already taught us that it was impossible to justify a point of departure absolutely'). What makes Derrida different from the cases suggested above (the anti-philosophical fundamentalist, the madman, the logic of the totalitarian state) – and this is crucial – is that he aims to ask these questions philosophically, to find the exorbitant within the text of philosophy, not without it (ignoring or censoring philosophy like a totalitarian regime) or with out it (outside or without philosophy like a madman or a mystic): he does not have an 'anti-philosophical attitude'.[17] (This is why he is not, for example, a religious thinker, but why his work has a lot in common with religious thought: God, after all, is exorbitant). All this is well known, too.

This sort of attack on what I have called elsewhere the 'metaphysics of comprehension' is not unique to Derrida. Indeed, as the work of Robert Bernasconi and Simon Critchley among others has shown, it owes a great deal to Levinas's analysis of how the relation to the other, the origin of ethics, both underlies and is covered up by philosophy. Adorno, too, thought that the 'system is belly turned mind' which consumed the otherness which exceeded it.[18] And, of course, it clearly echoes Heidegger's argument about how the meaning of the question of Being has been forgotten by philosophy: something outside a structure of thinking that grounds thinking. But where Levinas offers the Other, Heidegger Being and Adorno the Not-I, Derrida refuses to be pinned down to exactly what the exorbitant is. This is the significance of the 'trace' in his work.

b) Tracing the trace from Levinas...

> I relate this concept of *trace* to what is at the centre of the latest work of Emmanuel Levinas and his critique of ontology.[19]

Levinas introduces the idea of the trace at a key moment in his philosophical development. Levinas's work is not about creating new ideas: 'his task is to find the sense of ethics and not to construct an ethics.'[20] Levinas believes that 'ethics is first philosophy', that the ethical relationship to other people is the most basic thing about existence: indeed, it comes before our own existence. He doesn't *argue* this as this would presuppose that logic or reasoned argument would be that which justifies ethics, and so logic or argument would be ontologically prior to ethics. Rather, as a 'good phenomenologist', he aims to unveil how ethics – the relationship with the other – is the grounding of being. What he is interested in, then, as his phenomenological clue (to use Heidegger's phrase) is how the ethical appears in everyday life. And it is this question of appearance that marks the change between his two major works, *Totality and Infinity* in 1961 and *Otherwise than Being* in 1974.

In *Totality and Infinity*, the ethical appears in the actual, really present face-to-face relation of one to another. The face is not a metaphor: the moment of facing is the moment of ethics. 'To manifest oneself as face is to impose one-self above and beyond the manifested phenomenal form, to present oneself in a mode irreducible to manifestation, the very straightforwardness of the face to face, without the intermediary of any image, in one's nudity'.[21] For Levinas, the face is not a representation, even of itself but the actual moment in which the infinite responsibility of ethics appears. In order to stress that the face is *not* a representation, Levinas is forced to use phrases like 'true representation', 'nudity', 'present oneself in a mode irreducible to manifesta-tion', 'very straightforwardness', 'appealing to me in destitution'.[22] Levinas is trying to suggest that the face, although made manifest like objects, is beyond manifestation: it represents itself without representing itself, it has access to infinity. Even language – vital for Levinas – only is truly language if it guaranteed by presence: the speaker 'never separates himself from the sign he delivers' and 'must present himself before every sign – present a face'.[23] Writing is 'a language impeded' and to be expressed by symbols, 'by one's works, is precisely to decline expression'.[24] Although Levinas does trust that 'the interpretation of the symbol can assuredly lead to an intention divined', this interpretation is a 'burglary' and occurs 'without conjuring the absence' of the author.[25]

However, this causes a problem for his ethics: if the ethical moment is only the moment of facing, with the face actually present, then how are we responsible for those who are absent, who have no faces? How does the ethical relation appear in an absence, the absence of the past, for example? The answer to this problem, a major turning point in his thought and the clue that opens to the ethical discussion of language in *Otherwise than Being*, occurs in Levinas's discussion of the trace. This discussion begins in 'The Trace of the Other' from 1963 and is returned to in an essay on the ethical significance of culture in general called 'Meaning and Sense' from 1973.

For Levinas, the trace has a double meaning. The trace 'plays the role of a sign'.[26] It is a mark of the past in the present: the animal's spoor, the clues a detective finds, the 'vestiges left' by an ancient civilization uncovered by the historian or archaeologist.[27] However, it is much more than this: the meaning of the trace as material, as content *per se* is secondary. More impor-tantly, the trace is a mark of the other. Levinas writes that when 'a stone has scratched a stone, the scratch can, to be sure, be taken as a trace, but in fact without the man who held the stone this scratch is but an effect'.[28] It is in 'the trace of the other that a face shines'.[29] The trace, beyond its material, inaugurates the same ethical relation to the other in the past as the face does to the actually present other: it is a 'proxy' for the face, as Edith Wysgorod has it.[30] What a particular trace signifies is not central: that it signifies, and what the signification implies, is. The trace is to the absent other of the past what the face is to an other person actually here present. It is this idea of the trace – of how the absent other appears – that allows Levinas to develop his understanding of language as Saying and Said in *Otherwise than Being*. It is the trace that allows representation to have an ethics. The trace is how the other appears in representation. And it is the trace that, is a terribly fertile idea for Derrida.

c) ... to Derrida

As I have suggested, Derrida is keen not to give a particular name to 'the exorbitant', as that would both place it into a system and invoke a specific referent in the light of which a text was being read. So, where, for Levinas, the trace is the trace of the other (the other absent and present, disrupting presence), for Derrida, the trace is

> reconciled to a Heideggerian intention – as it is not in Levinas's thought – this notion signifies, sometimes beyond Heideggerian discourse, the undermining of an ontology which, in its innermost course, has determined the meaning of being as presence and the meaning of language as the full continuity of speech.[31]

The trace is, then, the moment of disruption in thought, it is what exceeds philosophy. It 'is nothing, it is not an entity, it exceeds the question "what is" and contingently makes it possible'.[32] In it, in fact, is

> the absolute origin of sense in general. Which amounts to saying once again that there is no absolute origin of sense in general... Articulating the living upon the nonliving in general, origin of all repetition... the trace is not more signification than an opaque energy and no concept of metaphysics can describe it.[33]

For Heidegger, Being-in-the-world (*Dasein*, which is also Being-with, *mitsein*) is the ground on which 'normal' truth, understood as agreement of judgement with its object, as assertion and discursive intelligibility, appears. For Levinas, it is the relation with the other that grounds intelligibility. For Derrida, here, the trace – outside any description or truth – is the origin of sense in general: but it is not one concept or thing (Being, the other) but the disruption of intelligibility (it interrupts systems of thought) and the limit of intelligibility (it cannot be described). Without the trace, deconstruction would be impossible.

It is to do with ethics because, although more Heideggerian, it is to do with the appearance, as absence, of the other before that other is given a designation or limited into a philosophical term. It is not humanist – as Levinas writes that humanism 'has to be denounced because it is not sufficiently human'[34] – but as the other coming to be telepoetically in the – infinite? – future, it is that which disrupts the systems of thought that turns otherness into sameness. Thus, the trace is the opening of justice.

The trace, then, is where what is outside philosophy – the other, however understood or manifested – is made manifest within philosophy: and the task of deconstruction is to reveal – to open – this. In *Positions*, Derrida says that to

> 'deconstruct' philosophy . . . would be to think . . . the structured genealogy of philosophy's concepts, but at the same time to determine – from a certain exterior that is unqualifiable or unnameable by philosophy – what this history has been able to dissimulate or forbid.[35]

The trace is the appearance of the exterior that is unqualifiable or unnameable by philosophy, not describable by metaphysics, the infinite responsibility that arises from the other appearing before (and so outside) reasoned thinking. Derrida's obsession with spectres and 'hauntology' in *Specters of Marx* and with ghosts, ashes, spirits and spirit in *Of Spirit* again show the importance of the trace: ghosts are both present and absent, a presence that marks an absence. This is not to say that the trace, and the deconstruction that opens and is opened by it, offers a new philosophy: Derrida argues that 'the passage beyond philosophy does not consist in turning the page of philosophy . . . but in continuing to read philosophy in a certain way'.[36] Derrida constantly renames his insights to avoid them becoming systematic and in order to fix them in definite responses to certain texts: a reading not a methodology. The trace, the opening of justice, is a constant pressure on thinking and on ways of reading.

As is well known, Derrida's readings are supposed to follow no method, but to be attentive to the text: but my suspicion is that the Derridian terms that emerge from very specific readings – 'circumfession' from reading Paul Celan, 'hymen' in 'The Double Session', 'pharmakon' from Plato, and so on – can all be seen as specific, located versions of reading under the pressure of the trace. The opening or unveiling of the trace is what deconstruction does: and, if deconstruction is justice, unveiling the trace in a discourse is justice.

d) Cinders

> Of course, the word trace doesn't mean anything by itself. [. . .] I would prefer something which is neither present nor absent: I would prefer ashes as the better paradigm for what I call trace: something which erases itself totally, radically, while presenting itself.[37]

The word 'trace' doesn't mean anything: like 'hymen' or 'pharmakon' it is one word taken from a certain context to describe what 'no concept of metaphysics can describe', what is not. Even the idea of trace as 'imprinting' is to force it too much into a conceptual framework: it appears each time in each context as different. But this constellation of words around trace, or ashes, could they be better understood? Is there a more significant term? Derrida said that the 'thought of the trace, without which there is no deconstruction, is a thought about cinders and the advent of an event, a date, a memory'.[38] Derrida turns to this in *Cinders*, a very oblique (to say the least) prose poem, written to be spoken and to be read, knowing it has been spoken – read knowing it bears traces in its production. It concerns an untranslatable phrase that haunts Derrida, '*Il y a là cendre*': there are there cinders, cinders there are. It seems to be about the relationship between singular moments, philosophy, writing and the Holocaust; Derrida goes further. Instead of developing other, context-specific terms for 'the trace', Derrida suggests that 'the trace' itself changes its name, is (or traces) something different.

The cinder

visible but scarcely readable... referring only to itself, no longer makes a trace, unless it traces only by losing the trace it scarcely leaves

– that it just barely remains.

– but that is just what he [Derrida himself? Heidegger? Levinas? the unnamed party being discussed?][39] calls the trace, this effacement. I have the impression now that the best paradigm for the trace, for him, is not, as some have believed, and he as well, perhaps, the trail of the hunt, the fraying, the furrow in the sand, the wake of the sea, the love of the step for its imprint, but the cinder (what remains without remaining from the holocaust, from the all-burning...).[40]

The 'trail of the hunt, the fraying, the furrow in the sand, the wake of the sea, the love of the step for its imprint' are all metaphors that imply that what makes the trace is still present chronologically, just are just over there, just charged through, on the other side of frayed material, the other side of the beach, three paces along. The cinder is temporal: that particular fire and that particular burnt 'thing' can never be recreated, bought back, bought to life. The cinder brings the trace into temporality: and into a specific temporality, of a Europe and America shadowed (if not overshadowed) by the Holocaust, what remains from the Holocaust. We live in a particular time, we reflect particular moments, dates (as Derrida writes on Celan). 'We must begin wherever we are' and the 'writer [Rousseau, Derrida] writes in a language and in a logic whose proper system, laws and life his discourse by definition cannot dominate absolutely'.[41] Like Celan and others he analyses, Derrida is set in time and makes no claim to a God-like view from outside of time and history. Other writers at other times did not, may not, might not have the same shadows, the same ashes. But for Derrida on

Derrida – and this is the significance of the fact that *Cinders*, unlike other texts by Derrida which discuss other writers, is a discussion of a phrase in his own work, a self-reflexive unveiling – for Derrida on Derrida, it's clear that the 'best paradigm' for the trace is the cinder 'what remains without remaining from the holocaust'. The cinder underlies deconstruction and the cinder is the cinder of the Holocaust. This is why Derrida said in interview that the 'thought of the incineration of the Holocaust, of cinders, runs through all my texts'.[42] The trace, for Derrida, for us (who could 'we' be? perhaps, for me) is best considered as the cinder.

I don't think this is the only 'haunting' through Derrida's work – although it is perhaps the most significant. The trace is the appearance of an infinite responsibility, after all, and Derrida's work has been concerned with deconstructing ethnocentrism, racism and so on. But, as Derrida has often made a point of claiming, deconstruction responds to singularities, to specific times, places and texts. For thinkers of Levinas's generation and then of Derrida's generation, in Europe, responding to the singularity of the Holocaust was and is thought of as being central, almost a *sine qua non* of thought. For Derrida, too, there was the trauma of the Algerian war, with its echoes of the Holocaust for the victims (those Algerians murdered with no reason, outside the law) and the perpetrators (the French torturers).[43] So what Derrida offers, developing a lacuna in Levinas's thought, is a philosophy haunted throughout by those events, a philosophy that can articulate the debt to what it cannot name.[44] A philosophy of the cinder, and it is in these cinders that Derrida' deconstruction originates. And, *pace* the interview above, this is to say nothing 'original or certain' about Derrida or about the Holocaust, save that it happened, an event, a date, a memory.

The Holocaust is both a universal injustice and a singular injustice. This has not yet been thought philosophically. (But perhaps memoirs and even some literature have attempted this). 'Deconstruction, while seeming not to address the problem of justice, has done nothing but address it, if only obliquely, unable to do so directly':[45] responding to a universal, ahistorical demand for justice. Deconstruction, while seeming not to address the Holocaust, has done nothing but address it, if only obliquely, unable to do so directly: coming from a particular, historical, located demand for justice. Both these demands – justice, which is unrepresentable 'as the experience of absolute alterity',[46] and the singularity of the Holocaust – are brought together in the figure of the cinder: this is how the demand of justice appears, by not appearing, for Derrida.

2   The philosophy of cinders

If deconstruction is the cinders of philosophy, what marks does it bear of this? In what way is this claim not empty rhetoric? It's certainly possible to read books that deconstruct 'the Holocaust' if this is taken to mean to 'deconstruct' how the 'Holocaust' as an event in history is represented, understood, exhibited and so on.[47] But this is not more than 'cultural critique', carefully describing and judging, implicitly or explicitly, how this most terrible event is presented and remembered. This is commentary, relying on an external referent, not opening a reading. James Berger, in his illuminating study of post-apocalyptic thinking, asks the question of how deconstruction views the Holocaust, too. However, as I have suggested, this is the wrong question. It presupposes that deconstruction is a method or a model of thinking, and the Holocaust is one event: as if the deconstruction is a telescope and the Holocaust a remote constellation on which it is focused. In fact, as I have suggested, deconstruction is already the cinders of philosophy. It is always already involved with, responding to, the Holocaust. It is also the philosophy of cinders, reflecting on and engaging with the events of the Holocaust: to illustrate this briefly, in relation to the past, the present and the future.

a) Cinders then

What is philosophy about? Michael Dummett argues that:

> Only with Frege was the proper object of philosophy finally established: namely, that the goal of philosophy is the analysis of the structure of thought; secondly, that the study of thought is to be sharply distinguished from the study of the psychological process of thinking; and finally, that the only proper method for analysing thought consists in the analysis of language.[48]

This approach – the analytic school – seems to claim to be ahistorical, and so unable to reflect, philosophically, on the Holocaust. (In the case of Dummett, this does not mean that he has no opinions on these matters: with his admirable work in anti-racist activity, it would be surprising if he did not. However, asked if his philosophical views 'impelled' him in the struggle against racism, he says that they did not).[49] Alain Badiou, too, argues that it is neither philosophy's 'duty nor within its power to conceptualize' the extermination of European Jews: it 'is up to an other order of thought [...] For example... History examined from the point of view of the political.'[50] In contrast, Derrida's form of philosophy/questioning of philosophy, developing in the European philosophical tradition where the 'natural affinities of philosophy have rather been taken to be with literary and artistic culture, and the concerns of the philosophy have centred on moral, literary, spiritual, socio-political and cultural questions rather than on the logic of the sciences', is not philosophy of this sort (but this is not to say, here, that there is anything wrong with the other sorts: there is not, or there is not now, one way of doing philosophy).[51] Indeed, he writes that deconstruction generally takes one of two styles (although it mixes them together): one 'takes on the demonstrative and apparently ahistorical allure of logico-formal para-doxes. The other ... seems to proceed through readings of texts, meticulous interpretation and genealogies.'[52] Both of these are profoundly historical (against apparent 'ahistoricism', through reading texts, contexts, traditions). Both forms – and they intermingle to make this distinction no more than a guiding thread – tend towards what Jonathan Rée, in the discussion of phe-nomenology which ends his book *I See a Voice*, describes as philosophical history. Not the 'history of philosophy' (a study of canonical texts, forced into dry, professorial narratives) but a way of thinking about 'the world in terms of what it can mean to us, to each of us, in whatever specific situations we happen to find ourselves' in a way which is 'mobile, complicated, strati-fied, detailed', making use of the 'rememorative methods of autobiography and the evocative polyphonies of fiction, as well as the exacting demands of historical research and philosophical criticism'.[53] It is this approach to think-ing, a way which admits the past and the thinker's finitude and historicity, that Derrida adopts – or, because of the thought of cinders, is forced to adopt. (Perhaps the difficult idea of the trace is no more than the awakening to the world that we are always already in, the others with whom we always already share it – the wonder that we are already here, that there is something rather than nothing: and the cinder is what, in the twentieth century, was made of this). A philosophy of cinders has already located Derrida (and we who live in Europe, physically, intellectually? We of the Graeco-European adventure? Or those who respond to those events? Or only me in my 'mine-only-ness'?) in a post-Holocaust world, with no way to escape that world: so, how were 'we'? An origin of deconstruction in the past. Cinders are what are left of the events of the past, are the 'past' and so are that with which we make 'history'.

b) Cinders now

But Cinders are also present. In the 'Post-scriptum' to 'Force of Law' Der-rida ventures to describe how Walter Benjamin might have responded to the Final Solution. There are two different versions. The first, Derrida sug-gests, corresponds to what might be a commentary on Nazism, on its use of language (evil is a possibility in all language), on its totalitarian 'logic' of the state and corruption of democratic institutions – especially the police[54] – and on its total, 'mythical', violence. But this is to think the Final Solution from the point of view of Nazism, to follow through Nazism's thought: a philo-sophical equivalent to perpetrator history, perhaps. This necessary 'doubling commentary ... is not easy and requires all the instruments of traditional criticism'. But it only comments on – guards – understanding. Derrida also suggests a counter-commentary from what the Nazis aimed to exclude: to read the Final Solution from the point of view of Nazism's other, 'that which haunted it at once from without and within'.[55] This means that it must be thought from the 'possibility of singularity'; as the Final Solution it aimed at and nearly succeeded in destroying not just 'human lives by the millions' but also their 'demand for justice'.[56] It must be thought of as a 'project of destruction of the name', meaning the destruction of each singular individual creed (think of the Nazis defining Jews by decree, as Hilberg has it, taking their names and replacing them) that as a singularity and as a more general naming binds and creates communities. Philosophically, perhaps akin to 'victim history'. 'From this point of view,' he writes,

> Benjamin would have judged vain and without pertinence...any juridical trial of Nazism...any judgmental apparatus, any historiography still homogenous with the space in which Nazism developed...any interpretation drawing on philosophical, moral, sociological, psychological or psychoanalytic concepts.[57]

That is, any concepts that developed in the same forest as Nazism, any trees that grew in the same soil, as Derrida put it in *Of Spirit*. Only that which is truly outside Nazism and the Final Solution could judge it or measure its significance. But, at this point, Derrida finds something 'intolerable' in this interpretation at which he bridles. If the Final Solution can only be measured by what is outside all these concepts, then this means that (I might say) 'only a God can explain this': the Holocaust as 'an uninterpretable manifestation of divine violence'. Derrida writes that one 'is terrified at the idea of an interpretation that would make of the Holocaust an expiation and an indecipherable signature of the just and violent anger of God'.[58] Derrida is not alone in this, or in following this path to this conclusion. It is in response to both Christians and Jews suggesting this that led to the thought of Richard Rubenstein in *After Auschwitz* (at least in the first edition in 1966). This is one of the terrible ideas (terrible in its proper sense) that Elie Wiesel wrestles with in much or perhaps all of his work. It is this idea that appears in *Yosl Rakover Talks to God* by Zvi Kolitz, which so affected Levinas. It is here – 'only a God can explain this' – that Derrida finds Benjamin, and these alternatives, 'too Heideggerian, too messianico-marxist or too archeo-eschatological for me'.[59]

Neither of these discourses, then, is enough response in the present to the past, or able to 'take the measure of the event'.[60] One is too complicit, describing the Holocaust through the logic of Nazism (nothing post-Holocaust about that, just the Holocaust written); the other – dismissing the first – is too much the opposite, in which no 'anthropology, no humanism, no discourse of man on man, even on human rights' could 'be proportionate' (the Holocaust has consumed everything: nothing post-Holocaust here, either).[61] Neither is an opening. Further, both correspond to Nazism: to its fake logic and premise, and to its appeals to myth beyond reason: or, looking into its abyss, into a complete opposition to that. For Derrida, this leaves us with the task of thinking about the complicity of the discourses (of right, of ethics, of identity, or race, say) that we still have with the Holocaust: 'Nazism wasn't born in the desert... it had grown in the shadow of big trees [...] In their bushy taxonomy, they would bear the names of religions, philosophies, political regimes, economic structures, religious or academic institutions. In short, what is just as confusedly called culture, or the world of the spirit.'[62] Mary Midgley offers a metaphor by asking if philosophy is 'like plumbing'.[63] 'Both activities,' she goes on, 'arise because elaborate cultures like ours have, beneath their surface, a fairly complex system which is usually unnoticed, but which sometimes goes wrong'.[64] The job of philosophy is to look at and, if possible, correct or suggest correction to the 'plumbing': 'to show the fly the way out of the fly bottle'.[65] But Derrida goes further, and is suspicious that the tools themselves may be complicit in the breakage. How are 'we'? An origin of deconstruction in the present.

c) Cinders to come

And cinders are also future. Are there dreams of a new future, one that comes from but is no longer not complicit with or contaminated by cinders – nor with the machine-gunned or mutilated or frozen or poisoned or radioactive or economically enslaved or just beaten traces/cinders/ashes/marks (the British at Amritsar, the Congo Free State, the Gulags, Bhopal, Chernobyl, 'the swoosh', the way men behave – and all the events and states for which these are metonyms, perhaps all with their different logic or perhaps linked by a shared logic, as Arendt suggests). An 'atheological heritage of the messianic'? A future both of and for justice?[66] If there were to be such a future, Derrida has projected (at least) two facets, and it's possible to show how these, too, stem from cinders.

The first is the question of the human. What is the status of the human after the Holocaust? For some survivors, like Robert Antelme – at least in Sarah Kofman's interpretation – a central contention is that the extreme situations of the camps is simply a magnification of what happens in the 'normal' world, that 'we the detainees are not animals; and you the SS are not gods. We are nothing more or less than men and there is nothing inhuman or superhuman in man'.[67] For Antelme, even the most basic vital functions show that a man is still a man and, he maintains, that because the SS 'sought to call the unity of the Human race into question... they will eventually be crushed'.[68] But Antelme was not a Jewish prisoner. Other survivors often say things like 'we were beings, but not human beings': at the end of *Night*, what looks back at Elie Wiesel from the mirror after liberation is 'a corpse', not a human being. (Derrida, but not a joke: 'How do you recognize a ghost? By the fact it does not recognize itself in a mirror'.[69]). As Agamben points out, the murder of the Jews 'constitutes... neither capital punishment nor sacrifice'; that is, nothing in the economy of human society.[70] It was

the actualization of a mere 'capacity to be killed' inherent in the condition of the Jew as such. The truth... is that the Jews were exterminated

not in a mad and giant holocaust [i.e., in a sacred event] but exactly as Hitler has announced, 'as lice' which is to say, as bare life. The dimension in which the extermination took place in neither religion nor law but biopolitics.[71]

The question is, then, what is the status of the human after the Holocaust. One current branch of this is the question – one Derrida returns to often – of the animal. That the Holocaust is the cinder for this, the trace that begets this question is illustrated by, for example, J. M. Coetzee's *The Lives of Animals*. Elizabeth Costello, the anti-carnivore activist and novelist, in despair at the end of the novel with words 'so outrageous that they are best spoken into a pillow or into a hole in the ground, like King Midas', compares the Holocaust to the slaughter, use and consumption of animals: 'a crime of stupefying proportions [. . .] It is as if I were to visit friends an remark about the lamp in their living room, and they were to say, "Yes, it's nice isn't it? Polish-Jewish skin it's made of" '.[72] The Holocaust marks the horizon of this debate. Derrida suggests in *Politics of Friendship*, reflecting in a way on Levinas's remark cited earlier – that humanism 'has to be denounced because it is not sufficiently human' – that what is to be 'human', or even what it is to demand justice, is yet to be decided or is yet to come as a process of *humanization*. It is to be aimed for, not a state from which we begin and this future-facing responsible shaping – *messianic telepoesis* – is the activity we should be undertaking.

The second is the question of the state and of democracy. This ground – the 'democracy to come' – has been very well covered by others. But again, it takes its origin from the Holocaust. Derrida writes that 'deconstructions have always represented . . . the at least necessary conditions for identifying and combating the totalitarian risk'.[73] Bernstein glosses this by arguing that the

> totalitarian risk is the risk of the coming into being of a totalitarian regime as a consequence of principled metaphysical totalization, even the principle of freedom. On this account no discrimination is made between 'good' and 'bad' acts of totalization since *qua* acts of totalization all entail the same risk.[74]

In this anti-totalitarian sense, Derrida's work echoes the work of 'classic' liberals like Isaiah Berlin and Karl Popper for whom the totalitarianism of Nazism and of the Soviet Union was the enemy. But his position goes further than theirs, not only because he is not defending a cold war *status quo* but also because he is more than cautious about liberalism itself.[75] But here, in this warning way, deconstruction projects itself into the future, resistant to those discourses that will reduce it or delimit the potential of the polis for justice. It aims for the 'democracy to come', the future.

These two are questions and demands projected into the future: how will 'we' be? An origin of deconstruction in the future.

Conclusion

This has been no more than a commentary. The Holocaust – the events, whatever we call them, if not 'The Holocaust', the subject of Holocaust studies – is not a subject on which deconstruction can focus, any more than an astronomer can focus on her telescope while looking at the stars. Deconstruction already *is*, in its origins, about the Holocaust, not least because the cinder, the trace, underlies the time in which Derrida (and 'we', perhaps) think. That this is the case can only be shown. I have chosen to show it in two ways: that it underlies the pressures that lead to deconstruction (the cinder) and – sketched in roughly – that it is ever-present in deconstruction's orientation toward the past, present and future. 'Least of all does it prove I have ever had anything original or certain to say about it': least of all does this prove I have ever had anything original or certain to say about it.

Notes

*This chapter first appeared as Chapter 10 of the author's *The Holocaust and the Postmodern* (Oxford: Oxford University Press, 2004).

1. Jacques Derrida, *Of Grammatology*, trans. Gayatri Chakravorty Spivak (Baltimore: Johns Hopkins University Press, 1976), 162.
2. Jacques Derrida, 'Canons and Metonymies: An Interview with Jacques Derrida', in Richard Rand (ed.), *Logomachia: The Contest of the Faculties* (Lincoln: University of Nebraska Press, 1992), 211–12.
3. Jacques Derrida, 'On Reading Heidegger: An Outline of Remarks to the Essex Colloquium', *Research in Phenomenology*, 17 (1987), 179.
4. Dan Stone, 'Paul Ricoeur, Hayden White and Holocaust Historiography', in Jorn Stuckrath and Zurg Zbinden, *Metageschichte: Hayden White und Paul Ricoeur* (Baden-Baden: Nomos Verlagsgesellschaft, 1997), 270.
5. In his influential book on the subject, Dominick LaCapra writes that one 'crucial undertaking of postmodern and poststructuralist approaches may thus be to explore more clearly their own relation to the Shoah in all its intricate dimensions', *Representing the Holocaust: History, Theory, Trauma* (New York: Cornell University Press, 1994), 223. As I have suggested, because of the nature of this relation, this can only be shown, as it were, inductively, and not deduced in a logical form.
6. See, for example, the work of Christopher Norris.
7. Other explicit discussions of this occur in Amanda Grzyb, 'Jacques Derrida and the Holocaust: Cinders, Deconstruction and Excessive Responsibility', unpublished MA thesis, University of Western Ontario (1996); James Berger, *After the End: Representations of Post-Apocalypse* (London: Minnesota University Press, 1999); Elaine Marks, 'Cendres juives: Jews Writing in French "after Auschwitz"', in Lawrence D. Kritzman (ed.), *Auschwitz and After* (London: Routledge, 1995). There are other discussions with Derrida in mind in a wide range of work on the Holocaust by James Young, Marc Taylor and Dominick LaCapra, to name just some.
8. Derrida, *Of Grammatology*, 158.
9. ibid.

10. Martin Heidegger, 'On the Origin of the Work of Art', in *Poetry, Language, Thought*, trans. and with an introduction by Albert Hofstadter (New York: Harper and Row, 1971), 37.
11. Derrida, *Of Grammatology*, 159.
12. ibid., 161–2.
13. Richard Kearney, *Dialogues with Contemporary Continental Thinkers: The Phenomenological Heritage* (Manchester: Manchester University Press, 1984), 108.
14. Derrida, *Of Grammatology*, 3.
15. Jacques Derrida, 'Force of Law: The "Mystical Foundation of Authority"', trans. Mary Quaintance, in Drucilla Cornell, Michael Rosenfeld and David Gray Carlson (eds), *Deconstruction and the Possibility of Justice* (New York and London: Routledge), 15.
16. Derrida, 'Force of Law', 15.
17. Kearney, *Dialogues*, 108.
18. Theodor Adorno, *Negative Dialectics*, trans. E. B. Ashton (London: Routledge, 1973), 23.
19. Derrida, *Of Grammatology*, 70.
20. Robert Bernasconi, 'The Ethics of Suspicion', *Research in Phenomenology*, 20 (1990), 9.
21. Emmanuel Levinas, *Totality and Infinity: An Essay on Exteriority*, trans. Alphonso Lingis (London: Kluwer Academic Publishers, 1991), 200.
22. ibid., 200
23. ibid., 97, 182.
24. ibid., 176.
25. ibid., 177.
26. Emmanuel Levinas, 'Meaning and Sense', in *Collected Philosophical Papers*, trans. Alphonso Lingis (Dordrecht: Kluwer Academic Publishers, 1987), 104.
27. ibid., 104.
28. ibid., 106.
29. ibid., 106.
30. Edith Wyschogrod, 'God and "Being's Move" in the Philosophy of Emmanuel Levinas', *The Journal of Religion*, 62 (1982), 150.
31. Derrida, *Of Grammatology*, 70.
32. ibid., 75.
33. ibid., 65.
34. Emmanuel Levinas, *Otherwise than Being: or, Beyond Essence*, trans. Alphonso Lingis (The Hague: Martinus Nijhoff, 1981), 128.
35. Jacques Derrida, *Positions*, trans. Alan Bass (London: Athlone Press, 1981), 6.
36. Jacques Derrida, *Writing and Difference*, trans. Alan Bass (London: Routledge and Kegan Paul, 1978), 288.
37. Derrida, 'On Reading Heidegger', 177.
38. Derrida, 'Canons and Metonymies', 211.
39. James Berger suggests unproblematically that this is Derrida: yet the terms used echo both Heidegger and Levinas, and so, perhaps, a whole philosophical tradition.
40. Jacques Derrida, *Cinders*, trans. and ed. Ned Lukacher (London: University of Nebraska Press, 1991), 43.
41. Derrida, *Of Grammatology*, 158.
42. Derrida, 'Canons and Metonymies', 211.
43. All this is, of course, to pass over an argument from biography. For this, see Geoffrey Bennington and Jacques Derrida, *Jacques Derrida*, 325–7.

44. Does Derrida think the Holocaust is unique? A hard question: he suggests that all events are unique and singular, but that we have no way, philosophically, of responding to this: indeed, the discourse of Western thought covers the 'singularity' of events up by turning them into examples or general cases. Part of the responsibility to and from the trace, the cinder, is to be aware of this and to deconstruct it and this is specific to Europe, to a certain time and a certain place. Derrida is a thinker of the particular, and for those in Europe, and those like Derrida with a slightly tangential relationship to Europe, this is the particular event which is thought of as the most damaging.

45. Derrida, 'Force of Law', 10.

46. ibid., 27.

47. For examples: Peter Novick, *The Holocaust and Collective Memory* (US title: *The Holocaust and American Life*) (London: Bloomsbury, 2000); Tim Cole, *Images of the Holocaust: the Myth of the Shoah Business* (London: Duckworth, 1999).

48. Michael Dummett, *Truth and Other Enigmas* (London: Duckworth, 1978), 441, 458.

49. Michael Dummett, *On Immigration and Refugees* (London: Routledge, 2001), xi, xii.

50. Alain Badiou, *Manifesto for Philosophy*, trans. Norman Madaraz (Albany: SUNY Press, 1999), 30.

51. Eric Matthews, *Twentieth Century French Philosophy* (Oxford: Oxford University Press, 1996), 7.

52. Derrida, 'Force of Law', 21.

53. Jonathan Rée, *I See a Voice* (London: HarperCollins, 1999), 384.

54. See, for a good account of this, Michael Burliegh, *The Third Reich* (London: Macmillan, 2000), 149ff.

55. Derrida, 'Force of Law', 60.

56. In D. M. Thomas's novel *The White Hotel*, the narrator writes of the 30,000 killed on the first day of the Babi Yar massacres that 'their lives and histories were as rich and complex as Lisa Erdman-Berenstein's [the character who has been the subject of the rest of the novel]. If a Sigmund Freud had been listening and taking notes from the time of Adam, he would still not have explored even a single group, even a single person. And this was only the first day' (D. M. Thomas, *The White Hotel* [London: Penguin, 1981], 220). This is one way of understanding singularity.

57. Derrida, 'Force of Law', 60.

58. Derrida, 'Force of Law', 298.

59. ibid., 62.

60. ibid., 59.

61. ibid., 61.

62. Jacques Derrida, Geoffrey Bennington and Rachel Bowlby, *Of Spirit: Heidegger and the Question*, trans. Geoffrey Bennington and Rachel Bowlby (Chicago: University of Chicago Press, 1991), 109.

63. Mary Midgley, *Utopias, Dolphins and Computers: Problems of Philosophical Plumbing* (London: Routledge, 1996), 1.

64. ibid.

65. Ludwig Wittgenstein, *Philosophical Investigations*, trans. G. E. M. Anscombe, 3rd edition (Oxford: Blackwell, 1968), 309, 103e.

66. Jacques Derrida, *Spectres of Marx*, trans. Peggy Kamuf (London and New York: Routledge, 1994), 168.

67. Robert Antelme, *The Human Race*, trans. Jeffrey Haight and Annie Mahler (Marlboro: The Marlboro Press, 1992), 60–1.

68. ibid., 69.
69. Derrida, *Spectres of Marx*, 156.
70. Giorgio Agamben, *Homo Sacer: Sovereign Power and Bare Life*, trans. Daniel Heller-Roazen (Stanford: Stanford University Press 1998), 114.
71. ibid., 114.
72. J. M. Coetzee, *The Lives of Animals* (London: Profile, 1999), 121.
73. Jacques Derrida, 'Like the Sound of the Sea Deep within a Shell: Paul de Man's War', *Critical Inquiry*, 14 (1988), 647.
74. J. M. Bernstein, *The Fate of Art* (London: Polity, 1992), 183.
75. On this, see, for example, Chantal Mouffe (ed.), *Deconstruction and Pragmatism* (London: Routledge, 1996).

13
The Beginnings of Art: Heidegger and Bataille

Gérard Bucher

> The 'man of Lascaux' created a world of art out of nothing at the primordial *locus* of communication between minds.
>
> *Georges Bataille*[1]

Two works in the twentieth century – Heidegger's and Bataille's – have taken up the challenge of questioning the work of art in a perspective which, in so far as it implies the deconstruction of our traditional aesthetic conceptions, sheds light on the *immemorial mytho-logo-poetic* 'disclosure' of the Dasein. The issue which we would like to raise could thus be summarized as follows: at the hypothetical point of intersection between Heidegger's and Bataille's (but also Nietzsche's) perspectives on art, will an original anthropologico-philosophical inquiry enable us to glimpse the 'end' of deconstruction as the a-theological *'poetic* scene' of language *and* death?

Although it may appear somewhat restrictive in scope, an investigation on the 'beginnings of art' may dramatically contribute to the project of a 'deconstruction of the history of being' which, as we know, has first been advocated by Heidegger in §6 of his Introduction to *Sein und Zeit*. (As a matter of fact, the author uses the word *'Destruktion'* but he will soon afterwards coin the word *'Abbau'*). In this context two points need to be stressed: 1) Heidegger's project of 'deconstruction' requires the elaboration of an 'existential' approach of the 'primitive Dasein' (*das primitive Dasein*, as outlined in §11); 2) the author, as he requests such an approach, *simultaneously brackets it off* due to the 'preparatory nature' of his quest, as well as of the 'abundance' (*überreiche Kentniss*) of the anthropological data at hand.

We will first propose a close comparative reading of Heidegger's and Bataille's discussions of the 'origin of the work of art' in order to outline, in the conclusion, how our double perspective may impact (and perhaps even programmatically 'fulfill') the task of deconstruction.

* * *

At a decisive moment of his itinerary, in November 1935, at a time when, coping with the so-called *Kehre* (turn), he was writing his *Beiträge zur Philosophie*, Heidegger delivered his famous lecture 'The Origin of the Work of Art'.[2] Divided into three parts ('Thing and Work', 'The Work and Truth' and 'Truth and Art'), the essay first summarizes in Part I the state of the author's philosophic inquiry in the wake of *Sein und Zeit*. In Parts II and III, it is by means of an unsettling encounter with the question of art, by means of a broadening of the notions of *energeia* and *techne* that Heidegger intends to achieve the reversal of all metaphysical positions after *Sein und Zeit*. Art is no longer considered as a regional domain within the realm of human life: its function is 'a setting to work of truth'[3] No longer characterized as a subordinate activity under the aegis of the gods, Art conditions the co-genesis of world, man and meaning on the horizon of an as yet unheard-of *poetic philosophy*. Once it is reworked as the explicit combination of poetry *and* thought and set free from the dominion of the gods, art will knowingly partake in the 'disclosure' or 'unconcealedness' of a world.

'The Origin of the Work of Art' thus presents itself as one of the most audacious essays of the author of *Sein und Zeit*, and hence also as one in which the aporias of his philosophy appear most symptomatically. Indeed, Heidegger was aware of the fact that, in this context, his thought was confronting the limits of the unthinkable/unsayable: 'A domain which escapes us [...] the reticent domain that is the source of what has to be thought'.[4] In his 1960 'Addendum', he asserts somewhat disconcertingly that: 'Art [...] belongs to *the disclosure of appropriation* [*Ereignis*]' by way of which the 'meaning of Being' (see *Sein und Zeit*) can alone be defined. '*What art may be* is one of the questions to which *no answers are given in the essay*.'[5] In 'The Origin of the Work of Art', precisely because the lecture is centered on the mystery of art, Heidegger's difficult confrontation with the *mythos/logos* caesura, in so far as it runs through the whole of the history of philosophy since the Greeks, appears more vividly than in any other text.

From the outset (as a matter of fact, from its very title) the essay raises the issue of origin (*Ursprung*) *per se* from a position which is still profoundly infused with mythical preconceptions: 'Origin here means that *from* and *by which* something is what it is and as it is. What something is, as it is, we call its essence or nature.'[6] However, as we shall see, this introductory definition which carries with it the classical motif of a *mythic causality*, will surreptitiously be undermined in the course of the demonstration, first by virtue of an ana-chrono-logical 'complication' introduced by an unpacking of the meaning of the German *Anfang* ('The beginning already contains the end latent within itself'[7]), then by means of a 'correction' of the original definition stated at the very end of the essay: 'To originate something by a leap, to bring something into being from out of the source of its nature in a founding leap – this is what the word origin [German *Ursprung*, literally, primal leap] means.'[8] While thus bridging the span between these two definitions present at both ends of the essay, but without ever stating it explicitly, Heidegger actually investigates the possibility of *a radical deconstruction, i.e., demythification of origins* by means of a paradoxical (tautological or 'medial') promotion of *the silent ex-nihilo re-invention of language as work of art*. As Heidegger will claim later in *On the Way to Language*, the complete reversal of metaphysics as *Ereignis* cannot be accomplished without 'bringing speech to speech as speech'.

As a matter of fact, Heidegger will draw our attention towards two major enigmas about art which confer to his investigation its singular originality and value. In a first phase, the work of art is assimilated to the 'temple-work', i.e., the construction which ruled the Greek city:

> A Greek temple portrays nothing. It simply stands there in the middle of the rock-cleft valley. The building encloses the figure of the god and, in this concealment, lets it stand out into the holy precinct through the open portico. By means of the temple, the god is present in the temple. This presence of the god is, in itself, the extension and delimitation of the precinct as a holy precinct. The temple and its precinct, however, do not fade away into the indefinite. It is the temple-work that first fits together and at the same time gathers around itself the unity of those paths and relations in which birth and death, disaster and blessing, victory and disgrace, endurance and decline acquire the shape of destiny for human being.[9]

Thus does Heidegger admit, without further elaboration, that art (insofar as it originally 'sets up') was always traditionally subordinated to the constraints of *mythos*, i.e., always already considered to be subservient to the manifestations of the gods:

> Such setting up is erecting in the sense of dedication and praise. Here 'setting up' no longer means a bare placing. To dedicate means to consecrate, in the sense that in setting up the work the holy is opened up as holy and the god is invoked into the openess of his presence.[10]

Indeed, as will be made more explicit later on, it is as if the motif of the 'temple' enables Heidegger to both *indicate and cover up* within his text, the pre-philosophical *locus* of religious experience inherent to *mythos* in so far as it conditioned the 'opening up of a world', not only within the boundaries of Greek culture, but for the whole of the traditional and/or prehistoric worlds which preceded the advent of rationality.

However, in a second phase, after renewing his question – 'What, however, is art itself that we call it rightly an origin?' – the author affirms abruptly that: '*All art*, as the letting happen of the advent of the truth of what is, is, as such, *essentially poetry*'.[11] The Work reaches its climax when the *thought invention* (or re-invention) of language performs truth in an original act of nomination, when it informs: 'beings *to* their being *from out* of their being.'[12]

We now must be aware of the fact that the *unthought dimension* of the essay, as well actually as in Heidegger's work as a whole, resides in this opposition between the work as 'temple', as it relates to *'mythos'* or to *'origin'* as *cause*, and the work as *language ex nihilo*. As a matter of fact, Heidegger will never clarify *the conditions of possibility of the 'historical' reversal* from the visible 'idolatrous' sacred to the *poetic* disclosure of language *as* language. In his eagerness to perform *Ereignis* (i.e., to assimilate the *poesis* of language to a work of art), everything happens as if Heidegger never realized that his project was in fact made impracticable by *lack of an archeology of the sacred*. The metaphysical occultation of *mythos* (i.e., of the beliefs and practices of the 'primitive Dasein') under the dominance of *logos* may have thus perpetuated itself *even in Heidegger's own philosophy*. Although, within the modern context of the ruin of all religious traditions, the author suspects that only the Epiphany of language as art could enable us to renew the *meaningful differentiation* of humanity from all 'natural' beings: 'Where there is no language, as in the being of stone, plant, and animal, there is also no openness of what is, and consequently no openness either of that which is not and of the empty'[13] (it is remarkable that for Heidegger such a reification of 'Nothingness' specifically pertains to the realm of the 'Poem').

As a matter of fact, this discussion, in 'The Origin of the Work of Art', latently extends a motif investigated at length by Heidegger in *The Fundamental Concepts of Metaphysics; World-Finitude-Solitude* (a book-length transcript of a seminar taught in 1929–30). The whole second part of said book – 'The Question: What is World?' – is indeed precisely devoted to an elucidation of the *difference* between the animal deemed to be 'poor in world' and man conceived of as 'the instigator of world'. This latter inquiry will ultimately, in the whole of the last chapter (Chapter VI) of *The Fundamental Concepts of Metaphysics*, focus on: 'a return to the realm of the origin... of logos'. Thus, we understand that the passage of 'The Origin of the Work of Art' that we have been discussing has to do finally with the possibility of *a renewed leap of humanization* (a 'new beginning', *der andere Anfang*) on the horizon of a *meaningful differentiation* – both primary and ultimate – between animal and man and indeed between man and the gods as well. However, Heidegger refused to draw such a conclusion insofar as he apparently deemed it necessary to prevent all 'contaminations' of his ontological project by anthropology, i.e., all lapse into aspects of ordinary idealism or materialism. In *The Fundamental Concepts of Metaphysics*, he warns us that an overcoming of the metaphysics of the *animal rationale* would first require:

...to make explicit what is meant by the essence of the animal and the essence of the humanity of man, to explain in which fashion we get access to the essence of such beings. The essence of the animal, we can in turn determine only if we would be in a position to clarify the nature of living beings in opposition to what is lifeless, of what does not even possess *the possibility to die*.[14]

In conclusion, we will admit that the essay implicitly postulates the *possibility* of the overcoming of the metaphysical differentiation between the animal world an humanity by means of a (re)creation of language *ex nihilo* on the horizon of a renewed awareness of 'the possibility of dying' or of man's *mortality*. Iconoclastic of all residual forms of 'idolatry' (including Greek *aletheia*), such a renewed epiphany of the innermost connection between language and death would command, for the first time, the advent of a radically new poetic or *poetic* humanity capable of freeing itself from the constraints of the primitive *mythos*, i.e., of all 'idolatrous' forms of religion.

We will now consider how the *correlative* investigation of the 'Birth of Art' according to Bataille will enable us to solve the 'historical' complexities left unexamined by Heidegger as the difference between the 'temple', as *mythos* both manifested *and* repressed, and the hypothetical flowering of language's *Ereignis* or demythified *logos*. Indeed, could it not be possible that prehistoric art, because it is unquestionably more 'originary' than any other art – namely the Greek 'temple-work' – stands essentially witness to the fact: 'that concealedness of what *is* has happened here, and that as this happening happens here for the first time, or that such a work *is* at all rather than is not ... is just what is extra-ordinary.'[15]

*　*　*

As is well known, beyond his fascination for the diversity of man's faces, Bataille incessantly scrutinized the enigma that man is for himself. As an assiduous reader of Nietzsche and Freud, a thinker who wanted to free himself from all the constraints of academic disciplines, he simultaneously investigated *philosophy* (particularly Hegel's in the wake of Kojève's teaching), *the history of religions* (singularly the Christian faith), as well as the vast domain of anthropology (notably under the guidance of Alfred Métraux, Roger Caillois and Michel Leiris). As a matter of fact, he constantly tried to achieve a critical *new stance* (he called it the 'inner experience') capable of transcending the shortcomings of contemporary nihilism: 'I have sacrificed everything to the discovery of a point of view wherefrom the unity of the human mind could be ascertained [...] nothing has motivated me more than the possibility of retrieving in a general perspective the image which obsessed my teenage years: that of God.'[16]

The two books which apart from his literary works coincide with the culmination of his work – *Lascaux or the Birth of Art* and *Death and Sensuality* (the original title is *L'érotisme*), published respectively in 1955 and 1957 –

deal decisively with the origins both of man and of art: from the outset work as *oeuvre* is distinguished from work as *travail*, the latter being assimilated to 'the birth of tooling' and referred as such to the realm of the 'profane'. Indeed, a number of cross-references between the two books stand witness to the fact that they constitute two versions of one and the same enterprise. To the evocations of the painted caves[17] and the birth of art[18] in *Death and Sensuality* corresponds the final discussion of 'Knowledge and Prohibition of Death' in *Lascaux or the Birth of Art*.

It is undoubtedly thanks to an extrapolation of the theses both of Roger Caillois in *Man and the Sacred* and of Kojève in his lectures on 'The Idea of Death in Hegel's Philosophy' that Bataille developed his original theory on the awakening of consciousness to death at the dawn of *Homo sapiens*. In his attempt to delineate what he calls 'a religious experience outside the realm of defined religions', by discussing facts drawn in particular from sacrificial and funerary rituals, Bataille demonstrates how the anthropo-genetic denegation of 'nature' in man, i.e., the denial *by* man of (*his*) *animality* (and of corruption or decay in particular) conditioned a paradoxical awareness of death inseparable from the emergent ritualized dichotomy of transgression and prohibition:

> We affirm with some confidence that in its essence, transgression can exist only in so far as art exists... in the frenzy of the celebrations depicted in the darkness of the caves by these figures bursting with a life which constantly transcends itself and finds its most eminent form of manifestation in the play of death and birth.[19]

The ambivalence of the primordial experience of nothingness as the *locus* of initial 'dis-closure' is here illustrating from the tensions between the *wish* to die and a way of *'acting out'* or overcoming the anguish of death: 'Religious sensibility... always links desire closely with terror, intense pleasure and anguish [...] anguish in the face of death, is what men desire in order to transcend it beyond death and ruination.'[20] In spite of certain obscurities and iterations, Bataille's argument fascinates us by dint of both its powerful intuitions and expressions. It will certainly remain an indispensable reference text for all future studies of the sacred, notably of the sacrificial[21] and funeral rites,[22] hunting,[23] violence,[24] war[25] and, of course, sexuality.[26]

If we now take a step back in order to consider Bataille's argument as a whole, we may say, from a Heideggerian point of view, that, despite its innovations, his approach is still impregnated with the metaphysical a priori of the *animal rationale*. Indeed, nowhere does Bataille's investigation call into question the 'ontical' ascendance of the concepts he utilizes as he draws his inspiration from three sources: 1) from Hegelian idealism, specifically in regard to Hegel's (and Kojève's) central theme of 'Death generating Man in Nature' (when he discusses the way prohibition lifts transgression without cancelling it, he writes in a note: 'There is no need to underline the Hegelian character of this operation which relates to the dialectical process described by the untranslatable German *aufheben*: to both overcome and preserve';[27] 2) from anthropological positivism since, for Heidegger, anthropology is unknowingly transfused by the materialist *and* idealist tenets that govern all the sciences; 3) from the 'Catholic phase' experienced by the author in his youth.[28] In spite of his attempts at radicalizing Nietzsche's critique of the Christian dogma and actually due to such endeavors, Bataille's thought remained imbued by his Catholic faith, as he willingly acknowledged.

More essentially still, and again in a Heideggerian perspective, we can postulate that the *flaw* of Bataille's demonstration both in *Lascaux* and in *L'érotisme* concerns his 'forgetting' of the poetic dimension and more broadly of his ignorance of the issue of the origin of language. Even if, in his Preface, the author briefly admits his limitations in this respect: 'I spoke of mystical experience, not of poetry. I could not have talked about poetry without plunging into an intellectual labyrinth. We all feel what poetry is. Poetry is one of our foundation stones, *but we are unable to talk about it*'.[29] Similarly, the book on *Lascaux* had remained silent about the *poetic* dimension immanent to cave art. Despite the vividness of Bataille's impressions and the beauty of his comments – 'These paintings, as we contemplate them, appear miraculous, they stir in us powerful emotions'[30] – never will Bataille assign, as did Heidegger, a primordial role to the 'Poem' or nascent language at the foundation of the arts. However, can we not suspect that the magical visions of something *in* and *beyond* nature (in the pictorial rendition of cave art) presuppose a capacity for speech?

Indeed, prehistoric art, precisely because it appears like a flash in the night, is unthinkable outside an already perfected access to language. When man projected himself into another being under the guise of an animal, he actually expressed the mythical truth of his mortal birth *already inherent* to the deployment of language. As Clayton Eshleman has shown, by means of what he names the 'Grotesque archetype',[31] it is both by overestimating *and* underestimating his animal double that man was able to poetically transport himself into the sphere of the invisible. It is remarkable that the rare representations of humans found in cave paintings are more crude than those of the animals. Sometimes we only catch a glimpse of man under the double guise of the god *and* the beast as is the case for the famous sorcerer of the Trois Frères cave. Since the dawn of time *Homo absconditus* must have been the blind spot of his own vision: 'animality was and still is for us the first sign, a blind sign, albeit a tangible sign of our presence [and I would like to add 'absence'] in the universe.'[32]

It now appears that Bataille's fascination for paleolithic art, which we may qualify as 'idolatrous' since it ignores the linguistic grounding of art, enables us to understand the strange correlation between his meditation on 'the essence of the work of art' and the focal role attributed by him to eroticism in his eponymous book. It is as if the aesthetic representation of the *difference* between the animal world and humanity in the upper paleolithic caves had to find its correlate in eroticism considered as the ghost-like figure of religion in the modern era. (The two first sections of Chapter I bear the following titles: 'The Decisive Importance of the Passage from Animal to Man' and 'Eroticism vs. Animal Sexuality'). However, in the contemporary climate of nihilism, it is the mere preservation of an ecstatic experience which may be at stake. How can it be possible to assign to Eros an eminent status when the event of 'being exposed without reservations to death, torture and joy, to horrific and ecstatic dying in an obscured flash of light, a divine illumination'[33] may no longer be perceived. The celebration in *L'érotisme* of a sense of beauty and terror, under the guise of the ecstatic animal, enables, in spite of the repression of the *poiesis* of language, an acute awareness of humankind's 'e-normity' (Heidegger): 'If beauty, whose fulfillment rejects the animal nature, is so passionately wished for, it is because, in it, the sense of possession introduces an element of bestiality and filth.'[34]

If we now take a second step back and consider the works of Heidegger and Bataille in the same purview, we will have to admit that they both evade, each time in specific but actually complementary ways, the anthropogenetic correlation between speech *and* the sacred (or death), i.e., the intimate link between *mythos* and *logos*. To the unexamined space between the dominant function of the 'temple' and the glimpsed flowering of speech as *Ereignis* in Heidegger corresponds the still 'idolatrous' approach of the ritualization of death in Bataille but also, as could be shown, in Hegel. Thus, on the one hand, the breach between *mythos* and *logos* is recognized by Heidegger but remains unexplained (in 'The Origin of the Work of Art' of course, but also in the author's work as a whole) while, on the other, the emphasis placed by Bataille upon primitive *mythos* circumscribes an 'a-theological' origin but leads him to renew the immemorial oblivion of logos' destiny *in* history or *as* history. In both cases, it is the task of deconstruction as a radical demythification of origins which remains unfulfilled.

It is now precisely in view of their mutual limitations that we should strive to bring to light the *latent complementarity* of the two positions under scrutiny. To Heidegger's inquiry about the *poiesis* of speech, what is secretly at work in the instigation of the 'idolatrous' visibility of the 'temple', must correspond the questioning of the mortal birth of man out of the animal world, beyond Bataille's (and Hegel's) stance, i.e., from a position capable of bringing into focus the 'historical' coincidence of aesthetics, ethics and alethics (or truth). We should note in passing that in his essay Heidegger does not refer to *Sein und Zeit's* motif of 'being-towards-death', even though, when discussing the 'Poem', he raises the issue of the genesis of language in mortality or *ex nihilo*: 'Poetic projection comes from Nothing, in this respect, that it never takes its gift from the ordinary and commonly accepted'.[35] In short, it would only be by means of the iconoclastic destruction of *all* religious myths (i.e., by means of a general deconstruction or an 'a-theological Summa') that the transformation of conscience called 'beginning anew, *der andere Anfang*' could take place. This Event (*Ereignis*) we can now conceive of as the initial metamorphosis of paleanthropian man as is reflected by *Homo Sapiens'* constant struggle to achieve humanity *in* history and *as* history.

At the juncture of Heidegger's and Bataille's perspectives, we should thus be able to access the 'Spiritual conception (out) of Nothingness' that the Poet (Mallarmé) contemplated. In this way alone, by completing the ordeal of the deconstruction of origins, can (or may) all restrictive or naive approaches of the passage from animal to man be overcome (as it successively stressed hunting, sexuality, violence, man's biological 'pre-maturedness', and so on). It thus is only by means of an ana-chronological dis-enclosure of all of history's 'ages' that the exposition of *an abyssal in-between dimension* can (or may) happen (be fulfilled) as the revelation of a 'symbolic matrix'.[36] At the secret *locus* of man's birth lies the *poesis*-of-language as Work of art, the *articulation* between nascent speech – voiced phonemes – and the 'vestiges' of the absented *other*. Thus could an Epiphany of 'true speech' (the inaugural deployment of language/conscience/world) be incessantly renewed both as 'allegory' (*'allo agoreuei'*: 'the work...manifests something *other*') *and* as 'symbol' of the *membra disjecta* of man's destiny ('To bring together is, in Greek, *sumballein*').

*   *   *

At a time when humanity seems more than ever trapped in the labyrinth of origins (as is illustrated precisely by the *seemingly irreducible differential* between Heidegger's and Bataille's conceptions), we are called upon once again to transgress the boundaries of the im-possible and renew the *Ursprung* of humanization. In revisiting our 'birth-place', we need to conceive of the deconstructed *myth-of-speech* in its 'as yet undiscovered essence'.[37] We simultaneously need to become aware of the fact that such a 'coming together' of our dislocated Dasein may have no other confirmation than the 'historical' transformation of our current modes of *conscience* or 'being-in-the-world'. In order to overcome the contemporary fragmentation of knowledge, the accumulation of data without any real communication between disciplines, we will have to envision, in the wake of a radicalization of Nietzsche's criticism of the 'idolatry' of science and the perspective of 'a tragic philosophy', a complete reformation of philosophy and of the 'human sciences' (notably anthropology, linguistics and psychoanalysis). When the 'a-theology' (Bataille) of Beginnings will finally come to be manifested, it is the paradoxical *in-coherence* of history (the trans-mythical 'deconstructed' unity of man or of the 'Poem') that will be 'revealed'. Beyond the post-archaic aporias of the sacred, it is then the exploration of the initial deployment of language (the exposition of the genetic coincidence of funereal traces *and* voice, of signifier *and* soul) that will give access to that *other truth* of which paleolithic art offers us an always already *striking testimony*. With the now close-to-being-fulfilled event of the 'fleeing of the gods', it is finally our rooting in the in-essence of the animal and of the earth that could be acknowledged: 'The work moves the earth itself into the Open of a world and keeps it there. The work lets the earth be an earth.'[38] Reciprocally, the mediation of language *in statu nascendi* would render forever more *fantastic* our relation to the *other world* (i.e., the abolished *and* resurrectional world of the gods).

We have indicated, in our introduction, that Heidegger, by advocating the need for an existential 'take' on 'primitive Dasein', programmatically bracketed off such inquiry at the inception of his 'deconstruction of the history of being' (*Sein und Zeit*, §6 & 11). Although he never mentions these antecedents, it is remarkable that Derrida, in his characterization of the limitations of Heidegger's 'being-towards-death' in *Sein und Zeit*, centrally questions the lack of a theoretical grounding for the distinction between *man* 'who is capable of dying' – *sterben* – and the *animal* who 'perishes' – *verendet*.[39] In the light of the general reading outlined above, it seems that it is not without reason that Derrida successively raises the issues of the animal/human divide and of Heidegger's 'delimitations' (*Abgrenzungen*) which lead him to blatantly ignore all paleo-anthropological data. (For his part Derrida insists that: 'There is no culture without a cult of the ancestors, a ritualization of mourning and sacrifice, sites and institutional modes of inhumation, be it just the disposal of the ashes of the incinerated corpse'.[40] It will here suffice to indicate that, as Derrida's discourse confronts its/our own limitations – 'without being able to engage ourselves [*s'engager*] towards the heart of things'[41]– as his discourse dramatically achieves a breathless climax/conclusion,[42] one wonders if it is not our globalized civilization which is running out of time.[43])

Will we then be able to still welcome without any restraint the chance event of the Beginnings of art (language *and* death) in such a fashion as to complete the *reciprocal conversion* of thought into poetry and poetry to thought? As 'truth at work' this project can only be in-finite since it will coincide, for a *Homo absconditus* initiated to the secret of his mortal birth, with the 'production of things' common presence'.[44] Then, suffused with a sense of renewed amazement/awe, will we be able to recognize with Hölderlin that: 'A measure of a being-together always was and [still] lies in the heart of the night.'

Notes

1. 'Lascaux or the Birth of Art', in *Oeuvres Complètes*, IX (Paris: Gallimard, 1979), 12.
2. In *Poetry, Language, Thought*, trans. Albert Hofstadter (New York: Harper Colophon, 1975).
3. ibid., 39.
4. ibid., 61, 87.
5. ibid., 86, my emphasis.
6. ibid., 17, my emphasis.
7. ibid., 76.
8. ibid., 77–8.

 9. ibid., 41–2.
10. ibid., 43–4.
11. ibid., 72.
12. ibid., 73.
13. ibid.
14. Martin Heidegger, *Les concepts fondamentaux de la métaphysique* (Paris: Gallimard, 1992), 269, my translation, my emphasis.
15. Heidegger, 'The Origin of the Work of Art', 65, slightly modified translation.
16. Bataille, *Lascaux or the Birth of Art*, 12.
17. Heidegger, 'The Origin of the Work of Art', 42, 74–5.
18. ibid., 258.
19. Bataille, *Lascaux*, 14, my translation.
20. ibid., 39, 87.
21. ibid., 21–2, 81–90.
22. ibid., 45–8, 67–70.
23. ibid., 73–5.
24. ibid., 41–4.
25. ibid., 71–3, 75–80.
26. ibid., 51–3, 96–116, 129–39.
27. Georges Bataille, *Eroticism: Death and Sensuality*, trans. Mary Dalwood (London: City Lights Publishers, 1986).
28. See Michel Surya, *Georges Bataille, La mort à l'œuvre* (Paris: Gallimard, 1992).
29. Bataille, *Lascaux*, 24, slightly modified, my emphasis.
30. ibid.
31. *Hades in Manganese* (Santa Barbara: Black Sparrow Press, 1997).
32. *Lascaux*, 12, my translation.
33. The quote comes from a preface published under Bataille's name to the 1956 edition of Maurice Blanchot's *Madame Edwarda*. The book was first published in French in 1941 (with the false imprint and date 'Éditions du Solitaire, 1937') under the pseudonym of Pierre Angélique; 2nd edition 1945; 3rd edition 1956. It has been published in English translation as *My Mother, Madame Edwarda and The Dead Man*, trans. Austryn Wainhouse (New York: Marion Boyars Publishers, 1969).
34. Bataille, 'Death and Sensuality'.
35. Heidegger, 'The Origin of the Work of Art', 76, slightly modified.
36. See Gérard Bucher, *L'imagination de l'origine* (L'Harmattan, 2000) and *L'autre commencement; Archéologie du religieux immemorial* (forthcoming).
37. Heidegger, 'The Origin of the Work of Art', 60, or 'in-essence'.
38. ibid., 46.
39. Jacques Derrida, *Aporias* (Paris: Galilée, 1996), 61–80; I am quoting the original French.
40. ibid., 79–86, 110–12.
41. ibid., 139.
42. ibid., 127–41.
43. One cannot but evoke here the work of Jean-Luc Nancy and notably *The Creation of the World or Globalization* (Albany: SUNY Press, 2007) and *Dis-enclosure: The Deconstruction of Christianity*, trans. Bettina Bergo, Gabriel Malenfant and Michael B. Smith, Perspectives in Continental Philosophy (New York: Fordham University Press, 2008).
44. Heidegger, 'The Origin of the Work of Art', 37, slightly modified translation.

14

Aesthetic Allegory: Reading Hegel after Bernal

Martin McQuillan

> The simple beginning is something so insignificant in itself, so far as its content goes, that for philosophical thinking it must appear as entirely accidental.
>
> *Hegel*, Aesthetics[1]

> The beginning is always constituted by what is abstract and indeterminate in its meaning.
>
> *Hegel*, Aesthetics[2]

One day I would like to write a book on Egypt and Derrida. The two proper names, if that is the right term here, are tethered together in suggestive ways. It would, of course, treat Freud's book on Moses, which appears so prominently in *Archive Fever*, as well as the god of writing, Thoth, who pops up in 'Plato's Pharmacy', the pyramids that serve for Derrida as an introduction to Hegel's semiology, the Egyptian stones that resonate at the end of *Glas*, the desert of Edmond Jabès and the Mount Sinai of Emmanuel Levinas that Derrida visits, and the hieroglyphs from 'Scribble (writing-power)'. This would be for starters before a full reckoning with that other border of Europe beyond Greece and Rome, imagined by the North African Derrida. Such a project will need to wait for another day. This present essay is concerned, as Derrida always is, with the place of Egypt (or more accurately the figure of Egypt) as an origin of Western philosophy. It attends to the place of Egypt in Hegel and the place of Hegel in Martin Bernal. It points to many of the places I would like to go to in such a book.

So, let us begin with architecture, archaeology and arche-writing.[3] This *arch* configuration will point us toward the troubling question of origins. It will be my contention that whenever the figure of Egypt appears in the text of Western philosophy it is always associated with the question of origins – not only with the architecture of the pyramids, or the archaeology of tombs, or the arche-writing of hieroglyphs, but with the very question of the origins of philosophy itself. The question of Egypt as a site of origin for philosophy is troubling because such a possibility challenges the primacy of Greece as the birthplace of Western thought. This assertion of the originariness of Egyptian philosophy for the European tradition is made, more or less explicitly, by Martin Bernal in his seminal study *Black Athena: the Afroasiatic Roots of Classical Civilization* (1987).[4] In brief, Bernal makes a distinction between 'the Ancient model' and 'the Aryan model' of European culture. In the former, Greek knowledge is said to be derived from Egyptian and Phoenician sources as a consequence of Egyptian colonization in Thebes, Athens and the Argolid and the Phoenician foundation of Thebes. For example, Plato, Aristotle and Pythagoras are all said to have studied in Egypt and consequently Greek philosophy and mathematics are Egyptian in origin. In the later model, which Bernal claims only succeeded the Ancient model in the European imaginary after the orientalist re-writing of nineteenth-century imperialism and race theory, Greece is named as the proper origin of Western thought.[5] This 'fabrication' of the origins of Western civilization occurred, according to Bernal, because the idea that Western culture is originarily the product of African and Semitic influences was intolerable to the euro-centric racism of the nineteenth century. In this essay I would like to challenge some of Bernal's work in *Black Athena*. I will do so not out of reactionary or even mildly conservative reasons; I have no interest in defending the Aryan model that Bernal so brilliantly dismantles and I am in broad sympathy with his attempt to recover the Ancient model of European civilization. Rather, I would like to take to task some of the critical reading Bernal offers (and offers by omitting) as justification for his thesis. In particular, as a way of opening up the complex question of the figurative place of Egypt in Western philosophy, I would like to push at Bernal's insistence on Hegel as a principal culprit in the fabrication of the Aryan model. It is not so much that Hegel is an innocent wrongly accused but that the text of philosophy, as a text and as philosophy, can no more yield to the reductionism of Bernal's Ancient model than it can succumb to the crudity of the Aryan model. Rather, I will argue that Egypt may be that figure which undoes the very possibility of all and every such model in philosophy. Whenever Egypt appears in the text of philosophy one can detect an uncontrollable undecideability in the epistemology, order, logic and axiomatics of that discourse. In part this is a result of the proximity of Egypt to the troubling question of the origin but it is also a consequence of the indissociability of Egypt and the problem of the material.

If Bernal is correct and Greece cannot be the origin of the West, then – for reasons I am perhaps too easily tempted too call deconstructive – Egypt can be no more originary than Greece despite its historically prior claims. If ancient Greek culture cannot attain to the Aryan ideal of the pure point of origin for European thought but is rather a space of cultural hybridity (a site of de-colonization, mis-appropriation and mis-understanding) between African and Semitic influences, then similarly ancient Egyptian civilization cannot be a fixed, stable or authentically autochthonous source. In this regard one need only consider the cultural differences between upper and lower Egypt, the Nubian Pharaohs, or the competing tendencies of monotheism and polytheism in ancient Egyptian religion. In fact, to follow Bernal's own argument, Egyptian colonization or trading practices must have ensured the hybridity of Egyptian culture, just as surely as all culture – which can never take place prophylactically – must be hybrid.[6] Rather, the experience of ancient Egyptian culture as the receptacle of an unchanging pre-historic mythos will only ever have been the effect of a certain European *nachträglichkeit*, to use Freud's analysis of the non-originariness of primal scenes. As such, to posit Egypt as a determinate beginning for Western thought would be, once again, to surrender the idea of Egypt to the very eurocentric model (and the eurocentrism of the model) from which Bernal has attempted to rescue it. Such a gesture sees the importance of Egypt in the effect it produces in the West rather than in the incompatibility between Egypt and the West.

To do justice to Bernal, his argument is never strong enough to make the outright claim for the originariness of Egypt with respect to Western culture. Rather, his aim in *Black Athena* is to open up new lines of inquiry regarding the supposed classical roots of European civilization by providing evidence of the 'dubious origin of the Aryan model' and the competitive plausibility of the Ancient model.[7] However, in saying this Bernal makes no attempt to identify pre-Egyptian or Phoenician cultural practices and so the originariness of Egyptian thought stands by inference. It is an inference picked up by Simon Critchley in the essay 'Black Socrates?'.[8] It is surprising that Critchley does not comment on what looks suspiciously like an onto-genetic historization in Bernal's argument. Recalling the classical account of the origin of philosophy as told by Hegel and Nietzsche (in which Socrates' death initiates the vocation of the philosopher as critique, replacing *mythos* with *logos*) Critchley seems to transfer Bernal's Aryan model on to the philosophical tradition. He cites (not unproblematically) Husserl's 1935 Vienna Lecture 'Philosophy and the Crisis of European Humanity' as exemplary of a certain 'Aryan' or eurocentric understanding of the history of philosophy, 'the belief in exclusivity of the Greek beginning of the philosophy and the centrality and linear continuity of the European philosophical tradition'.[9] While Husserl's rhetoric in this text is at times uncompromising, his own Jewishness and his subsequent treatment by his pupil Heidegger renders the 'Aryan' nature of his historical narrative somewhat ambivalent. Critchley suggests that similar positions can be found in 'Hegel, Nietzsche, Heidegger, Merleau-Ponty, Arendt, Gadamer, and an entire German and English romantic tradition'.[10] The list, I am sure, could be extended. Such testimonies, for the Critchley of 'Black Socrates', are a clear indication of philosophy's complicity with the orientalism (or outright racism) of the Aryan model of European civilization. He provisionally concludes the first movement of his paper with the question, if we 'admit that there is a racist or imperialist logic in philosophy – and this is as much an accusation against myself as against Husserl – then could it ever be otherwise?'[11] While I am willing to accept that certain texts in the canon of European philosophy force this reading upon us as part of our initial encounter with them, this essay may be an attempt to show how philosophy can be read otherwise.

Just as there are good reasons for wanting to relate Bernal's arguments to the philosophical tradition, there are equally valid grounds for being wary of mapping Bernal's historicism on to philosophical texts. Critchley provides a number of these reasons for himself. He concludes his essay with:

> Three important consequences for those concerned with philosophy and its history: i) The acceptance of the necessity of the Greco-European tradition as the linguistic and conceptual resource with which what 'we Europeans' (leaving the limits of this 'we' deliberately vague) call thinking takes place. ii) The necessary failure of any attempt to constitute an uncontaminated Greco-European tradition, a pure inside that would presuppose the European exclusivity of philosophy and the privileging of the European over the non-European. The identity of the European tradition is always impurely traced and contaminated by the non-European other that it tries unsuccessfully to exclude. iii) The acceptance of the impossibility of a pure outside to the European tradition for 'we Europeans', the irretrievability of another origin, the fantasy of a European anti-Eurocentrism, of anti-ethnocentrism, of romantic anti-Hellenism, of all post-Rousseauesque versions of what Derrida calls *nost-Algerie*.[12]

On the one hand, philosophy in its European moment is compelled to recount its own narrative of Greek origins in order to constitute the meaning of European philosophy precisely because this beginning can only be determined after the foundation of European philosophy, which is thus constitutively illegitimate.[13] In this way the Greco-European origin of philosophy works, as de Man says of Rousseau's account of speech as the origin of language, 'by means of causal categories that are themselves dependent on the genetic power of the origin for which they are supposed to account'.[14] This is the case even for those readers of European philosophy who only call themselves philosophers as an act of remembrance for the constitutive impossibility of the texts they read. On the other hand, if there is no proper point of origin for philosophy then there can be neither a determinate 'inside' to the philosophical tradition nor equally a definite 'outside' in which one could locate an alternative origin for philosophy, such as Egypt. This is the aporia of closure characteristic of all logocentric thought and which is perhaps the greatest single issue confronting the philosophical tradition that thinks of itself as having initiated the logos in the first place. In this sense the logos itself has no proper point of origin, or at least must be thought of in terms of a non-originary origin.

To question Bernal's argument is not to argue for a return to a Greco-European origin of philosophy, hedged around with the appropriate reservations. Rather, even if the academic institution of philosophy, characteristic of modernity (which depends upon a Socratic tradition of the critical articulation of origins as opposed to the amnesia of origins that comes with pre-philosophical doxa) is in some way – yet to be fully elaborated – complicit with the discourses of nineteenth-century nationalism and imperialism,[15] the work of philosophy itself cannot be reduced to this institutional apparatus. This irreducibility between philosophy and Philosophy takes several forms. Firstly, as we have seen, philosophy itself must pre-date the violent foundation of the institutions of Philosophy in order to constitute them. Accordingly, and secondly, philosophy is a form of knowledge which can take place outside of the legitimating channels of those institutions, even if – by the aporia of closure – these institutions define in advance, or *a posteriori*, what such knowledge looks like. Thirdly, it is the opening between philosophy and non-philosophy (which because it now falls within the ambit of philosophy must also be a form of philosophy or quasi-philosophy, or at least philosophy's 'past and its concern, its death and wellspring'[16]) that constitutes the historical as such. Thus, the questions of non-philosophy immediately pose themselves as, or in relation to, philosophical ones and so at once philosophy can always be outside of itself even if it is never free of itself. Fourthly, it may be possible to read philosophy without participating in, or seeking permission from, the institution of Philosophy. For example, deconstruction reads philosophy but it does not seek the approval of Philosophy to legitimize its readings. Conversely, however, since the history of Philosophy would seem to be merely the appropriation of everything outside of itself to itself then such illegitimate reading can only ever complete the work of Philosophy in its most classical sense.[17] Much will depend here upon how we are to define terms such as 'philosophy' or 'deconstruction'. Indeed this particular problem may be leading us back to a more fundamental and perhaps intractable question, 'what is philosophy?' Let us suspend this analysis for the moment, noting, as Derrida does in the opening of 'Violence and Metaphysics', that such problems are ones that philosophy itself cannot answer. At any rate it would be safe to assume (securely buffered by the limits of Bernal's own chronology) that the text of, say, Plato, a *sine qua non* of philosophy, cannot be reduced to the modern institution of Philosophy that reads it and takes it as its own origin. The same must be true, following Bernal, of all pre-nineteenth-century philosophical texts. Problems will begin to arise, and subsequently multiply, for Bernal's hypothesis when one attempts to draw a line in the sand by reading specific philosophical texts in relation to the Aryan model. In other words, given all that has been said above, how can one date or find the origin of such a model? Hegel is the earliest philosophical instance cited by Bernal, and later Critchley, in the genealogy of this – to borrow a term coined by Foucault – discursive formation. We will return to Hegel in a moment.

Bernal names a range of academics in post-Kantian Germany as being responsible for the Hellenomania which fabricated the origins of European culture and thus philosophy: the classicist Friedrich August Wolf, the educationalist Wilhelm von Humboldt, the historian Barthold Niebuhr, the philologist Karl Otfried Muller, the art historian Johann Joachim Winckelmann, and the philosopher Hegel. Bernal makes no real distinction between the dubious formulations of this collection of nationalists and race theorists and Hegel's philosophical system. The one is reducible to the other in the long historical sweep of Bernal's thesis. Herder, Schegel, Fichte, Schiller and Goethe are all gathered up by Bernal's broad brush as well but only Hegel and Schlegel are subject to any sort of critical reading. Bernal states 'it is noticeable that Hegel wrote exceptionally little about Egypt'[18] and turns to the *Lectures on the History of Philosophy* to identify 'Hegel's true feelings'.[19] He quotes Hegel twice:

> From Egypt Pythagoras thus without doubt brought the idea of his Order, which was a regular community brought together for purposes of scientific and moral culture... Egypt at that time was regarded as a highly cultured country, and it was so when compared with Greece; this is shown even in the differences of caste which assume a division amongst the great branches of life and work, such as the industrial, scientific and religious. But beyond this we need not seek great scientific knowledge amongst the Egyptians, nor think that Pythagoras got his science there. Aristotle (Metaph.I) only says that 'in Egypt mathematical sciences first commenced, for there the nation of priests had leisure'.[20]

And again:

> The name of Greece strikes home to the hearts of men of education in Europe, and more particularly is this so with us Germans [...] They [the Greeks] certainly received the substantial beginnings of their religion, culture... from Asia, Syria and Egypt; but they have so greatly obliterated the foreign nature of this origin, and it is so much changed, worked on, turned round and altogether made so different, that what they – as we – prize, know and love in it is essentially their own.[21]

On first appearance these citations (made to stand metonymically for the whole of the Hegelian system and thus they have their work cut out) may look as if they concur with Bernal's thesis on the repression of the afroasiatic (and more specifically Egyptian) roots of classical civilization. However, on close reading (and returned to the context of Hegel's philosophy) they might in fact suggest a richer and more complex view of Egypt in Hegel than Bernal may be ready to admit. As Hegel puts it elsewhere, 'when we first enter the world of . . . Egyptian shapes and productions, our footing is not really secure; we feel that we are wandering amongst *problems*'.[22] This will require a little unpacking.

Bernal never cites Hegel's *Aesthetics*. This is surprising because the lectures on Fine Art are not only the place in which the question of representation makes the whole of the Hegelian system tremble,[23] but it are also the place in which Hegel gives his fullest elaboration of his thoughts on Egypt. In brief, Hegel's system of aesthetics, which stands as a pivotal point in the greater project of Hegelian thought, divides into Symbolic, Classical and Romantic varieties of art. That art is itself divided into five strictly hierarchical classifications: architecture, sculpture, painting, music and poetry. Symbolic art, of which Egyptian artistic practice is, for Hegel, exemplary (although it is not the only variety of Symbolic art identified by Hegel) is the first order of true art because it contains within itself the idea of art as a defining property. While Symbolic art is said by Hegel to have 'in general the character of sublimity' it is 'to be considered only . . . as the threshold of art'.[24] Symbolism (such as the vertices of a pyramid representing the rays of the sun) involves, says Hegel, an intrinsic ambiguity between form (pyramid) and content or meaning (the power of the sun). This diremption between image and meaning ensures that Symbolic art will always fail to accomplish the true meaning of art which would be, for Hegel, an exact correspondence between ideal content and true form, which would express substantive subjectivity in its proper external shape. Classical art, however, while matching form to the individual spirit, also degrades art by 'providing an artistically formed inorganic environment for the spiritual meanings that for their part have now been independently realized'.[25] Romantic art, of which the art of Christian Europe is exemplary (although Hegel also identifies Moorish art as Romantic as well; this question of exemplarity is not insignificant), manages to combine, in appropriately dialectical fashion, a spiritual purpose for art while ensuring that art is framed and produced on its own account, as in the Symbolic. The divisions and exclusions upon which this system depends are put under tremendous strain in Hegel's elaboration of them and this system, as we shall see, is in constant contradiction and disarticulation (particularly whenever the figure of Egypt emerges within it). However, the initial point to make here is that while Hegel may view Egyptian art as in some way 'conceptually' inferior to Classical art, at no point does Hegel deny the historical relation between the two. In fact it is absolutely necessary for the Hegelian system that Classical art has its roots in something like Egyptian art in order for this system to operate in a dialectical way. On this point it may be useful to cut straight to the chase, as it were, to examine the moment in the lectures on Fine Art where Hegel seems to be at his most critical of Egyptian art, namely his account of Egyptian sculpture.

Here Hegel states that 'so far as sculpture goes we ought to call the Egyptians children'.[26] However, despite his seemingly derogatory opinion of the aesthetic merits of Egyptian sculpture – a point of view by no means applied universally by Hegel to Egyptian art and architecture – he feels it absolutely necessary to pass through Egypt on his way to Greece. He states:

> When we are on the point of studying the classical art of sculpture in Greece historically, we are met at once, before achieving our aim, by Egyptian art as sculpture too; as sculpture, that is to say, not in connection with enormous works produced in an entirely individual artistic style by supreme technique and elaboration, but as a starting-point and source for the forms of Greek plastic art.[27]

Now, it will be necessary to tread wearily around an explicit attribution of origins such as this, given all that has been said to date about the non-originariness of any and every such 'starting point and source', as well as the necessarily hybrid nature of ancient Greek culture. However, Hegel's position here, regarding the Egyptian roots of Greek art, is decidedly unambiguous. He continues:

> The fact that the latter is the case, that it is actually historically true that Greek artists did learn from the Egyptians and adopt shapes from them – all this must be made out so far as the meaning of the divine figures portrayed is concerned, on the field of mythology, and in respect of the manner of artistic treatment, by the history of art (ibid.).

One can begin to determine here a trembling in this dialectical system, a constant tremor which lends the *Aesthetics* the quality of a work in perpetual crisis rather than of systematicity. On a strong reading of Hegel (i.e., one which read Hegel in isolation from the other Germans labelled guilty by Bernal) this is a statement of fact ('it is actually historically true') and so runs counter to the idea that Hegel ever imagined Greece as the autochthonous origin of Europe. On a weak reading (one which keeps Hegel within the ambit of the discursive fabrication of Ancient Greece) this is an important concession ('the fact that the latter *is* the case, that it *is* actually historically true'). After Bernal's intervention the perceived difference between such readings may be importantly undecideable. Either way, this historical relation between Egypt and Greece cannot, by the very logic of Hegel's own system, be distinguished from the conceptual relation between Symbolic and Classical art of which Egypt and Greece would only be exemplary.

The point to be made here is that the artistic representation of mythology – whether it is the religious allegory of the pyramid or the Greek myth, say – is Symbolic in its nature. At the moment when Hegel explicitly admits the historic relation between Egypt and Greece he implicitly admits the conceptual relation, that he identifies elsewhere, which will act as a contaminatory force, spreading like a virus, undoing all the boundaries and classifications of his aesthetic system. While the dialectical method depends on something like the general correctness of its classifications in the greater sweep of its historical telos, in relation to the specific cases that Hegel examines to build this system there is always a certain inappropriateness to them. This system is built from pieces that never quite fit and which will have the accumulative effect of a structure in danger of constant collapse. In a previous lecture (introducing 'The Symbolic Form of Art') Hegel maintains, following Schlegel, that *all* mythology 'is to be understood symbolically'.[28] Thus, unavoidably, the Symbolic spills into Classical art (which is nothing but the representation of mythology, particularly in the case of sculpture[29]) and so Classical art in itself can never be absolutely Classical. Equally, Egyptian or any other mode of Symbolic art can never be purely Symbolic and must in certain respects duplicate the work of the Classical. Hegel seems willing to cede this latter point while going to great lengths to attempt to deny the former. He says in the section on 'Unconscious Symbolism':

> Egypt is the country of symbols, the country which sets itself the spiritual task of the self-deciphering of the spirit, without actually attaining to the decipherment. The problems remain unsolved, and the solution which *we* [Hegel's italics] can provide consists therefore only in interpreting the riddles of Egyptian art and its symbolic works as a problem remaining undeciphered by the Egyptians themselves.[30]

In this respect Hegel concedes that the avowed aim of Egyptian art, as a form of religious or spiritual expression, is the same as that of Classical and Romantic art – 'the self-deciphering of the spirit'. It is only the Egyptians' failure to make the necessary breakthrough (and it is not at all clear whether this is a question of technical skills, aesthetic forms or conceptual sophistication) into the true rendering of the spirit in its ideal form which relegates Egyptian art into the realm of the Symbolic, although such Symbolism can only be 'unconscious' since it was the conscious aim of the art to decipher the spirit. This is a problem (a problem more for Hegel than the Egyptians) which remains unresolved. On the one hand, the Egyptians are identified as 'the properly artistic people'[31] who have produced an undecideable quasi-Symbolic art:

> In a symbolism which confusedly intertwines meaning and shape, presages a variety of things in fact or alludes to them, and therefore already comes close to that inner subjectivity which alone can develop itself in many directions, the associations are ambiguous, and this is the virtue of these productions, although their explanation is of course made difficult owing to this ambiguity.[32]

The problem for Hegel is, as he states in his founding definition of Symbolism, 'the symbol by its very nature remains essentially ambiguous'[33] and correspondingly will not fit easily into the determinate place Hegel demands of it in order to secure the stability of his aesthetic system. It is the very ambiguity of Egyptian art, as a form of Symbolism, which allows it to touch on the definition of higher orders of art ('already comes close to that inner subjectivity'). A resolution to this problem (i.e., one that will definitively return Egyptian art to the Symbolic) is too difficult for Hegel to accomplish here – it has already forced him into the invention of this supplementary category of 'unconscious symbolism'. Rather, his pursuit of a solution here leads Hegel to concede that the meaning of Egyptian art lies in its interpretation rather than its essential characteristics and so hints at a far deeper problem for his entire aesthetic order: 'in this we regard the Egyptian works of art as containing riddles, the right solution of which is in part unattained not only by us, but generally by those who posed these riddles to themselves'.[34] If, for Hegel, the true work of art is one which rushes to reveal its meaning before us – by perfectly matching spirit to expression – and in so doing finds its place within an aesthetic schema as true art; then, correspondingly, in order to fit into this schema, Symbolic art must also render up its meaning immediately. Its meaning in this sense, in terms of the system, is that it fails to match spirit to expression. Thus for Egyptian art to work as Hegel wishes it to work it must be unambiguously ambiguous. However, if it is 'essentially ambiguous' it cannot be in any way unambiguous even in its ambiguity, or, if it is unambiguous it cannot be Symbolic. Thus, Egyptian art falls through the hole made for it in Hegel's aesthetic order.

If the figure of Egypt can be identified, following a favourite phrase of Paul de Man's, as the 'defective cornerstone'[35] of Hegel's aesthetic system, then Classical art (of which the figure of Greece is exemplary but not in an exhaustive sense) can also be read as undoing the classifications put in play under its name. In the introduction to 'The Symbolic Form of Art', Hegel is once again forced to amend the divisions of his aesthetic order by making additional distinctions between Symbolic and Classical mythology in order to maintain his restricted definitions of Symbolic and Classical. This double gesture of augmentation and contraction forces Hegel's argument into a moment of textual anxiety. The argument runs likes this. Classical art presents a problem because it contains its own 'aspect of ambiguity since in the case of the mythological productions of antiquity it may seem doubtful whether we are to stick to the external shapes as such and marvel at them as merely a charming play of a happy fancy – because mythology is indeed in general only an idle invention of fables – or whether we still have to search for a further and deeper meaning'.[36] Hegel feels it necessary to resort to this metaphorical structure of inside and outside (deep and surface meanings, a metaphorical arrangement on which the entire definition of Symbolic and Classical depends) because clearly, on face value, the fables of ancient Greece which he cites in reference to this problem 'would have to be regarded both as wholly beneath the dignity of the Absolute and as inadequate and taste-less inventions'.[37] In other words the mythological nature of Greek art is an inadequate expression of the divine spirit it is said to contain. Therefore, Greek art must be in some way, on Hegel's terms, Symbolic. Having dug this hole for himself Hegel proceeds to build a logical argument to extricate himself. Since such mythology concerns the supreme divinity, says Hegel, 'it may all the same be credible that still another, wider meaning, than what the myth provides on the surface, lies concealed under them'.[38] Thus, not unproblematically, Greek mythology if it is to be an adequate expression of the spirit must work by containing a deeper meaning than its surface expres-sion, even though such a non-consubstantiality between form and content would be the very definition of the Symbolic. Hegel points to two possi-ble solutions to his worry here. Firstly, on the one hand mythology, despite the grace and beauty of individual myths, is simply incapable of render-ing deeper meanings: 'mythology is therefore on this view to be considered purely *historically*'[39] because what you see is what you get and its elucidation is already conspicuous in its form. On the other hand, 'from the point of view of its historical *origin* [Hegel's italics]'[40] as a product of priests, artists and poets the meaning of a myth cannot be reduced to its purely external shape and must contain a deeper sense 'and that to know this sense never-theless, by unveiling it, is the proper business of mythology as the scientific treatment of myths.'[41] While this formulation may secure Roland Barthes as the most Hegelian of thinkers, it does present several problems for the *Aesthetics* because as Hegel states 'on this view mythology must therefore be interpreted *symbolically*'.[42] However, this imperative allows Hegel to work with a displaced definition of the Symbolic, 'for "symbolically" means here only that the myths, as a product of spirit...still comprise meanings, i.e., general thoughts about the nature of God, i.e., philosophical theories'.[43] In other words, this problem of the definition of the Symbolic (or perhaps more accurately this attempt to separate out the definition of the Symbolic and the Classical) enables Hegel to make a significant compromise on the relation between *mythos* and *logos* and between philosophy and non-philosophy. In a certain sense, if Classical art is mythological it is only because such mythol-ogy would in fact be philosophical. Hence, indirectly perhaps, the entire issue of the origins of philosophy is brought into question (or questioning) by the instability of the figures of Egypt and Greece in these lectures. Hegel continues by turning to Creuzer, his colleague at Heidelberg, and his *Symbo-lik und Mythologie*. Creuzer, says Hegel, has – contrary to traditional academic lines of inquiry – sought in the myths of the ancients 'inner rational mean-ings. In this enterprise he is guided by the presupposition that the myths and legendary tales took their origin in human spirit'.[44] According to this argument, 'reason is the inventor of shapes' and while it remains unable to unfold their inner meanings adequately, 'when reason invents the shapes, there arises also the need to know their rationality'.[45] The knowledge of this rationality is the only pre-occupation worthy of man, says Hegel, in contrast to the mere accumulation of 'historical external details'[46] that are only the product of accident and fancy. This justification of rationality in Greek myths has led Hegel into some very deep water indeed, for in order to pull off this claim he must in some way disentangle himself, even provisionally, from the progress of history, the very guiding thread of his aesthetic order and perhaps his entire philosophical edifice. For Hegel simultaneously formulates and absolves himself of the necessary historical objection to this line of thought, namely, that the producers of such myths 'knew nothing of such thoughts [i.e., Reason] which were incompatible with the whole culture of their age'[47] and that any attempt to uncover Reason in mythology is an achronological imposition of the modern on the ancient, *logos* on *mythos*, philosophy on to non-philosophy. However, this does not constitute a sufficient objection for Hegel because the composers of these myths 'lived in purely poetical conditions and so brought their inmost and deepest convictions before their minds not in the form of thought but in shapes devised by imagination without separating the universal abstract ideas from the concrete pictures'.[48] In this way not only would a pre-philosophical *mythos* have a philosophical content but the expression of this content would, under certain historical conditions, be adequate to their content and so not be Symbolic as such but would in fact be Classical. Thus Hegel invokes history in order to circumvent his own historical dialectic.

However, Hegel is not content with this as an explanation. He continues to push for a non-Symbolic-Classical mythology by distancing his definition of the Symbolic from the one proposed by Schlegel when he maintains that all mythology and art is to be understood symbolically and that in every artistic representation an allegory ought to be sought. It is not so much that Hegel wishes to relegate allegory to a lower, or supplementary, to use a loaded term, order of art; rather, he questions, despite his own characterization of Classical art as containing an element of ambiguity, whether all art is necessarily allegorical (i.e., it contains some meaning other than its external shape initially expresses):

> In that case [i.e., Schlegel's definition] the symbolical or allegorical is so understood that for every work of art and every mythological shape there serves as a basis a universal thought which, then explicitly emphasized in its universality, is supposed to provide the explanation of what such a work, such an idea really means.[49]

The problem of this approach to art, for Hegel, is that in its understanding of the work of art it separates form and meaning and so reaffirms the idea of a form of allegory:

> Understanding especially runs quickly to symbol and allegory, since it separates picture and meaning and therefore destroys the form of art, a form with which this symbolical explanation, aimed only at extricating the universal as such, has nothing to do.[50]

Thus interpretation of the work of art necessarily involves a separating out of content from the form in which it is expressed and so art criticism (or aesthetics as such) participates in the destruction of the art object, being unable to do anything with the artistic form it reads. Form for Hegel is the measure of true art. Hence, aesthetics (a general theory of the universal meanings of art regardless of its individual forms as elaborated here by Hegel) is itself a form of Symbolism because it necessarily separates form from content and the universal from its expression. To borrow from de Man and to play on Hegel, an aesthetics can only ever be an allegory of aesthetics; an aesthetics that failed to achieve the conditions of an aesthetics.

It may seem that Hegel now finds himself in irredeemable contradiction but what seems like a deconstruction of a central figure (aesthetics) will also contain within itself the demonstration of the impossibility of the reading that deconstructs the figure in the first place. The discovery that an aesthetic system is merely tropological would be only the first step of a deconstruction of Hegel, or, the deconstruction of Hegel by Hegel, by the text of Hegel. Rather, the corrective impulse within his own analysis is obliged to act out a second misreading in an attempt to establish itself as the true or corrected version of a deconstructed aesthetics. In other words, having demonstrated the invalidity of his own universal aesthetic system, Hegel proceeds to revisit all those tropes which lead him to this point (Egypt, Greece, the Symbolic, history and so on) in order to show the impossibility of the impossibility of aesthetics. This is not necessarily the same thing as the possibility of aesthetics, rather it is a demonstration by aesthetics of its own impossibility as the condition of its possibility. In this way, Hegel's edifice might be said to no longer resemble a precarious Classical ruin but rather a doubly folded plan of a pyramid which knows itself in its own transparent improbability, like the glass pyramid that now stands outside the Louvre in Paris.

Hegel proceeds to make an argument that might be characterized as saying, it is only on condition that everything not be Symbolic that the Symbolic has some chance of being thought. In this way he is caught up in the double-bind of closure in which it would be necessary to put down a definition of the Symbolic only to show that such a definition could never be saturated. Hegel notes that the 'extension of symbolism to *every* sphere of mythology and art is by no means what we have in view here in considering the symbolic form of art'.[51] For the *Aesthetics* it is not so much a question of discovering how far the terms 'symbolic' or 'allegorical' will take us in the interpretation of art; 'instead, we have to ask, conversely, how far the symbolical itself is to be reckoned an art-form'.[52] Hegel is not about to backtrack and declare Symbolic art non-art; rather he wants 'to establish the artistic relation between meaning and its shape, in so far as that relation is *symbolical* in distinction from other modes of representation'.[53] In other words, Hegel wants to ask what it is about the Symbolic that will allow us to think the symbolical as such. The task, he says, 'must therefore consist, not in accepting that diffusion of the symbolic over the entire field of art, but conversely expressly limiting the range of what in itself is presented to us a symbol proper and therefore is to be treated as symbolical'.[54] This is the very project of the aesthetics as it has been outlined by Hegel in the section on the 'Development of the Ideal into the Particular Forms of the Beauty of Art'. For Hegel, the symbolic is not to be associated with mere ambiguity; rather his 'meaning of the word at once stops short of the point where, instead of indefinite, general, abstract ideas, it is free individuality which constitutes the content and form of the representation'.[55] It is this independence – as in the case of Egyptian funereal architecture – which initiates the idea of art itself and which makes the Egyptians 'properly artistic people'. The ideal of art would be achieved, says Hegel, when 'meaning and sensuous representation, inner and outer, matter and form, are in that event no longer distinct from one another'.[56] In other words, the ideal of art would be that sublime object which undid the metaphorics of inside and outside upon which the Hegelian aesthetic order depends and, paradoxically, upon which thinking about the very ideal of art depends. Thus Hegel's aesthetic system is an attempt to know something which in its knowing will disarticulate or exceed the entire system that thinks it. For Hegel such an ideal is contained within the symbolic but is not reducible to the symbolic in which the differences between inner and outer 'announce themselves ... as merely related' rather than expressed 'as *one* whole in which the appearance has no other essence, the essence no other appearance, outside or alongside itself'.[57] Provisionally, this argument will free Hegel from this local difficulty of determining between Egyptian and Classical mythology. However, in the long run it will provide a definition of the ideal of art that will prove impossible to sustain in any exemplary instance of art, Symbolic, Classical or Romantic. Thus, the ideal of art will operate in the manner of a quasi-transcendental term for Hegel; at once enabling him to make the distinctions of his aesthetic system while always being caught up within the disarticulation of those distinctions and so finally exceeding the very logic of the system itself. In the short term Hegel is able to use his limited definition of the symbolic to say 'in so far as Greek art represents [the gods] as free, inherently and independently self-sufficient individuals, [they] are not to be taken symbolically', i.e., the stories of the gods are satisfactory in themselves without reference to a wider cosmogony or religion. Any attempt to generalize an abstract or universal meaning from such stories would be, says Hegel, seemingly forgetting his earlier appeal to Creuzer, to leave unnoticed and to destroy 'what in these figures is in conformity with art'.[58] This, however, leads Hegel into deeper water still. Having just identified something like a non-symbolic mythology in order to allow the category of the symbolic to be enunciated, he goes on to say that:

> For what we may think is left as an actually symbolic indication or allegory in the Classical and Romantic sort of artistic representation affects incidentals and is in that case expressly degraded to a mere attribute and sign, as e.g. the eagle stands beside Zeus, and Luke the Evangelist is accompanied by an ox; but the Egyptians had in Apis [the bull] a vision of God himself.[59]

Hegel thus turns back on to a distinction between sign and symbol introduced in his earlier elaboration of the Symbolic,[60] a full analysis of which we will postpone for another occasion when we will return to the question of the architecture of Hegel and his equally troubling distinction between the pyramid and the labyrinth.[61] However, needless to say, the division is not absolute. 'The symbol,' says Hegel, 'is *prima facie* a sign' although, unlike a sign, the relation between meaning and expression is not arbitrary but rather the symbol 'in its externality comprises in itself at the same time the content of the idea which it brings into appearance'. For example, a triangle suggests the idea of God because it contains the same number of ideas appearing in God. Nevertheless, the symbol does not present itself as God but only as the universal quality it signifies. And as we have seen while signifying this quality it also signifies the other attributes of its shape, such as the rays of light suggested by the sides of a pyramid, and so gives rise to ambiguity and confusion. Thus, while the relation between meaning and expression is not arbitrary it is importantly undecideable and so never saturated. Hence, this appeal to the difference between sign and symbol will not quite do the work that Hegel wants it to do here because while the bull may be symbolic of the Divinity it is no more divine than the triangle. Even if the bull in itself was divine for the ancient Egyptians as a sacred animal, this, according to an argument Hegel will make in the closing paragraph of his discussion of mythology, does not affect the realm of Symbolic art; 'however close the connection between religion and art may be, we still have not to go over the symbols themselves ... we have only to consider that element in them in accordance with which they belong to art as such. The religious element we must hand over to the history of mythology'. So, in order to preserve what is proper to aesthetics (art as such) Hegel must undermine the example (of Apis and Zeus) which preserved the distinction between Symbolic and Classical upon which his aesthetics is founded. Furthermore, as Hegel objects himself:

> The difficult point in this artistically adequate appearance of free subjectivity lies in distinguishing whether what is represented as person has also

actual individuality and subjectivity or whether it carries in itself only the empty semblance of the same as mere personification.[62]

Thus personality in a fable of Zeus or Apollo might be read not as subjectivity itself but as, undecideably, a superficial form whose external reality is indicative of some other meaning. This problematic, says Hegel, 'is the chief consideration in relation to the delimitation of symbolic art'. It is, however, a consideration that Hegel fails to resolve adequately, having used it as a conceptual division between Greek and Egyptian art only to imply later that as art no such reliable distinction can be made between Greek and Egyptian figures. Thus, while Hegel says that he does not wish to extend the notion of symbolism as ambiguity over the entire field of art, he pulls back from a definitive description of Classical mythology, wary of just such a possibility. Furthermore, having equivocated over the matter of history in his discussion of mythology Hegel now returns to the historical dialectic of the *Aesthetics* in order to conclude this definition of the symbolic:

> Our interest in considering symbolism consists in recognizing the inner process of the origin of art, in so far as this can be derived from the Concept of the ideal in its development up to true art, and so recognizing the sequence of stages in the symbolic as stages on the way to genuine art.[63]

Once again this problem of origins and the blurred distinction between a historical relation between Egypt and Greece as examples of Symbolic and Classical art and a conceptual relation between Symbolic and Classical which, as we saw apropos of Creuzer's search for rationality in Greek myth, would not be entirely dependent on history even if the thinking of its categories were the product of history. Symbolic art on this reading is not a unified thing but a series of stages; conceptual stages which could over-lap into the Classical and Romantic historical periods on the way to true art. Therefore, the exemplarity of Egyptian art as a form of the Symbolic would be thrown into reasonable doubt given that Greek art could historically be indicative of certain conceptual aspects of the Symbolic. If, as Bernal suggests, Hegel is responsible for the fabrication of the Graeco-European origins of western culture he is certainly going out of his way in the *Aesthetics* to show how this situation is necessarily otherwise.

In saying this Hegel still wants to maintain the division between Egyptian and Greek mythology, even though it puts the whole of his aesthetic order in peril. He closes the section on 'Unconscious Symbolism' with an account of a self-evidently rational Greek myth, which marks the passage from Symbolic to Classical, namely that of Oedipus and the Sphinx. Hegel states that 'the works of Egyptian art in their mysterious symbolism' are 'riddles; the objective riddle *par excellence*'.[64] Thus, Egyptian art is, for Hegel, exemplary of its ambiguity and so may not be exemplary of anything, exemplarity being conditioned by determinability. If Egyptian art is exemplary only of undecideability then it cannot be strictly exemplary and is in fact no more exemplary of ambiguity than the ambiguous aspect of Classical art. While Egyptian art may provide Hegel with access to the general structure of the Symbolic it is in itself no more exemplary of the Symbolic than in fact Greek art can be exemplary of the Classical mode. This is the situation which in fact allows Hegel to move from the historical difference between the examples of Egypt and Greece and the conceptual categories of Symbolic and Classical which are the proper object of study for the *Aesthetics*. In this way, Hegel's aesthetic order does not in fact need any work of art to operate but is instead troubled whenever it encounters examples of art.

However, Hegel turns to the example of the Sphinx because it represents the 'proper meaning of the Egyptian spirit' and is 'the symbol of the symbolic itself'.[65] This characterization ought to direct us toward the problems Hegel has been multiplying for his aesthetic system in this account of Egyptian art. Firstly, if the Sphinx is the proper expression of the Egyptian spirit then it is surely a Classical work rather than a Symbolic one because it matches the meaning of spirit to its external appearance. That is unless Hegel now wishes to introduce a supplementary distinction between Egyptian spirit and Greek spirit, which would produce as many difficulties as the supposed difference between Egyptian and Greek mythology. Such a distinction would in fact be indissociable from the problematic difference Hegel is attempting to resolve here. Secondly, if the Sphinx is symbolic of the symbolic then in the first place it cannot be Symbolic, because its meaning would no longer be a riddle but determinable (i.e., that it is definitely Symbolic or, again, unambiguously ambiguous). In this way the symbol of the symbol would escape the realm of the symbol. It would be that which, despite the exemplarity claimed for it by Hegel, the Symbolic as 'essentially ambiguous' could not account for. If the Sphinx is the most undecideable aspect of the field of the undecideable then its undecideability has been decided upon and so must in fact be decideable. Hence, the Sphinx falls outside of the Symbolic and by dint of its propriety as both example and expression of spirit must be Classical. The example of the Sphinx can only work in a pyrrhic way for Hegel, both constituting the terms of the Symbolic and undoing this category while finally moving beyond the very logic that initiates that conceptual order. Hegel states: 'out of the dull strength and power of the animal the human spirit tries to push itself forward, without coming to a perfect portrayal of its own freedom and animated shape, because it must still remain confused and associated with what is other than itself'.[66] In his attempt to return the Sphinx to the realm of the Symbolic, Hegel provides us with a definition of the Symbolic which might adequately account for the structure of the Symbolic and explain why that structure, despite Hegel's retreat from Schlegel, does indeed cover the entire field of art. The first thing to note here, however, is that Hegel does not seem to want to make a distinction between Egyptian and Greek spirit. Egyptian spirit is characterized as 'human spirit' and is therefore the same spirit at work in Classical and Romantic art; it is simply that Egyptian art is not an adequate expression of that spirit. This is necessarily the case for Egyptian art to be exemplary of the Symbolic and so represent a stage on the path to true art. However, if Egyptian spirit is the same as Greek spirit then several consequences follow. Firstly, the theological distinction that Hegel makes between Egyptian and Greek mythology will not hold as both forms of myth must be occupied by the same spirit. It follows from this that either Greek mythology and therefore Greek art is Symbolic or Egyptian art is Classical. Secondly, while Egyptian art may on Hegel's terms struggle to express this spirit properly were it ever to do so, then Egyptian art would indeed be Classical. Therefore, since the Sphinx is the proper expression of Egyptian spirit, then the Sphinx must be 'Classical'. However, of greater interest here is the description of the Sphinx as remaining 'confused and associated with what is other than itself'. In this way the Sphinx, simply put, is art; or, to use a Derridean formulation, the Sphinx is writing. Meaning haunted by and mistaken for its other is the very condition of meaning as such. The Sphinx in this way, as Hegel maintains, is representative of 'the symbolic as such which at this peak becomes a riddle'.[67] The Symbolic presents a riddle for Hegel. On the one hand, if the Symbolic is different from itself (it is said to only contemplate 'itself in what is related to it and brings itself into consciousness in precisely what is strange to it') then it must be the Classical; absolute difference being absolutely different from everything including itself and therefore being the self-same, to use an argument Hegel employs elsewhere.[68] On the other hand, despite his disavowal of Schlegel, Hegel cannot contain this otherness within the category of the Symbolic that he meticulously prepares for it and in fact the uncontrollability of the Symbolic turns the entire dialectical order around, allowing the Symbolic as the condition of all art to subsume the categories of the Classical and Romantic to itself. While Egyptian art may not be Classical or Romantic, all Greek and European art is in some way Symbolic and so Hegel's dialectical tripos is a pyramid turned on its side.

This situation is played out in Hegel's account of the Greek myth of the Sphinx, in which the Sphinx as the supplementary figure (or hinge) which connects the Symbolic Egyptians and the Classical Greeks is read as an initiator of Reason. Oedipus answers the riddle of the Sphinx and Hegel suggests that 'the explanation of the symbol lies in the absolute meaning, in the spirit, just as the famous Greek inscription [on the oracle at Delphi] calls to man: Know thyself'.[69] While this may look like an allegory of *logos* superceding *mythos* and so another repetition of the Greek origins of philosophy (although a story that pre-dates Bernal's eurocentric cabal by several thousand years) it should be noted that the riddle of the Sphinx was not a riddle to the Sphinx, who upon having it answered threw herself down from her rock. Only two paragraphs earlier Hegel had insisted that not only were the riddles of Egyptian art riddles to 'us' but also to the Egyptians. The story of Oedipus and the Sphinx surely demonstrates that the answers to such riddles are not only obtainable by 'us' but were also known by the Egyptians. Therefore, if the Sphinx as the symbol of the Symbolic is 'the objective riddle *par excellence'* then she demonstrates the answerable nature of such riddles and in fact their non-mysteriousness and indeed their non-Symbolic nature. The Sphinx knew the answer was 'man' and posed the question in an adequate form so that it might be answered. In this way the riddles of Egypt are not indecipherable or inadequate expressions of the spirit but questions directed to Greece. The fact that Greece, in the figure of Oedipus, is able to answer them is indicative of their rational content. If the Sphinx threw herself down from her rock this may say more about the andro-centric exclusions of Western humanism and the absolutism of the spirit than it does about the rationality of Oedipus, who remains a figure confined to mythology and, even in Hegel's account of him, in the realm of the Symbolic. His answer represents something other than his own self-conscious spirituality, namely, the universal abstract quality of Reason. Thus, Oedipus is symbolic of the non-Symbolic or, if you prefer, exemplary of the ambiguity of the Classical.[70]

After this lengthy aside it is now possible to return to Hegel's account of Egyptian sculpture. Several details regarding the place of Egypt in the Hegelian system have emerged from reading the lectures on Fine Art. Firstly, at no point does Hegel deny the historical relation between Egyptian and Greek art. He states this again in the text on sculpture:

> That there was a connection between Egyptian and Greek ideas of the gods was believed and proved by Herodotus [ii. 41ff.]; an external connection in works of art Creuzer thinks he thinks he can find most obviously in coins especially, and he rests his case above all on old attic ones. In Heildelberg [in 1821] he showed me one in his possession, on which the face indeed, in profile, had exactly the cut of faces on Egyptian pictures.[71]

This historical relation is enforced by a double appeal to authority. On the one hand, a Classical source, Herodotus, whose claim that the Greek gods are later versions of Egyptian gods that Hegel quotes with approval on five separate occasions in these lectures.[72] On the other, a Romantic source, Creuzer, whose investigations Hegel had leaned upon in the discussion of Greek and Egyptian mythology. Hegel also makes an appeal to the authority of the visible, having recognized Egyptian physiognomy in attic coins for himself. However, Hegel maintains here that the connection in works of art is an 'external' one. This seeming distinction might pose problems when we recall that both Egyptians and Greeks share the same spirit and so external agreement in their art would tend to suggest a match in-between spirit and expression in Egyptian as well as Greek art. Whatever the case, it would seem to be a crude reduction to suggest that Hegel denies the afroasiatic roots of Greek culture, given the importance of the aesthetic realm to such culture. However, this is not to deny Hegel's eurocentrism. Just as the dialectic, by necessity, cannot deny the relation between Egyptian and Greek art, the 'ontological imperialism'[73] (to borrow a phrase from Emmanuel Levinas) of its method simultaneously places symbolic (and so Egyptian) art in subservience to classical (and so Greek) art. Greek art is, however, equally deferential to Romantic art in this scheme. So while the historical link is a dialectical necessity, Egypt remains at the bottom of Hegel's conceptual order. Yet, as we have seen, Egypt (and the category of the symbolic in general) refuses to conform to the position offered to it by the dialectical method, constantly transgressing the boundaries of its classification and so threatening to unseat the entire aesthetic order.

This has consequences for the greater work of Hegelian philosophy, since the *Aesthetics* is a key text in the elaboration of that philosophy (the question of aesthetics, or representation, acting as the crucial link between real events such as history or politics and philosophical texts). Far from formulating an adequate notion of aesthetics that will help Hegel develop his philosophical system (that will require a detailed account of the representation of the spirit in historical and political forms), Hegel's text only succeeds in undoing the aesthetic as a valid philosophical category. Thus Hegel cannot close off his philosophical system because it cannot ground its discourse on a principle internal to the system. Since the system cannot be closed it cannot be systematic or ensure its own propriety. In attempting to validate the aesthetic by placing Egypt at the threshold of art, the text of Hegel presents the aesthetic as a trope which deconstructs, or disarticulates, itself and so sends a shudder through the larger system in which it operates. This trembling in the axiomatics and logic of the entire Hegelian system begins, let us repeat, wherever we find the figure of Egypt. This is a situation which Hegel simply cannot control and which will effect every thetic and theoretic statement he makes.

For example, if we continue reading in the section on sculpture, Hegel states of the factual (i.e., historical) relation between Egyptian and Greek art:

> Here, however, we can leave this purely historical question alone and have only to see if, instead of this, an inner and necessary connection can be exhibited. This necessity I have touched on already. The ideal, and art in its perfection, must be preceded by imperfect art, and it is only through the negation of this, i.e., through getting rid of the defects still clinging to it, that the ideal becomes the ideal. In the instance before us, classical

art of course *comes into being*, but that from which it develops must have an independent existence of its own outside it, because classical art, as classical, must leave behind it all inadequacy, all becoming, and must be perfect in itself. Now this [pre-classical] process of becoming classical consists in the fact that the content of the presentation begins to meet the ideal, yet remains incapable of an ideal treatment because it still belongs to the symbolic outlook which cannot form into one the universality of the meaning and the individual visible shape. The one thing that I will briefly indicate here is that Egyptian sculpture has such a fundamental character.[74]

The problem of Egypt (the riddle Egypt presents to Hegel) forces the dialectical method to renounce history. Knox writes in a footnote to his translation of the *Aesthetics*: 'nothing is more striking in Hegel than this dismissal of "purely" historical questions, although history is the guiding thread through all his major works, including these Lectures'.[75] Hegel's translator quickly explains away the difficulty by distinguishing between the work of the historian and a philosopher's study of history (i.e., between 'purely historical questions' of fact and the interpretation of their spiritual purpose). However, Hegel is not just any philosopher and the question of history is not just any question for Hegel. The problem here is that while the relation between symbolic and classical is one of inner necessity (i.e., a conceptual relation rather than a purely historic one) it must also be, by inner necessity to itself as a conceptual relation, a historic relation of dialectical becoming. Thus, Hegel finds himself in the double bind of at once grounding his conceptual order in history and removing it from history. The need to suspend history (and so displace, even provisionally, the dialectic) arises here for Hegel because the historic relation of becoming which characterizes the field of art history as well as the limits of the conceptual order must breach the integrity of any such limits. The symbolic-becoming-classical must remain in proximity to the classical proper right up until the classical proper comes into being, thus not only forming a constitutive outside for the classical proper but also remaining a presence within the classical's knowledge of itself as classical. Thus, the independence of the classical would always be in doubt and so the perfection of the ideal could never be fully realized without knowledge of the becoming perfect of imperfection. In other words, just as an Egyptian work of symbolic-becoming-classical can never be purely symbolic and so entirely contained within the aesthetic order, so a Greek work of the symbolic-becoming-classical-becoming-romantic cannot define a sufficient area beyond the becoming-classical and before the becoming-romantic which could adequately constitute the perfect, independent of all other concerns. To ensure the propriety of such classifications and remain within purely historical terms Hegel would have to identify a moment in art when becoming-classical stopped and perfection began. This would require

Hegel to select a single work or a single artist as the origin of classical art, a trick he can no more perform than the death of Socrates can deliver the origin of philosophy. Hegel does not attempt to name such an origin. On a weak reading of Hegel this would be the result of an anxiety over the necessary Egyptian origins of Greek art, which pushes Hegel into contradiction and compromise. On a strong reading this would be the result of Hegel's understanding that the problem posed by Egypt outflanks every attempt to classify it according to the dialectical method. Either way, while Egypt may seem to appear at the bottom of Hegel's conceptual order it is in fact the key to understanding the structure, operation and limitations of that order. Accordingly, if Egypt is that which troubles the dialectic in both its Socratic and Hegelian forms then Egypt is the question that outflanks the ontological question itself. It is the question which undoes the founding axiomatic of the European tradition, perhaps of Europe as such. Egypt is the difficulty that places Europe in deconstruction. If Hegel describes the Egyptians as children it may on the one hand be because historically they are the children who grew to manhood in European thought. This would at least correspond to Bernal's ancient model even if its patronizing eurocentrism continued to flatter Greece. On the other hand, it may be a calculated and ironic reversal of a famous passage from the *Timaeus* that Hegel no doubt knew well. In the Platonic text, Critias recounts to Socrates the story of Solon who is told by an Egyptian priest: 'Oh Solon, Oh Solon, you Greeks are all children, and there's no such thing as an old Greek.'[76] Solon asks what the priest means by this and is told 'you are all young in mind...you have no belief rooted in old tradition and no knowledge hoary with age'.[77] The priest goes on to explain to Solon how the Greek myth of Phaethon can be interpreted according to Egyptian knowledge of astronomy. The priest then recounts the story of Atlantis for Solon, saying that the absence of written records of antiquity makes the Greeks think 'like children, in complete ignorance of what happened in our part of the world or in yours in early times. So these genealogies of your own people which you were just recounting are little more than children's stories'.[78] Perhaps the lectures on Fine Art, if they can be said to repeat the narrative of Greco-European origins, are nothing more than children's stories. On this account they would be considered ignorant of history just as they initiate the model of art historical inquiry. Perhaps Bernal's genealogy of post-Kantian conspiracy is also just a child's story, replete with bogey-men and heroes; too black and white to be read. Either way, if the Egyptians are said by Hegel to be children it may be because their sculpture seems to him to have no ancient roots of its own and so is the proper origin, historically speaking, of Greek plastic art. Much will depend for us, in understanding this problem, upon these questions of origin, propriety, history, text, symbol, order, the archive, narrative, philosophy, culture, archeology, architecture and arche-writing. Even now posing the question of Egypt is only in its infancy.

Notes

1. G. W. F. Hegel, *Aesthetics: Lectures on Fine Art*, vol. 2, trans. T. M. Knox (Oxford: Clarendon, 1975), 630.
2. G. W. F. Hegel, *Aesthetics: Lectures on Fine Art*, vol. 1, trans. T. M. Knox (Oxford: Clarendon, 1975), 317.
3. Here I am echoing and augmenting the opening line, 'we shall begin with architecture', of Denis Hollier's *Against Architecture: The Writings of Georges Bataille* (Cambridge MA: MIT Press, 1989), 3.
4. Martin Bernal, *Black Athena: the Afroasiatic Roots of Classical Civilization (Volume 1: The Fabrication of Ancient Greece, 1785–1985)* (London: Vintage, 1991 [1987]).
5. Here and elsewhere I will use the term Orientalism, following Edward Said, *Orientalism* (London: Routledge and Kegan Paul, 1978).
6. A minimal reference for this understanding of hybridity might be Homi K. Bhabha, *The Location of Culture* (London: Routledge, 1994).
7. Bernal, *Black Athena*, 443.
8. Simon Critchley, 'Black Socrates? Questioning the Philosophical Tradition', *Radical Philosophy* 69 (Jan/Feb) 1995, 17–26. Reprinted (in part) in Martin McQuillan (ed.), *Deconstruction: a Reader* (Edinburgh: Edinburgh University Press, 2000).
9. Critchley, 'Black Socrates', 19.
10. ibid., 18.
11. ibid., 20.
12. ibid., 24–5.
13. This is also Geoffrey Bennington's reading of Martin Bernal; 'Mosaic Fragment: if Derrida were an Egyptian…', in *Legislations: The Politics of Deconstruction*, (London: Verso, 1994), 223. Here Bennington compares the 'amateur' Bernal's intervention in another 'professional' academic field to the figure of the Lawgiver in Rousseau, who must always arrive from outside to impose the Law. On one level this is as far as Bennington's interest in Bernal extends. However, he does quote Bernal with approval on several occasions within the complex patterning of this essay and this comparison (a privileged one within Bennington's writing) would seem to imply an uncharacteristically uncritical regard for Bernal's argument. Nevertheless, on the question of the figurative place of Egypt, Bennington's essay simultaneously would seem to undo Bernal's onto-genetic historization, as incidentally does Critchley.
14. Paul de Man, *Allegories of Reading: Figural Language in Rousseau, Nietzsche, Rilke, and Proust* (New Haven and London: Yale University Press, 1979), 142.
15. An example of what this elaboration might look like can be found in Gayatri Spivak's reading of Kant; see *A Critique of Postcolonial Reason: Toward a History of the Vanishing Present* (London and Cambridge MA: Harvard University Press, 1999).
16. Jacques Derrida, 'Violence and Metaphysics: an Essay on the Thought of Emmanuel Levinas', in *Writing and Difference*, trans. Alan Bass (London: Routledge, 1997 [1978]), 79.
17. This is a paradox first formulated by Geoffrey Bennington in *Jacques Derrida* (Chicago: Chicago University Press, 1992), which I take to be axiomatic of the work undertaken in this book.
18. Bernal, *Black Athena*, 256.
19. Bernal, *Black Athena*, 294.

20. G. W. F. Hegel, *Lectures on the Philosophy of History*, vol. 1, trans., E. S. Haldane and F. H. Simson (London: 1892), 197–8, quoted in Bernal, *Black Athena*, 295.
21. ibid., 149–59, quoted in Bernal, *Black Athena*, 295.
22. Hegel, *Aesthetics*, vol. 1, 308.
23. I am thinking here of de Man's readings of Hegel in his *Aesthetic Ideology*, ed. Andrzej Warminski (Minneapolis: University of Minnesota Press, 1996). I will return to this point momentarily. See also my *Paul de Man* (London: Routledge, 2000).
24. Hegel, *Aesthetics*, vol. 1, 303. When reading these lectures on Fine Art one should remember their own origins as the amalgamation of lecture notes from Hegel's students – in the manner of Saussure's *Cours General* – and so the problems involved in attributing any or all of the ideas and words contained within them to Hegel.
25. Hegel, *Aesthetics*, vol. 2, 634.
26. ibid., 783.
27. Here and subsequently Hegel, *Aesthetics*, vol. 2, 779–80.
28. Hegel, *Aesthetics*, vol. 1, 312.
29. See, for example, Hegel's discussion of 'Silenus with the Infant Bacchus', *Aesthetics*, vol. 1, 202.
30. Hegel, *Aesthetics*, vol. 1, 354.
31. ibid, 354.
32. ibid., 360.
33. ibid., 306.
34. ibid., 360.
35. Paul de Man, *Aesthetic Ideology*, 104.
36. Hegel, *Aesthetics*, vol. 1, 309.
37. ibid.
38. ibid., 310.
39. ibid.
40. ibid.
41. ibid.
42. ibid.
43. ibid.
44. ibid.
45. ibid., 310–11.
46. ibid., 311.
47. ibid.
48. ibid.
49. ibid., 312
50. ibid.
51. ibid.
52. ibid.
53. ibid.
54. ibid., 312–13.
55. ibid., 313.
56. ibid.
57. ibid.
58. ibid.
59. ibid.

60. ibid, 304.
61. This is the starting point for Derrida's reading of Hegel in 'The Pit and the Pyramid: Introduction to Hegel's Semiology', in *Margins of Philosophy*, trans. Alan Bass (Brighton: Harvester Press, 1982).
62. Hegel, *Aesthetics*, vol. 1, 314.
63. ibid.
64. ibid., 360.
65. ibid.
66. ibid., 361.
67. ibid.
68. See Geoffrey Bennington, 'Inter', in Martin McQuillan et al. (eds), *New Directions in Criticism* (Edinburgh: Edinburgh University Press, 1999).
69. ibid.
70. A fuller elaboration of the figure of the Sphinx awaits us in a future reading of Freud in Egypt.
71. Hegel, *Aesthetics*, vol. 2, 780.
72. Hegel, *Aesthetics*, vol. 1, 394, 444, 477 and *Aesthetics*, vol. 2, 780, 1047–8.
73. The Hegelian dialectic as a philosophical structure appropriates the other as a form of knowledge and brings it into the unity of the progressive narrative. There is then an economy of inclusion at work in which all otherness is subsumed into the singular otherness of its privileged term and, as in the case of the *Aesthetics*, all art (symbolic and classical) is incorporated and absorbed into romantic art. The dialectic follows the same conceptual strategy as the colonial expropriation of the non-European by the West. The dialectic as a form of historicism results in one order of human history incorporating all heterogeneous and non-synchronous histories into an homogenizing historical schema. This privileged vantage point which absorbs all difference into itself is inevitably Western because Romantic art *qua* concept emerges from the Modernity which gave rise to both Enlightenment rationality and the European Colonialism which relies on its categories and assumptions. Robert Young uses this phrase after Emmanuel Levinas in *White Mythologies: Writing History and the West* (London: Routledge, 1990), 13.
74. Hegel, *Aesthetics*, vol. 2, 780.
75. Hegel, *Aesthetics*, vol. 2, 780, fn 1.
76. Plato, *Timaeus*, trans. H. D. P. Lee (Harmondsworth: Penguin, 1965), 34.
77. ibid., 35.
78. ibid., 35–6.

Index